THE 1980 SYNOD OF BISHOPS
"ON THE ROLE OF THE FAMILY"

BIBLIOTHECA EPHEMERIDUM THEOLOGICARUM
LOVANIENSIUM

LXIV

THE 1980 SYNOD OF BISHOPS
"ON THE ROLE OF THE FAMILY"

AN EXPOSITION OF THE EVENT
AND
AN ANALYSIS OF ITS TEXTS

BY

JAN GROOTAERS

AND

JOSEPH A. SELLING

1425

LEUVEN
UNIVERSITY PRESS

UITGEVERIJ PEETERS
LEUVEN

1983

ISBN 90 6186 153 5

D/1983/1869/16

Leuven University Press/Presses Universitaires de Louvain
Universitaire Pers Leuven
Krakenstraat 3, B-3000 Leuven-Louvain (Belgium)

Uitgeverij Peeters, Bondgenotenlaan 153, B-3000 Leuven (Belgium)

PREFACE

This book owes its existence to the cooperative effort of two authors, Jan Grootaers and Joseph Selling. The first has for many years closely followed the events and currents within the Catholic Church and has already provided numerous excellent publications on the Church in the World in our time. The second, a moral theologian, has spent a considerable amount of time studying the teaching of the Church on marriage and sexuality. He has written important commentaries on the chapter of *Gaudium et spes*, 47-52, on marriage and the family, in light of the *Acta Concilii* and the historical documents pertaining to this area, and has in particular accomplished a penetrating study of *Humanae vitae* and the reactions to that encyclical by the episcopal conferences.

The contributions of both authors complement each other and shed light upon the work of the 1980 Synod in broad historical perspective. They are clearly written and demand no outside explanation. I do not think it is necessary to give any commentary on the content of these studies. However, I would like to state that the reading of this joint work has thoroughly convinced me of the importance of its publication.

In the first place, I find it impressive that this study of a Synod which dealt with the role of the family has been written by two married christians. They write in a realistic way, informed by their own daily experience. They are also rather hesitant to accept a deductive method of reasoning which too easily results in abstract conceptions having little to do with reality. Both contributions demonstrate the enriching character of their reflections which are grounded in the personally experienced givens of marriage and family life. In reading their text, I have continually been struck how elucidating their commentary is and how much it follows the method of *Gaudium et spes* (4, 11, 33, 46), considering the signs of the times and human experience in the light of the Gospel.

Before I had the opportunity of reading the manuscript for this book, I had already gone through the preparatory texts for the Synod (*Lineámenta* and *Instrumentum laboris*) as well as the official documents that followed («Message to Christian Families» and *Familiaris consortio*). I had thought that I had gained an insight into the events of the Synod. It was thus something of a pleasant surprise for me to learn from the first contribution of this book, as well as from the second, that the work of the Synod was much richer and much more diversified than the official documents might lead one to believe.

The description of the general exchange of ideas (first phase of the Synod) demonstrates how conscientiously the Synod was prepared for in the young churches (Africa, Asia) and in the rejuvenated churches (Latin

America), as well as in the Western Church. The bishops had carefully described the situations and circumstances in their cultural contexts and outlined the concrete problems of their pastoral tasks. They did not shrink from considering the difficult questions of pluriformity, inculturation and the competence of the local churches. Equally interesting are the details of the small discussion groups (second phase). These clarify how various proposals were set forth either in the direction of a deductive method (as in the Latin Language group under Card. Felici) or in a more inductive way (as in the French group of Card. Etchegaray).

Special attention is focused upon the redaction work that resulted in the 43 Propositions (third phase). In my humble opinion, the accurate analysis of the content and the import of these Propositions will be the most stimulating part of the book, especially for theologians. It is clearly shown that the Propositions — at least the majority of them — were drawn up in the spirit of Vatican II and that the Synod fathers approached the urgent problems of the contemporary pastoral situations from the perspective of the Council. Expectations were formulated with respect to ecclesiological issues, such as that the Church, as much as possible, in her own life should promote the equal rights and dignity of her own members, especially women, that the bishops of the local churches should enjoy more competence in the areas of the inculturation of the faith, mixed marriages, etc. There were also questions in the area of sacraments: the bishops desired further study of the relation between faith and sacrament, especially with respect to marriage now that we are more and more confronted with baptized persons who have lost the faith and yet request a church wedding. Then there were problems of a pastoral nature: the bishops asked for a new and extensive study of the pastoral care of the divorced and remarried and hoped that this would take account of the practices of the Eastern Churches; they also wished for a study of the phenomena of experimental marriages, including the psychological and sociological aspects. The bishops hoped that the magisterium would reformulate the teaching of the Church on marriage and human sexuality, giving it a "fuller, more organic and more synthetic explanation», and so forth.

These are only a few of the issues present in the richness of the Propositions. I must go further, however, and say that the whole of this study shows how the Synod bishops shed valuable light on the contemporary problems concerning marriage and the family. By accomplishing this, the present work will stimulate theologians to deal further with the urgent problems that have been put forth by the bishops in the 1980 Synod.

Leuven, 7 March 1983   Prof. emer. Louis Janssens

INTRODUCTION

On 15 September 1965, Pope Paul VI instituted the permanent Synod of Bishops with his motu proprio, *Apostolica sollicitudo*. In the years that followed, the General Synod has been convened six times. In 1967, the first "Ordinary Synod" dealt with a number of topics which had grown directly out of the "unfinished business" of the Second Vatican Council. These were: the revision of canon law, dangerous opinions, seminaries, mixed marriages, and the liturgy. The second meeting, held in 1969, constituted an "Extraordinary Synod" called by Pope Paul VI to discuss the nature of collegiality as well as the relations of the episcopal conferences with the Holy See and with each other. Many saw this meeting as an attempt to deal with a certain "crisis of authority" in the Church revolving around the need to elaborate upon the doctrine of collegiality, revived in Vatican II, and to address the specific application of that doctrine. The period of the late 1960's has often been characterized as one of social upheaval and ecclesial tension, not the least cause or example of which was the reaction prompted by the *Humanae vitae* event. The Synod of 1969 was an attempt to deal with questions of authority and dialogue within the Church, subjects which ultimately have a bearing upon the synodal process itself.

The second "Ordinary Synod" was held in 1971 and was dedicated to the topics of priestly ministry and world justice. This meeting might be seen as a major step in the synodal process and the first attempt to give that process more coherence. On the one hand, there was the significant learning that the Synod was a much too limited event to deal with more than one topic. On the other, this period witnessed the beginning of a more structured approach to these episcopal gatherings. More order was needed to channel the complex input of the world episcopacy, especially since the specific contributions of the so-called "young churches" were becoming more well-defined. However, the introduction of more structure into the synodal process was not without a certain ambiguity. The attempt to deal with greater and more diverse types of input was inevitably linked with the formulation of a structure that tended to reduce the diversity of opinion itself. As that structure became more rigid, the end produce of synodal discussion was less capable of reflecting the broad scope of episcopal input. The difficult process of attempting to draw conclusions and produce a final document during the last days of the bishops' gathering became more problematic. The Second Ordinary Synod of Bishops would be the last occasion on which this form of gathering would be able to produce something of a final episcopal text.

After 1971, the Synod assumed the pattern of a triannual meeting. The Third and Fourth Ordinary Synods, in 1974 and 1977, on evangelization and catechesis respectively, took on the outward appearance of an organized process. In actual fact, however, what was gained in systematization represented a certain loss in the strength of the bishops' effective contribution to the Church as a whole. In 1974, the failure of the Synod to produce a final document would be accompanied by the bishops' abandonment of undertaking that process in the future. In place of the Synod's own attempt to draw conclusions from the bishops' discussions, then, the decision was made to submit the synodal findings to the Holy Father for his study and eventually his own statement. As a result, the synodal event itself would begin to recede into the background. Whatever focus of attention the episcopal gathering might generate, either in its preparatory phases or in the meeting itself, would be overshadowed by the knowledge that the Pope would have the "last word". At least officially speaking, the meetings of 1974 and 1977 would be generally remembered because of the publication of *Evangelii nuntiandi* (1975) and *Catechesi tradendae* (1979). The 1980 Synod was similarly followed by the apostolic exhortation, *Familiaris consortio* (1981). It should become evident from the present study, however, that the comprehension of this Synod, and by implication other Synods as well, should not be reduced to the content of the papal reflections on the topics which had been discussed.

The Synod of Bishops in and of itself is a significant event in the life of the post-conciliar Church. Its very existence is the result of the achievements of Vatican II in a number of ways. On the one hand, we cannot ignore the "rediscovery" of the concept of collegiality in conciliar theology and practice. A deeper appreciation of the functions of the bishops in the Church as well as the integrated relationships among the local churches and with central authority had led to a rather obvious need to provide a forum for continued dialogue and exchange of ideas. On the other hand, it does not appear an exaggeration to say that the Council was only a preliminary step in the process of renewal, and that its work might best be characterized as "unfinished". Many questions and problems remained unanswered in Vatican II and what was achieved there still needs to be integrated into the life of the Church. The application and working out of conciliar theology, itself in need of much integration and understanding, was viewed as a continuing process in 1965. The institution of the Synod of Bishops was one attempt to carry out that process in a collegial way. In historical perspective, it can be said that we are still involved in the nascent stages of that process.

The subject of the present study is the Fifth Ordinary Synod of Bishops called by Pope John-Paul II shortly after his election to the papacy. The topic officially designated for discussion in this episcopal gathering was "The Role of the Christian Family in the Modern World".

At first sight, one familiar with the recent history of ecclesial events may be struck by the significance of this choice. Since Pope Paul VI issued his encyclical *Humanae vitae* in 1968, nearly every aspect of conjugal and familial life has been under discussion throughout the Church. When the pontiff not only recognized but even encouraged this "lively debate", he confirmed that much work still had to be done before the People of God would come to a clear understanding of marriage and the family in the light of the Gospel and according to the signs of the times. The controversy over the issue of regulating fertility, the topic of the 1968 papal letter, was only one small aspect of that much wider debate. In the years following *Humanae vitae* and the 1969 Synod on questions of authority, Paul VI did not feel that the time was yet ripe to raise that debate to the level of synodal discussion. After his death in 1978, the first General Synod to take place turned its attention to this vital area of christian life.

When the topic for episcopal consideration was chosen, it appeared that discussion would be limited to the specific function of the christian family in the life of the Church. This would involve the role of the family in evangelization, catechesis, and various other apostolic and ecclesial tasks. It soon became clear, however, that such a limitation would be impossible. Determining the "role of the family" depended upon an understanding of the identity of the family. This, in turn, could not be undertaken without a consideration of marriage itself, not only as sacrament but also as a human, cultural, social and moral reality. The topics of discussion inevitably grew beyond their official designation and eventually encompassed nearly every aspect of conjugal and familial life, from the wide perspective of situating the family against social structures to the more specific questions of marriage preparation and contraception. All of this, quite naturally, could not escape the fact that the episcopal meeting was a post-conciliar and post-*Humanae vitae* event. The challenge of the 1980 Synod was aptly met by the bishops chosen to represent the World Church. The comprehensiveness of their preparations, the richness of their discussions and the broad spectrum of their suggestions for papal consideration represent the real achievement of this meeting. The papal response to that achievement, *Familiaris consortio*, is only one, small facet of a much larger historical occurrence with far-reaching implications touching upon ecclesiology, sacramentology, conjugal morality and even social justice. It is the purpose of this study to bring to light the significance of the 1980 Synod in this broader perspective by examining that event in its many aspects. It is an attempt to expose this one Synod in such a way that it may be appreciated in itself and not seen merely from the point of view of the public image that was presented by the bishops' closing "Message to Christian Families" and the Pope's exhortation. To accomplish this task, two different kinds of analyses were undertaken.

The first part of this book examines the 1980 Synod as an event in the life of the Church. Unlike the genre of text that might be written by an official chronicler of ecclesial events, this is not limited to the publicized and officially recognized facts and sources. After starting with a brief reminder of the global context in which the Synod took place, this contribution offers a detailed analysis of some of the unpublished position papers drawn up by episcopal conferences in preparation for the 1980 meeting. This provides a first glance at the richness of the bishops' own contributions that has largely gone unnoticed by most commentators. With this as a background, the actual events of the Synod itself are then examined in a way that goes far beyond the usual commentaries and reports that were provided at the time of the meeting or its immediate aftermath. The broad understanding in this analysis was only possible after the Synod could be approached as a whole. This demanded a certain passage of time, the accumulation of sources, and the ability to situate each facet of the episcopal gathering into a more comprehensive picture.

The underlying theme of the first analysis is that the Synod itself is a process. In its present, concrete form, the triannual episcopal gathering presents a forum for an exchange of views and an articulation of pastoral problems facing the Church both universally and locally. The contributions brought to the Synod from the local churches represent a broad spectrum of information about and testimony to the daily life of the living Church. At the same time, however, the Synod as process is also subject to the restrictions of its own structural procedure. Since that procedure has become more imposing, the diversity and richness of episcopal input has been gradually narrowed down to a limited set of statements and closing texts that barely resemble the complexity of the initial phases of the entire process. Of particular interest in the 1980 Synod were the list of 43 Propositions that were prepared for presentation to John-Paul II. These suggestions are viewed from the perspective of the episcopal event itself and an attempt is made to answer the question how and to what extent the Propositions reflected the discussions that had taken place. Especially valuable is the description of the process by which the Propositions were drawn up and amended. The commentary on these events will likely be interesting not only to those who observed the Synod from afar, as it were, but even to some of the bishops who attended the meeting itself. Both the secrecy and the rush of last minute events have obscured a clear picture of precisely what had been happening. The exposition of these occurrences may very well be of aid to future Synod bishops in avoiding a repetition of the problems faced in 1980.

The first contribution closes with an assessment of the Synod on the family which, in historical perspective, can at best be described as provisional. It is still too early to judge the ultimate impact of the 1980 meeting on the Church as a whole. Nevertheless, some significant conclusions are drawn with respect to both the procedure of the synodal process and the richness of episcopal contributions to the topics under discussion. The first part of this work, originally written in Dutch by Jan Grootaers, was translated into English by Joseph Selling.

The second part of the text seeks to analyze the 1980 Synod from a rather different perspective, namely the theological content of the major documents related to the episcopal event. In setting out a proper background, it is postulated that the Synod must be theologically situated within the historical development of the Church's teachings on marriage and the family. This includes a brief overview of that historical perspective concentrating on the single most important factor against which the 1980 event must be viewed, the teaching of Vatican II on marriage and the family, *Gaudium et spes*, 47-52. Recognizing the nature of the renewal that was begun at the Council, one must judge the episcopal discussions taking place fifteen years later in light of what Vatican II had accomplished. The theology of marriage and the family found in the conciliar document is summarized under twenty points which are elaborated elsewhere, in a previous publication. What is presented here is given in the form of an introduction.

The specific analysis of the Synod itself, in some contrast to the first contribution of this book, then concentrates on official documentation. Rather than studying the synodal procedure itself, attention is drawn to the fact that the episcopal gathering takes place under the auspices of officials who represent the central authority of the Church. It was those representatives who were responsible for the preparatory documents leading up to the Synod. The bishops were expected to react to those documents and use them as guidelines, even though they were presumably not to function as schemas for the outcome of the meeting. A detailed study of the *Lineamenta* and the *Instrumentum laboris* are thus provided to explain how the officials of the Church's magisterium envisioned the scope and the subject matter of the episcopal discussions.

The heart of this analysis, however, rests in the commentary on the 43 Propositions which resulted from the bishops' work. Comparing the two versions of that text, as well as the official explanation of the amendment process, reveals that, despite the tone set for the bishops in the preparatory documents, the Synod's findings and suggestions closely reflect the theology of Vatican II. With the possible exception of the final thoughts on *Humanae vitae*, the Propositions are shown to contain a wealth of theological and pastoral insight that could potentially bring about the next major step in magisterial teaching on marriage and the family as well as in the related areas of ecclesiology, sacramentology and even authoritative teaching itself.

The commentary on the Propositions is followed by some brief observations on the closing "Message" and the Homily of John-Paul II. The following section of this second part then goes beyond the first and offers an extensive analysis of *Familiaris consortio*. The principal point of reference taken here is the work of the Synod as embodied in the Propositions. While a great deal of the apostolic exhortation deals directly with the bishops' text, attention is also drawn to those parts of the episcopal findings and suggestions which are passed over in silence. For, while the papal document might conceivably be read as a self-contained text, its ultimate reason for existence, as well as its explicitly stated purpose, was to respond to the work of the Synod. Close analysis reveals that the theological perspectives operative in *Familiaris consortio* are rather different from those underlying the Propositions. In fact, there is a striking similarity between the papal text and the Synod's preparatory documents. The details of this analysis demand a sometimes rather technical exposition.

The final reflections of this contribution examine the work of the Synod as a whole with special reference to the apostolic exhortation. Although this may be a sufficient approach for gaining an insight into the Synod and its ultimate impact upon the contemporary teaching and life of the Church, a broader perspective is invoked that draws attention to the need for understanding the Synod, as well as the papal response, in the light of the Council. In the end, the Church must confront the question of the current status of conciliar theology with respect to marriage and the family. It is only in this perspective that the events of 1980 and 1981 can be properly understood.

The main point at which the two studies of this text may appear to overlap is in the commentary on the 43 Propositions presented to Pope John-Paul II by the bishops of the 1980 Synod. However, these two commentaries were written from two, independent perspectives and can be seen to complement rather than conflict with each other. It has become part of the general consensus that the Propositions form the most substantial "results" of the Fifth General Ordinary Synod of Bishops. Although these suggestions for papal consideration have been published in a number of translations, their central role in both the episcopal gathering and in the commentaries that are offered here are so important that it was felt necessary to publish the final text of the Propositions in their original form. Therefore, an appendix containing the *textus emendatus* of the 43 Propositions is provided at the end of the work. It will become clear in the commentaries provided how this text is to be understood. The difference, for instance, between plain and italicized text signifies the incorporation of amendment(s). The original text of these propositions should provide the serious reader with a valuable key for understanding the events of the 1980 Synod.

It is hoped that this understanding will itself contribute to the ongoing renewal of the function of the Synod of Bishops in the Roman Catholic Church. The Synod is a collegial event without decision-making power. It is an executive function without a clear definition as to its purpose. In the understanding of its official status, it is an advisory body without any guarantee of how its advice will be used. Ultimately, the Synod of Bishops is a process in search of identity. It is sincerely hoped that the present study will provide a reflection upon that process that may influence the unfolding of a collegial identity of the Synod. Any results that this may have on the areas addressed by the 1980 gathering of bishops, especially in light of the current *status quaestionis* of the theology of marriage and the family in the contemporary Church, cannot be anything but beneficial.

Jan Grootaers
Joseph A. Selling

TABLE OF CONTENTS

BIBLIOGRAPHY

Aʙʙʀᴇᴠɪᴀᴛɪᴏɴs

The following abbreviations appear in the text where reference to the document or phenomenon under discussion is clearly evident. Three of these, GS, HV and LG, are used throughout the text since their continuous reference is unavoidable. One of them, EM, it might be noted, refers to two different documents: that commenting on the final text of *Gaudium et spes* and that dealing with the amendments to the Propositions. The use of EM, however, is completely clear from the context in which it is used.

EM	Expensio modorum
FC	Familiaris consortio
GS	Gaudium et spes
HV	Humanae vitae
IL	Instrumentum laboris
ITC	International Theological Commission
LG	Lumen gentium
Lin	Lineamenta
NFP	Natural Family Planning
PBCC	Pontifical Birth Control Commission

The bibliography provided here first lists official texts to which reference is made and then studies and secondary sources which have been referred to in the text and footnotes.

Acta Synodalia Sacrosancti Concilii Oecumenici Vaticani II, v. 4, VI & VII, Vatican City, 1978.
Apostolica sollicitudo, in *AAS* 57 (1965) 775-780.
Casti connubii, in *AAS* 22 (1930) 530-592.
Declaratio de quibusdam quaestionibus ad sexualem ethicam spectantibus, Vatican City, 1975.
Documentum circa sterilizationem in nosocomiis catholicis (Responsa ad quaesita Conferentiae episcopalis Americae septentrionalis), Vatican City, 1975.
Familiae Christianae in mundo hodierno: Elenchus Propositionum; exitus suffragationis cum expensione modorum propositionum, Vatican City, 1980.
Familiaris consortio, in *AAS* 74 (1982) 81-191.
Gaudium et spes, in *AAS* 58 (1966) 1025-1115.
Humanae vitae, in *AAS* 60 (1968) 481-503.
Lumen gentium, in *AAS* 57 (1965) 5-71.
De muneribus Familiae Christianae in mundo hodierno (ad usum conferentiarum episcopalium), Vatican City, 1979.

De muneribus Familiae Christianae in mundo hodierno: Instrumentum laboris ad usum sodalium Quinti Coetus Generalis, Vatican City, 1980.
Populorum progressio, in *AAS* 59 (1967) 257-299.

ABBOTT, W.M. (ed.), *The Documents of Vatican II*, New York, 1966.
Annuario Pontificio per l'anno 1965[-1981], Vatican City, 1966-1982.
L'Attività della Sante Sede nel 1965[-1981], Vatican City, 1966-1982.
BEULENS-GIJSEN, H. & L., GROOTAERS, J., *Mariage catholique et contraception*, Paris, 1968.
CAPRILE, G., *Il Sinodo dei Vescovi: Quinta Assemblea Generale (26 settembre-25 ottobre 1980)*, Rome, 1981.
La charge pastorale des évêques (Unam Sanctam, 74), Paris, 1969.
CONGAR, Y., *La Commission Théologique Internationale (déc. 1977) et le Canon 1012*, in *Revue des Sciences philosophiques et théologiques* 65 (1981) 295-298.
CONGAR, Y., *Un problème ecclésiologique non résolu: le rapport entre le pouvoir papal et le pouvoir épiscopal*, in *La Croix* (19 Sept. 1969) 1.
DAVEY, T., *Divorce: The State of the Question Within the Catholic Church*, in *The Month* 242 (1981) 185-216.
DELHAYE, P., *L'encyclique Humanae vitae et l'enseignement de Vatican II sur le mariage et la famille (Gaudium et spes)*, in *Bijdragen* 29 (1968) 351-368.
DELHAYE, P. (ed.), *Problèmes doctrinaux du mariage chrétien*, Louvain-la-Neuve, 1979.
DE WOLF, A., *Lambeth 1930 over huwelijk en contraceptiva*, in *ETL* 48 (1972) 509-541.
Documents officiels de l'Assemblèe Générale, XXVII Session, Séances III, New York, 1964.
DOHERTY, D. (ed.), *Dimensions of 'Human Sexuality'*, Garden City (New York), 1979.
DOMS, H., *Du sens et de la fin du mariage*, Paris, 1937.
DONAHUE, J.R., *Divorce: New Testement Perspectives*, in *The Month* 242 (1981) 113-120.
FELICI, P., *Della Costituzione pastorale 'Gaudium et spes' alla enciclica paolina 'Humanae vitae'*, in *L'Osservatore Romano* (10 Oct. 1968) 3.
FELICI, P., *L'enciclica paolina 'Humanae vitae' e la Costituzione pastorale 'Gaudium et spes'*, in *L'Osservatore Romano* (7 Sept. 1968) 1.
FELICI, P., *L'Humanae vitae, la coscienza e il Consilio*, in *L'Osservatore Romano* (9 Oct. 1968) 3.
FRANCHINI, E., *Un sinodo per recominicare*, in *Il Regno* 30 (1980) 478-489.
FRISQUE, J., *Le Synode sur la famille: l'apport des églises locales*, Brussels, 1981.
FLANNERY, A. (ed.), *Vatican Council II: The Conciliar and Post-Conciliar Documents*, Dublin, 1975.
GAUDET, P., *Synode des Evêques 1980*, Paris, 1981.
GREEN, T., *The Revised Schema De Matrimonio: Text and Reflections*, in *The Jurist* 40 (1980) 57-127.
GROOTAERS, J., *De onverwachte wending*, Beveren, 1981.
— *De Vatican II à Jean-Paul II; le grand tournant de l'Église catholique*, Paris, 1981.
— *Dal Concilio Vaticano II a Giovanni Paolo II; una grande svolta della Chiesa cattolica*, Torino, 1982.

GROOTAERS, J., *Les synodes des évêques de 1969 et de 1974: fonctionnement défectueux et résultats significatifs*, in *Les Églises après Vatican II: dynamisme et prospective*, Paris, 1981.

GUINDON, A., *The Sexual Language: An Essay in Moral Theology*, Ottawa, 1976.

HÄRING, B., *The Synod of Bishops on the Family: Pastoral Reflections*, in *Studia Moralia* 19 (1981) 231-257.

HARRIOT, J.F.X., *The Synod's Absent Auditores*, in *The Tablet* 234 (1980) 986.

HARVEY, J., *Expressing Marital Love during the Fertile Phase*, in *The International Review of Natural Family Planning* 5 (1981) 203-220.

HASTINGS, A., *Christian Marriage in Africa*, London, 1973.

HEBBLETHWAITE, P., *The Pope and the Family*, in *The Tablet* 236 (1982) 29-30.

HENRION, M., *Les Nations Unies et la planification de la famille*, in *Société et procréation* (ed. R. GUBBELS), Brussels, 1981.

HEYLEN, V., *La Note 14 dans la Constitution pastorale, Gaudium et spes, P. II, Ch. 1, N. 14*, in *ETL* 42 (1966), 555-566.

HORGAN, J. (ed.), *Humanae vitae and the Bishops: The Encyclical and the Statements of the National Hierarchies*, Shannon, 1972.

JANSSENS, L., *Chastité conjugale selon l'encyclique Casti connubii et suivant la Constitution pastorale Gaudium et spes*, in *ETL* 42 (1966) 513-554.

JOHN-PAUL II, *Closing Homily to the Synod*, in *Origins* 10 (1980) 325-329.

KELLEHER, S.J., *Divorce and Remarriage for Catholics? A Proposal for Reform of the Church's Law on Divorce and Remarriage*, Garden City (New York), 1973.

KOSNIK, A., et al., *Human Sexuality: New Dimensions in Catholic Thought*, London, 1977.

LIO, E., *Natura sacra ed ordinazione intrinseca del matrimonio nella dottrina della Gaudium et spes*, in *Renovatio* 15 (1980) 9-63.

MACKIN, T., *Conjugal Love and the Magisterium*, in *The Jurist* 36 (1976) 263-301.

MANIGNE, J.P., *Un laïc italien invité au Synode*, in *Informations Catholiques Internationales* 557 (1980) 39-40.

MARSHALL, J., *NFP: The Facts*, in *The Tablet* 234 (1980) 1197-1198.

MARTELET, G., *L'Existence humaine et l'amour; pour mieux comprendre l'encyclique Humanae vitae*, Paris, 1969.

MARTHALAR, B., *The Family in Global Perspective: Synod 1980*, in *The Living Light* 18 (1981) 57-74.

MCCORMACK, A., *Humanae vitae Today*, in *The Tablet* 232 (1978) 674-676.

MCCORMACK, A., *Wie steht die Kirche zur Bevölkerungsexplosion*, in *Herder Korrespondenz* 34 (1980) 455-462.

— *The Population Problem and the Synod on the Family*, in *The Clergy Review* 65 (1980) 328-338.

MCCORMICK, R.A., *Sterilization and Theological Method*, in *Theological Studies* 37 (1976) 471-477.

Morality in Sexual Matters: Observations of the Sacred Congregation for the Doctrine of the Faith on the Book 'Human Sexuality' (July 13, 1979), in *The Pope Speaks* 25 (1980) 97-102.

O'RIORDAN, S., *The Synod on the Family, 1980*, in *The Furrow* 31 (1980) 759-777.

ORSY, L., *Faith, Sacrament, Contract, and Christian Marriage: Disputed Questions*, in *Theological Studies* 43 (1982) 379-398.

PAUL VI, Allocution of 31 July 1968, *AAS* 60 (1968) 527-530; in *Herder Correspondence* 5 (1968) 336-337.

PIUS XII, Allocution of 29 October 1951, in *AAS* 43 (1951) 835-854.

Postkonziliare Hintergründe einer Enzyklika, in *Herder Korrespondenz* 22 (1968) 525-536.

POTIN, J. (ed.), *Aujourd'hui la famille: Principaux documents du Synode des Evêques 1980*, Paris, 1981.

Pour relire Humanae vitae: Déclarations épiscopales du monde entier, Gembloux, 1970.

Reconciliation and Penance in the Mission of the Church, in *Origins* 11 (1982) 565-580.

REESE, T.J., *Reporting on the Synod*, in *America* 143 (1980) 407-411.

SCHMEISER, J.A., *Marriage: New Alternatives*, in *Worship* 55 (1981) 23-34.

SCHMEISER, J.A., *Marriage: New Developments in the Diocese of Autun, France*, in *Église et Théologie* 10 (1979) 369-385.

SCHOOYANS, M., *La Conférence de Puebla: un risque, un espoir*, in *Nouvelle Revue Théologique* 101 (1979) 641-675.

SEGUNDO, J.L., *A Theology for Artisans of a New Humanity*, v. 5, *Evolution and Guilt*, New York, 1974.

SELLING, J.A., *A Closer Look at the Text of Gaudium et spes on Marriage and the Family*, in *Bijdragen* 43 (1982) 30-48.

SELLING, J.A., *Moral Teaching, Traditional Teaching and Humanae Vitae*, in *Louvain Studies* 7 (1978) 24-44.

SELLING, J.A., *Re-reading Gaudium et spes on Marriage and the Family*, in *Louvain Studies* 8 (1980) 82-94.

SELLING, J.A., *Twenty Significant Points in the Theology of Marriage and the Family Present in The Teaching of Gaudium et spes*, in *Bijdragen* 43 (1982) 412-441.

SHANNON, W.H., *The Lively Debate: Response to Humanae Vitae*, New York, 1970.

VORGRIMLER, H. (ed.), *Commentary on the Documents of Vatican II*, 5 vol., New York, 1969.

WILLIAMS, G.H., *The Mind of John-Paul II: Origins of his Thought and Action*, New York, 1981.

WOJTYLA, K., *Amour et responsabilité: étude de morale sexuelle*, Paris, 1965.

WOJTYLA, K., *Karol Wojtyla e il Sinodo dei Vescovi*, Rome, 1980.

WRENN, L.G. (ed.), *Divorce and Remarriage in the Catholic Church*, New York, 1973.

ZALBA, M., *Ex personae eiusdemque actuum natura, GS 51, 3*, in *Periodica de re morali, canonica, liturgica* 68 (1979), 201-232.

AN EXPOSITION OF THE EVENTS OF THE SYNOD

by

Jan Grootaers

PART ONE

THE BACKGROUND

I. General Political and Economic Background

It would appear to us to be impossible to understand the real significance of the Synod of 1980 if we do not situate the general tendencies and particular interventions of this gathering of bishops in a broader context. The international discussions and polemics regarding the population explosion and family planning, which had already occupied the United Nations and other conferences for years, constituted a general background for the exchange of views on the family at the Synod. Between 1960 and 1980 there had been remarkable development in this area, the complete description of which is beyond the scope of this work. We would like to highlight only one aspect of that development: the gradual growth of consciousness regarding the connection between demographic factors and economic development.

For years, the view of capitalist economics had held sway: the rapid growth of the world's population, especially in those lands with low standards of living, was considered a contributing factor to continuing underdevelopment. But as early as December 1963, particularly under the influence of India and Pakistan, an "Asiatic Conference for Population Problems" was set up in Tokyo, the recommendations of which confronted the U.N. with another approach to the question[1].

For the first time this conference affirmed the *priority* of socio-economic progress which would bring the population problem closer to a solution. But, paradoxically enough, this new standpoint was coupled with an indictment of the rapid growth in population which was proposed as the source of underdevelopment in the lands of Southeast Asia. The main request made to the U.N. by the Asian governments represented at the conference was to provide international technical assistance on the level of family planning. Similar requests were repeated later on other occasions, including the U.N. General Assembly in December 1966, the Economic and Social Council in August 1967, and the General Assembly in October, 1970.

In the meantime, more significant shifts had occurred in international opinion. In December 1962, voting at the U.N. on a proposed Swedish resolution favoring universal birth control demonstrated that the Nor-

---

1. M. HENRION, *Les Nations Unies et la planification de la famille*, in R. GUBBELS (ed.), *Société et procréation*, Brussels, 1981, p. 238.

thern hemisphere was divided into 3 blocks: an Anglo-Saxon-Scandinavian group which advocated birth control, a West- and South-European group which opposed it and a group of Communist countries which abstained from voting. The Third World nations were equally divided with Arabic and Asian delegates speaking in favor of birth control and representatives of Black-Africa and Latin America, with some exceptions, opposing it [2]. +

During the course of the 1960's there was a growing realization that the effort to limit population growth in the poor countries was inspired by the self-interest of the economically developed lands: either to guarantee political or military superiority or to maintain their economic tutelage. This less than admirable motive was clearly expressed in the well-known remark of L.B. Johnson; in June, 1965 the U.S. president declared: "Five dollars that are invested in population control are as effective as a hunderd dollars spent on economic development". In contrast to this, during the discussion about development strategy for the second decade (October 1970), it was expressly declared that assistance provided for the regulation of births could be *no substitute* for development aid. In 1972, a declaration was prepared which stated that economic progress and social development were preliminary conditions to an efficient population policy. The proposition, originating with the Economic and Social Council of the U.N., provoked much disunity. While some Council delegates affirmed the need to intensify effort towards the greatest possible dissemination of contraceptives, other spokesmen seemed to defend the view that *only* economic and social development could provide a satisfactory resolution to the problems of population. During the World Population Conference in Bucharest, in August 1974, these two tendencies were clearly manifest. Representatives of the Far East, with the support of Anglo-Saxon nations (of the Protestant tradition) continued to be the most convinced advocates of birth control. The other camp consisted of the Southern European representatives (of the Catholic tradition), the representatives of Latin-America and Africa (suspicious of foreign intervention from the wealthy North), and the East European delegates who managed to couple Marxist anti-Malthusianism with political interests.

But despite these differences of opinion the participants at the conference still succeeded in setting up a *plan of action* designed "to promote the coordination of demographic tendencies with the tendencies to social and economic development". The Bucharest plan of action, especially in view of its six main points, allowed a compromise to be worked out on the basis of its indication of an *essential priority*: "The resolution of the problems of population growth demands, before

2. *Documents officiels de l'Assemblée Générale, XXVII session. Séances V. III*, Nations Unies, New York, 1964, p. 1263.

anything else, the realization of a socio-economic transformation". The action plan regarded the population policy as a portion of — but no substitute for — socio-economic development. Moreover, this policy must be compatible with recognized "human values" such as individual freedom, justice and the right of minority groups to exist. At the same time, there was a recognition of the right of each couple and each individual to decide, in a responsible way, on the number of children. In this context, both demography and development, in their mutual influences, were accorded equal status.

In any case, the main objective of development must be pursued, i.e. the improvement of the standard of living and the quality of life of each human being. Demographic policies must constitute an integral part of this development. In a searching analysis of this evolution, (a source which provided this writer with much information), Ms. M. Henrion concludes that out of all this a *new strategy* was born[3]. The consequence thereof is that family planning will play an ever more integral role in many social education and health service programs. In addition, since 1974, all governments have recognized that simply controlling the population explosion of Third World countries is no solution. Consequently, the great contrast between those who proposed birth control as the solution to underdevelopment and those who saw development as an adequate response to all problems has lost some of its sharpness. Recently, the celebrated Brandt-report of the North-South Commission, which was composed of a large number of politicians and experts from rich and poor nations, advanced a similar consensus. A large increase in population constitutes for many less developed countries a dangerous obstacle to necessary development, but this must be seen alongside many other causes of poverty which demand equal attention.

On the eve of the General Synod of Bishops of October, 1980, the well-known demographer Dr. Arthur McCormack, making reference to this, observed that it would simply be intelligent to combine "population and development" with one another[4]. The author then expressed his conviction that the Church, if she was to be credible, should attack the problem of world poverty on two fronts: first, by promoting, in every conceivable fashion, social justice and solidarity with the oppressed, while, secondly, at the same time helping to control the rapid population increases. Frequent Vatican statements relevant to the second proposal have created the impression that the Church's position in this regard is ambiguous and hesitant. McCormack also observed that there exists in the Church a peculiar alliance between some conservative and progres-

---

3. M. HENRION, *Les Nations Unies et la planification de la famille*, pp. 285-287.
4. A. McCORMACK, *Wie steht die Kirche zur Bevölkerungsexplosion*, in *Herder Korrespondenz* 34 (1980) 455-462; *The Population Problem and the Synod on the Family*, in *The Clergy Review* 65 (1980) 328-338.

sive tendencies. The former are inclined to ignore the population problem because they fear that any clear acknowledgement of its existence could spark a new struggle within the Church regarding the means of birth control. The progressives, for their part, fear that the control of births could become a substitute for genuine development; in this they simply overlook the increasing proof provided by demographers that rapid population growth is one of the obstacles to the conquest of world poverty.

Nevertheless, it is clear to others that it would be as unreasonable to tackle all the other causes of the problem while ignoring population growth, as it would be to contend only with the latter while leaving all other factors out of consideration. It might be a simple matter to ponder such a position on a theoretical level. However, when the subject was considered in the atmosphere of emotion and charged discussion that was to be expected at the Bishops' Synod, many more accents would emerge. Thus, for example, the statement about the waste that characterizes Western consumerism which was more than once passionately denounced. But at this point we are getting ahead of ourselves!

II. Specific Ecclesial Background

Because the specifically theological analysis of the *Lineamenta* for the 1980 Synod is treated in another part of this work, discussion of that document here would be superfluous. Our concern will be for the responses which the bishops sent to Rome in reaction to that document. It is important to concentrate our attention on the episcopal responses as part of the preparatory phase of the Synod. There is all the more reason to pursue this study in that most of the relevant documents have never been published.

In light of the virtual flood of episcopal response to the *Lineamenta*, our intention has been to choose examples which would be representative of four major areas: Black Africa, Southeast Asia, Latin America and the North Atlantic Region. An advantage to this method will be to review reactions from bishops coming from different backgrounds with respect to the problems of population growth and economic development. Although it is understood that the contributions about to be exposed are situated in the context of explicit reactions to the questions posed in the *Lineamenta* which was put forth as an inquiry, the content of these reactions goes much beyond that limited framework. The documents from Zaïre and the Philippines clearly went their own way and do not relate to the *Lineamenta*. The Korean bishops use the *Lineanmenta*, but they approach it critically because they considered it to be weak in its support for the pastoral experiences of the laity and superficial in its approach to the deeper causes of present conflicts and abuses. The thinking of the Indonesian bishops appears to be the most critical towards the *Lineamenta* in both form and content. The bishops of India give occasional reference to those portions of the document with which they were in agreement. The Brazilian bishops used the document as a point of departure but not without critical observations to the effect that the Roman suggestions were built upon elements and approaches which were already generally well known and open to very broad interpretation.

Because these documents have not been published and because we wish to represent their content as accurately as possible, we will borrow very liberally from the texts themselves. Frequent use of these texts will be incorporated into our own without necessarily using quotation marks which would be extremely cumbersome. Every care has been taken to insure that the meanings of the episcopal reactions have been accurately represented.

A. Black Africa

1. *Position Paper of the Bishops' Conference of Zaïre.*

Conférence épiscopale du Zaïre — BP 3258, Kinshasa — Gambe.
Mariage et famille au Zaïre — Contribution de l'Episcopat au Synode des évêques 1980 (typed test of 34 pages). No date or signature provided.
Structure (translated from the French): I. Marriage and the family in Zairese tradition. II. African marriage and family against the challenge of contemporary life (modernization). III. The African marital covenant in the light of Christ.
Note: This text was prepared by the Doctrinal Commission of the Bishops' Conference of Zaïre which is made up only of bishops. Theologians were only consulted with respect to some specific points.

In the General Introduction of the Zairese bishops' paper, it is noted that for many years the bishops have been concerned about questions concerning christian marriage and family life in their own particular context in order to construct an appropriate pastoral approach to these issues. Naturally, they also hoped that the Synod would take up these questions. But there is yet another reason why these bishops had been working toward effective pastoral care for the family, namely, the search for a more profound evangelization to awaken "living christian communities". If we consult the remarks made by Bishop Kaseba to Pope John-Paul II during his visit of May 1980, we find the observation that "the dynamism and the balance of these communities as well as their stability rest in large part in the vitality and stability of the family which simultaneously forms the basic cell of human society and the primordial basic community of the Chruch". In the eyes of the bishops, the family plays an irreplaceable role in the fundamental evangelization of the people and culture of Zaïre.

Furthermore, at the same time that the ecclesial community of faith is brought into existence as a response to the message of the gospel, it must fulfill four functions: liturgical, ethical, juridical, and theological. With respect to the last, one expects the development, almost spontaneously, of an African theology: a critical, systematic and rigorous reflection on the *fides africana*, the faith experience of the African covenant with Christ. This ecclesial function properly belongs to the normal responsibility of the christian community with its own structures that always remain open to reevaluation and that always remain at the service of life. It is in this perspective of inculturation and profound evangelization of the people and culture of Zaïre that the bishops put forth their reflections on problems of marriage and the family.

a. *Marriage and the family in Zairese tradition*

The bishops begin their treatment of the subject with the recognition of a wide diversity of traditions in Zaïre with respect to marriage and the family. This diversity is by no means a state of confusion, for it is based upon the deep convergence of a more general conception of things. Despite the existence of evil, it is an expression of the richness of the peoples of which Christ is the inheritance (Ps. 2:8). The fundamental conception of mariage and the family is characterized by the following four aspects.

1) The marital convenant is a personal and a communitarian undertaking. Ancestors are and remain essential members of the wider family concept. Each person belongs to a particular lineage. This is evident not only in the visible world but also in the unseen world of the hereafter. Against this background, marriage takes on the meaning of a sacred deed, an office in service to life oriented to the future of the race or tribe. Moreover, marriage as the immediate cause of the rapproachment and true joining together of the tribes/clans/families involves a bond which continues to exist after separation or death.

2) The institution of the marital covenant takes place in a dynamic process of stages. The importance which is attached to the marital bond by the family is evident from the care with which the family group prepares for and progressively works out its institution. One state follows the next until the bride has entered the new household or until the first child is born. Each stage has its own meaning, with its own rights and duties. But the whole process, to which objection can be made at any stage and which can sometimes last two years, constitutes a dynamic and existential whole.

3) The covenant is a profoundly religiously act. Through the various stages by which the marital relationship is gradually built, one finds continuous reference to the unseen world: God, ancestors and other persons, each contribute to the success of the marriage. This reference is realized through the action of certain mediators.

4) The family, which is brought into existence by this covenant, is the source of fruitful love. In the first place, God is "Father", the creator of life and the beginning of all things. He is the realization of fatherhood and motherhood in the most excellent way. The principle of the cohesive universe is evident in human "polarity" or the attractive power of different beings for each other. The fundamental polarity is the basis of nuptial universality which brings man and woman together. The ultimate culmination of this plan is the transmission of life. The principle of

"polarity" is worked out further through the establishment of concrete families. The demands which are placed step by step upon the bride and bridegroom must also be seen as a progression of involvement by the partners. This is especially evident with respect to oneness (an understanding relation), lastingness (a relationship formed between two clans which is not broken by separation) and fruitfulness (the absence of procreation can lead to separation).

b. *African marriage and family against the challenge of contemporary life (modernization)*

The bishops begin with the observation that through the importation of foreign cultural, religious, political and economic models, the Western world made its influence felt. This caused a situation of maladjusted relations among the people. During the colonial period, the method of evangelization had a negative effect on the institution of the family. In 1923, the so-called "ancestor cult" was the subject of an official anathema by the (Belgian) ecclesial authorities and was accomplished through an appeal to the secular authority of the colonial administration. This masterpiece of intolerance led to a cultural and religious alienation which was inseparably bound up with social and political subjugation. The consequent maladjusted relationships found expression in the subjection of the "assimilated", in the opportunism of the "ambitious", or in the closedness of the "integrist".

The ruinousness of foreign influences should not mean that Africa is threatened with the loss of its own identity. To that end, the original criteria should be once again reevaluated. In a spirit of critical openness, both the new influences and the old customs should be evaluated together. The challenge of modernity will function as a meeting of many different ideas leading to exchange and the reciprocal enrichment of every sector of life. With respect to marriage and the family, both the personal and the social aspects of the covenant can be maintained in order to work against substantial abuses. The notion of the nuclear family is not pertinent in Zaïre today. If the dynamic and step by step process of the institution of marriage cannot be totally maintained, it is still desirable that its spirit be protected so that the profundity and seriousness of the preparation for marriage as a meaningful, vital act can be insured.

c. *The African marital covenant in the light of Christ*

Taking as their point of departure the papal homily of 3 May 1980 delivered in Kinshasa and which is quoted at length in their text, the bishops of Zaïre touch upon evangelization, considering it from the geographical and cultural perspective of the African people. It is where people live, in their own situation, that Christ is to be met and to take hold. In this specific context, the Tabor — or Emmaüs — experience can be lived through. In the light of Christ, human experience and traditional religion can grow into a new relation. The African person can discover the great themes of the covenant, the mystical body, and the communion of saints in accordance with his own family experience.

As practical examples of valorizing christian elements in an African perspective, the bishops point to four ideas. First, the notion of God who is the source of family. In the religious experience of the African people, God is the creating presence, the axis around which the entire universe turns. The "awakener" is experienced as the supporting force behind all that is. Secondly, this entails a notion of family which is wider and broader. The family of the Trinity is the foundation of the brotherhood of man and the model for family, society and Church. Thirdly, there is the christian profession that God is married with His people. This is the spousal relationship par excellence and leads to the fourth element, namely that the covenant between persons is a sacrament of the Paschal Lamb. The marital relation formed between mortal persons becomes an efficient symbol of the spousal covenant between God and His people, between the Son and His Church, a new and everlasting covenant after the image of the trinitarian model. On the divine model one can ground a forceful marital spirituality. This would encompass the moral and spiritual fruitfulness of the spouses, the fulfillment of their wishes and a realization of the demands: an integrated fruitfulness and the missionary service of the family.

By way of conclusion, the bishops of Zaïre say that God has willed a large family, based upon the model of the Holy Trinity: the Father (père surgisseur), who takes all fatherhood up into Himself; the Son, the first born of all brothers who are united by His Cross; the Holy Spirit, who comes through the Son to lead us to the Father. The African family, in its broadest context, offers its members the opportunity to stand open to the mystery of salvation which has been accomplished by Christ. This figure will help them better comprehend its deepest meaning which is revealed by the family. The evangelization of the people of Zaïre and their culture will profit from the penetration and transparence, the appropriateness and applicability which would flow from integrating the fundamental givens which have fascinated man since the "beginning of time". The christian community which has been born in Africa and which carries with it the dynamics of the African family and its cultural patrimony responds to the model of the Holy Trinity. In its own living traditions, as well as in Christian thought and celebration, it expresses its own original life-form. This is, therefore, the language with which to announce the Message of Christ. Only then can the people of Zaïre be addressed in the deepest part of their being, only then can the Church be entirely catholic, only then is she worth the name of the Bride of the Lamb.

B. Southeast Asia

2. *Position Paper of the Bishops' Conference of Korea*

Conferentia Episcoporum Coreae — C.P.O. Box 16, Seoul, Korea.
Comments on "The Role of the Christian Family in the Modern World" (typed text of 5 unnumbered pages). Dated 3 November 1979 and signed by Vitorius K. Youn (President of the Korean Bishops' Conference).

Although the Korean document, in its opening words, commends the *Lineamenta* as a useful starting point for study and reflection, it nevertheless speaks quite critically of the Roman proposals. The document is described as displaying too much "book-knowledge" with countless quotations from previous Church documents, while drawing too little from the actual experience of married couples or from the pastoral experience of those actively engaged in the family apostolate. What is more, families are given little, if any opportunity to explain what help they expect from the Church in living their family life. The bishops suggest that the Synod should deal with these omissions. With regard to the reception of HV, the Korean bishops determined that the initial hesitation of many episcopal conferences had given way to a stronger supporting stand. The time is ripe, they say, for the body of bishops to show their unconditional support for the official and certain teaching of HV. With this in mind the Korean bishops noted that the *Lineamenta* contained many quotations from Vatican II but too few references to HV. The "natural family planning" programs throughout the world were also felt to merit encouragement.

Another part of the Lineanenta was faulted for containing no deep examination of the causes or the weakness of contemporary family life. The deep concern of the Church in this regard was not made abundantly clear, they say. With respect to the transmission of life, it was pointed out that no mention is made of the lack of pastoral effort in some places. The wholesale rejection of the teaching of the Church on the regulation of births by the faithful, priests, and theologians, should also be dealt with. The "verbosity" of the document's formulation is said to have the effect of concealing the doctrine rather than revealing it. Married people, they say, would be edified by the sublimity of the doctrine, but they might find it hard to take away anything that would be of practical use to them in their own family life.

Regarding part three of the document, the Korean bishops point clearly to the danger of clericalism. They propose that the Church's interest in the family gives the impression of being motivated not for the sake of the family but in view of the family's "usefulness to the Church". Rather than the family's being for the Church, they comment, the Church is for the family. Finally, the whole of the pastoral section of the *Lineamenta* is said to rely too much on quotations from other Church documents and not enough on the actual experience of family life. Many of the quotations appear to be little more than slogans (catchphrases) concerning the social role of the family. They are not concrete enough to be of real help.

3. *Position Paper of the Bishops' Conference of Indonesia*

Indonesian Bishops' Conference (MAWI) — Jakarta, Indonesia.
Remarks of the Bishops' Conference of Indonesia (MAWI) on: "The Role of the Christian Family in the Modern World" (typed text of 28 pages). Dated 31 January 1980 and without signature.
Structure: I. Sources. II. General remarks on the paper as a whole. III. The content. IV. Remarks concerning the different parts of the Vatican working paper.

The remarks submitted by the Indonesian Bishops' Conference to Rome are highly critical of the form as well as the contents of the *Lineamenta*. The text, comprising 28 pages in large format will be treated here only in its major lines.

a. *Sources*

According to the Indonesian bishops, the Vatican working document barely touches upon the central theme of the Synod. Moreover, very few things are said about the actual role of the family (the real situation), about the modern world of today or about the role christian families can and should play therein. Above all, they say that there is hardly any pastoral orientation, nor any practical hints as to how that role can be executed. Well known doctrine on christian marriage and family is simply repeated again and again under more modern-sounding titles and chapter headings. However, they ask, what does the Synod hope to achieve? And can a synodal document provide the help that the Synod hopes to give? There should be clarity about what is needed most urgently by most christian families and how and to what extent the Synod can and should answer real needs.

b. *General remarks on the paper as a whole*

1) The Indonesian bishops displayed little enthusiasm for the contents of the *Lineamenta*. The invocation of the duty of man and wife to be

obedient to the ethical order as regards the honorable performance of the generative role gives the document a moral orientation that could be seen to reflect an outdated point of view, the bishops observe. In contrast to this view, they recall the contemporary theological perspective that begins by emphasizing first of all that which is most basic in the theological attitude of man toward God: accepting or rejecting His sacrifice and His salvation, and evaluating behavior as a statement guided by that norm. It comes as no surprise, they say, that the standpoint of Paul VI on birth control methods is reconfirmed in this working paper. But, note the Indonesian bishops, it gives cause for deep concern that the same upheaval may occur when the matter is discussed again. In this context, they call attention to the article of Philippe Delhaye, "L'encyclique *Humanae vitae* et l'enseignement de Vatican II sur le mariage et la famille (*Gaudium et spes*)", published in *Bijdragen* 29 (1968) pp. 351-68 which they point out as demonstrating a rather clear difference between the two documents.

The Indonesian position points out that several bishops opposed the reiteration of HV as something that could only do damage in many parts of the world where a restriction of births is a necessity, while one bishop wished to stress the importance of the teaching of HV. But there was general agreement that the question of birth control should not become the focal point of the Synod's teaching. This was also desirable in the interest of keeping peace. The problem involved too many factors which had not yet been adequately examined.

The possibility is put forth that the movement of "natural family planning" might in the future produce some new experience. On the other hand, it is warned that the pressing problems of overpopulation must not be overlooked or dealt with in a sketchy manner such as by simply quoting documents of more than ten years of age. The last 15 years have been a period of radical change which renders useless any mere repetition or quotation of previous statements. It is not merely the constant tradition of the Church but also the problems that beset society in general and family life in particular that constitutes the *locus theologicus* for the magisterium in order to build up the faith community as a whole. In this connection, the bishops made reference to passages from *Lumen gentium* and *Gaudium et spes* which concerned the *sensus fidei*, the need for dialogue with those who live in the world, the natural autonomy of earthly reality, the obligation on the part of theologians to listen to the voices of the present age, etc.

2) The Indonesian bishops also criticized the pre-eminently Western outlook of the *Lineamenta*. What the Roman document describes as the "Modern World", they comment, really should be entitled the "Western World" in view of its being limited mainly to Western cultural and philosophical concepts as well as Western European/American ex-

perience of the modern world. The Roman document does not speak of or to the non-western, the missionary and the developing world. This limitation is considered to be one of the most serious weaknesses of the document. If the Synod wants to speak to the whole Church, it must pay attention to universal problems, difficulties and ways of thinking and doing. What other institution, they ask, is more deeply colored by local and regional cultural traditions than marriage and the family? Therefore, it is said that it may be wise to limit the scope of the topic to some more urgent, (almost) universal phenomena and problems faced by christian families all over the world, or try to penetrate to a level where such problems are more or less common. To obtain this universal character not only the voices of the bishops should be heard, but also those of experts – christian and non-christian. The synodal document, they say, is intended for the community, and not only for libraries.

3) Nearly all bishops of the Indonesian conference are described as deploring the lack of pastoral orientation of the *Lineamenta*. The real knowledge, concern and care for the actual joys, aspirations and difficulties of christian families, they say, should be felt by the reader on every page. It is not enough to add some practical advice at the end. The whole approach and orientation of the document must be pastoral. In order to achieve a pastorally useful discussion and paper, the bishops offered as a proposal that it may be good to state clearly the new possibilities that give reason for hope, the most common and pressing problems, and successful approaches to pastoral care that have already been tested.

4) In the opinion of the Indonesian bishops, the Roman document showed little coherence. The descriptive portion of the *Lineamenta* followed an inductive method, they observe, but little advantage was taken of it: its significance is not highlighted from a theological perspective and its concluding section contained only a string of lamentations without any critical analysis of why things may have come to such a pass. For example, the complaint that the Church teaching on sexuality is rejected even within the Church itself is made, but there is no investigation of why this is the case. In its doctrinal section, the Roman document is said to adopt an all too defensive attitude. There is an excess of quotations, as for example, the numerous references to HV during the discussion of aspects of fecundity. The bishops comment again that, in this connection there seems to be little wisdom in stirring up all the controversy about HV. The lack of coherence between the descriptive and doctrinal portions of the Roman paper is a failure that extends to the relation between the pastoral section and all that has preceded it. That portion of the *Lineamenta*, they say, is no more successful than the descriptive and doctrinal sections in pointing to the positive role of the family in the Church and in society.

5) Finally, the bishops declared that the language and method employed in the document were reminiscent of clericalism. The working paper, they say, used language that would not be attractive to the laity and which is not suitable for the direct instruction of the laity. There is an excessive use of quotations and a bothersome use of inappropriate philosophical terms. The impression of triumphalism is reinforced by the exhortative tone of the whole text. It is almost as if there is nothing new to proclaim so many years after HV. If the Church really wants to provide leadership for the faithful to take an active part in building the world in which we live, adapting the traditional teaching to today's situations is just not enough.

c. *The content*

From the Indonesian point of view, Part I of the *Lineamenta* elicited a few observations. They point out, for instance, that in a non-christian society the christian family is required to live in isolation which is not simply geographical. There is also a moral and cultural estrangement, especially regarding the customs concerning marriage. While in the West the limited family predominates, in Indonesia the extended family remains the norm. Indonesian Catholics are a minority in the midst of a predominantly Islamic population and tolerance is closely tied to religious relativism. For many families the most pressing problem is the population explosion and birth control. Considering this situation, the Catholic family in Indonesia stands in need of help to maintain evangelical ideals and Catholic principles.

Regarding Part II of the Roman document, the bishops expressed criticism of its rationalism and voluntarism, and its total failure to speak about happiness and the experience of unity and joy. They also pointed to the document's apparent preoccupation with the old "ends of marriage" and their "vital connection". This concern creates the impression that this whole part is engineered to culminate in the reference to those ends (HV, 12) and to indissolubility. While admitting that these were important questions, the bishops maintained that restating former arguments and explications certainly does not help very much. This whole part lacks inspiration, they say, and the type of orientation necessary for our time.

As to whether this document meets contemporary pastoral needs, the bishops answer in the negative: "pastoral" means contact with human beings who in concrete circumstances must try to find out how to follow the law of Christ and their conscience. The document should be called doctrinal and not pastoral. Among those doctrinal points which needed to be stressed nowadays, the bishops mentioned the following: pre-marital relations, abortion and responsible parenthood, the position of the wife in the family, the right of full-grown children to choose their own path of life, and the Catholic education of children by parents.

The bishops remarked that it hardly can be said that the specific role of the christian family in the modern world is evangelizing. When this role is broken down into a prophetic, priestly, and social mission, they declare, it seems to be farfetched. On the positive side, the bishops comment that the consideration of collaboration with young people is a very good point and should be developed. The Church must try harder to speak the people's language and to offer answers to the questions posed by other religions so that Catholics are able to defend the Church's position and carry on a dialogue with men of other beliefs.

The Indonesian bishops were also of the firm opinion that population growth is a very serious problem. While acknowledging that people want children who are considered as 1) a blessing of the Lord and 2) a help for parents in their old age, they point out that excessively rapid procreation gives rise to enormous problems which are not solved by the teaching of HV. On the other hand, they state that in some districts abortion is committed rather frequently without any scruples and that the Indonesian divorce rate is very high, especially among the Moslem people. Toward the end of their response, the bishops offered the following as priority items:
1) Deepening the sense of community — emphasizing likeness with one another, both as individuals and as families. This is the call of Christ. All men are called in the same way to save themselves and others.
2) As a consequence of this fundamental truth, every believer, no matter where he is, should try to search out his fellow believers and form a community. This effort at building community is most needed by the faithful in *diaspora*, those who live in isolation from their fellow Catholics.

In conclusion, the Indonesian document spoke of the obligations of the Church toward families, for example, preparation for marriage, giving greater attention to cultivating husband-wife relationships, and helping parents. In other words, wrote the bishops, what we need is a credible approach to the pastoral care of the family.

4. *Position Paper of the Bishops' Conference of India*

Communication to the Synod of Bishops 1980 on its theme: "The Role of the Christian Family in the Modern World" (typed text of 23 oversized pages).
No date or signature provided.
Structure: Introduction. I. The christian family in the Indian context. II. The christian perspective on the renewal of marriage and family in India. III. The role of the christian family in a non-christian India. IV. The christian family and the local church.

The Indian Bishops' Conference opened its statement with an expression of appreciation for the theme chosen for the Synod — a theme described as a fitting complement to the three previous Synods. The document submitted by the Indian bishops consisted of four major sections which treated the material in an ordered fashion.

a. *The christian family in the Indian context*

India, a land with many divergent cultures and customs, does not lend itself easily to generalizations about the family, they observe. Even the christian families (a tiny minority) differ from region to region. What is noteworthy, however, is the deep religious life of the people which exerts great influence on every event which occurs in and to the family. This is especially manifest in their vision of life as a unity of life and death, in the acceptance of children as a gift of God, etc.

Sociological factors also influence Indian family life. So, for example, the caste system continues to be a major obstacle to the integration of the social strata, and "communalism" stands as an obstacle to unity. There exists a wide spectrum of family types, depending on the geographical area: rural culture is characterized by the joint family, a close-knit group of people whose relations are patriarchal and extend over three generations; urban settings more commonly contain the nuclear family; then there is a third type of family structure which embraces a large section of the christian population, the tribal family which is by and large monogamous and in which women enjoy a greater freedom in their social life. The bishops note that social customs prevailing in India have far-reaching consequences on the Indian family. One still finds child marriages where the marriage promise is already made by the parents at a very early age and is ratified when the girl comes of age, and arranged marriages in which the parents impose their choice on their children. The custom of demanding a dowry from the bride is sometimes the source of much conflict.

The great underdevelopment which is part of the Indian socio-economic situation means that nearly 70% of families live below or just above the poverty line. The rapid population growth is also a cause for concern. However, the real problem is not only this increase but the over-consumption by a relatively small minority, widespread illiteracy, inadequate educational facilities, and the maldistribution of the resources available. Drastic measures have been taken by the government to control the size of the family but these are generally in conflict with prevailing religious sentiments. Finally, the bishops point out that the stability which was once a hallmark of the Indian family has suffered greatly under the influence of urbanization and industrialization. In spite of enormous changes, however, typical Indian values have been preserved such as family identity, marital fidelity, care for children, and attention to the needs of the aged.

b. *The christian perspective on and renewal of marriage and the family in India*

Vatican II described the christian family as the domestic church, in the sense that God Himself has ascribed to the family the mission of being the primary, vital cell of the Church by the mutual affection of its members, by common prayer and participation in liturgical worship, and by the practice of social justice. With this as a starting point the Indian bishops describe the christian family as a community of faith, love and hope.

1) As a community of faith

Under this aspect of family life the bishops considered the importance of family prayer through which the family becomes a listening and receiving church; family catechesis, through which family members share their faith experiences and seek renewal; and the preparation for family life, including sex education in the context of a communication of the right values. They understand the importance of home para-liturgies and the Indian traditional forms of prayer. The faith formation of both adults and children, they say, must convey the new orientations of the Council: ecumenism, concern for the world, religious freedom and respect for and relation with non-christian religions. Parents should be urgently helped through proper training sessions to fulfill their educational responsibilities. In addition to pre-marital preparation, follow-up programs for newlyweds are also a crying need of the time.

2) As a community of love

The threefold family relationship (conjugal, parental, and fraternal) helps each member grow to full maturity. This pattern of relations is a reflection of the Blessed Trinity where each person, by existing for the other, is his fullest self. Such a family constitutes a true home for all and therein the children learn to resist every form of social injustice. It is within the family that the vocation to marriage and family life as well as priestly and religious vocations develop.

3) As a community of hope

Hope is essential to family members, who often experience and must deal with their own shortcomings. For the Indian family, contraception is one of the most serious and critical problems, due to the rapid increase in the population and the strong measures adopted by the government in its policies of family planning. In this context, wrote the Indian bishops, we once again fully endorse the teaching of the Church which has come out very clearly on this matter through Vatican II, Pope Paul VI and Pope John-Paul II. In view of this, it is expected of married couples that they choose for responsible parenthood realized according to natural methods and in genuine love for one another and for God. However, it is also specifically noted that it is important that the Synod give attention to the problem of parents, many of them sincere and responsible christians, who find that natural methods are not workable in their cases for the time being. The bishops declared that they would appreciate very much a pastoral statement on such situations, already foreseen by the Council (GS, 51), particularly as there seems to exist much confusion in the minds of some priests, religious and faithful.

The legalization of abortion in India has created an extremely distressing situation where an increasing number of women, allegedly even among Catholics, are seeking abortion. The bishops proclaimed their support for the teaching of the Catholic Church which clearly condemns direct abortion as the killing of human life, but requested that the teaching be more actively promoted through educational institutions and the mass media. In spite of the traditional stability of marriage in India, they go on, divorce is on the increase. An enlightened program of pastoral action for marriage, particularly through the setting up of counselling centers, will go a long way to prevent, or at least reduce, the incidence of marital breakdown. Whenever there seems to be a valid reason for declaring the nullity of marriage or for requesting a papal dispensation from a non-consummated marriage, they say, the process must be speeded up at the various levels. Special pastoral care should be extended to those experiencing marital difficulties.

c. *The role of the christian family in a non-christian India*

As the christian family is the domestic church, there should be found in it the various aspects of the universal church. Hence, it is the place where the gospel is transmitted and from where the gospel radiates. According to the preparatory document, it can be said that the christian family has a single function or role, that of evangelizing, as evangelization has been described in the previous Synods (*Lineamenta*, III, 2). This missionary dimension should be present in all christian families, especially in a country like India where the overwhelming majority of the people have not yet accepted the message of Christ.

The bishops observe that unfortunately, for historical reasons, most Indian christian families have been encouraged to protect their faith by living in complete isolation from their non-christian brothers and sisters. It is time to help them emerge from this isolation, they say, and open up to the non-christians around them with an attitude of selfless sharing and service. Openness would help eliminate all sorts of fears, suspicions and prejudices. An attitude of tolerance can contribute a great deal to win over people inclined to friendliness and sympathy. For the christian, there should be openness and sharing, on both the material and spiritual levels, of whatever we possess, without any trace of discrimination.

Dialogue also means appreciation of and respect for whatever is true and holy in other religions. Another way of developing an open spirit would be fraternally to collaborate with people of all creeds in the pursuit of a more human society: peace, freedom and social justice, etc.

In preaching, more and more stress should be laid on the fact that all christians, without exception, are called to a fundamental witness which is already a silent but very powerful and effective proclamation of the Good News, "an initial act of evangelization". It is a known and encouraging fact that Jesus Christ is held in high regard and esteem by most Indians irrespective of their religious beliefs. Like the early christians heard and experienced, christian families should be helped to grow in a deeper personal commitment to Christ. A christian family which is truly conscious of its specific mission in the Church cannot help becoming the evangelizer of many other families and of the neighborhood of which it forms a part.

d. *The christian family and the local church*

One of the chief tasks of the whole local church according to the Indian bishops is the safeguarding and strengthening of the life of its primary vital cell, i.e. the family. This responsibility falls first of all on the laity from whose ranks come the builders of the christian family, as indicated in the texts of Vatican II. Yet the same Council reminds us that priests should consider married people and parents as committed to their care in a special way. Many priests and religious feel themselves inadequately equipped to meet the pastoral needs of the family today. To come to terms with this problem, it is urged that effective in-service programs, focused on family life, be planned and executed in accordance with the directives given by the Council (GS, 52). The task of the pastor is to sustain family life constantly and not merely on occasions of crises. Hence, regular family visitation is encouraged. The priest ought to know each family member personally, and help them to grow into Christ both as individuals and members of the family and parish community. The bishops expressed the hope that this solicitude might find tangible expression through the setting up, where feasible, of "Family Service Centers", where the various aspects of the family apostolate are adequately attended to and furthered by all the means available.

Conclusion

In the last analysis, concluded the Indian bishops, the well-being of the Church in any country depends very largely upon the quality of the christian family. The Church as a whole has received the promise from the Lord that she will last until the end of time. (The original apparently contains an error here by saying that the Church will *not* last. We have taken the liberty to correct the text). So it is that, in this time, she relies especially upon those christians who are joined in marriage and building domestic churches. "This and nothing else is the need of the hour and merits a common pledge at the hands of pastors and people to work together to make it a shining reality."

5. *Position Paper of the Bishops' Conference of the Philippines*

Catholic Bishops' Conference of the Philippines — General Secretariate, Catwelo, Manila, Philippines.
Position Paper on the Role of the Christian Family in the Modern World (condensed version, typed text of 6 pages). Dated 8 August 1980 and signed by Jaime Cardinal L. Sin, D.D., Archbishop of Manila.
Structure: I. Filippino cultural values related to the family. II. The situational context. III. Results of a survey on issues relevant to family life. IV. The work of the episcopal commission on family life (E.C.F.L.). V. Theologico-pastoral reflections.

The Philippine document opens by declaring that for over ten years the Church in the Philippines through the instrumentality of the Catholic Bishops' Conference of the Philippines (CBCP) has been officially committed to the ministry of the care of family life. The Family Life Apostolate (FLA) constitutes the pastoral response to the existing needs of the Church in the Philippines. In preparation for the October 1980 Synod, the CBCP developed a position paper divided into five major sections.

a. *Philippine cultural values related to the family*

The bishops begin by declaring that there exist certain spiritual values that, although not necessarily articulated, are certainly lived among the majority of the Filipino people. Marriage, in particular, is seen as an event involving whole families and even the whole community. For the most part, too, the typical average Filipino family is still largely unaffected by the technological mentality. Two particular features which are said to characterize the Filipino family are that it is strongly child-centered and tightly knit, with the whole family involved in the education of the children at home, and that it is deeply God-centered and the divine influence is experienced whether in favorable or in adverse circumstances in the daily lives of the people.

b. *The situational context*

The proper understanding of the meaning of the realities connected with family life is becoming crucial due to factors that challenge attitudes and the sense of values. The bishops therefore attempt to describe some of those factors. Filipino society is a society in search of development and thus undergoing changes which effect both socio-economic activities and the family. For instance, families are forced to separate for the sake of job-seeking, loneliness sets in, marital stability is threatened and breakdowns are increasing, especially in the higher social strata and among couples who were too young when they entered into marriage. The crisis is aggravated by the fact that a majority of the population is under 25 years of age. Often young people call into question values that are part of the Filipino culture and tend to give excessive importance to the ambiance of self-indulgence sometimes prompted by the Department of Tourism. All this easily leads, especially in the urban centers, to a growing loss of esteem for chastity, the pursuit of the erotic, the mechanization of conception and pregnancy control. This, simply put, represents a loss of the sense of the true of meaning of God-given sex.

c. *Results of a survey on issues relevant to family life*

In order to secure a fairly representative picture of the Filipino family situation, a survey was conducted covering 20 dioceses, geographically well distributed over the whole archipelago. Among the results, it was found that the family remains the first institution where the child is educated and that love is the most important thing that sustains family relationships. A good number of families still observe some traditional religious practices.

On the negative side, the bishops describe some conditions as not universally satisfactory: the family's participation in the socio-political affairs of the community, its freedom to voice their opinion especially in matters affecting the family, and the influence of the political conditions of society to strengthen families. More special problems include those of divorce; abortion as a means of birth control, especially in cases of unwed mothers; the changing status of women, bringing with it more and more involvement in out-of-home jobs and activities for economic reasons; and the parent-child relationship which threatens to become a growing problem as children manifest the need for love together with a great desire for freedom. Nevertheless, it is also observed that the laity are becoming more interested and involved in "Family Life Programs" as a realization of the duties incumbent upon them in virtue of the sacrament of marriage.

d. *The work of the Episcopal Commission on Family Live* (E.C.F.L.)

In 1969 the Episcopal Commission on Family Life was established in response to the needs of the moment with a general direction toward the formation of a value system in the lives of the people. Four aspects were discernable in the development of this project.

1) Preoccupation with technology (family planning)

Due mainly to the discussion about the escalation of population growth and the agitation for contraceptive family planning as a public policy, the overriding problem of family life came to be identified with the need for family planning. The effects of that sustained propaganda are still felt today. The CBCP joined the government's Commission on Population and issued a statement on "Population Growth Control" where the principles for collaboration were clearly spelled out. The bishops expressed genuine concern about the demographic problems of the country at that time, but stated unequivocally that there are basic values at stake affecting the more intimate aspects of married life in the Philippines.

The objectives of public population policy and of the family planning movement are not identical. Family planning aims at family welfare, while population policy aims at family limitation. Simply to reduce the number of children cannot be normative for the population, since it leads to abortion and masked infanticide as components of the program, as well as conditions that lead to the violation of the conscience of the individual. Population control is not and cannot be an absolute and ultimate value. When, less than two years after the beginning of their collaboration, it was dicovered that the CBCP's presence was being exploited to promote programs which in conscience it could not approve, the CBCP withdrew from the government Commission on Population. The bishops proclaimed that the problem of mass indigence was primarily not the result of the so-called population explosion, but of structured selfishness in the socio-economic-political order. The program petered out in 1975 with a clear conclusion: the solution to the problem of family size regulation does not lie in techniques nor is it merely a matter of methods.

2) The human dimension

Marriage in the Philippines is undergoing a transition from the functional to the personalist type of relationship. In response to the problems inherent in such a change, the Bukidon Family Life Seminar developed a program of sex education conducted by parents in rural homes to help young people approach marriage with a christian outlook and a sense of values and to revitalize the sacrament of marriage in the lives of the people. It was observed that when what is being sought after is not mere knowledge but change in the value system of people, the most effective tool is not scientific knowledge but witnessing. A program for pre-marriage instructors organized by the government in 1974 was found inadequate to meet the demands of a personalist type of marriage relationship since the instructors were trained to operate with the vision of a functional society. In response to this, the CBCP drew up the following guidelines: the main thrust of the Family Life Apostolate is evangelization of christian marriage and family life, not family planning; all family life programs must be integrated in the overall pastoral program of the diocese; and financial support from the government Population Commission is only to be accepted if certain conditions (freedom of action, no image of association) are met.

3) The theology of marriage

The theology of sexuality and marriage emerged very gradually. Couples became aware of the sacramental dimension of christian marriage, of the duty to evangelize each other that springs from the sacrament itself, and of the possibility of living the gospel in spirit and in truth.

4) Community orientation

The family contributes to larger communities by the formation in values that it gives. But it is in turn influenced by the system of values the community wants to promote through its laws and the control of the mass media. The CBCP issued a document (July, 1978) critically singling out the pagan character of the public program for population control and protesting against the use of outside experts for planning and programing the country's material development. Some principles were eventually formulated into "conclusions" reached in the Bukidon Seminar (October, 1978) and were later endorsed by the bishops (January, 1979). These pointed out that family life education is directed toward the development of the human person in the context of his family relations in the building of basic christian communities. The formation of these core groups is the beginning of a self-reliant, self-nourishing, and self-governing process, in coordination with the thrust of the local, regional, national and universal Church. The target audience should be people from the lower socio-economic strata or the grassroots level. Finally, funds should be generated from local sources and if outside funding is accepted there must be full freedom in using the funds according to the needs.

Other points touched upon were the involvement of priests in the Family Life Apostolate (FLA), the problem of systematic recording for natural family planning programs, and the use of mass media and promotional activities for effective support of family life programs. Shortly afterwards, the CBCP issued a strong pastoral letter entitled "Thou shall not kill", on the life of the unborn child. All these activities and processes of reflection made possible some conclusions with pastoral implications: the importance of human, not material, resources which can be found anywhere; the importance of knowing the needs of the people before starting any program; the observation that witnessing to real human values is very evident at the grassroots level; and that the Family Life Apostolate needs all the charisms in the Church: that of priests, married people and those vowed to the evangelical life.

To assess the situation and properly evaluate the activities of the FLA, seven regional consultations on family life were held during April and May 1980. The results in most of the aspects are confirmative of the facts and ideas presented above with a clearly expressed need of insisting on value-formation, closer coordination of many scattered activities coming from different groups, and diocese/parish-centered orientation. In such an atmosphere a declaration on the rights of the family was a welcome development. The "Declaration on Family Rights" was formally launched on 29 June 1980 with the participation of the private and religious sectors of the population with clear collaborative and ecumenical tone.

e. *Theologico-pastoral reflections*

The Christian Filipino family is seen to be one of the value-forces called to help in the evengelization of the Filipino people, particularly in the present existing conditions of social tensions and value crises. Marriage and family are conceived — and in many cases lived — not simply as a state of life bound by laws and duties, but as a community willed by God where mutual solicitude and care for one another and for the extended christian community is lived to the full. In the evaluation of the FLA four developments are worth mentioning:
1) The apostolate of the family constitutes a solid foundation for the formation of base-level ecclesial communities.
2) The central focus is to be placed on the christian vision of the person as a key to the pastoral approach to the problems of development and evangelization, the christian family being a counter-sign to the climate of manipulation that fosters artificial contraceptives, sterilization and abortion.
3) One of the theological insights brought about by the reflection of grassroots families refers to the role of charism in the evangelization of the family. A noticeable interplay of the three major charisms in the apostolate — the marital, sacerdotal, and religious charisms — has been deeply felt and its need strongly concluded: this is a genuine movement of the total ecclesial community.
4) The role of the christian family must be placed in and understood within the context of the Church's mission in its double parameter of

inward and outward movement if it is to actually be the domestic church (LG, 11). It is in this sense that we speak of the role of the family both as an evangelized and an evangelizing community.

In summary, then, what is expected of the Church — universal, local, domestic — is that she lives her vocation in earnest and exercises through word and life her right and her duty to be the true pedagogue of faith; the shaper of the christian community, where families are not just groupings of baptized persons but fully dynamic christian communities. There is a deep interrelationship between the destiny of the two churches, the "domestic church" of the family and the wider church — parish, diocese, universal church. The universal church, or for that matter the local church, will be as strong and vibrant as its communion of "domestic churches", the christian families, will be.

C. Latin America

6. *Position Paper of the Bishops' Conference of Brazil.*

Conferência Nacional dos Bishops do Brazil — CNBB, Comissão Representativa. As funçôs da familia cristã no mundo atual (Documento de sugestões para o texto fundamental do Sínodo mundial de 1980). Dated 30 October - 3 November, 1979, with no signature.
Structure: General Observations. I. SEE: The situation of the family in today's world. II. JUDGE: Doctrinal questions on matrimony and the family. III. ACT: Functions of the christian family.
Note: Only the English version of the Brazilian original was available to us: Christian family role in today's world (typed text of 10 oversized pages).

The method employed by the largest bishop's conference of Latin America, and one of the world's most important, was one previously put to use at the conference of Medellin and Puebla and consists of three phases: See, Judge, and Act. In their introductory "General Observations", the bishops remark that a doctrinal exposition cannot be extra-historical, but rather, should help judge reality. Applying the inductive method, for which the young churches had already pleaded, the Brazilian document expresses the conviction that their own proposed pastoral orientations respond in fact to the appeals made by reality but judged in the light of the Word of God. They comment further that it is necessary to clarify beforehand the concept of family which should not merely portray the traditional family of industrialized societies, solidly composed, without economic, habitational, or educational problems, but should embrace the various types of families existing in the world, especially in underdeveloped regions.

The consultation document contained elements and ideas which were said to be extremely vast and already generally known. For this reason, it seemed necessary that a reformulation give emphasis and order, distinguishing what is fundamental from what is secondary or peripheral. The *Lineamenta* was said to convey the impression that the family stands in the center of the social system. Much to the contrary, they observe, it seems that the family in Latin America is only a link, the weakest link, of society. It is more a victim than a transforming agent of society. It is therefore suggested that the synodal document begin with an anthropological reflection, of a moral form, so that it might receive more universal acceptance, and present the biblical doctrine and the magisterium only afterwards. It should take into account the ecumenical dimension, both in the doctrinal and pastoral parts. Finally, it is hoped that the Synod reinterpret the doctrine on family beginning with today's reality, in confrontation with the Word of God, and be more in the prespective of quality and liberation than that of moralizing. The three parts of the document develop these themes as follows.

a. SEE: *the situation of the family in today's world*

The bishops of Brazil begin by describing the major factors which determine the type of family present in their country. Family movements are said to exert little influence upon these factors. Action to change the vast causes (economic, social and cultural) which condition the family, is of prime importance if action at the level of family, and family movements, is to be successful and have lasting effect. The family is more a victim than an acting agent in relation to macro-economic factors. The bishops point to the problematic of poor families (the great majority) and to the vast social problematic which weighs heavily upon the family. Unjust societal structures impact on the structure of the family. The adverse social conditions (such as the problems of appropriation and use of land, the rural exodus, chaotic urbanization, lack of professional preparation, malnutrition) reach most especially the "populous classes", not only destroying many families, but preventing the sound formation of new families. The problem in developed nations is different: there, it is abundance and consumerism which drains the spiritual sense of the family. The bishops felt that it is necessary to denounce imperialist interests and the imposition of birth control programs. They also observe that political repression, realized by many regimes, destroys numerous families.

On the cultural level there is a new mentality of equal rights as regards family, man and woman, etc. In addition, children's rights have greater consideration. However, there is no uniform concept among the people as to what constitutes matrimony. There exists greater consideration for family cultural differences according to ethnic backgrounds but North American culture has a very strong influence today in Latin America. With regard to historical factors, attention must be given to the inheritance left by colonialism and slavery in the Third World. Only the master had a "family", the slaves cohabited. A negative factor for the family is the loss of its historical memory, its ethnic and cultural origins. Psychologically, the immaturity of engaged couples affects their ability to assume the obligations of the sacrament of matrimony. There is a need for an analysis of the factors and consequences of premature weddings which (at 13 or 14 years of age for women) are common among the poor classes of the Third World. The question of homosexuality and the problem of the non-acceptance of the elderly by the family also ought to be examined.

Insufficient evangelization, they say, has led to a faith disconnected from concrete life. The Brazilian situation is influenced by the great spread of the Western understanding of love, making conjugal love and sex in general an individual question of personal gratification without commitment. An abortive and contraceptive mentality is the result of poor formation. The celebration of matrimony is regarded as a private matter. Generally speaking, christians are ignorant about matrimony as a sacrament and present canonical legislation on matrimony is outdated. In some regions of Brazil, many couples are neither married civilly nor religiously. They live in fidelity as a natural attitude; other unions are fruitful but unstable. Still others do not marry because of exorbitant social costs or because of the complexity of religious and civil bureaucracy. Also, a prolonged and adequate matrimonial catechumenate is lacking.

In response to these factors, the bishops propose that basic ecclesial communities should be formed in rural areas and on the periphery of large cities as these lead to new forms of socialization or communitarianism of family units. The social factors are of prime importance. For instance, the bishops take the example of the indigenous extended family: in diverse regions of Brazil, godfathers and godmothers become co-fathers (compadre) and co-mothers (comadre) with the parents of the child and thus exert a great deal of influence. Nevertheless, there is a great deal of pressure brought upon the family because of changing social factors. As a matter of fact, they observe, the family has lost various traditional functions or has divided them with other intermediary social structures: economic functions have been assumed by social welfare and security systems, for instance. The bishops urge that the family exercise those functions which seem to be truly essential, namely, formation, affectivity, social consciousness, catechesis, and family liturgy.

b. JUDGE: *doctrinal questions on matrimony and the family*

The ground and judge for theological doctrine is said to be Scripture. This includes reflection on marriage and the family. The sensitive areas

of human sexuality, responsible parenthood and the regulation of
fertility are said to be in need of distinctions between definitely established doctrine and points which are in need of further elucidation.
The approach to sexuality and conjugal love, say the bishops, should be
positive and avoid a widely held negative and manichaean attitude. The
concept of love, likewise, which is the basis for family relations, needs to
be reaffirmed, as well as the dignity of virginity. They say that it is most
positive to speak of "conjugal chastity". However, the way it is done it
not so positive in the preparatory document for the Synod. It is an
extremely abstract exposition, without connection to lived daily life. In
the *Lineamenta*, conjugal chastity is poorly treated. Nevertheless, in
today's world, it is enormously important.

From a sociological point of view, the family is seen as an "intermediary
body" (unit), since it fulfills certain basic functions for persons and
society such as: procreation and the first socialization of children,
affective functions (socialized love), the individualizing foundation of the
offspring, the offering of privacy in a home and protection against the
risks of existence. From a psychological point of view, the environment
conditions the person's life. Family and conjugal therapy can help, but it
is not a panacea, since the greatest distortions of family life have origins
outside it, in the social and economic fields. From a theological
standpoint, the family is seen as a domestic church and marriage as a
sacrament, a sign of Christ's love for the Church, a gift of God, a state of
grace, and a visible sign of love. It is necessary to undertake a profound
study to allow the distinction of that which is related to a culture and that
which is a basic value of the family institution. There ought to be a
serious study of the doctrinal aspect: the coinciding of the validity of
marriages among the baptized and the sacrament of matrimony. The
bishops ask whether the distinction between "intentio Dei Creatoris"
and "intentio Redemptoris" is justifiable when the impression given is
that there is no relationship between them? There ought to be a study of
the dignity of the conjugal union as a human value, they say, even when
it does not reach the sacred, the sacramental. Special emphasis ought to
be given to the family/community aspect, seeking integration in society
and the Church.

The problem of justice in today's world needs to be more accented
because of institutionalized injustice; today the great majority of this
world's people are deprived of a worthy family life. It would be necessary
to accent more human freedom and the value of the human person as
opposed to the secular oppressor mentality of our days. The phenomenon of "domination" will affect more and more of our family life.
With regard to the moral question of matrimony, the bishops issue a call
to reaffirm the fundamental values of christian matrimony: love and
fidelity, fecundity and paternal responsibility. The Church should offer

norms related to marriage and sex as an ideal and help the people pastorally to reach the proposed ideal while understanding the weakness of whomever does not reach it. Further, it is observed that the value of the sacrament of matrimony should be the point of departure for a spirituality of marriage and family: as means to salvation and forgiveness in Christ, freedom in Christ, with sanctification being the social dimension of the sacrament and with an accent on the dynamism of growth in love as an essential part of marriage, and the family as community.

Given the population problems, certain demographic policies gravely affect families, especially in underdeveloped countries, and birth control methods continue to cause much unrest and suffering. It is indispensable, they feel, that the Synod debate these questions with the necessary amplitude and depth. They recommend that representative couples from different regions of the world participate fully in the preparatory reflections of this Synod and be present at the Synod itself.

In a more general vein, it is observed that the pastoral problems raised by the crisis in married life are so complex that canon law and the theological presuppositions on which it is based seem insufficient as just and merciful solutions. There is a felt need to profoundly rethink all biblical and systematic moral theology of marriage in order to reach a renewal of canon law and a more solid and adequate pastoral vision. They recommend, in particular, that the following guidelines already available and elaborated, be examined and studied in depth: respect for marriage as an earthly reality, incarnated in concrete cultures; the coming to be of marriage as a dynamic process and its existential consummation in faith; the real and juridical indissolubility of marriage; the ability to separate a real marriage (natural) and the sacrament of the New Law for the baptized; the sense in which love is constitutive of matrimony; a pastoral orientation for remarried divorcees; the "economy" of the Oriental Churches.

c. ACT: *functions of the christian family*

In approaching pastoral problems, the bishops criticize the *Lineamenta* for being strong on theory and weak on practice: the "how" of the family fulfilling its many roles. More attention needs to be given to the future as well as to the present, real problems and concrete solutions — which should be illuminated by the Gospel. The working paper is said to be lacking in its understanding of reality. The systematic approach which is taken there, the vision of prophet, priest and king, does not respond to the reality in Brazil which is marked by transformation, injustice, secularism and egoism. That reality must be faced before solutions can be found.

Calling upon the Synod to be more realistic, three levels are singled out for special attention: society, the Church and the family itself. As for the first, the bishops observe that the notion of the family being the basic cell of society obscures the fact that more often than not the family is limited and determined by society. By generating new lives, the already existing system of social inequality in Latin America and more specifically in Brazil is reproduced by the family. This should be a primary concern of pastoral work. Specific examples given are the appropriation of resources, funds and land, the dislocation of people and discrimination against the working class. Other examples are offered to illustrate how Third World societies sin against the family. Most of what is said can be summarized by the use of the term "unjust social structures" which turn the family into a victim that does not respond to the middle clase notion of the "traditional family". These structures need to be transformed. The Church, it is said, should take a lead in the process of transformation and the Synod would be a good forum for doing so. Other recommendations made by the Brazilian bishops to the Synod concerned the following topics: political parties; the struggle against moral decline; the right to constitute a family; radical change of political regimes and economic systems; the right to exist of ethnic minorities; and the need for good social communications.

In what is perhaps their most pointed criticism, the Brazilian bishops write that "family-ism" is a pastoral attitude present in the Church which consists in entrusting to the family only the satisfaction of affective needs of persons while accepting passively that all other social structures be controlled by efficiency and dominated by impersonal imperatives of greater production and profit. This approach produces the image of a serene family world, distant from the real world and a model for a-political and passive consumerism. Such a theory leads to the overestimation of the possibilities of the family, thus collaborating in preparing its downfall. There is also included in this pastoral choice of "family-ism" a way of ignoring the Gospel demands in political, social and economic life, while in Latin America there is a recognized oppressive, exclusive class society. Further, they say that a pastoral vision of the family which gives first place to moralizing and juridical considerations obstructs the real mission of the family in the Church. Family pastoral care must be, in the first place, founded on the proposals of the Gospel. A spirituality of marriage and family life unrelated to a lived understanding of love, to an understanding of sexuality as a source of happiness and pleasure and to the sacrament of matrimony as a dynamic of growth and renewed fidelity, impedes the mission of the family. We must avoid a pastoral vision that treats the laity only as objects of evangelization and does not assume christian couples and their children as the subject of pastoral action, thus making the mission of the family in the Church more difficult. It is urgent that the laity be given their proper and inalienable place; not only the laity of the middle clase, but also the poor. The Synod ought to listen to the poor when preparing guidelines with respect to matrimony, sexuality and family life.

In a historical vein, the observation is made that in past centuries, when the Church exercised a certain social control, the family was a part of community life and was the object of general pastoral orientation. Baptism and matrimony contributed to social cohesion. In those times, a certain christian family was born and the parish was considered the family of families. Times have changed and society is now pluralistic. In many of her juridical, theological and pastoral writings, the Church has not succeeded in understanding the consequences of this new and very real situation. In losing a part of her social control, the general pastoral orientation is forced to face specific questions. Within this context, the pastoral experience of Basic Church Communities is an indispensable contribution to be taken to the Synod. In a Basic Church Community, the bishops observe, the family is no longer a specific pastoral area; it becomes an integrated pastoral experience. A Basic Church Community unites families (sometimes husbands, wives, youth and children) and not individuals as in traditional Church societies or specific married groups. Family pastoral care is not reduced to family movements but realizes its mission in and through each and every community. The Basic Church Community leads to greater communion and participation. They go beyond consumerism. They offer new models of family life and christian living. From them new ministerial roles evolve. It is from this perspective that study of the possibility of conferring the priestly ministry on heads of families should be considered. Also, it is precisely amongst the ordinary people, whether in cities or country places, that the Basic Church Community springs up with a new style of interfamily relationships, giving rise to new types of family life and even of social relationships and structuring. Families evangelize one another, and are characterized by mutual solidarity at all times. They prepare young people for marriage and other sacraments.

Other family pastoral initiatives have contributed to the christian formation of families. These include various types of movements of married couples and courses of preparation for engaged couples, parents, and godparents. These should be integrated among themselves and with organic pastoral planning so that all dimensions of pastoral life may be enriched by them and they, in turn, enriched. The Church ought to purify marriage celebrations and adopt other means so that religious weddings be more than simple social events. Furthermore, the Church should organize "Family Counseling Centers", with the cooperation of universities and other centers for higher learning. Also, care should be given to the remote and immediate preparation for matrimony, the celebration itself, pastoral care for special situations, and an adequate preparation for priests and married couples who work in family movements.

With respect to the functions of the family, the bishops enumerate that they are: to form persons, conscious of their political and social responsibilities in view of a global transformation of society and the implementation of Gospel values; to be a faith educator by also developing a critical conscience illuminated by faith; to transmit fundamental values and enable one to integrate new values; and to be a center for communion and participation, of learning to write one's own history and give value to human life. Dialogue must be used daily in the family in order that union between parents and children may grow. Families should feel their responsibility as the first educators in the faith of their children and be reminded of their role in fostering vocations. The family ought to value confirmation as the time to conscientiously integrate youth into the community. The Synod ought to encourage family prayer, giving value to creative forms of family liturgy. The family should be the first to promote and defend the value of human life.

Finally, reiterating their social perspective, the bishops state that a critical christian conscience should lead the family to a discovery of political and social responsibilities and to organized action for a global transformation of society imbued with Gospel values and the creation of new social systems free of injustice. The family should assume a united front in civic and social organizations, and in unions in which its members participate. As a kind of postscript, the position paper puts forth some proposals about special cases. The bishops say that an effort must be made to hear the people involved when seeking to reflect theologically and pastorally reach dismembered families, the separated and divorced, remarried couples and unwed mothers, so that within the Church there are no marginalized or humiliated persons.

D. North Atlantic

We face a danger of being one-sided at this point since we have hardly any preparatory documents from the bishops' conferences of the North Atlantic region. Two possible exceptions might be the Netherlands and Belgium. However, the documents from these two countries are not position papers in a completely representative sense. The document from the Netherlands was not drawn up by the bishops' conference itself but by the Secretariate of the Roman Catholic Church Province of the Netherlands which is not necessarily comparable with the position of the bishops themselves[5]. The Belgian document was not officially endorsed

5. *Commentaar bij de Lineamenta Algemene Synode 1980*, introduction by A.F. VERMEULEN, Secretary SRKK, dated 18 Oct. 1979, 12 typed pages.

by the bishops' conference but was actually drawn up by the Doctrinal
Commission of the Belgian Bishops' Conference and sent to Rome as an
official reaction to the *Lineamenta*[6]. In some West European countries a
kind of preparatory document was published but these were actually
messages which the bishops had directed to the faithful of their own
churches and were not direct reactions to the *Lineamenta*[7].

Because of this situation we will attempt to fill the lacuna by reporting
on some of the speeches which were delivered during the opening week of
the Synod. With our own plan in mind, we have chosen those which most
closely resemble reactions to the preparatory documents of the Synod
and which put forth the majority opinion of the conference of which the
individual bishop functioned as a representative. We thus follow the
loose structure which parallels that of the already mentioned position
papers. In this case, we have also limited ourselves to representatives
from North America, namely, the U.S.A. and Canada.

7. Contributions in the name of the National Conference of Catholic Bishops of the United States

a. Intervention of Archbishop John R. Quinn (San Francisco)

The intervention delivered by Archbishop Quinn on 29 Sept. was
entitled "Contraception: a Proposal for the Synod", and was brought
forward in the name of the National Conference of Catholic Bishops of
the U.S.A. At the outset, the speaker affirmed that his paper was based
on an acceptance of the teaching of the Church as it had been enunciated
by Pope Paul VI in HV and by Pope John-Paul II in his address to the
bishops of the United States in October 1979. With respect to this
teaching, queried Quinn, are the only three options available: silence, a
mere repetition (of magisterial teaching) or dissent? His own intervention, declared the Archbishop, is based on the belief that there is another
course suggested by the words of Paul VI shortly following the
publication of HV. The encyclical, said the Pope, "is not a complete
treatment regarding man in this sphere of marriage, of the family and of
moral probity. This is an immense field to which the magisterium of the
Church could and perhaps should return with a fuller, more organic and
more synthetic exposition".

Having pointed to the fact that the majority of U.S. Catholics reject

6. *Extrait du rapport de la Réunion de la commission doctrinale de la conférence
épiscopale de Belgique. Examen du document préparatoire au Synode des Evêques*, dated 12
Sept. 1979, 13 typed pages.

7. Cf. *Documentation Catholique* 77 (1980) for statements of the bishops from
Switzerland (7 Sept. 1980) 823-824; Italy (7 Sept. 1980) 824-825; and France (19 Oct. 1980)
936-938.

HV's teaching on contraception, the speaker raised the central question, which might be summarized as follows: what reflection can this Synod bring to bear on this opposition which is found even among those who are otherwise good and faithful Catholics and whose dedication to the Church is beyond doubt? Archbishop Quinn continued that there is no doubt that the teaching of HV on contraception is authentic teaching of the magisterium of the Church. Yet the Church has always recognized the principle of doctrinal development, for example, in the area of Scripture studies, in canonical jurisprudence and notably in the Second Vatican Council. In the area of contraception, then, Quinn asks whether there are not nuances and clarifications, further considerations and greater pastoral insights still to be elaborated? Consequently, the Archbishop proposed the following considerations in an effort to remove the harmful impasse" on this moral teaching.

1) The issue of contraception should be treated in a new context.

The teaching on contraception rests in a broad perspective but this context is either unknown to many or not recognized. Many priests and laypersons see it simply as negative, a prohibition against contraception, and as narrow, concerned only with the morality of the marital relationship. The prohibition of contraception is understood as if the Church teaches that married couples must have all the children they can.

In addition, there is a serious population problem confronting the world. We cannot credibly treat the problem of contraception without clear and honest recognition of the grave demographic problem of our times. It is a fact that the Church's teaching in this area is almost unknown. The Archbishop pointed out that the Church has a clear doctrine of responsible parenthood. And it is with this, he proposed, that the Synod begin its treatment of the issue of contraception: place it in the context of a developed teaching on responsible parenthood. On this point there is a continuing line of thought from Pius XI in *Casti connubii* through Pius XII and the acknowledgement of infertile periods, Vatican II in *Gaudium et spes* regarding responsible parenthood, and Paul VI in HV. The first coordinate for creating a new context for treating contraception, then, would be a doctrine fairly well developed already in magisterial teaching and one which enjoys a wide consensus within the Church. The second, and broader, coordinate should be an articulation of the Church's teaching on human sexuality. This is one of the major problems of the world today and it has never been dealt with in any comprehensive way be the magisterium.

2) There should be a widespread and formal dialogue with theologians.

The fact that a significant number of theologians do not accept the teaching of the magisterium on contraception constitutes a grave problem for the Church. Of this number, many do indeed hold that there is an intrinsic link between the unitive and procreative aspects of marriage.

Many would hold that contraception is not simply something good, desirable or indifferent from a moral point of view. Their ultimate problem with the teaching of the church lies precisely in *quilibet actus ...*, or that "each and every marriage act must be open to the transmission of life" (HV, 11). This dissent by theologians has serious implications in three areas.

a) *The faith of the people.* Public dissent by well-known theologians leads many to call into question other teachings of the Church.

b) *Practice.* As the representative of the teaching authority of the Church, the priest is expected to uphold the teaching of the magisterium. As a pastor he is also expected to aid people in the shaping of their consciences. The dilemma places a disproportionate burden on the capabilities of the average confessor.

c) *Ecclesiology.* The fact that in practice the widespread non-observance of the teaching is coupled with widespread reception of the eucharist means that the moral issue as such has been resolved by many. But the remaining ecclesiological issue is an explosive question, for "disserters" and for all who believe in and reverence the teaching authority of the Church.

How, then, can the Church prevent the results of the contraception debate from eroding the role of the magisterium in the Church? In summary of these points, Archbishop Quinn observed that Catholic theological tradition has always insisted on the complementarity of faith and reason. For many, this is precisely the heart of the present ecclesiological crisis: they find the rational basis for the Church's teaching unconvincing. This, therefore, would seem to be an area of special concern to the Synod in its effort to support and uphold the doctrine of the magisterium. The speaker then proposed the following approach to resolving the problem.

a) The Holy See should initiate a formal dialogue with Catholic theologians, including a recognition that the teaching on contraception is a serious and authentic doctrine of the ordinary magisterium coupled with the recognition that there can be development and amplification of this teaching just as there has been in other areas.

b) This dialogue should have two stages or phases. The first would be a listening phase including both theologians who support the Church's teaching and those who do not, bearing in mind Pope Leo XIII's principle that "the Church has nothing to fear from the truth". At the same time, the theologians should be encouraged to listen in a spirit of faith and openness to the magisterium, to its position and its assumptions. The second phase should be comprised of the effort to work toward a resolution of this problematic situation in the light both of the dialogue itself and of the Church's experience since HV.

c) The more permanent result of such a dialogue might well be the recognition that an institution such as the International Theological

Commission should be strengthened to ensure a continuing means of ongoing communication of a direct nature between theologians and the Holy See. A second major fruit of such a dialogue would be the development of a better understanding of some specific guidelines about dissent within the Church.

3) Careful attention should be given to the process by which magisterial documents are written and communicated.

To some degree, the credibility problems of the magisterium are caused by a failure to get an adequate hearing for what is being taught. This may indeed derive from media distortions, but we cannot deny that another major reason lies in a failure to communicate the teaching of the Church adequately. It would seem useful, then, that an international staff be created to collaborate in writing such magisterial documents in a language which would be directly comprehensible to moderately educated people in today's world, for instance, as comprehensible as the daily newspapers are to the general readership.

In his general conclusion, Archbishop Quinn pointed to the main intention of his intervention: an attempt to respond to the serious obligation of taking part in this Synod. The time has come, he said, to take up the challenge of Paul VI when he noted that "this is an immense field to which the magisterium of the Church could and perhaps should return with a fuller, more organic and more synthetic exposition".

b. *Intervention of Archbishop Joseph Bernardin (Cincinnati)*

It was also in the name of the National Conference of Catholic Bishops of the U.S. that Archbishop Bernardin, on the same day as Archbishop Quinn, initiated the general synodal discussion with an address dedicated to "the need for a more positive theology of sexuality". In many parts of the world, he pointed out, there is a significant gap between the teaching on sexual morality and the ideas and attitudes on the same subject held by many of the laity and even many priests. Departing from this enormous problem, as the Archbishop calls it, the credibility of the Church is seen to be undermined when the proposals of the bishops are simply ignored. On this level, two needs must be addressed:

1) the manner of conceptualizing and presenting our teaching on sexuality and the ethical and moral norms which flow from that teaching;

2) helping people not only to understand the teaching more fully but to respond to it in an affirmative way.

A more positive theology of sexuality is needed, he says, not to replace this moral teaching with a substantively different one, but to help people see more clearly why the tradition takes the position is does. A moral teaching is seldom accepted solely on the basis of authority. It is accepted only if it is perceived as reasonable, persuasive and related to actual experience. It is important to highlight some elements which might be part of a more positive theology of sexuality:

1) Sexuality is a gift from God, good in itself, and used as God intends, enriching. Hence, all dualism and denigration of sexuality must be counteracted.

2) Sexuality is a relational power. It is not merely a capacity for performing specific acts. It is part of our God-given natural power or capacity for relating to others. It colors the qualities of sensitivity, warmth, openness and mutual respect in our interpersonal relationships.

3) Understood in this way, sexuality cannot be equated with genitality, which is a narrower concept referring to the physical expressions of sexuality leading to genital union. The special context of marriage is demanded to serve human love and life generally.

4) It cannot be taken for granted that people understand and accept a natural law ethic, or that citing natural law principles will be persuasive. This does not mean that the natural law tradition should be abandoned, but it needs to be expanded. The complementarity of sexuality must be seen as reflecting in human terms the dynamic unity within the triune God. Light must be shed on the need for both physical and psychic integrity in the act of sexual union through which spouses express and accomplish self-giving.

5) As the development of a more positive theology of sexuality proceeds upon such lines as these, it should become both more urgent and more simple to situate within it our traditional teaching on such issues as premarital sex, homosexuality and contraception. This can be done by linking the "nuptial meaning of the body" with the human procreative potential (in the marriage context). Then, in this context, the high value placed on the child as an expression of the patent's love and generosity can be emphasized. Pope John-Paul II expressed this beautifully and forcefully in his homily at the Washington Mall last October.

6) This "nuptial meaning of the body" is also realized — admittedly in a different way — in those who are single or celibate for the sake of the kingdom. A single or celibate person must also be generative, life-giving and life-producing, not in a genital physical sense but in a genuinely personal sense through a wide range of loving relationships. It would be much more productive for the Church if we could look upon celibacy in a more positive, enriching way. This would be more in line with our understanding of sexuality as a relational power.

7) Finally, an integral theology of sexuality must also take into account the reality of original sin and its concomitant, concupiscence, without however slipping into a Jansenistic mentality. Original sin results in a tendency toward defective relationships both with God and with our fellow human beings. Theologically, we use the term concupiscence to

describe this disintegration or fragmentation. When sexuality, which is so expressive of the person, contributes to the integration of our inner selves, it is healing and good. When, however, sexuality is expressed in a way that runs counter to the God given orientation of the human person, it becomes destructive.

In his conclusion, Archbishop Bernardin observed that most institutions in recent years have suffered from a credibility problem. As noted, the Church faces a similar situation in the area of doctrine. The Church's teaching concerning human sexuality, marriage and social justice simply does not have the impact it should on many people. Too many people, he said, look on our moral teaching as a laundry list of do's and don'ts based more on historical accident or institutional concern than on the gospel mandate. So they pick and choose what appears convenient to them and reject the rest. In confronting this problem a greater evangelistic effort is needed. Without minimizing the intellectual dimension we must recognize that this alone is not sufficient. Before people can fully live by the values Jesus taught us, they must experience conversion. Only then will they be willing to commit themselves to Him and accept the demands that He makes. Persons who have experienced conversion begin to understand that we are called to a totally new way of life involving new personal and societal responsibilities — a way of life, furthermore, which runs counter to many of the values of our contemporary culture.

8. *Contributions of the Canadian Conference of Catholic Bishops*

a. *Intervention of Archbishop Henri Légaré (Grouard-McLennan)*

In his capacity as deputy chairman (vice president) of the Canadian Conference of Catholic Bishops, Archbishop Légaré, in the name of that conference, focused attention on the problem of marriage and family in the industrialized countries. In these countries, the institution of the Church has ceased to exercise a normal function. The Canadian delegate is convinced that the construction of a theology of marriage and the family must find its point of departure in those values which belong to the real experience of married couples. In the opening of his address, Archbishop Légaré pointed to the importance of the Synod as a privileged opportunity to investigate the experience of people. The principle points of his talk elaborated upon four topics.

1) A new meaning for marriage and family
For a large number of young people today in the industrialized countries, he observed, marriage and the family no longer mean what they did for previous generations. For them, the couple relationship is based on love. Love is readily taken as an absolute which justifies sexual relations and premarital cohabitation. The radical changes in percep-

tions of sexuality include: fertility control, feminine and masculine roles, and the functions of the family in modern society. If some of these attitudes are full of hope, others are full of ambiguity. They are an expression of a search for a new balance between personal love and institutional constraints. They show the effort required for establishing a new relationship between women and men and family and society, as well as a new way of situating oneself in the Church. If we, as Vatican II asked, scrutinize the signs of the times, we must encourage a theology that would start with today's experiences, without, however, neglecting the riches of the past.

2) The validity of marriage

The first question here that is becoming more and more painful is divorce. The fact that divorces have increased dramatically is in itself a reason for restudying the requirements for a valid marriage, taking into account the findings of modern psychology, especially regarding the conditions for freedom and maturity. From a socio-cultural perspective, attention must be paid to the phenomenon of premarital cohabitation, in which thousands of young people are involved.

3) The indissolubility of marriage

These first observations bring us to the deeper questions of the indissolubility of marriage. We have an obligation to re-examine certain aspects of doctrine upon which the indissolubility of marriage is based, taking as our point of departure the pastoral ministry to the divorced-remarried. The indissolubility of christian marriage is based on a number of realities: the necessity of faithfulness inherent in human love, the good of the children, the good of society and the design of God. But the ultimate foundation upon which the Church's doctrine rests is the symbolism of the union of Christ and His Church. Christian marriage thus becomes the image, the sign, and the witness of this indissoluble union. This teaching which is undeniably rich, leaves two questions unresolved.

The first, which is theological, is linked to the experience of the pilgrim people of God who welcome salvation within a history where grace and sin are mixed. How does one speak of marraige as a privileged sign of the convenant between God and man? How express the difference between the relationship of Christ to the Church and the relationship of the Church to Christ? This latter relationship cannot simply be equated with the first since it is marked by human frailty. The essentialist philosophy within which the theology of the sacrament of marriage evolved can lead one to think that the Church is already in a state of perfection, that it has in some sense arrived at its end. But that approach forgets that the Church is truly in a pilgrim state, that it is constructed in history. Therefore, should we not rethink the theology of marriage in a more existentialist and personalist framework?

The second, pastoral question arises from the situation of the divorced who are remarried. Present pastoral ministry does not pay enough attention to the situation of those who, after experiencing the loss of a first love, live another in fidelity, are involved as christians in the name of their faith and want to enjoy full participation at the eucharistic table. There is need for a ministry of mercy which continues to welcome people without denying the evangelical demand for conjugal fidelity.

4) Baptized non-believers

A final situation which demands attention is that of the baptized non-believers. This involves the refusal of sacramental marriage on the grounds of incapacity (since marriage is an affirmation of one's faith). The consequence of relegating these people to the condition of public sinners bespeaks the denial of their right to a natural or civil marriage. First of all, what is the relationship between the marriage sacrament and the human institution of marriage? And then, what of the relationship between baptism, faith, intention and the marriage sacrament. By way of conclusion, Archbishop Légaré observed that these are admittedly difficult questions. But he thought that to face them in this assembly constitutes an act of confidence in the Spirit who does not cease to guide His Church.

b. *Intervention of Archbishop Joseph N. MacNeil (Edmonton)*

Archbishop MacNeil, president of the Canadian Conference of Catholic Bishops, spoke, at the opening of his intervention, about the intensive preparations for the Synod undertaken by the Canadian delegation in the preceding eight months. It is to the members of families, the laity, those who are called to be "agents of history" that the Synod must turn its attention since these are the bearers of such heavy responsibilities. The Synod must recognize that it is the family members who are responsible for the growth of family life and the progress of society. In the course of this Synod, he said, we are invited to listen to what the Lord says through families, to discover how we should multiply, through the Church, opportunities for family members to hear, respond to and express the Lord's call.

1) The Lord's call

Couples and their children are called to love their Creator and each other, to join others in co-creating the future of mankind, to cultivate and care for the plants and animals and all the other resources that the Lord gives for all people. Family members are called to build up the kingdom by bringing God's plan to reality in all aspects of family life and indeed in all situations where they are present.

2) People respond

Just as we can say that the Lord calls family members to lives of active love, we can equally affirm that countless people are responding to that call. One of the most noteworthy signs of the effort being made to bring God's plan to reality is the movement, almost everywhere in the world, to allow women to come to full dignity and recognition, personnally and socially. This Synod must see how we pastoral leaders can do more to bring this movement to full realization in the institutional Church.

Yet another sign of our times is the special difficulties of troubled marriages and broken families to whom we must listen with special care. Archbishop MacNeil wished to emphasize that no families, even those considered to be the best and most successful, are immune to suffering and sorrow. Furthermore, when we say that family members are the Church, and when we also say that they need the support of the Church, then we are saying that families need to support and assist one another. The Lord's promise to be in the midst of two or more gathered in His name applies very clearly to those times and places in which family members and groups of families gather to pray and celebrate and work together. Self-help among members and groups of christian families is one of the forms of help that they need from the Church in order to continue responding positively to the Lord's call. Reference was specifically made to christian experience. There is no claim that the majority of families are active in this way, but growing numbers are. The Synod can celebrate the fact that very many christian families are in fact helping one another and especially those afflicted by poverty and oppression.

One important common characteristic of all these families is that they do not stay by themselves in isolation but are open to the needs of others. We can distinguish several kinds of these self-help and mutual-support groups in Canada. There are people who suffer personal and family tragedies, such as loss of a partner, separation, divorce, rejection, abandonment. Others are afflicted by other kinds of needs: poverty, unemployment, racial discrimination, economic injustice and oppression. The conclusion is made that the Conference of Canadian Bishops urges that more and more christian people in all walks of life should unite for mutual encouragement and support and to help those who are weaker.

PART TWO

THE SYNOD IN THREE PHASES

Considering the bishops' reactions during the preparatory phase of the Synod which we have introduced in Part One, it is logical to give some serious thought to the first phase of the Synod itself which was devoted to the interventions of the bishops during the first week of general sessions. This will be done in the following section. What follows immediately is an exposure of the themes of the Synod as they actually emerged and an accounting of the general development of the synodal events. The Synod of Bishops on the Family began its work on 26 September and was officially closed on 25 October 1980.

III. THE THEMES AND DEVELOPMENT OF THE SYNOD

A. Composition and Opening

It is important to take account of the nature of the Synod's membership, for the composition of bishops will have its own characteristics. Similar to the previous ordinary meetings of the Synod of Bishops, one finds various categories of members taking part in the 1980 Synod:

148 delegates of the bishops' conferences
 13 representatives of the Eastern Churches
 24 participants named by the Pope
 20 leaders of Roman curial departments
 10 general superiors of the religious orders
 43 auditors including 16 couples.

Cardinals Primatesta (Cordoba), Picachy (Calcutta) and Gantin (*Justitia et Pax*) were named as presidents of the Synod. During the course of the Synod's work the importance of its official leaders became very evident; the key role of Card. Ratzinger (at that time, archbishop of Munich) who had been named *Relator* of the Synod, that of Bishop Lozano Barragàn (Mexico City) who was the *Special Secretary*, and the ten *Adiutores of the Special Secretary* (or *periti*) who assisted them both.

If we divide the 148 representatives from bishops' conferences and those of the other categories along the lines of geographical distribution we come to the following schema[8].

8. Here we are making use of the documentary work on the Synod by G. CAPRILE, *Il Sinodo dei Vescovi*, Rome, 1981, pp. 36-37, and later, 39-40.

	Representatives of the bishops	Other categories[9]	Total
Africa	36	7	43
Asia	22	11	33
Latin America	36	6	42
Europe	41	36	77
North America	8	7	15
Oceania	5	1	6
Totals	148	68	216

These figures indicate the relative weight of the continental representation of bishops. The percentages with respect to that representation, taking all categories into account, are:

Africa	20%
Asia	15.2%
Latin America	19.5%
Europe	35.6%
North America	7%
Oceania	2.7%

One will notice that the unproportional weight of the European representation is due in large part to the inclusion of members from "other categories" who came chiefly from centralized, authority functions such as the leaders of the curia and the General Superiors of the religious orders. If we consider the figures only from the "pure" representation of the local churches, namely those who were chosen as representatives by the bishops' conferences themselves, it appears that the bishops from the Third World count the greatest weight with 94 out of the 148 representatives, while the churches from the First and Second Worlds were only represented by 54 out of the 148.

It is further evident that this type of weight or strength represented by the numbers of those present should also be balanced by the authority and dynamism of the churches from the different geographical locations. This will become clear in the study of the actual contributions which came forth from the local churches.

Another characteristic of the 1980 Synod can be seen in the extensive change which took place in the personel of the delegations. If we postulate that already in the 1974 Synod a type of phenomenon began to appear which at that time established a new generation of post-conciliar bishops and saw the beginning of a new style typical of the "young churches", in 1980 we see that this trend had progressed even further. Of

9. Other categories include representatives of the Eastern Churches, members named by the Pope, leaders of the curia, General Superiors of the religious orders, and the General Secretary, Bishop Jozef Tomko.

the 148 representatives from bishops' conferences who were chosen for 1980, no less than 94 were taking part in the Synod of Bishops for the first time. This in itself points to a significant evolution which must be taken into account to appreciate the atmosphere of the 1980 Synod.

To take just one example of this development, for the majority of bishops present at this Synod, the events of Vatican II already belonged to a historical period. At the same time, this period was sufficiently removed from the historical elements leading up to the publication of HV and from the events which characterized the *reception* of that encyclical both of which remained more or less *terra incognita* for those bishops or at least only part of a vague memory. The only categories which remained relatively uneffected by this evolution were the representatives of the Eastern Churches and the heads of the curial departments.

Turning then to the events of the Synod itself, the official opening took place on 26 September and was highlighted by an introductory speech by Bishop Tomko, permanent Secretary General of the Synod since July 1979, and one by Card. Ratzinger who, as *Relator* of the Synod delivered a kind of keynote address. For John-Paul II who as archbishop already had considerable experience with the bishops' Synod[10], this would be the first gathering that he himself as Pope had called together. At the opening, he limited himself to delivering a homily. It was striking to the bishops that the Pope delivered no official address and at the same time that there was no preplanned *perspectus* or general description of the overall pastoral situation in the Church along the lines of geographical division. This was felt to create a regretable lacuna[11]. In his opening report[12], Bish. Tomko gave a summary of the activities of the General Secretariate between 1977 and 1980. When all the bishops' conferences were consulted in the beginning of 1978 about the choice for the topic of the next Synod, the Secretariate received no fewer than 68 answers. A summary was made from the analysis of this material according to the following categories presented in the order of frequency:

1. themes which were connected either with marriage or the family
2. themes on the Church (either as sign of the Gospel or as the mission of the faithful)

10. On the eve of the 1980 Synod, the Vatican press published an extensive work on the participation of Cardinal K. WOJTYLA in previous Synods. It appeared under the title *Karol Wojtyla e il Sinodo dei Vescovi*, Vatican City, 1980 (432 pp.), and included both a description of Card. Wojtyla's synodal contributions and his synodal addresses. Copies of the publication were distributed to the participants of the Synod.

11. The general overview was first suggested in the 1969 Synod and since 1971 had become part of the general process. In his opening report (p. 13), Bishop Tomko justified this lacuna because of a lack of time. There was a need to create more time for the interventions and exchange of views.

12. *Relatio de laboribus secretariae generalis synodi praesertim consilii eiusdem secretariae inter duos coetus generales synodi episcoporum: 1977-1980 (sub secreto)*, Vatican City, 1980 (14 pp.).

3. questions with respect to christian life (moral principles, Catholic institutions, youth, vocations, the catechumenate)
4. the theme of faith and culture (as well as human rights)
5. under the rubric of varia, seven other categories

During the meeting of the Concilium of the Secretariate for the Synod (18 May 1978) which was presided over by Card. Wojtyla, then arch-bishop of Cracow, it was suggested that the theme should be "The Family in the Modern World". This proposal was accepted by Paul VI and approved by John-Paul I two days before his sudden death. On 17 November 1978, the sugested theme was once again approved by John-Paul II and was renamed with the title "The Roles of the Christian Family in the Modern World", whereas under John-Paul I the title had more simply been designated as "The Christian Family".

In giving his report, Bish Tomko also mentioned other events such as the preparation of the *Lineamenta* for the 1980 Synod, the Special Synod for the Dutch bishops, and the working out of the *Instrumentum laboris* for 1980. In the content of his exposition one finds another point that deserves special mention: since 1971 the Concilium of the General Secretariate had received numerous suggestions and requests for further study on many points of the roles and procedure for the Synod which had often been rather critical. From Bishop Tomko's report it appears that Paul VI refused to deal with these suggestions for changing the pro-cedure and wished to wait for more time before considering them. The Secretary General let it be known that an entire dossier containing all the earlier and most recent suggestions for amendments (over the period from 1971 to 1980) had been prepared for consideration but that this project would only be possible when the pope himself decided that it should be done.

B. The Theme of the Synod

We have already noted that the precise formulation of the theme for the 1980 Synod had gone through meaningful change under the three popes: from *De familia in mundo hodierno* (Paul VI) to *De familia christiana* (John-Paul I) and finally *De muneribus familiae christianae in mundo hodierno* (John-Paul II). In principle, only the last of these would define the topic of the 1980 Synod. But in reality the majority of the members of the Synod would give their greater efforts to widening the scope of their task. The circumstances which led up to this have up until now received too little attention.

Significant change of accent
After the trauma that was caused by the poor reception of the encyclical HV (1968) in the Western christian world, attempts to place

"marriage" on the agenda for a Synod had not previously been successful. This was especially true in the case of the 1974 Synod; the subject was taboo at that time. The 1980 Synod was called together to exchange ideas on "the family". The difference between the two themes is not insignificant. The difference becomes even sharper when we take account of the fact that John-Paul II had specified the topic to be "The Roles of the Christian Family in the Modern World". In the first place, the question is raided about the precise idea that the Pope had in mind when he took over this theme from his predecessors and specified it in his own way. The primary purpose of the Pope was not to bring forth the questions of conjugal morality. His geatest concern lie elsewhere, namely in the valorization of the christian family as *ecclesia domestica* (domestic church) in order to lend support for the future of christianity and to compensate for the languishing of other supportive structures.

In an earlier time christian morality had found its basis and support in the establishment of civil law which was inhibitive on certain points (e.g., by making divorce impossible and annulment extremely difficult, by discriminating against the children of adulterous relationships, by pros-ecuting abortion, etc.). It could also lean against organs of christian opinion and other social forces which lent themselves to the defense of a certain "moral conformity". Setting out from the perspective that these various means of support were disappearing, even and especially in countries which had a Catholic or at least christian tradition, and even in a part of Europe where the faith is being prosecuted and a process of demoralization is taking place, the Pope saw sanctity itself to lie in a confirmation and a *mortification of the family as bulwark of faith and morality*. It was an institution which in the future could even possibly take the place of disappearing apostolic movements or fulfill the function of priestless parish structures.

The Pope had been warned that the theme chosen could lead to a renewal of the heated arguments around HV. Although John-Paul II was little interested in reopening the discussion over methods of regulating fertility, he did not shrink from taking on that risk.

A Synod which was dedicated to the mission of the family would in fact be compelled to deal with pastoral questions about the experience of marriage. It would soon become evident in the synodal discussions that the bishops, for sometimes divergent reasons, would extend the points of the agenda and go much beyond the intention of the Pope. The bishops from the North Atlantic World wished to return to the poor reception that HV had undergone in their countries and to the need for a new pastoral consideration of the question of methods of birth control. Many of these even spoke in terms of a crisis of civilization.

The Synod fathers from many of the young churches where the reception of HV caused no great problems wished to give expression to the aversion felt in the Third World for the "anti-life mentality" which was being propagandized among their peoples. They saw factors of economic and political regression present in that trend which they considered to be unacceptable. Further in conjunction with this position, to which one had already been exposed in the previous synodal meetings, the tenor of the theme returned in 1980 but with various nuances: the African representatives demonstrated their concern for vitality and fertility while they reacted against the international attempts at demoralization; those from South-East Asia voiced their objections against their own governments which were attempting to impose methods of lowering fertility on their own people; Synod members from Latin America placed themselves in opposition to North American interventionism but also emphasized structural poverty which prevented the development of normal marital life. This last group also delivered the strongest criticism against the background of the theme of "the mission of the christian family".

The actual broadening of the agenda was in fact much wider than that concerning the problem of fertility regulation. The following problem areas also received a great deal of attention: mixed marriages; pastoral care of the divorced-remarried; economic pauperism which hinders the young from marrying; inculturation of the forms of marriage in Africa; the relationship between faith and sacrament and the situation of dechristianization. Eventually these subjects were justified as valid points of the agenda because of their intimate connection with the main theme: the function of the family in society is ultimately dependent upon a more integrated conception of marriage itself. Here we have given only the broad lines of the overall perspectives within which the exchange of views during the Synod can be better understood.

C. The General Development

In order to summarize the development of synodal events in a graphic way, it can be compared with a "funnel": indeed the general interventions *in aula* consisted in the widest influx of contributions and represented the broadest mouth of the funnel; this was gradually narrowed down when the *circuli minores* or small language groups went to work during the second week; the neck of the funnel exemplifies the stricture of synodal substance during the redactional work on the project of the Propositions which would incorporate the official advice of the Synod. At the very end of the funnel one finds an even further narrowing: here we point to the voting on the final text as well as the "Closing Homily" of the Pope. The general picture is one of an event ending in a sort of anti-climax which, up to the present, has come to characterize just about every Synod. In the end, one cannot avoid noticing the wide contrast between the high expectations which were brought to the Synod and the enormous imput which the participants gave during the first week on the one hand, and the rather impoverished result on the other which, at least formally speaking, the bishops would have to bring home with them.

On occasion some have spoken of movements which have come from the bottom up within the Synod and those which emanated from the top (authority) down. In so far as one thinks of the composition of the Synod as the delegates of the bishops' conferences and thus the representatives of the local churches, the Synod has demonstrated a clear tendency toward this upward movement. However, in so far as the Synod has been led according to pre-programmed givens and unarticulated limits, it has exhibited a more downward movement. On the eve of the opening of the 1980 Synod one can again find speculation about the possibility — or the impossibility — that the upward tendencies would be held in check by the downward ones[13].

After the Synod it was almost certain that the publication of the apostolic exhortation *Familiaris consortio* would neither reflect a spirit of unifying these tendencies nor remove the feeling of disillusionment. The painful disproportion between the stakes involved and an eventual, disappointing outcome has been characteristic of the Synods of the most recent years.

Returning to the actual events, however, it is perhaps notable that each of the three phases of this Synod culminated in some form of documentation: the first phase was summarized in the "second report" of Card. Ratzinger, the second phase was represented by the reports of the eleven discussion groups, and the third phase culminated in the redaction of two dissimilar and unequal documents, the 43 Propositions and the "Message" of the Synod to the christian families of the world. The progression of events in the general development of the Synod is made all that much clearer through consideration of these end-documents which simultaneously form a break in that development and contain a clear description of the meaning of each phase.

1. *The first phase*

The first phase of the Synod began with the introductory report of Card. Ratzinger, the *Relator*. Following the three-fold style of the preparatory documents (description of the situation, the family in the plan of God, and pastoral problems), he highlighted the principle aspects of the general theme to which the Synod was to address itself. He also made reference to the reactions which the bishops' conferences had made with respect to the preparatory documents.

13. These thoughts were voiced by Prof. G. Alberigo in a lecture given to the *Centro culturale per l'informazione religiosa* at Rome on 30 Sept. 1980.

Between 29 Sept. and 3 Oct. there were ten plenary sessions held during which the vast majority of speeches were delivered. In one week there were a surprising number of interventions delivered, no less than 162 out of the 216 participants were heard from. There were also 51 written interventions which were handed over to the secretariate. If one leaves aside the interventions of the General Superiors of religious orders and the members of the curia, one can speak of a very impressive contribution emanating from the local churches. Most of the interventions during the first week describe the situations in the local regions of the bishops and deal with the pastoral needs that they felt were the most important in their own countries. The weight of this material was that much greater because the bishops were acting as delegates of their respective conferences and were delivering the results of a communal effort put forth by those gatherings in preparation for this particular Synod, often with the help and advice of priests and laypersons who took part in their deliberations.

The contributions from the local churches can be divided geographically as follows:

Africa:	37 speakers of the 43 bishops present
Asia:	25 speakers of the 33 bishops present
Latin America:	30 speakers of the 42 bishops present
Europe:	38 speakers of the 77 bishops present
North America:	11 speakers of the 15 bishops present
Oceania:	5 speakers of the 6 bishops present

We will return to the content of these many interventions in the following section. Their contribution to the Synod was summarized by Card. Ratzinger in his "second report" (*relatio altera*) delivered on 6 October. Without exaggeration this report at the end of the first phase can be looked upon as the central point of the 1980 Synod. Card. Ratzinger, who is also a theologian and was at that time archbishop of Munich, composed a voluminous and comprehensive overview of all the material in a single document which was structured along the lines of six principle themes. These six "chapters" were then handed over to the discussion groups and made it possible for the second phase to go forth with a certain amount of consideration of the many opinions which had been expressed.

2. *The second phase*

The second phase of the Synod at first appears to be a sort of calm period after the first week, but in fact it was a privileged moment in the series of events. It lasted the whole of the week from 6 to 10 October during which the eleven *circuli minores* discussed the principle themes which had been put forth. The reports of these smaller groups were delivered during plenary sessions on 13 and 14 October.

The groups, which were made up of 10 to 28 members on the basis of a common language, offered the opportunity for the bishops to function in a more normal, human way. During a much more free exchange of ideas they were able to put forth their views in a much more concrete and detailed manner. While the official speeches given in plenary session were more stylized as a series of monologues, in the small groups it was evident that much more dialogue could take place.

After the end of the previous Synods, many complaints were heard about the way in which these small groups work. These groups were determined neither on the basis of geographical lines nor according to subject matter for the discussion of specific points of the agenda, methods for which the bishops had expressed their preference. Rather, the organization was done on the basis of language which resulted in a rather arbitrary grouping even though it was left up to the bishops themselves which language they would choose[14]. In 1980, there was again an expectation that this method would be reevaluated. But that hope was not realized. Nevertheless, the present system is not without some advantage. The arbitrariness of the division insured that each group would contain bishops of different persuasions and with interests in different points of the overall agenda so that in most of the groups there would be an impetus for genial dialogue to take place between bishops who were not necessarily in full agreement.

The division of the eleven groups, along with the names of their *moderator* and *relator* are as follows[15]:

Latin	Card. Felici and Card. Palazzini
German	Card. Höffner and Fr. Pfab
Italian	Card. Bellestrero and Archbishop Martini
French A	Card. Etchegaray and Archbishop Danneels
French B	Card. Zoungrana and Bishop Monsengwo Pasinya
English A	Archbishop Bernardin and Card. Cordeiro
English B	Card. Hume and Archbishop Hurley

14. The arbitrariness of the division rested not simply on the fact that the groups were divided according to language but also because the members of language groups themselves were divided alphabetically. Thus, the French A group included bishops Batantu to Margeot; French B, Marie-Sainte to Zoungrana; English A group, bishops Alberto y Valderrama to Finau; English B, Francis to O'Fiaich; English C, Otunga to Zubeir Wako, etc...

15. In the allocation of functions one can find a certain continuity despite the fact that there had been change in the membership of the Synod participants in general. Thus, Card. Felici had already been the moderator of a group three times before (1971, 1974 and 1977), Card. Enrique y Tarancón twice (1974 and 1977) and Card. Etchegaray and Archbishop Ryan each once before (1977). Three *relators* had also fulfilled this function before (1977); Archbishop Hurley, Archbishop López Trujillo and Fr. Pfab. In 1980, 7 of the 22 directive functions of the small groups were performed by those who had done so before.

English C   Archbishop Ryan and Archbishop Quinn
Spanish A   Card. Enrique y Tarancón, Bishop Mendes de Almeida
                and Bishop Acha Duarte
Spanish B   Card. Landázuri Ricketts, Archbishop López Trujillo and
                Bishop Llaguno Farias
Spanish C   Card. Pironio and Bishop Quarracino

The largest language group was the Italian one with 28 members and the smallest was the Latin with 10 members. The latter, presided over by the very accomplished lawyer, Card. Pericles Felici (who has since died) included influential voices from the curia (Cards. Pallazzini and Seper as well as the moderator) four bishops from Eastern Europe and three from the Eastern rite (including two from India). It is also clear that there was a significant representation of African and Asian bishops in the English groups, while Spanish group B was primarily composed of Latin Americans and French B had a large representation from French-speaking Africa[16]. With respect to the tenor of the groups, it is evident that there were divergent characteristics. The small Latin group represented the clearest articulation of traditionalist positions while the Italian group sought to find a balanced middle ground wherein the divergent tendencies among the Synod fathers could reach some sort of compromise. In the latter case, Archbishop Martini from Milan and *relator* for the Italian group, played a vital function. In a later section we will discuss the contributions of the various group discussions.

3. *The third phase*

With the work of drawing up the Propositions and composing the "Message", the Synod faced its most difficult task which can be described as "the neck of the funnel". This was also the most secretive phase of the Synod: there was not a single press communiqué issued between 16 and 20 October whereas the official press service of the Synod had indicated that there would be an official release at least twice a day with regard to the progress being made and a daily briefing of a more informal nature.

The turning point occured on 14 October when the bishops were asked to vote on two important points. The first had to do with procedure: the bishops were asked whether they wished to present the Pope with "Propositions" based upon the results of their discussions. This proposal was passed with an overwhelming majority. The same results were reached for the approval of issuing a "Message to Families" and a

---

16. The nationalities were also widely mixed. French A included 23 members from 16 different countries; French B, 23 members from 21 countries; English B had only one member from Great Britain, and Spanish C, only one from Spain.

committee was appointed for the project: Card. Zoungrana (Upper Volta), Card. Lorscheider (Brazil), Archbishop Bernardin (USA), Card. Cordeiro (Pakistan) and Archbishop Danneels (Belgium).

The first vote with respect to procedure left a number of bishops feeling rather uneasy, they were of the opinion that an alternative should have been offered so that the participants could have had some sort of a choice. It is entirely possible that the majority of bishops were unaware of the fact that earlier Synods — up to and including that of 1974 — had attempted to draw up their own statement of conclusions. Other bishops felt that the presentation of a restrictive set of Propositions could have been avoided if all the various interventions presented at the Synod without differentiation or limitation would be transmitted to the Pope.

On 15 and 16 October there was again the opportunity present for speeches. This consisted of reports from the representatives of the curia who explained their administrative accomplishments as well as a platform for the defense of some more traditionalist perspectives. However, behind the scenes there was a much more important series of events taking place of which the majority of bishops remained unaware. Although there had been no official announcement of these events, we are in possession of a sufficient amount of data gathered from numerous sources of reliable information which has allowed us to put forth a working hypothesis concerning what took place[17].

The experts (or *periti*) who were at the service of the *relator* — the so-called *adiutores secretarii specialis* — were requested on 14 October to draw up a plan for the Propositions within a day and a half. This was to be done on the basis of the discussions of the language groups and their respective final reports. This development of events does not appear to have been in conformity with the expectations of the leaders of the discussion groups: when, in the afternoon of 15 October, Card. Ratzinger attempted to discuss the plan of the text with the representatives of the *circuli*, they refused to accept the plan as the basis for discussion. According to some of the *periti* this refusal was caused by the suspicion of the bishops who were on their guard against possible interventions on the part of the curia, which had not been unknown in previous synods. According to a spokesman for one discussion group, the refusal rested upon the conviction that the work of drawing up this text belonged to the bishops themselves as members of the Synod and not to the experts who were in no position to make the necessary judgments. Actually, these reasons do not exclude each other and can be seen as complementary[18].

17. This working hypothesis has been substantially verified by some witnesses of the events in question. The calendar which appears in the last part of this section also provides a substantiating overview to the procedure of events.

18. In the work of G. Caprile, for many years the official chronicler of the Bishops' Synod, we surprisingly find the report of a meeting taking place on the morning of 15

The leadership of the discussion groups made it very clear that the composition of a draft text should be entrusted to those *circuli*. As a result, in the afternoon of 16 October Card. Ratzinger appeared before the Synod with empty hands and, in somewhat concealed terms, was forced to admit to the misadverture [19]. Consequently, two precious days of work were lost which the bishops could well have used to bring the Propositions into a more ripe form [20]. Nevertheless, at this point the *circuli minores* were immediately called back together, not to discuss an existing text as was originally planned, but to get to work themselves in drawing up a draft text to have ready the following day and put forth for general discussion. According to some official communiqués, the groups should have received a general list of themes from Card. Ratzinger, but in the documentation of several bishops there is no sign of any such text [21].

October between Card. Ratzinger, the Special Secretary, and the experts (*periti*), with the *relatores* of the *circuli*, to draw up the first draft of the text. Cf. G. CAPRILE, *Il Sinodo dei Vescovi*, p. 421. This is completely at odds with every testimony which we received on the matter.

19. According to one source, Card. Ratzinger announced *in aula* that "the grapes are not yet ripe"; according to another (H. FESQUET, in *Le Monde*, 18 Oct. 1980), "after we fished all night, we came up with nothing". While the press office of the Synod remained silent on the matter, in some unofficial newspapers the chain of events was reported before they happened by correspondents who had no idea that a "short circuit" would change the planned program. Cf. *La Croix* and *L'Avvenire* (both of 15 Oct. 1980).

20. According to J. P. MANIGNE, in *Informations Catholiques Internationales* n. 556 (1980) 30 & 39, there were 4 days planned to prepare the first draft of the text; half of these were lost because of the "incident" between the bishops and the *periti*.

21. The laconic character of the press release for 16 Oct. 1980 appears, after some research, to be very misleading. The English text read "Cardinal Ratzinger briefly presented a list of 'proposals' for the discussions in the 'circuli minores' ", the French text had, "la série de propositions" and the German, "die Serie der 'Propositiones' ". The work of P. P. GAUDET, *Synode des Evêques 1980*, Paris, 1981, presents a list of 8 themes (pp. 182-184) entitled "Propositions issues des groupes de travail", dated 15 Oct. According to information which the author was very willing to share with us, this had to do with a first plan that Card. Ratzinger provided for the discussion groups. According to some participants of these groups whom we have personnally asked, this document was unknown. Because of these circumstances and because of the date which has been assigned to the supposed text, we propose that such reports refer to the text which was drafted by the experts at the request of Card. Ratzinger and which was rejected by the *relatores* of the discussion groups.

In a letter written by Card. Ratzinger to the clergy of his diocese (8 Dec. 1980) one reads the following report: "Daraufhin wurden die Sprachgruppen damit betraut, je für eine bestimmte Anzahl von Themen, die den Schwerpunkt ihrer Interessen bildeten, den Text der "Propositiones" vorzubereiten, die das Hauptergebnis der Synode bilden sollten. Meine Aufgabe war es nun nur noch, aus den sich etwas überschneidenden und ungleich formulierten Produkten der einzelnen Sprachgruppen eine logische Abfolge der Proposi-tionen zu bilden sowie ihren sprachlichen und gedanklichen Duktus aufeinander abzustimmen". Cf. *Brief an die Priester, Diakone und an alle im pastoralen Dienst Stehenden*. (s.l.s.d.), p. 6.

After all the *relatores* delivered the proposals of their respective groups on the evening of Friday (17 October) the intervening weekend (18-19 Oct. 1980) was dedicated to the coordination of all these contributions. Together with the leadership of the *circuli*, Card. Ratzinger and his aids put together the draft text of the Propositions that was presented to the general session of the Synod on Monday (20 October). Between the vote on the first reading (21 October) and that on the second reading (24 October) of the text one could observe a great deal of tension. Many of the bishops were dissatisfied with the manner in which their suggestions concerning the first draft were handled. The commission in charge of this project was not chosen by the Synod participants but was appointed by the Synod's officials (*presidium*). As a result, the amendments were dealt with by small groups of a few *periti* and *relatores*, and no one even knew the composition of any of the groups. Finally, the report about the handling of amendments — *Expensio modorum* — was insufficiently discussed in a general meeting so that the bishops received the impression that there was little if any control of the process leading toward the formation of the final text. There are some who would consider these procedural questions to be relatively unimportant; however, we believe that they are important to explain the critical reactions of some of the bishops who were at the Synod[22].

Indeed, during the last days of the Synod (23 and 24 October), the bishops did get the opportunity to put their critical reactions into work. In a manner similar to that of the events of the 1974 Synod, the bishops' gathering of 1980 underwent an examination of conscience during their final plenary sessions. Under the work of putting forth "suggestions" about the function of the Synod[23] the entire procedure of the recently completed session was brought into question by more than one bishop. In the course of this evaluation a proposal was also made that the Propositions and the "Message" be discussed in plenary session (by Cards. Lorscheider and Zoungrana); and another that the amendments to the first version of the Propositions similarly be discussed (Card. Hume). It was also suggested that in order to provide for a certain maturation in the processes of thought and drawing up texts there be another gathering six months later (Archbishop Martini). These are merely samples which suggest that the general impression held by the bishops was that the general discussions and those which took place in the small groups had not yet been satisfactorily represented in the final

---

22. The previous Synods have exhibited a very similar kind of tension which can only be understood through attention to events which took place behind the scenes. Cf. J. GROOTAERS, *Les synodes des évêques de 1969 et de 1974: fonctionnement défectueux et résultats significatifs*, in *Les Églises après Vatican II: dynamisme et prospective*, Paris, 1981, pp. 303-328.

23. This is alluded to in an abbreviated fashion in the chronicle of C. CAPRILE, *Il Sinodo dei Vescovi*, pp. 794-795.

texts of the Synod. Through a consideration of procedure it had become clear that something had to be done with respect to future planning. But this had also happened in the previous synodal gathering. In the present situation, it was not just the Propositions which had to be drawn up in the final week. There was also the text of the "Message" which had to go through a number of editions and eventually be agreed upon.

The handling of the so-called "Message to Christian Families" suffered from a pressing lack of time. The committee in charge had the task of summarizing a list of twelve priorities. It further had the problem of finding a compromise between the two major tendencies present at the Synod: the defenders of the doctrinal aspects and those who put forth a more pastoral approach to the text. The first and last paragraphs of their text gave a certain satisfaction to the latter but the majority of the body of the document was dedicated to the doctrinal approach. Many bishops were of the opinion that the "Message" had failed in accomplishing what they felt to be a necessary dynamism. When the text was finally presented to the Synod, after its difficult process of coming into being (and three different versions), its reception was less than enthusiastic, but there was no time left to change anything. The Closing Homily that Pope John-Paul II delivered on the final day of the Synod will be dealt with in a separate, conclusory section.

D. The Role of the Lay Representatives

Any sketch of the events of the 1980 Synod would be incomplete without a general description of the special role that was set out for the lay participants and the way in which they carried this out. In the official synodal reports, it appears what there was little importance attached to the activities of this group, although this is one more reason why the phenomenon should not be neglected.

The official purpose for inviting 43 *auditores* to the Synod was so that twelve family movements could be represented. Close examination reveals that 22 *auditores* were members of either W.O.O.M.B. (World Organization Ovulation Method Billings) or I.F.F.L.P. (International Federation for Family Life Promotion), which means that the NFP (Natural Family Planning) movement enjoyed a monopoly position of representation. The Billings advocates made up two thirds of the delegates because even within the NFP movement the advocates of the sympto-thermal method had been shut out by this group[24].

24. During the preparatory phase of the Synod, this monopolized position was secured with the greatest care. A world congress of the "International Confederation of Christian Family Movements", planned for October 1980 was in fact cancelled under pressure from the Synod Secretariate because the position of the "World Organization Ovulation Method Billings" had to be preserved.

The remaining minority of the *auditores* was made up of representatives of other movements such as the Equipes Notre-Dame, Communione e Liberazione, Marriage Encounter, Foccolarini and Opus Dei, all of which are well known for their conservative tendencies. This imbalance of representation in the lay participation in the Synod would be all that more sharply felt when Archbishop Quinn openly admitted that in his country 80 % of Catholics do not follow the teaching of HV and when Card. Hume and other bishops offered similar observations[25].

If one consults the latest yearly volumes of the *Annuario Pontificio*, they will discover an additional aspect of this selective choice in *auditores*: eight of the representatives had for years already been members of the "Comitato per la Familglia", an important subdivision of the consultative organizations of the Roman curia[26].

The various and sundry activities of these *auditores* played a continuous role on many fronts. Within the official program of the Synod itself, there was only one short series of interventions presented on Monday, 6 October. It included Mr. and Mrs. N. Martin (West Germany) who gave a presentation on appropriate family spirituality, Mr. and Mrs. Z. Goma (Congo) who sketched out the situation of the christian family in Africa, and ended with Morther Teresa (India) who spoke about education for responsible parenthood.

Of more importance were the two "academic sessions" which took place in the Synod aula but outside of ifficial session on the afternoons of 10 and 22 October[27]. During the first of these, there were five interventions from *periti* and *auditores* with respect to philosophical, theological and biological principles[28]. The second "academic session" was opened with an appeal made to the bishops by Dr. Mascarenhas (India) in the name of the medical doctors of the group. There was also the testimony from five couples about the apostolate of the family and from two other

25. Two interviews with couples who were members of the *auditores* revealed a clear image of embarrassment when the question of representativeness was raised. Cf. J. F. X. HARRIOT, *The Synod's Absent Auditores*, in *The Tablet* 234 (1980) 986, which recounts an interview with one of the American couples given to the B.B.C.; and J. P. MANIGNE, *Un laïc italien invité au Synode*, in *Informations Catholiques Internationales* nr. 557 (1980) 39-40, which was an interview with the Italian couple, Pino and Marielle Quartana.

26. This Committee was established by Pope Paul VI in January 1973 to pastorally study the spiritual, moral and social problems of the family. In December 1976 it was absorbed by the "Papal Commission for the Laity" but retained its own structure. The Committee played an important role during the preparation and meetings of the 1980 Synod and in May 1981 was "elevated" to an independant "Papal Commission for the Family" chaired by Card. James R. Knox and led by a commission of bishops. Cf. *Osservatore Romano* (French edition) 32 (19 May 1981) 5.

27. We are omitting the intervention of Brother G. B. Rueda on 23 October. Br. Rueda should be considered not as an *auditor* per se but much more as a Superior of the Marist Brothers.

28. Among the speakers one should be aware of important figures such as G. Martelet and Dr. Billings himself.

couples on their personal experience, all of which was complemented with interventions from a cloistered sister, two priests, a jurist and a demographer.

A thrid event occurred in a broader context during the public celebration of the "World Day of the Family" on Sunday, 12 October. In the large Paul VI Hall, the afternoon was dedicated to fifteen witnesses for family life and was attended by numerous Synod bishops and representatives of ecclesial family movements from a large number of countries[29].

However, it was behind closed doors that the select group of lay participants had their greatest influence. When the bishops divided into the eleven language groups, the auditores were spead out among the circuli minores with the result that one can find their practical influence in each report of the discussion groups. One of the few published testimonials to this was very specific about what happened. "While they could only intervene during the plenary sessions by speaking with the bishops, it was only in the discussion groups that they could express themselves freely"[30].

The one-sidedness of the tendencies that were represented and the emphatic stress that was delivered to the bishops by the periti and the auditores, whether in the medical field or in the experiences of the lay representatives, was not welcomed wholeheartedly by all of the bishops. A number of them received the impression that a very specific kind of atmosphere had been created to bring pressure upon them. Some Synod bishops reacted against this. One example is Bishop Jullien (Beauvais, France) who was the first to call into question the general applicability of "observation techniques" (1 October) and consequently expressly disputed the interventions of experts during the first "academic session". Their arguments, he said (14 October), are supported by intuitions which are benefical for themselves but which remain unconvincing for others who base themselves upon other intuitions[31].

29. See L'Attività della Sante Sede nel 1980, Rome, 1981, pp. 1114-1116 and 1146; and Sala Stampa della Sante Sede, Bolletino 440 and 441.

30. During the Synod the lay auditores lived completely apart, without any contact with the outside world. The editor of the French weekly Famille Chrétienne (30 October 1980, p. 15) deserves all the more credit for his interviews. In this report, the Argentinian lawyer Mr. Mazzinghi said that the most interesting work of the laity was done in the circuli minores; in his own group he saw fit to declare "que très souvent l'église n'imposait pas une discipline qui lui était réservée, mais qu'elle prenait la défense d'exigences relevant de la loi naturelle, donc commune à tous les hommes".

31. The secrecy that reached never before seen proportions in October 1980 had as at least one effect that prominent theologians whom bishops had brought to Rome to advise them were given no admittance to the synodal hall, not even to the entrance hall of the building. There was thus a glaring contrast between the privileges enjoyed by the periti and auditores named by Rome and the way in which the advisers brought to Rome by the bishops were shunted out.

E. The Calendar from 14 to 24 October 1980

Because of the importance of the turning-point that took place during the third week of the Synod, it seems advantageous at this point to sketch the chronological order of events, mentioning the most important ones which would have an effect upon the outcome.

Tuesday, 14 Oct. (AM): Two points are submitted for a vote: 1) the bishops decide to present Propositions to the Pope and 2) it is decided to issue a "Message to Christian Families".

Tuesday, 14 Oct. (PM): After the *predidium* consulted with the Pope about the coming events, a group of the *periti* of Card. Ratzinger and Bishop Lozano Barragàn are put to work on drawing up a set of "Propositions".

Wednesday, 15 Oct. (PM): The proposed text which Card. Ratzinger presents to the leadership of the *circuli* in rejected by them; they voice the opinion that the work of the drawing up of Propositions belongs not to the *periti* but to the bishops themselves.

Thursday, 16 Oct. (PM): Card. Ratzinger announces to the general assembly that the initial plan has not worked and that the *circuli* would again be called together to put forth suggestions for the Propositions. It is unlikely that there was a list of concrete proposals provided at this point.

Friday, 17 Oct. (PM): The *relatores* of the various discussion groups deliver their drafts for the Propositions; the Synod begins to come under pressure of its pre-programmed date of closing because of the loss of two valuable days of work.

Saturday and Sunday, 18-19 Oct.: The representatives of the small groups work together with Card. Ratzinger to draw up the Propositions on the basis of the work of the *circuli* accomplished in the two previous days.

Monday, 20 Oct. (AM): For the first time since 16 October the entire Synod meets to receive the first text of the Propositions.

Tuesday, 21 Oct. (AM): The bishops of the Synod vote on the first text of the Propositions and on the "Message"; there are more or less 750 votes "placet iuxta modum" resulting in the proposal of amendments for the Propositions.

Wednesday, 22 Oct.: Limited "ad hoc" committees composed of *periti* and *relatores* (no more than two of three members) study the amendments and decide which will be incorporated into the text. (According to one source, 144 changes would be accepted.)

Thursday, 23 Oct.: Card. Ratzinger presents the *textus emendatus* of the Propositions along with an explanation of the amendments, the so-called "Expensio modorum". The bishops perform a general evaluation of the Synod itself and, among other things, criticize the final texts for their lack of representation of the actual discussions which had taken phace.

Friday, 24 Oct.: Vote taken for choosing the members of the Concilium for the following Synod; final vote for the Propositions; final vote on the Message; continuation of evaluation of the synodal process.

Saturday, 25 Oct.: Official closing of the Synod with a "Homily" by John-Paul II.

IV. The Contributions of the Local Churches

First Phase: The General Exchange of Ideas

As was already mentioned, the first week of the 1980 Synod, from 29 Sept. to 3 Oct., was dominated by the flood of 162 interventions delivered during plenary sessions. Most of the audience had probably never been exposed to such a large amount of input that, despite the limitless juxtaposition of so many monologues, in fact managed to cover most of the relevant aspects of the Synod's theme. When one attempts to group the principle contributions according to continent and to classify them under a few general headings, a certain impression can be created.

The observers as well as the members themselves attached particular significance to the positions put forth during this first week. Indeed, upon reflection, one is aware of the fact that the majority of the members of the Synod were representatives of their bishops' conferences and that their first interventions were precipitated by previous collegial efforts that in many cases also involved the participation of priests and laypersons. This resulted in the fruits of communal consultation in which the contributions of the local churches had been formulated. In many cases it appeared that the free expression of a number of bishops was subject to a certain amount of cautioning. The impression was sometimes created that some of the too outspoken bishops were given signs to tone down their remarks[32]. In the end, however, experience has taught that the direction of opinion which was expressed in the first plenary meetings would only be partially reflected in the Synod's final texts.

A. The Main Issue

For various reasons, the first week of discussions for this Synod deserves more than ordinary attention. It is regrettable that most commentors have placed greater emphasis upon the later events in the synodal procedure and upon their expected or actual outcome than on these contributions from the local churches. Seen historically, it is this first phase which has always been the richest in synodal gatherings, for it has brought together the most information[33]. At the risk of doing

32. Such signals did not necessarily have to emanate from the highest levels of authority; often they had their origin in the circles of certain curial leaders.

33. It is disappointing that there are few publications which have recorded these many contributions. As far as we know, the most complete compilation is J. Potin (ed.), *Aujourd'hui la famille. Principaux documents du Synode des Evêques 1980*, Paris, 1981.

damage to the many nuances of the entire spectrum of opinion expressed during that week, we will attempt to put forth an interpretive summary.

Such a summary can be done by applying different kinds of criteria: there is the geographical distribution according to various regions, there are also the main topics which were addressed in the bishops' speeches. The first method was used with excellent results by the recently deceased and much missed Jean Frisque, a prominent theologian and editorial chief of the center of studies "Prospective"[34]; the second was applied in an interesting study on the Synod by Enzo Franchini[35]. For our own purposes, we will attempt to follow a different method based upon a listing of a number of principle themes and incorporating various points of the two studies mentioned here. We will not restrict ourselves to a chronological unfolding of the interventions nor feel bound by the "rubrics" which Card. Ratzinger enunciated at the end of the week as guidelines for the smaller discussion groups.

At the outset of the Synod, the first contribution was delivered by Card. Ratzinger, as *Relator*, who offered a preliminary report based upon the *Instrumentum laboris* (IL) and upon the reactions which had been received from the different bishops' conferences. This report followed the three part structure which had been employed by IL:

I. The situation of the family in the world today
II. God's plan for the contemporary family
III. Pastoral problems

One can interpret this general introduction as an attempt to "reconcile" some of the "polarity" present in the synodal gathering without losing sight of its overall task. The latter was understood as a need to speak out in a critical and prophetic manner against contemporary ideologies which are abusive of the person, and at the same time thereby to proclaim the Gospel call for conversion. Great importance was thus attached to what was called "the crisis of traditional culture" which, under the influence of a technological and rationalist mentality, threatens to discredit important values. At the conclusion of this first *relatio*, Card. Ratzinger returned to the subject which had been put forth by the Pope as the principle theme of the Synod, namely the moral revolution which, based upon responsibility to one's neighbor and to God, would fight against the tyranny of the consumer mentality and would find its foundation within the christian family.

In their responses to the preparatory documents many bishops declared that the Catholic family as such should be seen as the image and realization of a new humanity in the midst of a society characterized by

---

34. J. FRISQUE, *Le Synode sur la famille: l'apport des églises locales*, Brussels, Prospective international, 1981.

35. E. FRANCHINI, *Un sinodo per ricominicare*, in *Il Regno* 30 (1980) 478-489.

materialism, hedonism and permissiveness. These families should see their duty as one of giving witness to values which are radically opposed to those of the world around them. There was, therefore, a certain agreement about some general lines of approach. In contrast to this, one of the most striking areas of the "polarity" mentioned above was the problem of methods for regulating fertility: the generally acknowledged fact that the teaching of HV had not been accepted in the Western World was ignored by Card. Ratzinger and his report can be understood as an attempt to reconcile HV's rejection of contraception with pastoral solicitude as well as with a more personalistic conception of marital life. This should be seen against the background of the issue itself.

During the discussions about conjugal morality that developed during the 1960's, in the time of Vatican II and especially the Pontifical Commission for the Family and in the period just prior to HV, the protagonists could be divided into four groups: the maximalists, the pragmatists, the pastoral conservatives and the authoritative conservatives[36]. After the rather unsuccessful Pontifical Commission completed its work (1966), and during the final redaction phase of HV, only the last two groups were consulted. While the "authoritarians" had their influence in parts one and two of HV (among other things with respect to the individual marital act remaining "open to procreation"), the third part was much influenced by the "pastorally oriented" approach. Gustave Martelet, one of such theologians and very close to the final text of HV, published a commentary on the encyclical immediately after its appearance in which he reacted against what he felt was an exaggerated preoccupation with part two of the text. It is significant that commentaries that Paul VI himself had provided for the encyclical stress the pastoral interpretation of that document, a fact cited and referred to on a

---

36. The terms are used in the following manner: The *maximalists* sought a fundamental solution which would provide the greatest amount of openness toward contraception (and not simply the pill). The *pragmatists* were of the opinion that social and demographic arguments were sufficient reason to find a practical approach without an official judgment upon the principles involved (for instance, allowing for the use of the pill because it hinders ovulation and does not really "sterilize"). More moderate pragmatists held that, on the basis of pastoral care, it was possible to appeal to a real need of married couples to permit the use of regulatory methods in some circumstances (such as therapy in physical or psychological cases or in the period following childbirth). The *pastoral conservatives* based themselves on a continuity with the teaching of Pius XI but also held that while maintaining unchangeable principles there should be some justification of accomodation. They were opposed to negative declarations and strove for a positive approach, placing the accent upon conjugal love and personal development which would lend more credibility to the practice of periodic continence. (During the 1960's there was not yet any discussion of "Natural Family Planning", especially along the lines of the so called "Billings method"). The *authoritative conservatives* were in favor of a strict reading of *Casti connubii* as an exercise in preserving the function of authority against every form of decay. They believed that it was necessary to follow the classical teaching on conjugal purposes (Augustine) and especially wished for an official declaration to be put forth infallibly.

number of occasions during the 1980 Synod. It is just as significant that Fr. Martelet was one of the limited group of *periti* who contributed a great deal to the Synod.

With this perspective, another look at the introductory *relatio* of Card. Ratzinger (26 Sept.) reveals that although its approach was a long way from the conciliar commission for GS, it was equally dissimilar from the position of the authoritative conservatives (1966-1968) and more closely resembled the pastoral conservative position which became preeminent after 1968. Observers who thought that the 1980 Synod would reopen the question of the fundamental problematic behind HV were to be greatly disillusioned[37]. It was insured that any "polarity" which would surface during the Synod discussions would be limited to a tension between the authoritative and pastoral conservatives[38].

Finally, the beginning of a new pontificate under John-Paul II was not about to re-open a dossier which was felt to have been closed with HV. On the contrary, the fact that so many convinced Catholics had failed to follow the teaching of HV was invoked during the conclaves of 1978 to call for a greater amount of strictness. A significant portion of the electoral college held the opinion that the wrongs done to Paul VI were among the causes of the enduring uncertainty in public opinion at the end of the 1960's. It was explicitly expected that the new Pope, with greater clarity and fortitude, would take a sure and strong line in the coming years in the areas of faith and morals.

Another characteristic of the 1980 Synod that became evident at its very beginning was that the influence of the bishops from the so-called "rich churches" of the Northern hemisphere remained that of a minority. The representatives of "Western Christianity" formed a minority not simply because of their numbers — though a consultation of the proportional representation is not unimportant —but also because of the "quality" of the topics which they brought forth for discussion that were more typical of the problems facing the representatives of the older local churches. These were in marked contrast to the sometimes effervescent approach of the young churches that dealt with the dynamism of the faith. This was certainly no new phenomenon since it had already been characteristic of the earlier Synods. However, this time the contrast was

37. *In tempore non suspecto*, we had warned against this illusion during a lecture given in Rome at the *Centro culturale per l'informazione religiosa* (30 Sept. 1980).

38. The voices of the *maximalists* and the *pragmatists* had long been overwhelmed and completely rejected in Rome during the preparation of the documents for the Synod. The moral theologians being consulted were concerned with the authoritative versus pastoral interpretation, handling questions such as the relation with *Casti connubii* and the controversy over the "primary end" of marriage. It is sufficient to refer to two articles here, M. ZALBA, *Ex personae eiusdemque actuum natura, GS 51,3*, in *Periodica de re morali, canonica, liturgica* 68 (1979) 201-232, and E. LIO, *Natura sacra ed ordinazione intrinseca del matrimonio nella dottrina della Gaudium et spes*, in *Renovatio* 15 (1980) 9-63.

more pronounced by the fact that the subject to be discussed was so bound up with cultural elements that play an important role in discussions on marriage and the family. Those elements came forth many times, especially in the contributions of the African and Asian bishops which emphasized their opposition to Western life styles.

In any case, it is sufficient to observe that the predominant tone of the 1980 Synod was set by the bishops from the Third World. While many expected that the Asian bishops, even with their rather small number of 22 representatives, would present more influential contributions, it was the African bishops, with 36 representatives, who were the most prominent, especially during the first week. The bishops from Latin America were divided between a more conservative tendency, under the influence of the leadership of CELAM, and a more progressive one, more or less under the leadership of the Brazilian episcopacy.

B. The Themes

1. *The deductive or inductive approach*

The first theme that came forth from the interventions of the first week and that would appear later in the texts of the Propositions (especially 2-6) concerned the tension between the deductive and inductive methods of approaching the questions at hand. This discussion had been present since the time of Vatican II and in fact had been becoming more important, as the 1974 Synod in particular and the conference of Puebla in 1979 had shown. It played a very significant role in the 1980 Synod. The causes of this difference of opinion are many sided. On the practical level, there was the judgment of many bishops that discussions about marriage and family life should include the participation of laypersons and especially married couples. And on a more theological basis, there was the reference to the *sensus fidei* (cf. *Lumen gentium*) and the need to take into account the "signs of the times" (cf. *Gaudium et spes*).

In the minds of the African bishops, no true renewal in the pastoral care of the family was even thinkable without both a general Africanization of the Church as a whole and a rethinking of the entire theology of marriage. In Africa, there is hardly any reality which is as profoundly rooted in cultural givens as that of marriage, and this same reality has been raised to the dignity of a sacrament in the Catholic Church. It comes as no surprise, therefore, that the African bishops were very much in favor of an inductive method for approaching the entire question: the Synod must begin with the given situation rather than with principles. In the thought patterns of Vatican II, it must recognize that the "worldly reality" of the family rightly belongs to the autonomy of the temporal.

The Latin American bishops, by contrast, were divided on this question. There were, on the one hand, the advocates of an "essentialist theology" defended by, among others, the Mexican episcopacy and the leaders of CELAM. On the other, were the advocates of an inductive method led by the bishops from Brazil and Peru. The former group believed that the first step consisted in cataloguing those values which necessarily belonged to the reality of the family. According to these standards, the concrete givens of the family itself should be examined to determine the present changes taking place in those values and to warn against the dangers presented by this mutation. The latter group, led by the Brazilian bishops wished first to consult the existing situation from a sociological perspective in order to determine the actual social context which threatens to isolate the family from its proper context. The family is not an autonomous, isolated reality but a given which is very much determined by its social environment. Thus, the Brazilian bishops began with the reality of the families of the poor which, in Brazil as well as in the whole of the Third World, form the majority of the population. The Brazilian speakers such as Bishops C. Hummes (Santo Andre) and L. P. Mendes de Almeida (Sao Paulo) and the Peruvian representative Bishop Irizar Campos (Yurimaguas) felt that problems for the family were essentially social problems. From the perspective of their experience, the family is not so much the basic cell of society as it is its victim.

In contrast to this, the Mexican delegation put forth the idea that God directly willed the institution of the family as an image of the love relationship in the life of the Trinity. From this it is deduced that the family itself is a conservatory of values, whereas one could conjecture that such an image functions in service to the "established order". In the same direction, representatives from Argentina and Colombia placed the highest priority on the statement and preservation of pure teaching. The Brazilian standpoint on this last issue emphasized the historical dimension of salvation and the need to avoid blindness toward events and circumstances which can be understood as the signs of the times.

2. The special role of cultural values

During the last decade, the problem of rooting christianity in given cultures has assumed a high place on the agenda of the young churches. Since the 1974 Synod the term "inculturation" has become the shibboleth of the African churches. It therefore was not unexpected when Card. V. Razafimahatratra (Tananarive, Madagascar) proposed that inculturation be chosen as the principle theme of the next Synod and pleaded for a substantial decentralization of the competence for determining the ecclesial rules governing marriage. In the Synod in general, then, the discussion of inculturation became one of the central points.

A number of speakers from Black Africa put forth the indisputable cultural value of traditional marriage and the force that this institution continues to exhibit. Because of the fact that there is a sharp difference between this custom of "marriage coutumier" and christian marriage, it was important to underscore the disadvantages that this causes for pastoral care and for the general living of the christian faith[39]. A few bishops also expressed their own uneasiness with respect to deep changes that are threatening the African family, and others, especially from East Africa, reflected the Brazilian position of placing justice high on the list of priorities[40].

All things considered, one could say that while marriage in Western tradition had moved toward the model of an interpersonal relationship between two individuals, African marriage had gone in the opposite direction, toward the notion that the vitality present within the community is entrusted to the persons marrying. Traditional African marriage is characterized by two aspects: it is solemnized in a purely communitarian context and style, and the drawn out process of solemnization can last for months or even years. In contrast to this stands christian marriage which springs out of an entirely different anthropology and which comes into being through a short ritual exclusively involving the partners and a witness who is certainly not representative of the two families of lineage. Through this discrepancy between two different processes of institution and two different images of person and society it can easily be seen that christian marriage carries little weight in the perspective of the African people. As a result, at least according to the African episcopal representatives, it is necessary to be careful that customary African marriage is not looked upon as a form of concubinage but rather is correctly appreciated as a type of progressive marriage. Furthermore, the majority of African christians do not find Church marriage to be meaningful and many are uncomfortable with the idea of the indissolubility of christian marriage because it does not take into account or in any way guarantee the fertility of the couple. The question with respect to this complex situation, therefore, touchs upon the notion of the sacramentality of marriage in all its dogmatic, canonical and liturgical aspects. There are more questions here than what a single Synod of Bishops could handle[41].

In the expressions of Card. L. Rugambwa (Dar-es-Salaam, Tanzania), customary traditions of marriage and family life belong to that extremely

---

39. Cf. J. FRISQUE, art. cit., p. 9.

40. For instance, we refer here to the intervention of Bishop D. H. De Jong (Ndola, Zambia).

41. Bishop B. Batantu (Brazzaville, Congo) for instance, concretely suggested that "marriage coutumier" should be declared reconcilable with a minimal canonical form so that the later phases of the process can be open to pastoral guidance and the admittance to the eucharist allowed for its solemnization.

important area with which the message of the Gospel should be engaged to find and work out its own incarnation. The history of the Church's coming to be in diverse cultural worlds demonstrates that this process can only bear fruit in the actual establishment of particular churches. Thus, it is the proper task of the local church in Africa to deal with the encounter between christianity and African cultures in order to find the necessary solutions for this meeting on a pastoral level. The development of ecclesial legal codes must be fundamentally reviewed, according to the conclusions of the Cardinal as well as the opinion of a number of other African bishops.

It can be summarized that in the minds of the majority of African bishops the first theological principle concerning the teaching of the Church is precisely the need for Africanization. According to Bishop J.C. Bouchard (Pala, Chad), the center of gravity of christianity has shifted from Europe to Latin America and Africa. Evangelization in Africa should not contribute to the attack and destruction of the human values which already exist among these people: it should bring liberation and not threat.

The problem of inculturation in Asia, however, takes place in a totally different context: with the exception of the Philippines and in contrast to the African churches, the christian churches and communities in Asia remain small minorities. The Asian family is also a pluriform reality, influenced by a great diversity of models. While in Africa there is a relative underpopulation, Asia suffers from the real threat of overpopulation. Also, the wide cultural diversity of Asia weighs heavily upon the christian churches which still bear the character of their Western origin.

It was pointed out by Bishop P.D'Souza (Varanasi, India), that ceremonial marriage according to Hindu customs is a generally accepted obligation which estabishes legal status. Indian converts who do not wish to be alienated from their families and local communities must also accept this ceremony. Consequently, they are also obliged as christians to repeat the rites of marriage according to the Catholic Church. It is therefore necessary to create a christian marriage rite which can be integrated with the existing local customs. In the same respect we encounter here the difficulties surrounding mixed marriages which were considered a number one problem among all the Asian bishops' conferences. In this area, as in several others, there was a call for greater manoeuverability within the particular churches.

Turning to Latin America, Bishop Quarracino (Avellaneda, Argentina), secretary general of CELAM, pleaded for more attention to be given to the question of the "evangelization of culture" which had been neglected in the preparatory documents but was nevertheless part of the point raised in the papal address to the Conference of Puebla. Culture itself, considered as a totality of values by which the person is modeled, also embraces religious attitudes and one's relationship with God. The family is inescapably a cultural reality that every particular culture expresses and passes on. There is a reciprocal influence and interplay between the family and society to which Bishop Quarrarino attached great importance[42].

With all this said, and being aware of the fact that the observation might be less pointed, we should not hesitate to give attention to a similar concern for the cultural situations of the developed countries which were contributed by Western representatives. A single example would be the thoughts of Archbishop G. Danneels (Mechelen-Brussel, Belgium) on the roots of the present crisis, the atmosphere of anxiety about the future that touches young people who, consciously or unconsciously, are afraid to take on the project of marriage and raising a family. This anxiety goes hand in hand with the gradual loss of the meaning of God and of human existence. When the Father disappears, the children are afraid and cold. Thus, the Synod should not only inform people's conscience but warm their hearts as well.

3. *Birth control and the anti-life mentality*

The two, combined terms which form the designation of this topic signal in themselves the diverse points of view held by church leaders from the Northern and Southern hemispheres which treatened to lead this exchange into a discussion between the deaf. The bishops were virtually cast into contradictory positions because of the structure of the agenda which was dedicated largely if not exclusively to "the roles of the christian family". The bishops from both North and South wanted to deal with the problem of limiting births. However, those from the so-called North wished to return to the problematic of HV because this encyclical had not been accepted by a large portion — perhaps the vast majority — of the married faithful, while those from the South generally had no problem with the papal letter itself but wished to stress the issue

42. The allusion of Bishop Quarracino leads us to take note of the ambiguous function of the notion of "culture" at the CELAM Puebla Conference (1979). While the majority of bishops took the position neither of a "return to Christendom" nor of a kind of "diaspora Church" — thus, a minority church — most had recourse to a sort of middle position of "christian culture". It was hoped that, on the basis of the Latin American tradition, the Gospel could be passed through the general culture of society. Christianity would thus lend its support to a society which found itself in the midst of a crisis. One interpretation of this point raised at Puebla can be found in M. SCHOOYANS, *La Conférence de Puebla: un risque, un espoir*, in *Nouvelle Revue Théologique*, 101 (1979) 641-675, p. 660: "L'évangélisation n'est certes pas pensée en termes de chrétienté: mais elle est pensée en fonction d'une culture incluant explicitement la référence au christianisme". We must admit that this idea is very close to an ideal of veiled "christendom", a perspective that perhaps can also be found in the 1980 Synod when we consider that the family is expected to perform the same function.

in an entirely different perspective, namely the economic and political regression of the Third World which gives rise to an "anti-life mentality"[43]. The oppositions on this point were not new during the Synod.

Nonetheless, the episcopal gathering had its own particular characteristics to add. For one, the participants in the discussions of 1980 were largely members of a new generation (namely, the post-HV generation). For another, there was a new pope (who was chosen with the idea that authoritative teaching should be presented more strongly). Finally, there was a moral and economic crisis going on in the world which was having a profound effect.

Bishops who were representatives of the developed countries of the North, and were aware of a crisis largely attributable to the consumer society, wished to insist upon the need for a new pastoral approach to the question of contraception. In their eyes, the gulf between teaching and pastoral practice had become too great to be bridged effectively. This was the general thrust of the interventions presented by, among others, Archbishops Quinn (San Francisco, USA) and Danneels (Mechelen-Brussel, Belgium), Bishops Ernst (Breda, Nederlands) and Jullien (Beauvais, France), and Card. Hume (Westminster, England).

On the other side were the bishops from the developing countries of the South who protested against the economic and political pressures which were threatening their people on all fronts, including the demographic level. The families of these regions for the most part did not live under the influence of the consumer society as such but were often confronted with coercion from their own governments (India) or from international organizations (Philippines) to drastically limit the number of children they might have without any respect being shown for the freedom of conscience of the couples themselves. This was a concern not only in the regions of Southeast Asia but in countless countries of Latin America where the economic influence of North America was working to neutralize the demographic pressure on the poor by promoting the limitation of family size. In Africa the meaning of vitality and fertility was so strong that not only did the population reject the influence of international organizations but the bishops even went so far as to reject the pastoral problematic of the Western churches as being almost meaningless or at least hardly understandable.

There is probably no more striking example of the difference of opinion we are describing here that that which can be found in the intervention of Bishop Patrick D'Souza (Varanasi, India). "The dis-

---

43. We have already attempted to describe these two readings of HV which are indicated here. In short, one could say that the bishops from the North were chiefly concerned about HV, 10-14 while those from the South concentrated on HV, 23. Cf. J. GROOTAERS, *Humanae vitae et les réactions dans les pays du Tiers-monde*, in *Pour relire Humanae vitae*, Gembloux, 1970, pp. 51-66.

contentedness of young people has become a universal phenomenon which is undoubtedly in contradiction with the ideal of christians. But while this phenomenon is, in abundant societies, an expression of the disputation of the culture of the welfare society, that disputation in a developing country such as India gives rise to substantial despair caused by a situation of misery and injustice. In the same consequent factors are the causes which urge the use of prohibited methods of controlling births when a family lives in inhuman conditions or a couple lives in a developed country. One should be able to enumerate all the evils which touch upon family life here and indicate how these evils differ from region to region".

This brief sketch, however, does not relieve us of the obligation to expose more clearly some points of the debate which took place. The phenomenon of the population explosion was repeatedly brought to the fore. The interventions of the Filippino Bishops Th. Alberto y Valderrama (Caceres), J. Varela (Ozamis), and Card. J.L. Sin (Manila) were very much to the point on this issue. The Asian bishops opposed the standpoint of the demographers and the economists that the number of births had to be drastically reduced without including any ethical considerations or any concern for finding alternative ways of aiding human misery and poverty. They criticized this approach for being backwards: it is not overpopulation which causes misery but the other way around — the evidence of more global study shows that as the standard of living rises the growth of population slows down. Therefore, according to Card. Sin, the false propositions of the demographers should be rejected. It is dangerous to preach a morality based on efficiency in place of a value-oriented morality. The real cause of mass poverty which needs to be addressed today, as indicated at the Bucharest Conference of 1974, needs to be exposed: "The present situation in developing countries is due to the inequality of socio-economic systems which has divided people since the beginning of modern times. This inequality remains today and is even becoming more intense".

It was Bishop D'Souza who used the term "anti-life mentality", which he said was precipitated by government programs in India which did violence to traditional values that have always considered life as sacred, as was pointed out in the statements from Tagore. What is needed is an international strategy to eliminate not life but poverty and underdevelopment. Many of the speakers clearly recognized that a real problem existed in this area but insisted that any solution must be situated in the whole context of the development problematic.

There were others, however, who would not even admit to the problem such as Archbishop López Trujillo (Medellin, Colombia), President of CELAM, who warned against the exaggerations of the prophets of doom who were predicting a population explosion. The rich countries had to be convinced that they must stand open toward and work together with the poor countries, he said[44]. The Brazilian bishops approached the increase in world population from the perspective of denouncing the social structures of an unjust world order. According to Bishop Mendes de Almeida (aux. of São Paulo, Brazil), the excessive cultivation of nature caused by the overconsumption of the rich countries is a more serious problem than the increase of the population in the Third World. By imposing birth control, the multinationals and the governments of the powerful countries have manipulated people of these regions.

Taking a completely different tack, the interventions of the Bishops from the West were more prone to address this issue from an individual, micro-ethical perspective. The principle concern of most of these opinions, expressed both in and out of the Synod, emphasized, as we have indicated, the gulf between official teaching and pastoral practice which was attributable to the non-reception of HV. Bishop Jullien (Beauvais, France) ventured to speak of a "no man's land" created by the distance between the position of the Church with respect to the methods of regulating fertility on the one side and the justification of this position on the other. Bishop Ernst spoke of the gap between the teaching authority and the experience of many. Archbishop Quinn provided a clear illustration with the results of a recent survey by Princeton University that revealed that 76 % of Catholic women in the U.S. use some form of birth control and 94 % of these Catholic women use methods which are prohibited by HV; only 29 % of American priests considered artificial methods immoral and only 26 % of the priests would refuse absolution to those who refused to give up using them. Most especially, it was observed that opposition to HV was common among those who lead an engaged christian life, including theologians and spiritual leaders, and who exercised common sense and an otherwise undoubting dedication to the Church[45].

All these speakers professed their adhesion to the principle points of HV. What they sought was to situate the encyclical in a broader context — as they interpreted the words of Paul VI himself a few days after he issued the letter — and to review, widen and deepen the arguments upon which the teaching was based, the notion of "gradualness" in the "pedagogy" of the faithful, and a more pastoral approach to the regulation of fertility. In short, they were not seeking to change the teaching of HV but to deepen it. Yet, by taking this point of departure, the representatives of this position did not create an easy task. A

44. In an interview given to the French weekly *Famille Chrétienne* (16 oct. 1980), Archbishop López Trujillo referred to the "terrorism of demographers" and the absence of ethical norms in, for instance, the final report of the Brandt Commission.

45. A more detailed report of Archbishop Quinn's intervention was presented in Section II. Cf. *supra*, pp. 57-60.

continuous investigation of the encyclical would demand a great deal of time and would probably result in a lack of clarity if not complete vagueness.

The most outspoken suggestion came from Bishop Ernst who pleaded for a greater freedom of movement in approaching sometimes very diverse situations. By using the example of the social teaching of the Church which addresses itself to the direction of human activity but leaves the details of concrete action to those who are involved (as, for instance, John-Paul II indicated during his trip to Brazil) the teaching authority of the Church should use the same approach with respect to marriage and the family, by presenting general principles while restraining judgment on their concrete application which christians themselves would make after consulting the realities in which they live in the light of the Gospel and Church teaching[46].

Another remarkable intervention was that of Archbishop Danneels who pointed to a disjointedness in this area between teaching and spirituality. We spend a great deal of effort on morality, he observed, and miss the inspiration of the mystical, but "being comes before acting". Rules for moral behavior in the absence of marital spirituality lead to exaggerated feelings of guilt; without spirituality, morality is reduced to voluntarism. It is necessary that the Synod find a pastoral approach which can be followed.

Finally, it goes without saying that in the course of such a landslide of opinion in this area, the Synod would also hear from the representatives of the "natural methods" and more particularly from the often well received proponents of the so-called "Billings method"[47]. One came across these advocates among the bishops and curial leaders who defended on absolutist position with respect to Church teaching and held that pastoral practice could only be built on the basis of this doctrine. Card. Felici, who was very much involved in the defense of HV, held the bishops of the West responsible for the reservations expressed over the encyclical. His reaction against the exposition of Archbishop Quinn in this context received much attention. However, his remarks left these bishops unconvinced. Many of them reacted critically to the sometimes unbridled propaganda that extolled the values of the "natural methods". Some expressly noted that the question of applied methods was not necessarily the ethical crux for approaching the limitation of births. Bishop Jullien declared that, "the methods are important, but they are not the most important". Bishop Ernst expressed the same opinion and Bishop Hadisumarta (Malang, Indonesia) reminded his colleagues that natural methods could also be used for realizing an "anti-life mentality".

46. We will return to this topic in the following sections, on the small group discussions.
47. The sixteen couples who were, without exception, chosen from this direction, were heard from repeatedly.

4. *Faith and the sacrament*

The Synod was welcomed by many as an opportunity to approach another pressing issue that had been causing problems for pastors for many years. We refer to the difficult case of "marginal believers", the nominal Catholics who, without really participating in the life of faith of the Church, sought a church wedding for reasons which apparently had nothing to do with the experience of christian faith. Whereas on the one hand the local churches of Africa had laid emphasis upon the differentiations between "marriage coutumier" and ceremonial christian marriage, on the other, the problem of the "marginal believers" was one of the principle agenda points that was of paramount concern among the bishops of the older christian traditions.

Of course, one should not consider this observation to be absolute. It is indeed the case that tangential questions with respect to faith and the sacrament came from a number of quarters, be it the situation of the divorced-remarried, especially in the West but also among the East European churches, or from other concerns that were prevalent in Third World countries. In contrast to the discussions about birth control and HV in which there was a clear division between the representatives from North and South, the exchange of views about the relation between faith and the sacrament of marriage sometimes revealed comparable pastoral problems in different parts of the world, even though they might not be equally distributed. One could even say that this thorny question was central in the synodal discussion.

In an earlier time, one looked upon the simple request for a church wedding to be sufficient to accept a marriage in the Church. This admittance was based upon the traditional theory of "implicit belief", meaning that the request itself signified that the baptized person intended to do what the Church intended. In the contemporary situation, the applicability of this theory has been seriously brought into doubt, a fact that was reflected in the episcopal discussions. The questions being posed clearly pointed out that the intention to do what the Church does was no longer the minimum requirement to establish that one believed along with the Church. Nominal christians who were baptized at birth (and thus not by personal choice) and yet who were not believers were faced with an impossible choice according to the presently existing norms: either to refuse a church wedding and thus enter into a marriage which is not considered valid by the ecclesial institution, or to request the sacrament of marriage and "undergo" the process without belief. In the contemporary situation of the fragmentation of christendom, this phenomenon could also undermine the hope that the children of many such unions would receive an education in the faith. The cases of baptized non-believers who request a church wedding had become increasingly numerous and in some places even prominent. In such a situation, conscientious pastoral care had become inevitably restricted with no apparent way out.

In the name of the French conference, Bishop G. Duchêne (Saint-Claude, France), chairman of their Commission on the Family, addressed this issue in a way that logically connected with other, similar interventions. What was the reason, he asked, for the disconcertedness of parish priests with respect to the sacrament of marriage? Since Vatican II, priests have become aware of the prerequisite of faith for the solemnization of the sacrament. Too many pastors have found themselves uncertain of at least the feeling that engaged couples were in search of an authentic experience of faith; too many of them were asking the Church merely for a religious gesture which was often very ambiguous. More serious still was that the engaged would sometimes simply feign belief in order to obtain an exterior ceremony. It is the message of the Church itself that is falsified by these sham and even hypocritical relationships. Whether the priest refuses the sacrament because he judges that there is insufficient faith present, or he admits the marginal believers to the sacrament because he wishes to maintain some bond with the Church, neither solution gives him any true peace.

The Bishop of Saint-Claude then asked where the sacramental demands of unity, faithfulness and indissolubility might lie in such circumstances? And what may happen to the credibility of the Church? He referred to a study done by the International Theological Commission in this area in which their report clearly recognized that the sacramental celebration of marriage for non-believers leads to a new problematic which for the present found no solution. Finally, Bishop Duchêne recommended that the Synod establish a work group of bishops and theologians to study this point so that a satisfactory theological and canonical solution could be suggested without delay.

When, during the third week of the Synod, the leaders of the Roman congregations and curial departments gave a series of speeches that countered requests for more openness and adaptation, Card. Knox (Cong. for Sacraments and Liturgy) took the opportunity to give the diocesan bishops a lesson and, despite pastoral difficulties, to remind them again of the classical position of canon law that binds pastors to do everything possible to bring the baptized to a minimum of faith prior to their contracting marriage. This intervention did not go unanswered by Bishop Duchêne, for he pointed out that the obvious rule, of which pastors were being reminded, was not always realizable in a world which was characterized by dechristianization and indifference, as Card. Ratzinger himself pointed out in his first report. The French bishops asked why a question that had been recognized by the ITC was not allowed to be heard. "I fully understand the concern of the

Congregation, he said, but it is my wish that one, in fraternal and constructive dialogue, would listen to the doctrinal and pastoral questions which have been put forth in this area".

It was not difficult in this whole exchange of views to discern a tendency which was seeking to distinguish better between the validity and the sacramentality of marriage and thus in a certain sense to return to a situation which resembled the time before the Council of Trent that had fused both aspects into one, single concept of marriage.

5. The need for a theology of marriage

One of the most articulated needs put forth at the Synod was undoubtedly that of an applicable theology of marriage. This question, which was posed very clearly by the African representatives, was also heard from bishops of other parts of the world. Alongside the classical reference to the close bond between Christ and His Church which served as a ground for theologizing about christian marriage, a number of other voices were heard with the suggestion of moving away from this foundation and valorizing other conceptions.

This had already been put forth in the preparatory document from the bishops of Zaïre[48] who touched upon the notion that the "family" of the Trinity provided a ground for the brotherhood of all men and a model for marriage. Then, Card. A. Lorscheider (Fortaleza), speaking for the Brazilian bishops, was opposed to the strict preservation of the idea that the sacrament of marriage was a sign of Christ giving Himself to His Church; such a symbol is more appropriate for the Eucharist. The specificity of marriage as sacrament, he said, lies in its value as a sign of God's creative love. Bishop Marie-Sainte (Martinique) was also convinced that the essential reality of the christian family was best understandable by rising to the source of life which is the Trinity, as the Father has revealed it to us through the Son.

For his own part, Archbishop Légaré (Grouard, Canada) understood the difference between the relationship of Christ to His Church and that of the Church to Christ; the first is one of unconditional faithfulness but the second is a case of human uncertainty. Essentialist philosophy has influenced us to think of the Church as completed, but historical reality and existential perspectives must change this view of the Church[49].

The point already made with respect to theological method had touched upon the question of working along with married laypersons in this area. A large number of bishops had established that the christian experience of spouses was one of the sources which belonged to theological consideration (cf. Cards. Enrique y Tarancón, Hume, Bishops

48. Cf. *supra*, Section II, pp. 30-34.
49. Cf. *supra*, Section II, pp. 62-64.

Bouchard, Ernst, and many others). With respect to method, various African representatives insisted on keeping apart the central truths and peripheral elements: Bishop Monsengwo Pasinya (Inongo, Zaïre) wished to distinguish two series of domains within marriage: on the one side, the essential, solid and permanent elements of revelation; and on the other, the contingent and improvable elements such as cultural givens which evolve in the course of centuries. On the basis of the law of the Incarnation, the local churches (first among them in this being the bishops' conference of Zaïre) made an appeal for the cultural values of their people.

Going even further than these suggestions, we find a number of bishops who were looking for a pastoral solution to the countless and varied kinds of cases of irregular marriage about which the existing norms could do nothing. In this connection, Bishop L. Tienchai Sawanchit (Chanthaburi, Thailand) appealed to the Word of the Lord that "The Son of Man has come to seek those who were lost and to save them", in order to encourage the Church's special attention and willingness to help the "lost sheep". The Synod in general exhibited great concern for the many marriages which are not in line with the Church's norms: polygamy, mixed marriages, remarried divorced persons. This last category was the cause of the most thought and concern for bishops from every part of the Church universal.

With respect to polygamy, Archbishop Arinze (Onitsha, Mozambique) drew attention to the fact that marriage is a very complex institution, closely tied to local culture; it is therefore not surprising that the ideal of christian marriage can only take hold after the passage of some time. Thus the Church must take on a pastoral attitude of patience and compassion, without rushing in to condemn things on the basis of the clarity of her teaching. Similarly, Bishop J. Hardy (Superior General of the African Missions) recommended a pedagogy of gradualness supported by dialogue and patience as well as a spirituality of hope.

As far as the great number of "irregular families" of Latin America are concerned, those bishops who were involved in this area drew attention to the present conditions under which the faithful are forced to live and for which they are not responsible. In this whole area, according to Bishop J. M. Ruiz Navas (Latacunga, Ecuador), the Church is not only the "mistress" of a doctrine, but also a "mother" who will exhibit loving concern. Bishop Dammert Bellido (Cajamarca, Peru) pointed out that in the poor regions of the Andes where a true evangelization has not yet penetrated, there exists no christian marriage. There are, of course, natural unions which are lasting and unbreakable and which are loving centers for the true upbringing of children, despite the fact that they are neither civilly nor ecclesially recognized. This is not a phenomenon of secularization but of simple ignorance. Here is where a profound evangelization is needed, one that takes into account the ancestral traditions of these peoples.

Of all those spouses who are not living according to the norms of the Church, the Synod bishops demonstrated special interest for christians who were divorced and remarried and yet, despite this irregular situation, wished to re-establish a close relation with the Church and her life. Of particular interest is their recognition that some of these partners are the guiltless victims of the breakdown of a first marriage who have built a second marriage and a lasting family which can insure the upbringing of children. In response to these concerns of both the Western and non-Western members of the Synod, the representatives of the Eastern Rite Churches made reference to the centuries-old practice of the Orthodox, namely, the recognition of a second, non-sacramental but valid marriage wherein the remarried, after the passage of some time, may completely partake in the life of the Church. A figure as well known as the Patriarch of Antioch, Bishop Maximos V Hakim, declared, "Since the contemporary Catholic theologians and canonists cannot accept the grounds for divorce given by Justinian in the time before the division of the Church, let them give more thought to the ideas that were generally accepted in the first centuries of the Eastern Church to understand that only a first marriage was considered to be a sacrament while the following marriages were not. Later marriages were also sometimes admitted by the Church and even blessed, but without the liturgy of 'crowning'. The Fathers of the Church at that time accepted that the divorced-remarried could again be admitted to the eucharist. On the basis of the principle of 'Oeconomia', often invoked and applied in the East, the Synod would be in a position to approach this question and find a practical solution"[50].

The last but certainly not least category of "abnormal" situations that we will mention in this brief summary is one about which a large number of bishops had something to say, namely mixed marriages. In the pastoral situation of the Western Churches, these situations form a substantial subdivision of the question of the relation between the Catholic Church and other christian churches, especially the Protestant and Anglican traditions. In the whole of the exchange of views on this point, the Synod demonstrated a much broader outlook in which the classical questions of ecumenism played only a marginal and exceptional role. The large scope of the problem of mixed marriages throughout the world was perhaps best illustrated by the exposition of Bishop B. Halem' Imana (Kabale, Uganda) who addressed the various types of situations that needed to be dealt with in East Africa: the mixed marriage between

---

50. In a second intervention, ten days after the first, Bishop Maximos V Hakim made reference to the legislation of the Sixth Ecumenical Council (691), thus signaling a return to ancient sources.

a Catholic and a non-Catholic (which was steadily growing in number); between a Catholic and a non-christian (the Islamic faithful, but also members of the traditional African religions); between members of different ethnic lineage; and between persons of different race.

While mixed marriage had for the most part been looked upon in countries with a Catholic tradition (or in which Catholics formed a majority of the population) as a threat to the faith of the Catholic partner, in a remarkable intervention Archbishop Yasuda (Osaka, Japan) opened a completely different perspective: just as in the time of the primitive church, mixed marriage is a form of missionary task intended by Providence to aid in the spread of the faith. In such families, the Catholic partner has an exceptional opportunity not only to lead their partner to conversion, but also to provide for the Catholic upbringing of the children. In his written remarks to the Secretariate, the bishop tried to put his pastoral position into a more theological context. For his own part, Archbishop Foscolos (Athens, Greece) made reference to mixed marriage with a partner of the Orthodox tradition. If such a marriage is considered to have come to an end on the side of the Orthodox, the Catholic remains "bound", a paradoxical situation which is even more complicated by the fact that in Greece there is no practice of civil marriage.

All in all, it was the Asian bishops who were most hard pressed with the care of marriages between a Catholic and a non-christian which is very frequent in their region of the world. In this line, the Indian Bishop D'Souza insisted upon the competence of the local church to draw up guidelines for mixed marriages that could be appropriate for the local needs. The situations in the christian world are so diverse, he suggested, that it was not possible, for instance, to apply the same rules in his own diocese, with 15.000 Catholics among 20 million inhabitants, as those which apply to a christian country.

As representative of the Secretary of Christian Unity, Card. J. Willebrands gave a detailed exposé of the ecumenical aspects of the Synod's theme. He expressed the wish that the Synod would fulfill its pastoral task in a positive way that promoted the courage and the hope of the gospel message. The Cardinal also posed the question whether the time had come "to once again study the possibility that non-Catholic partners could be admitted to eucharistic communion in the Church, at least in certain cases". Such a study would also have to give its attention to the pressing question of "reciprocity", namely the permission for the Catholic partner to receive the eucharist in another church.

6. Open or closed concept of the family

There remains the question of how the entire problematic of the "function of the family in society" would be handled in the 1980 Synod.

As we have already mentioned, the majority of bishops were reluctant to deal with this theme. A great number of speakers certainly recognized and even emphasized the role of the christian family as domestic church or as the basic cell of society, just as those who had prepared for the Synod had want to do. But at the same time one can also observe a contrasting flow of opinion that wished to draw attention to the danger of segregating the family from society, both with respect to sociological analysis and in the formation of a plan for the future. A number of bishops considered the theme of the Synod itself to rest upon an idyllic conception of the family that some saw as romantic and others too moralistic. It was an image that did not correspond to reality very well and that could only offer a shaky basis for a real diagnosis.

The call for a more realistic approach was most clearly put by the Brazilian representatives, but was discernable in more or less cautions terms by others who referred to the need for more openness. The Western bishops could hardly ignore the fact that in their region the concept of the nuclear family was prominent and that former family traditions were being largely rejected by the younger generations. Most of the African (and Asian) bishops, addressing their own cultural situation, drew attention to the extended family which provided significant social norms and functions and was in no way related to the Western nuclear family that they considered to be an intensive part of the Western model of society. The Latin American representatives emphasized the romanticism of the presupposed image of the family and denounced the social and economic oppression of the poor who could not even establish a family.

In view of this general exchange, the designation of the family as "object" or "subject" also contributed to the confusion and added a certain ambiguity to the discussion. Indeed, when the Latin American bishops (e.g. A. Lorscheider, Llaguno Farias, García Gonzáles, and others) drew attention to the fact that the family is an "object" of social structures, they based themselves on a totally different foundation than that of Archbishops J. MacNeil and C. Martini who put forth the idea that the family is the "subject" of pastoral care. The first perspective was primarily social while the second referred to an ecclesial relationship. Perhaps the core of this important difference could be described as the tension between an open or closed concept of the family.

The emphasis that was placed upon the family as domestic church during the preparatory phase of the Synod included an inevitable danger that the family would be understood without direct reference to its social context. Placing the accent upon ethical norms and diminishing the fundamental givens of sociological analysis resulted in an undoubtable misconception. This tendency appeared strongest in the West where the family was understood as a reality in itself, even though it was seen to have a distinctive role on the individual and social levels, that was considered structurally independent from the more general model of society. This obviously included the risk that the stabilizing role of the family would remain subject to the dominant social patterns while those patterns and the influence they exert would remain unknown[51]. It is striking that the bishops of the Western churches were very much concerned with the reevaluation of traditional ethics, indeed on the basis of a renewed ecclesiology, rather than with exposing the causal connection between the situation of the family and the questionable model of the dominant social givens. In a word, micro-ethics was given preference to macro-ethical considerations.

Those who subscribed to an open conception of the family, however, by no means remained silent during the Synod. For one, there were the various representatives of the Brazilian church who, as already pointed out, recognized that the family was not as much the basic cell of society as it was its victim. Bishop Lorscheiter (Santa Maria) rejected "every idyllic and utopian concept of the family ... not only as meaningless but also as a source for new, serious frustrations for the family". Since the family is in fact more a victim of society, it would be more appropriate to direct pastoral action to a more global evangelization, stressing the role of the basic christian communities. According to Bishop C. Hummes (Santo André, Brazil) poverty in the Third World is structural and continuous, and the fault of this social sin lies with the First World and the christians who live there. Pastoral care for the family must in the first place be directed to dominant social structures and work toward a dismanteling of their injustice. Again, Bishop Mendes de Almeida (aux., São Paulo) pointed to the exploitation of nature caused by the over-consumption of the rich countries that forms a larger threat than the increase of world population. The multinationals have manipulated the poor like machines, and it is necessary to appeal to a change of heart among the rich[52]. Bishop Irizar Campos (Yurimaguas, Peru) emphasized that the family is not an autonomous reality that can be considered independently from the more global reality that surrounds it. There is a close relationship between the problems of society and those of the

51. According to J. Frisque (*art. cit.*, p. 57) sociologists have already revealed how far the Western privatization of the family is a direct result of dominant forces that are at the service of the consumer society. The Western churches have given much attention to the moral position of the family but too little to its social position.

52. Bishop Mendes de Almeida formed three conclusions: 1. public opinion in the *developed countries* should be substantially formed with respect to programs of development in the Third World which often include the use of contraceptives; 2. one needs to appeal to christian communities; especially in the *developed countries*, to see to it that poor families in the Third World will be given a proper formation in order to practice responsible parenthood; and 3. all christian families should strive toward a simple, sober and strong style of life which would serve as an example for the *developed countries* to conserve natural resources and would give expression to the liberating power of the Gospel.

family; the situation of social injustice has a direct effect upon the inner life of families.

Other, similar ideas were presented by bishops from other parts of the world. Two African representatives in particular, Bishop D. De Jong (Ndola, Zambia) and Archbishop G. Daniel (Pretoria, South Africa) defended very much the same position. The former noted that the effort necessary to reform unjust social structures must begin with ourselves, while the latter believed that it was the responsibility of the Church to fashion and promote a pastoral theology of social change. The Synod should apply itself to enlightening governments as to the heavy moral obligations they have for guaranteeing the basic requirements for marital and family life. Finally, the Asian bishops were not silent in referring to the misery of countless families and connecting this to the injustice of dominant economic structures. This was the case with Bishop T. Gomes (Danajpar, Bangladesh) who considered it the task of the Universal Church to critique these structures because it carried much greater weight than any particular church. Archbishop Datubara (Medan, Indonesia) also rejected the nostalgic view of an idyllic situation.

In so far as the bishops defended something of an open or closed concept of the family, their pastoral conclusions would be opposed to each other along the same lines. It was primarily the bishops of the Third World, who emphasized the social influences upon the family, who pointed out that a pastoral approach built up in a vacuum would have no meaning and called for pastoral action that would reach society as a whole. In the same lines, these bishops gave special attention to ecclesial basic communities and the role that such groups could fulfill. This was expressly stated by the representatives of AMECEA (Association of Member Episcopal Conferences of Eastern Africa) as well as by Card. Cordeiro (Karachi, Pakistan) and Bishop Tzadua (Addis Ababa, Ethiopia).

By way of summary, the six principle themes which we have developed here to sketch an image of the first week of synodal discussions is by no means totally exhaustive. But we hope that they have clarified the meaning and special importance of the contributions from the local churches. In light of the great diversity of these major lines which sometimes give the impression of real polarization, it is evident how impossible it would be to simply characterize the different opinions as falling into clear tendencies toward "progressivism" or "conservatism". Nevertheless one can still attempt to draw positive conclusions from these discussions by outlining a few major lines of development[53]: in general, there was a preference given to spirituality and a pastoral perspective over that of an abstract doctrinal one; the need for a renewal

53. We make specific reference to the article of E. FRANCHINI, art. cit., passim.

of a theology of the family was underscored, to be based upon the experience of married laypersons (in this area, the "creational" values of the family were also brought to the fore); in consultation with a proper hierarchy of priorities, the socio-economic situations of the local churches were seen to be of decisive importance; and in connection with this last point, one can also see the division lines between the rich North and the poor South with respect to the use of contraceptives, the general (open or closed) concept of the family, and the need to indict unjust social structures which affect the family. This difference can also be referred to as a polarity between micro- and macro-ethics.

In Third World countries, the question of regulating fertility could only be experienced as a frustrating exception in reference to the "cosmic value of the flow of life". (In the Western world, the problem was a more private one having to do with the tendency toward hedonism.) Also, many peoples of the Third World considered fertility to be a social phenomenon, against which contraception was seen as fundamentally negative, a lack of trust in the future and destructive of social living. (The privatizing tendencies of the West consider a child exclusively in terms of the welcoming benevolence of the parents.) Consciousness of these deeper differences in basic perspectives was, at the same time, a source of enrichment in the results of the Synod for it gave another dimension to the dialogue.

C. The "relatio altera" of Card. Ratzinger

Our own analysis of the major lines of thought present in the general discussions of the first week does not dismiss us from making reference to the official report of the *Relator*, Card. Ratzinger, on 6 Oct., that was dedicated to the same purpose. As we have already said, this was one of the best texts of the Synod, and it served the bishops well in providing the outlines for discussion in the *circuli minores* which would take place in the following days. The *relatio altera* thus came to be a pivotal point in the Synod [54].

In the beginning of his report, the Cardinal gave a sketch of the two major methodological tendencies which divided the participants of the meeting. Some fathers, he said, have emphasized the avoidance of static formulations, as if teaching has been closed for all time: reality cannot simply be summarized by theoretical, doctrinal statements but should be considered from the perspective of the pilgrim people of God. The criterion for this accounting, which is always in development, is the

---

54. *Synodus Episcoporum 1980 Relatio Altera* (16 pp. with an 8 page appendix consisting of detailed proposals intended for the *circuli minores*). A condensed version of the text appeared in *Osservatore Romano*, 120 (8 Oct. 1980), (French edition) 31 (21 Oct. 1980). We base our commentary here on the complete, original text.

appreciation of the faith that includes the experience of married christians, the work of theologians, philosophers, scientific experts, and the
value judgments of Church teaching authority. The principle categories
of this method are historical (the signs of the times) and experiential
(enlightened by the appreciation of the faith) from which it follows that
pastoral action in a real sense precedes doctrinal judgment and therefore
guides it.

The representatives of the other tendency maintained that the principle
pastoral task lies, first and for all, in remaining true to Church teaching
because salvation can only be found in truth, according to the word of
the Sacred Scripture. The Church should not be led by trends in opinion,
as if the law is a mere consequence of sociology. On the contrary, the
prophetic role of the Church is to denounce evil in the world by utilizing
the gospel, that is, by the power of the Cross and of Christ's
Resurrection. In the minds of these fathers, the Church can only truly be
at the service of the world by proclaiming the light of the Gospel clearly
and without hesitation. Because mankind is seeking salvation, it is
necessary to resist the injustice and sin that fundamentally penetrates the
structures of the world. The development of doctrine, which is in no way
ruled out, takes place insofar as faith penetrates and converts the life of
man and thus the structures of the world as well. In this conversion the
Word-Incarnate is advanced and the world slowly moves toward "the
fullness of the life of Christ" (Eph. 4:13). In this perspective one of these
bishops has aptly said: "We are the sailors of the ship of the Church,
guided by the Holy Spirit. By the Word of God, culture is broken up and
reformed. The Word is in a position to give direction to a helmsless
civilization. It beckons to the way of conversion and it brings an end to
moral pessimism".

As a middle position, several fathers wished to find a way to reconcile
these tendencies. They spoke of the way that the teaching of the Church
must find a connection with the life of persons and emphasized the need
for a pedagogy that would lead persons gradually toward a life inspired
by the Gospel and bridge the gap between the ordinary customs of life
and the christian vocation. Such was Card. Ratzinger's description of the
general tendencies.

According to the commentary of E. Franchini, there were two general
tendencies in the Synod which might be classified as "personalist" and
"classicist", those who wished to review doctrine along the lines of
experience and those who, in contrast, would correct experience on the
basis of Church teaching[55]. This was the nucleus of the entire synodal
debate: a significant, subsequent tendency was born to attempt to go

---

55. Our own classification would prefer the words "pastoral" and "doctrinal". It is a
contrast which has been present in the Church since the time of Vatican II and which we
have described at the beginning of this section.

beyond these contrasting views and to include the values present in each, a pedagogical method in which science and experience, doctrine and life could grow together[56]. Archbishop Martini's press conference of 15 Oct. can also be understood as an honest attempt to bridge the polarity. It is something of a disappointment that these and other attempts at a compromise were not evident in the final text of the Propositions. We will return to that in the next section.

This sketch of the tendencies present in the general discussions was only a first part of Card. Ratzinger's report which was divided into six rubrics. These general topics were:

I. de methodo adhibenda
II. de situatione familiae christianae in mundo hodierno
III. de sacramento matrimonii, ubi imprimis etiam de eius indissolubilitate agendum erit
IV. de munere vitae transmittendi
V. de spiritualitate familiae, ubi etiam de educationis quaestionibus tractandum erit
VI. de actione pastorali quoad familias

The first subject, on the method to be followed, has just been discussed. The second, on the situation of the christian family, noted various aspects of the topic. As a result of increasing permissiveness and secularism and the negative influence of the developed countries upon the Third World, social conditions have been drastically changing, contributing to the disintegration of the family. In the prevailing economic circumstances, the meaning of progress and development is placed in question. When external, material success is looked upon as the criterion, conscience is seriously undermined. Then, there are political systems which threaten the being of the family itself (e.g. by permitting abortion and divorce) or the proper rights of the family (e.g. by imposing contraception). Cultural conditions were also considered and a suggestion was noted to draw up a declaration for the rights of the family.

Under the heading dealing with the sacrament of marriage there were four different problems dealt with which the Synod had indicated as

56. Cf. E. FRANCHINI, *art. cit.*, p. 480. This commentator made an attempt to develop an inventory of the two tendencies. In his analysis, the fathers calling for a renewal of moral theology in the sense of openness, spirituality, and personalism were: Freeman, Enrique y Tarancón, A. Lorscheider, Légaré, Monsengwo Pasinya, Duchêne, Hurley, Callens, Boyle, Winning, Perkins, Huynh-Dông-Các, Dorado Soto, Lópes Fitoria, Khoarai, de Couesnongle, de Araújo Sales, Delhaye, Hume, Bernardin, Zubeir Wako, Fernandes, and Ruiz Navas. Those who represented the more classicist position were: Beltritti, Laguna, López Trujillo, Mercieca, Ryan, Suquía Goicoechei, Bianchi di Cárcano, Höffner, Benelli, Padiyara, Thiandoum, Cooke, Baum, Vagnozzi, Ekandem, and Knox (plus most members of the Latin language group). The intervention of Card. Poma was considered to be representative of the middle, or reconciliatory, position.

needing specific attention. After some general remarks which pointed to some anthropological givens and a theological approach to the sacrament as well as a warning against a false romanticism of the family, the Cardinal dealt with the relation between faith and the sacrament (including marginal believers or baptized non-believers) and the great attention that was given to the call for mandatory marriage preparation programs. Also, the relation between traditional marriage customs and the form of christian marriage was noted to be an important point of discussion, especially in connection with the application of inculturation. Then, according to traditional Church teaching, the word sacrament referred immediately to the unbreakableness of the marital bond, but today we are confronted with a growing number of divorces and with the situation of the divorced-remarried who are not allowed to approach the sacraments. A series of concrete proposals were noted to have been put forth in this area. Lastly, with respect to mixed marriages, the *Relator* noted that the opinions of the bishops were divided. In one region these could be considered as promoting evangelization while in another they might have disadvantageous consequences. Also, the divergent practices of the different churches with respect to indissolubility remained an unsolved problem.

The fourth topic, dealing with the transmission of life, was the subject of approximately half of the episcopal interventions. The bishops of the Third World denounced the anti-life mentality, caused in large measure by anxiety about the future and the absence of God. In this connection the Synod called for the neccesity of a new attitude toward life. They also focused attention on the forms of pressure which were brought to bear on the Third World to promote a limitation of births without any respect for the conscience of persons or for the independence of people. Finally, the bishops recalled the "objective difficulties", already mentioned in IL, 64, which played a role in the problem of accepting HV by priests acting as counselors. Therefore, the unfinished character of the encyclical was invoked and the gradualness of personal development was underscored.

The subject of family spirituality was roughly divided into four aspects: the development of conscience, sacramental life, family prayer and christian education. Because the family is not only the subject but also the object of evangelization, a proper development of conscience is demanded so that the faculty of discernment of spirits will not fall short of its task. In the same context an appreciation of the faith is formed and the people of God participate in the teaching office of the Church. It is also noted that through the sacraments of the New Covenant, christians become deeply rooted in the visible community of saints: marriage is a continuous sacrament which man and woman bring to fulfillment throughout their lives.

Some speakers warned against a romantic conception of family life which would forget the place of daily sacrifice. Participation in the celebration of the eucharist should be one of the constituting factors of christian family living. Not to be neglected as well, however, is that through family prayer the family itself becomes a domestic church. A number of meaningful remarks were presented in this area. Also, the movement of the family to transcend itself forms a part of its own proper spirituality.

The project of christian education is based upon the dynamic of love whereby the members of the family learn to care for each other in the spirit of the beatitudes. With respect to the relation between family and school, the inalienable rights of the former were confirmed.

Finally, the last topic of this second report touched upon pastoral action for the family: graduated phases of preparation for marriage, pastoral action in helping marital life, the useful role of small communities including the parish or associations, the extended family or "basic communities" depending upon the situation and the appropriateness. In the same connection it is noted that many bishops desired that a directory for the pastoral care of the family be drawn up.

The *relatio altera* delivered by Card. Ratzinger also included an eight page appendix of more concrete and detailed questions concerning the six rubrics. These questions were intended for the smaller discussion groups which were now at the point of beginning their work.

V. SACRAMENTALITY AND THE TRANSMISSION OF LIFE

Second Phase: The Small Discussion Groups

The six rubrics and accompaniying, more detailed questions put forth by Card. Ratzinger in his *relatio altera* were handed over to the smaller groups for more concrete discussion. We have already drawn attention to some of the disadvantages present with respect to the way that these groups, the *circuli minores*, were drawn up. Yet, just as with the previous Synods, this phase of the event was a significant moment in the entire process. The first question that may be asked in whether the major tendencies that surfaced during the general discussions were also evident in the smaller groups. It is entirely possible that the counterpositions of the pastorally oriented and the classically conservative bishops would be found again in the *circuli minores*[57]. However, while the members of the Latin group had, with the greatest clarity and determination, defended the classical perspective (taken from the traditional handbooks), in the other groups there was a discernable effort to go beyond this kind of polarity by utilizing, for instance, the categories of spirituality which were most evident in the French A and the Italian groups.

In regard to the problem of the divorced-remarried, the strictest representatives would be found in the Latin, English C, Spanish B and C groups; the other groups did not take a strong position on this issue and many wished that the problem be looked at from the Eastern Orthodox tradition. The question of the *sensus fidelium* and theology in respect to the people of God was taken very seriously by French A which attempted to develop criteria whereby pastors and faithful could be attuned to each other; while English A, Spanish A and the German group also came to the conclusion that doctrine needs to be renewed through the theological reflection upon experience. In this area, the Latin group gave preference to doctrine over experience.

The basic concept of the family itself was far from consistent between the groups. French A expressed the opinion what an overused term such as the "domestic church" should probably be left to the side. Both this group and Spanish C recommended that the trinitarian dimensions of the family should be rethought with respect to its christological interpretation. They also called for more attention to be given to the vocation and the office of spouses in exercising the "ministry of the family", specifically in a way that would avoid clericalism; Spanish C took an even broader approach to this, stipulating that a theology of community

57. We refer here to the broad conclusions drawn by E. FRANCHINI, *art. cit.*, pp. 480-481.

would apply to the family and to all families. For its own part, the Italian group emphasized that encounters between the local churches and more centralized authority could be beneficial in preventing some local episcopates from falling into a certein particularism.

It should be evident from these preliminary remarks that the many themes and opinions expressed by the small groups are too varied and diverse to lend themselves to a complete analysis in the space available to us here. We will thus have to limit ourselves to a more specific study in order to demonstrate the events that were taking place in the *circuli minores*. From the six rubrics proposed in Card. Ratzinger's second report, we will follow two themes which carried significant weight in the course of the Synod, namely: the sacrament of marriage, with particular reference to its indissolubility; and the task of transmitting human life. Furthermore, we will also limit the study to four groups which are representative of the major tendencies present in all eleven. These are, English B (presided over by Card. Hume), French A (Card. Etchegaray), Spanish C (Card. Pironio), and the Latin group (Card. Felici). Our analysis is based upon the final reports of these groups as drawn up by their secretaries for presentation to the entire Synod[58]. It is thus unnecessary to refer to the summaries of these reports which were prepared for the press service. The membership of the four groups is given below.

1. *English B*

Francis, Michael Kpakula Francis	Monrovia (Liberia)
Freeman, James Darcy	Sydney (Australia)
Gaines, Edward Russel	Hamilton (New Zealand)
Gaviola, Mariano	(Philippines) Secretary General F.A.B.C.
Gomes, Theotonius	Dinajpur (Bangladesh)
Gran, John W.	Oslo (Norway)
Hakim, Maximos V	Patriarch of Melkite Rite (Antioch)
Halem'Imana, Barnabas	Kabale (Uganda)
Hume, Basil	Westminster (England)
Hurley, Denis E.	Durban (South Africa)
Huýnh-Dông-Các, Paul	Qui-Nhon (Vietnam)
Iteka, Patrick	Mahenga (Tanzania)
Jadot, Jean	Pro-president of the Secretariate for Non-Christians (Rome)

58. The reports were in Latin except for that of French A which was in French. The specific titles are: 1. *Relatio circuli minoris anglici B* (without date or signature; 12 typed pages and an included appendix); 2. *Relatio circulus minor linguae gallicae A* (10 Oct. 1980, signed by Archbishop G. Danneels; 12 typed pages); 3. *Circulus Linguae hispanicae C* (without title, date or signature; 13 typed pages and an appendix); 4. *Circulus Linguae latinae post examen singulorum propositionum haec patet dicenda* (without date or signature; 11 typed pages).

Jatau, Peter Yariyok	Kaduna (Nigeria)
Karlen, Henry	Bulawayo (Zimbabwe)
Khoarai, Sebastian Koto	Mohale's Hoek (Lesotho)
Kim, Stephen Son Hwan	Seoul, (Korea)
Knox, James R.	Prefect of the Congregation for Sacraments and Worship (Rome)
Kocisko, Stephen J.	Metropolitan Byzantine Rite Pittsburgh (U.S.A.)
Lubachivsky, Myroslaw	Lwow & Philadelphia (U.S.A.)
MacNeil, Joseph N.	Edmonton (Canada)
Naidoo, Stephen	Capetown (South Africa)
O'Fiaich, Thomás	Armagh (Ireland)

Moderator: Hume, Basil
Relator: Hurley, Denis E.

Peritus: Pedro Richards (Uraguay)
Auditores: Dr. and Mrs. Mascarenhas (India)
            Dr. and Mrs. Szymanski (Poland)
            Dr. and Mrs. Lanctôt (Canada)
            Mother Teresa (India)

2. *French A*

Batantu, Barthélémy	Brazzaville (Congo)
Bouchard, Jean-Claude	Pala (Chad)
Buller, Gabriel	Lausanne-Genève/Fribourg (Switzerland)
Callens, Michel	Mossori (Tunesia)
Danneels, Godfried	Mechelen-Brussel (Belgium)
de Gouesnongle, Vincent	General Superior of the Dominicans (Rome)
Delhaye, Philippe	Secretariate, International Theological Commission (Rome)
Dosseh-Anyron, Robert Casimir	Lomé (Togo)
Dubois, Gauthier Pierre	Istanbul (Turkey)
Duchêne, Gilbert	Saint-Claude (France)
Ernst, Hubertus C. Antonius	Breda (the Netherlands)
Etchegaray, Roger	Marseille (France)
Gagnon, Edward	Saint-Paul/Alberta (Canada)
Gahamanyi, Jean Baptiste	Butare (Rwanda)
Hardy, Joseph	General Secretary of African Missions (Rome)
Hermaniuk, Maxim	Winnipeg, (Canada)
Jullien, Jacques	Beauvais (France)
Kaseba, André	Kalemie-Kirungu (Zaïre)
Lebel, Robert	Valleyfield (Canada)
Légaré, Henri	Grouard-McLennan (Canada)
Ligondé, François-Wolf	Port-au-Prince (Haiti)
Macharaski, Franciszek	Cracow (Poland)
Margeot, Jean	Port Louis (Mauritius)

Moderator: Etchegaray, Roger
Relator: Danneels, Godfried

Periti: G. Martelet (France)
        D. Tettamanzi (Italy)
Auditores: Dr. and Mrs. Goma (Brazzaville, Congo)
          Mr. and Mrs. Vercruysse (Belgium)
          Mrs. Poltawska (Poland)

3. *Spanish C*

Mojica, Juan Eliseo	Garagoa (Colombia)
Muñoz Duque, Aníbal	Bogotá (Colombia)
Piñera Carvallo, Bernardino	Temuco (Chili)
Pironio, Eduardo	Prefect of the Congregation for Religious (Rome)
Primatesta, Raul	Cordoba (Argentina)
Quarracino, Antonio	Avellanedo (Argentina), General Secretary CELAM (Bogota, Colombia)
Revollo Bravo, Mario	Nueva Pamplona (Colombia)
Rivera Perez, Hector M.	San Juan (Puerto-Rico)
Rodríguez Figueroa, Alfredo José	Caracas (Venezuela)
Rossi, Agnelo	Prefect of the Congregation for Evangelization (Rome)
Ruiz Navas, José Mario	Latacunga (Ecuador)
Seijas, Herbé	San José de Mayo (Uruguay)
Sin, Jaime	Manila (Philippines)
Suquía Goicoechea, Angel	Santiago de Compostella (Spain)
Terrazas Sandoval, Julio	La Paz (Bolivia)
Varela, Jesus	Ozamis (Philippines)
Viganò, Egidio	General of the Salesians of Don Bosco (Rome)

Moderator: Pironio, Eduardo
Relator: Quarracino, Antonio

Auditores: Dr. and Mrs. Cifuante (Colombia)
          Br. Gusmann Rueda, General of the Marist Brothers.

4. *Latin*

Felici, Pericle	Apostolic Signatura/Commission for the Revision of Canon Law (Rome)
Gábriš, Julius	Trnava (Czechoslovakia)
Hirka, Jan	Presa-Byzant. ritus (Czechoslovakia)
Jakab, Antal	Alba Julia (Romenia)
Lékai, László	Esztergom (Hungary)
Palazzini, Pietro	Prefect of the Congregation for the Canonization of Saints (Rome)
Parecattil, Joseph	Metropolitan Malabaren Ernakulam (India)
Seper, Franjo	Prefect of the Congregation for the Doctrine of the Faith (Rome)
Slipyj, Josyf	Metropolitan Ukrainian Rite (Rome)
Thangalathil, Gregorio B.V.	Metropolitan Malankaren Trivandrum (India)

Moderator: Felici, Pericle
Relator: Palazzini, Pietro.

A. The Sacrament of Marriage and the Life of Faith

1. *Proposals of the group English B* (Card. Hume)

The first group we have chosen to study approached the theme of marriage as sacrament under five headings.

a. *African marriage*

First the group touched upon three uneven elements which are characteristic of traditional African marriage ("marriage coutumier"), namely, the essential participation of the families of both spouses, the gradual process of solemnization and the (decisive) importance of fertility for success and for the lastingness of the marital bond. They expressly distinguished the essential components of marriage from those which are added on and culturally determined. With respect to the rite itself, the "Ordo Celebrandi Matrimonium" (art. 17) encompasses the possibility for episcopal conferences to draw up their own forms for local use and to present these to the Holy See for approval; it is already permitted for laypersons to witness the marriage ceremony. The *circulus* formally put forth its own recommendation for the Synod's consideration: bishops' conferences should be urged to set up commissions to study the forms in which the celebrations of marriage would be culturally most appropriate so that these can be proposed to the Holy See for confirmation.

With respect to marriage by stages, the group recognized that such a practice could only be approved when cohabitation is allowed after the definitive creation of the bond. The fact that fertility is a demand expected for validity in African marriage customs sometimes led to questions which were not reconcilable with the Catholic tradition of indissolubility. This was said to stand in need of further study by the African bishops' conferences.

b. *The admission of the divorced-remarried to the eucharist*

The results of this discussion group recommended that persons who were divorced from a first marriage and had begun a second should be handled, as members of the Church, with pastoral care and compassion. They expressed the wish that authority would draw up objective criteria for admitting such persons to the sacraments and recommended that the Latin Church initiate a study of similar practices in the Eastern Church.

c. *The presumption of validity*

It was also noted in the report that the presumption in law of recognizing marital validity rests upon concern for protecting the marital bond and the innocent partner. Some persons who were validly baptized but then became atheists have contracted a civil marriage. Such a marriage is considered to be a sacrament in the Catholic Church. However, this group suggested that faith should be recognized as a condition for the creation of sacramental marriage. The vote taken on this point resulted in 12 *placet* and 8 *non placet*.

d. *The preparation for marriage*

The greatest importance needs to be placed upon preparation for marriage both in the long term (through the education and catechesis of young persons) and the short term (for those who are about to marry). With respect to immediate preparation, the group felt that the individual bishop has the right to determine the length and method of this preparation, although it is equally advisory that the episcopal conference come to a common agreement about this program. One should also devote special attention to the admission to the program of those with little understanding or a minimal practice of the faith.

e. *Mixed marriages*

The marriage between a Catholic and another christian, it was observed, should be looked upon in a less negative manner, and pressure for the conversion of one of the partners should be avoided. The possibility should also be carefully investigated for admitting the non-Catholic partner to eucharistic communion. In determining the discharge of canonical form for the celebration, bishops' conferences and synods should have the right to decide whether a dispensation can be granted by an *ordinarius* even though he may not be the bishop of the place in which the marriage is occurring.

It is, further, not infrequent that special difficulties are encountered when one of the partners is not a christian. It falls upon the bishops' conference to provide special care in these cases for the Catholic partners of such marriages. In regions where the faith of the Catholic partner might be placed in danger, the bishops' conference should have the possibility of demanding a promise or guarantee from the non-christian partner.

2. *Proposals of the group French A* (Card. Etchegaray)

In contrast to the previous group which put forth its principle reflections around the problematic of African marriage, French A dealt with the subject in more general terms: how can one help the engaged couple realize the transition from the human reality (of their marriage) to the sacred reality (of the scrament). This notion cannot be achieved without observing the faith from which it springs and which supports it with a clear and spirited proclamation. To this end, various models of catechesis can be invoked. In summary, they presented the following.

a. *The mystery of the pre-existence of Christ*

b. *The Covenant*

Marriage is situated in the history of salvation through the Covenant. In this, one can better understand the dramatic dimension of the history of the couple in the dialectic of grace and sin, faithfulness and unfaithfulness; a dialectic which is also representative of the Covenant between God and His People.

c. *The oneness of Christ and His Church (Eph. 5) sheds light upon the deeper oneness of the couple, their faithfulness and their fruitfulness.*

d. *Marriage as sign of the domestic church*

Through marriage, children are introduced as new members of the Church and contribute to the eschatological building of the Church.

e. *The Trinity*

There is a bond between the mystery of the Trinity (the plural oneness of God) and the mystery of man (the oneness of man and woman). Person, a sexually determined being, is created in the image of God (Gen. 2). This suggests an analogy: oneness within differentiation. With this in mind, it is also proposed that it is not possible to speak about the sacrament of marriage without first building a theology of sexuality (not genitality).

In this connection, the African bishops have introduced a corrective: in Africa, sexuality is not emphasized as a catechetical model. Preference is given not to the oneness of Christ and His Church but to the images of sharing in the life of the Trinity, the Covenant between God and His People, and participation in the creative power of God.

f. *There are models which originate in human experience (the process of maturation though giving and receiving) in which many men and women acquire the premonition of the Other.*

g. *The family as domestic church*

All the members of this group were convinced that the concept of the domestic church was justified (cf. John Chrysostom and LG, 11) but that it needed to be specified. For instance, it should not emphasize blood relation in place of the bond of faith. The proclamation of the Word and the experience of the sacraments are not always guaranteed in marriage associations; on the other hand, too great of an accent upon the domestic church could lead to the danger of clericalism. In some parts of the world, the image of the domestic church functions well (e.g. Haiti,

Rwanda), but other bishops expressed their reservations about the difficulties of imposing this ideal on a secularized society.

However, the feasibility of various models was not the only notion that was put forth by this group. Another question posed was the possible use of different language, e.g. poetic, prophetic or mystagogical language. Another of their principle points concerned the pastoral care of the divorced-remarried. This group of bishops expressed the wish that the Church, itself a community of sinners on the way to conversion, would come to the awareness of the new situation which was being caused by the continually growing number of divorces. The group suggested that an atmosphere of acceptance and care be promoted with respect to the divorced-remarried. Again, there was reference given to the report of the International Theological Commission (with a prefatory note by Card. Ratzinger)[59]. There was also a request to set up a special commission of pastoral counselors and canonists to study the principles of "oeconomia" in the Eastern tradition and determine if these principles could have application in the present situation. Finally, the criteria for annulment and determining the absence of required consent were said to be in need of review with attention both to tradition and human experience.

3. *Proposals of the group Spanish C* (Card. Pironio)

The greater part of the report from this group dealt with the sacrament of marriage. They felt that the three aspects (creational, christological and trinitarian) which the previous group distinguished almost to the point of separation needed to be handled together and in a more global way, although the christological should be given preference. In doing this, further, it was considered important to be attentive not only to persons for whom the teaching is intended but also to the way that the teaching is put forth. The group observed that the marital bond should be seen in the light of the Kingdom. It is therefore appropriate to evaluate the reality of marriage against the reality of the Kingdom in order to avoid both romanticism and minimalism.

With respect to the notion of the *ecclesia domestica*, it is proposed that the family as domestic church means, by analogy, the same as the Church itself: the covenant between Christ and His People through the Paschal Mystery, a community which stands open to the Kingdom and the future completion of time. Similarly, the family is a community of belief, worship and love which also defines the ecclesial community. Just as the Church was established in the service of mankind, so is the family as domestic church open to all the problems of life and of society and thus in service to the Lord. Praiseworthy are families that dedicate themselves

---

59. P. DELHAYE, who is secretary general of the ITC and responsible for the publication of this report, was appointed to the Synod by the Pope and was a member of this discussion group of Card. Etchegaray.

to mission or that are active in the diocese to complement the work of pastoral care.

Priestly and religious vocations develop within the family which is a sign of fruitfulness in the Church community. It is here that children should be given the choice to answer the call to serve God and to serve mankind. Therefore, the family should be supported and urged on in this task. The report of this group also took note of the necessity for providing families with the required pedagogical means for passing on the truths of the faith. Catechetical texts are needed that are appropriate for use within the family and that can easily be memorized.

In the extended list of questions that was given over to the *circuli minores*, there was a special sub-question included: what should serve as criteria for marital validity, especially in respect to the question of marital consent in the present circumstances? The report from Spanish C gave particular consideration to this question. The problem is said to appear in the experience of different kinds of situations such as in the many cases of insufficient maturity on the part of the engaged or when there is an absence of faith since the sacrament itself is supposed to be a sign of faith. In this connection the problems of the churches in Africa and those of the peoples of Latin America were felt to be pertinent and it was recognized that a first consideration should be given to the requirements of inculturation.

There are other points which came forth in the preliminary discussion of this language group:

A relational commitment occurs in stages, although that commitment is a real one from the starting point. In a christian perspective the acceptability of sexual relations is dependent upon the commitment.

Alongside forms of cultural expression, the elements of purification or elevation also have a bearing on validity.

Neither cultures nor their existing elements can be considered absolute values, for they must be subordinate to the Word of God. It is even advisable to look at these things as subject to the process of change.

Freedom is essential for a commitment. Therefore the decision belongs to the person who brings the commitment into existence and not to someone outside the agreement or to the family.

The assertion that infertility leads to the invalidity of marriage appears to be unacceptable. However, the situation is different when there is a voluntary denial of fruitfulness or in cases of sexual impotence.

Returning to the central question about the norms for validity, whether with respect to maturity or to the absence of faith, it was evident that there are some circumstances in which neither of these criteria are adequate in themselves to render judgment. Yet, in the area of faith, the group proposed that an acceptable criterion that should be further investigated was in what state of mind and with what meaning the engaged were willing to do "what the Church does". When there are doubts about the validity of a marriage, despite attempts to make a declaration on the matter, the presumption should remain "in favorem iuris" on the side of validity, taking into account the general good that demands the stability of the institution of marriage. Nevertheless, some members of the group defended the opinion that there could be cases in which the declaration of validity can have serious and even scandalous consequences and thus, to protect the common good, a decision against validity may be required.

The more specific problem of admitting divorced persons to the eucharist was also dealt with but in a more specific manner than the other two reports we have discussed. Some members of this group pleaded for this admission on the grounds that it was impossible to judge the deepest conscience of a person, that there was a very heavy burden being carried by many who had been divorced but were now in a new relationship of love, and that it was necessary to avoid all scandal for the children and for those who were ignorant of the situation. In contrast, it is also true that the great majority of participants of the *circulus* could not be in agreement with such admission because they were looking at the problem on the basis of church doctrine: the eucharist is the sign of the sacramental fullness of the Church and of the integral community, but this is not present in cases of divorce. To admit these people to the eucharist, which has a communitarian function, would create the impression that their situation had been sanctioned and simultaneously that the dissolubility of marriage had been accepted. However, this does not mean that the Church should pastorally abandon those who have accepted a divorce. It should be increasingly kept in mind that, outside of participation in eucharistic communion, there are other sources of grace and christian life such as prayer and the Word of God (not only individually but *in* and *with* the Church), presence at the celebration of the mass, and participation in works of charity which are undertaken by the christian community.

The final result of the exchange of views was the conclusion that the present discipline should remain in effect.

4. *Proposals of the Latin language group* (Card. Felici)

This smallest of the *circuli*, under the leadership of Cards. Felici and Pallazzini dealt with the question of sacramentality in six well-defined points. It appears from the report that there was no divergence of opinions among the members of this group who consistently took the most conservative position within the Synod[60]. The first two points

60. A human factor which undoubtedly played a role in the conservatism of the Latin group was the age of the participants from the Curia and the Eastern Churches. These two categories as well contain representatives who had generally not followed the trend of

underscored the importance of preparation for marriage and the maintenance of the norms for validity put forth in the decree *Tametsi*. The fundamental criterion for validity is still *consensus*. In the present situation it was felt that valid consent could be hindered more easily through ignorance or as a result of prejudices on the part of those marrying who have been influenced by the contemporary state of society.

With respect to the question of admitting divorced-remarried persons to the eucharist, the recent instruction from the Congregation for the Doctrine of Faith was said to be sufficient: such persons may be admitted to the eucharist when they seriously promise to change their way of life and when all possibility of scandal can be avoided. In the meantime, they should be spiritually assisted to continue to serve God though prayer and through charitable works so that they will be able to overcome their situation. Outside of participation in eucharistic communion, other means should be applied to prevent such divorced persons from being completely closed off from the ecclesial community. Indeed, it would be unjust and incompatible with pastoral care to deal with these persons, who are more or less in a state of being unfaithful, in the same way as those who continue to respect their marital obligations. The Latin group also supported the idea that preparation for marriage should be promoted but said that it should not be looked upon as a *conditio sine qua non*. Finally, the report was of the opinion that the present legislation on mixed marriages should be observed since it already provides for maximum permission.

Although we have only given the broad lines of development here in dealing with the theme of sacramentality, one can still form a general idea of the diversity and richness of the proposals as they were expressed in 4 of the 11 *circuli minores*. As a transition point between the general discussions and the later work of redacting the Propositions, the smaller groups of the Synod progressed a step on the way to clearer proposals and a more outspoken consciousness of the problems that were posed.

B. The Task of Transmitting Life

In the more detailed list of questions provided for the *circuli minores*, the first question about the transmission of life was formulated in the following way.

In which manner can the Church today proclaim to married couples and to the world of our time the plan of God with respect to the complete truth of human sexuality? In which manner (can she announce) the correct way of acting in the area of marital fertility which will neither fall under the influence of the

replacement in the synodal membership and could be considered "veterans" of the whole process. Cf. G. CAPRILE, *op. cit.*, pp. 39-40.

contraceptive mentality, nor rest only upon obedience to a law, but rather would flow from a free docility to the call of God and support a deeper insight into human sexuality? Furthermore, this leads to the question of the way in which the sexual culture of our time should be judged and what theological concepts are present in the Church today that, on behalf of the welfare of the faithful, should not be restrained?

1. *Proposals of the group English B*

In the section of their report dealing with this question, the bishops of this group emphasized that they first had a long exchange of views and that they then approved their conclusions unanimously. These conclusions consist of five sections, all of which are related to HV.

a. The members of the group declared their recognition of the prophetic character of HV for our time in the sense that this document declared anew the handed down teaching of the Church by virtue of which marital love should be fully human, faithful, exclusive and open to new life (HV, 9).

b. The bishops wished (nevertheless) for a theology which would be fuller and clearer with respect to human sexuality, love and marriage in the context of "responsible" parenthood. The faithful who are of good will would be better prepared to give assent to such a teaching. (This proposal received one *non placet* vote.)

c. The scientific grounds for the natural methods of limiting the number of children were said to be clearly established. The members of the group urgently asked that education in these methods be widely spread and that they be promoted through further research. The natural methods were recommended as safe, efficient and appropriate means for exercising conscious parenthood.

d. It is not possible to deny that there are numerous Catholics in very many countries who, in all sincerity, have not been able to accept the arguments and conclusions of HV. Many theologians and pastors have encountered serious difficulties in this connection. There are those, especially, who have come to the conclusion that in practice the use of artificial contraception no longer needs to be looked upon as sinful. The bishops thus declared to be moved by pastoral solicitude on behalf of those faithful who were disturbed on this point and, because of that disturbance, they asked for a more detailed declaration on the correct interpretation of some key words of the encyclical, especially the term "intrinsece inhonestum".

e. In a last paragraph it was also asked that the norms in this area be clarified. Such a clarification, following the pastoral aims of HV itself, should make it possible to lead married couples more safely along the road to holiness by bringing their marital love to maturity without discouragement when they might fall short of the ideal. It was also hoped that in counseling and hearing confessions priests would assist the Catholic faithful with prudence and fortitude to deal with guilt as well as the progress which is and must be reachable in their married love. (HV, 25).

The clarification of norms is also desirable to prevent that couples who find themselves in difficulties of many sorts, and because of which they could hardly respond to the demands of HV, might be alienated completely from the Church or from the sacraments. It is further desirable so that many non-Catholics who are married with Catholics should be able to see proof of the beauty and the soundness of the Church's moral teaching. They must themselves become convinced before there can be hope that the teaching of HV will be accepted. It is thus also necessary to give witness to the human and biblical values of this teaching.

2. *Proposals of the group French A.*

This discussion group included a large number of leading speakers in the synodal debates over HV. One must also call attention to the fact that P. Delhaye and G. Martelet were members of this group, the former being secretary of the International Theological Commission and the latter being the principle inspiration for the pastoral sections of Paul VI's encyclical. It was consequently in this group that one finds the repeated call for a "deepening" of HV's teaching.

The report of this group thus began by expressly declaring their adhesion to the teaching of HV, recognizing it as an authoritative proposal of the teaching office: the human and evangelical values which are present in HV must be protected and promoted and strongly declared in order to fight against the dominant hedonism, the atmosphere of permissiveness and the contraceptive mentality of our time. It is hereby specified that the deepening of HV should in no way cloud the benevolence and the prophetic character of the text. This deepening must be realized with a great deal of nuance. During these times, according to the proposals of the bishops, there exists a feeling of perplexity in the Church[61], both in respect to the arguments of the encyclical as well as to the form of its teaching. A literal repetition of that teaching would not

---

61. The report uses the word "embarras" which is possibly better translated as perplexity or confusion rather than embarassment.

solve the problem. The following points can be singled out for our attention.

It is proposed that HV be placed in a broader and more positive context, according to the words of Paul VI (31 July 1968). HV is only a small part of the teaching with respect to marriage and the human person. It is appropriate to situate this in "a broader, more organic and more synthetic approach".

The pastoral application of the encyclical should take account of various factors: the gradual progression of the christian married couple toward the ideal; the fact that failures should be dedramatized and interpreted; and the given that no persons of good will should live "in anxiety or fear" (Paul VI, to the Equipes Notre Dame, 1970).

Finally, one must not lose sight of the fact that the spread of contraceptives in the Third World is often linked to programs of economic aid from the industrialized countries and international organizations that make the limitation of births a condition to the help. It is even more serious when methods such as sterilization and abortion are imposed. All these occurrences are in contradiction to the rights of the human person and threaten to assault the spirit of a people, especially the poor.

The report of French A also provided a separate subsection on the theoretical argumentation of HV for the purposes of both critical analysis and positive development.

a. *Critical elements*

Some bishops were of the opinion that the dichotomy between strict law and flexible application did not provide an adequate solution[62]. One bishop[63] proposed that the questions of conjugal morality should follow

---

62. When this issue was presented in the Latin group, one of the members remarked "compassio non est principium moralitatis". It seems that this would be the point of encounter between the maximalist positions of conservatism and progressiveness.

63. As is generally known, this was the position of Bishop Ernst (Breda) put forth in his intervention of 1 Oct. 1980. We provide a translation of a portion of that speech here. "When one consults the social teaching of the Church, from the encyclical *Rerum novarum* of Pope Leo XIII (15 May 1891) to the address of Pope John-Paul II during his visit to Brazil, it is evident that the Church makes declarations about the direction of moral activity in community living ... but that it leaves the concretization of this to those who are involved. ... When we wish to give the proper place to the development of the appreciation of the faith of the whole People of God with respect to the life of married couples and the family, within the context of the experience of the married, the work of theologians, philosophers, experts in the human sciences and the exercise of the teaching authority, and when we wish to overcome the distance that exists between the living faith of many christians and the pronouncements of the magisterium, would it not be good if the teaching authority presented its moral teaching on marriage and the family in the same way as its social teaching; it means that, where possible, a certain reservation should be practiced for

the analogy of the Church's social ethical teaching. The Church should be satisfied in giving general principles while their concrete application should be left to the individual or the couple. The decision of personal conscience is grounded in an analysis of the concrete situation and supported by the findings of the human sciences as well as in the light of the gospel and the teaching of the magisterium. Other members were opposed to this approach and appealed to the difference between sexual and social morality.

According to several of the bishops it is necessary that the question of methods be "unobstructed". To this end, it is required to make the very narrow link between the promotion of the deeper values for which HV stands and the moral judgment about the choice of methods for regulating fertility more flexible. One member recalled a passage of the gospel wherein it is stated that too heavy burdens should not be imposed where they are not absolutely necessary, We should grant time for couples to live through the experience of marriage and for priests to build up attendant pastoral care. In the meantime, we should be extremely prudent in the moral judgment of the different methods. Other members of the group were clearly opposed to this image. As soon as one gives up a morality based upon human nature, they will find themselves in a void since personalist morality, as it has developed up to this point, has not found general approval among theologians. There is, therefore, need for a new fundamental morality.

b. *Positive development*

Filling out the argumentation of HV, as presented by French A, involves three aspects: the integration of the values of human and christian morality, giving up the vocabulary based on "nature", and an investigation of the declaration of "intrinsece inhonestum".

First, the argumentation can be improved by emphasizing and integrating the values of human and christian morality: values such as staidness and self-control but also trust in grace, faith in the sacraments, and the joy of the christian experience of marriage. However, the experience of weakness must also be integrated: the consciousness of sin, the need for and promise of forgiveness; we should know that we are sinners and have contrition without trauma. In this way, contrary positions and too strong judgments of Church morality will be avoided

its concrete application and that it should encourage and support christians to find concrete moral truths by examining the reality in which they live in the light of the gospel and the teaching of the Church. ... Such an approach in the words and activities of the pastors of the Church can also lead to an integration of the doctrinal and pastoral moment". Cf. *Archief van de Kerken*, 36 (1981) c. 117.

and will no longer be exacerbated with regard to the encyclical and its teaching on the regulation of fertility.

By giving up the vocabulary based on "nature", the argument can also be improved. In contemporary understanding, "nature" is inevitably understood on the physiological and biological level. Sexual morality will be more convincing if it is supported by the image of the couple's participation in divine love. The spouses are created in the image of God, who is inseparably "oneness and fruitfulness". This double dimension of oneness in difference and of the awakening of new life is reflected in the married couple. God is present in it, even in the corporeal representation of the couple. Consequently, the couple should undertake nothing that would break apart the double symbolism of participation in the mystery of God (oneness and fruitfulness). By living out this divine symbolism, which is reflected in the marriage act, the married couple sanctify their corporeality and proclaim God's glory.

Finally, it will be necessary to put forth certain concepts, such as "intrinsece inhonestum" and "peccatum per se grave", in a much more appropriate way.

The report of this group concluded with a reflection upon the necessity of pastoral care. The bishops were convinced that HV would be better understood if it were presented as a prophetic call to continuous self-transcendence (rather than as a code of moral commandments). The language in which the encyclical has been drafted has not been beneficial for such an interpretation. In pastoral action, one should respect the gradual progression of the spouses toward the christian ideal, which presupposes human and spiritual maturity. It should be a pastoral care that can find inspiration in scripture for dealing with failure. These bishops also considered the natural methods to be genuinely trustworthy, even though they are not always practicable. In every case they provide a wide space within which the couple can manage their fertility. Finally, the group underscored that no form of practicing responsible parenthood would be completely free from suffering and from sacrifice.

3. *Proposals of the group Spanish C*

It was equally understood by this group that the teaching of HV remained valid. At the same time, they also indicated that a new presentation and clarification of its content would be appropriate, as well as a broadening of the teaching. They mentioned, among other things, an explanation of the concepts "natural" and "fruitfulness". This presentation should confirm the teaching of Paul VI and work to remove the ambiguity that exists in practice. It should take into account all the new knowledge from scientific research, in education and in the experience of families that has come forth in the years since the encyclical. One of the members of the *circulus* expressed the opinion that human fruitfulness should be viewed in the wider context of a socio-cultural and economic perspective.

During the exchange of views, attention was also paid to the "conflict of duties" and the choice of "the lesser evil". Some bishops took the standpoint that since this deals with a natural ordering of the purposes and the duties of marriage, which have been determined by God, is it not possible that there can be an objective conflict between them, or this conflict may only be limited to the conscience of the subject (subjective conscience). The concept of "the lesser evil" was just as questionably posed, first because it is not possible to proceed directly from an evil in order to accomplish a good, but secondly, it is not possible that one of the natural purposes of the totality can be sacrificed for the well-being of the whole marriage.

The group was of the opinion that one should expressly point out that the teaching of HV does not consist of only specific prohibitions. This teaching must be presented as a great confirmation of life, of human love and of the progress of the spouses, the family and society. It is a true call to responsibility for both spouses, and is not so much a formula and even less a code for applicable methods. Another important point raised during the discussions touched upon the role of spirituality. It is not possible, they observed, to separate morality from spirituality. Without marital ascetics, sacramental life and prayer, in a word, without spiritual life, the problems of the transmission of life can easily fall into an unsolvable casuistry. The reality of original sin has brought about a lack of clarity, insight and balance whereby the competence to see one's obligations and the will to fulfill them is weakened[64]. It was in this same context that the opportunity was offered to underscore the necessity of providing for an education in love appropriate to the period of life and an education in sexuality in a christian perspective. In this educative process, a model should also be presented toward which christian marriage should strive as well as the meaning of gradualness and continuous conversion that is demanded by christian life, whether one is married or not. The presence of the cross also belongs to this consideration.

Finally, the group also wished to speak a word of praise for the groups and organizations that defend life and all those who have been and still are dedicated to discovering and promoting the natural methods for achieving responsible parenthood. They also had a word for govern-

64. In the whole discussion around HV, this accent on the importance of the role of spirituality was one of the most prominent contributions of the Synod. For many of the bishops in 1980, this point showed the greatest vacuum in which the encyclical of 1968 had been situated and because of which it lacked strength.

ments that are charged with defending the rights of man with respect to life, as well as a word of condemnation for those organizations which violate those rights.

4. *Proposals of the Latin language group*

The concern of this small group to put forth the authoritative function of the magisterium as primary and to guard against every possible form of dispute was self-evident, especially in the discussion about HV. The second paragraph of the report of the Latin *circulus* was dedicated to the primacy of doctrine. The question of procreation must be dealt with first in its doctrinal aspects and only then in a pastoral context. It is necessary to hold to the teaching of HV (as well as to substantiate it with better arguments if that is possible) because this is an exercise of the ordinary magisterium of the Church (LG, 25) which always remains consistent with itself. Consequently, contraception is intrinsically illicit and may not be directly sought after. A teaching defended by theologians, especially when it leads to differences of opinion, does not constitute a valid "locus theologicus" for the formation of conscience for the faithful (cf. Paul VI, A.A.S. 67 (1975) 13; Congregatio pro doctrina fidei, A.A.S. 68 (1976) 739).

The report then made reference to the antecedents of the 1968 encyclical: after very many important discussions held in different groups, HV repeated the doctrine which was handed down and which was further developed in the Council. This doctrine, among other things, expressly argues (cf. GS, 50) that in order to reach a moral judgment about the sexual act one must keep in mind the nature of the marriage act and its intrinsic purposes. Thus, it is not permissible, continues the report, to speak in an objective manner about a conflict of the spouses' duties in some circumstances, quite less in the subjective sense. In other words, general principles can be diverted in the case of a malformed conscience. The prophetic competence which has been ascribed to some married couples bristles with ambiguousness. Subsequently, it is not admissible to make a distinction between a doctrinal and pastoral perspective, since pastors may act in no other way than that which has been taught by their Divine Master, the Lord, either in His own preaching or in that of His Church.

The Latin group went even further on the difficulties that have arisen since HV. Many of the bishops supported consideration of the problems that some bishops and priests have had with the encyclical and with the difficulties (in some circumstances) of following the law which forbids a direct intervention in the process of transmitting life. It is true that the first point was foreseen in HV itself. In number 28, priests in particular were encouraged to be obedient to the teaching authority of the Church. For some of them, it was in vain. As for the second point, it would be good to recall the statement of Jansenius who was condemned, "Some of God's commandments are impossible for just persons to fulfill, etc." (DS 2001). The task of pastors does not lie in improving God's laws or making them easier but, with the greatest love for the faithful, in helping persons to follow them. A frequently occurring violation of the law, moreover, is no argument against the fundamentals of the law or its sure existence.

The report prepared by Card. Pallazzini closed the chapter on the transmission of life in stating: we do not deny that it would be helpful to support the teaching of the encyclical HV with stronger arguments. The greatest kindness, he said, must also be shown to couples who are beset by difficulties, despite the fact that it appears, objectively speaking, that the law has been violated, though subjectively it is possible that they cannot be held responsible for a grave fault because of the circumstances in which they acted. This, in fact, has already been suggested by the encyclical itself.

The Neck of the Funnel

Rather unexpectedly, on 14 Oct. the bishops were asked whether they wished that (advisory) propositions be drawn up to be presented to the Holy Father. Since the question was put in this form it was, of course, approved. It was in this way that the Synod approached "the neck of the funnel" in which the richness of the interventions during the first week and the exchange of ideas coming from the small language groups would be severely limited and selectively chosen.

In order to summarize the 43 Propositions, the content of which went through two redactions, it would be advantageous to construct a logical ordering of the themes with which these texts dealt. It is not our purpose here to fundamentally examine the meaning of these advisory statements. It is rather to situate the contents of the Propositions in the context of the dynamics of the discussions which had taken place. Therefore, a few words of background appear necessary.

To be consistent with what we have already set forth, we will here distinguish two sets of subjects: on the one hand, five *principle themes* and, on the other, five *pastoral problems*. This distinction is parallel to the broadening of the agenda upon which the bishops had insisted. As *principle themes* we mean the "roles and function of the christian family in the world" which, according to our interpretation, were the chief concern of John-Paul II but which were only passingly dealt with by the bishops. In contrast, the *pastoral problems* refer to the various pressing questions which the bishops wanted introduced from the very beginning in order to move toward solutions for the urgent needs experienced in pastoral care.

To follow the general lines of development and the logic of the final texts of the Propositions, we will first deal with the pastoral problems. For the same reason we will proceed from what were the more general perspectives. What follows is a division of the content of the Propositions constructed in logical order for the purpose of comparison with the events of the Synod itself. Included are the numbers of the Propositions as they appear in the final text[65].

---

65. Reference to the Propositions will be supported with the original Latin version of the *textus emendatus* published as *Synodus Episcoporum: De muneribus Familiae Christianae in mundo hodierno. Elenchus Propositionum (sub secreto)*, Vatican, 1980 (100 pp.). This booklet was given to the bishops for the purpose of their voting on the final text (50 votes) and contained places for indicating the results of the votes taken. See the appendix at the end of this book. We will be using our own translation as well as those found in *Archief van de Kerken* (4 March 1981) and *Documentation catholique* (7 June 1981), taking into account that the text which appeared in *Archief van de Kerken* contains

Proposition numbers

inaccuracies in several places. The schema provided here is *thematic* and was drawn up for the purpose of relating the Propositions to the actual work of the Synod as a whole. This is different from the actual, official schema of the text of the Propositions itself. That schema is provided in the second part of this work, p. 259-260.

A. General Preliminary Perspectives

1. *Anthropological and theological foundation of marriage* (*Proposition 8*)

"God, who is love, created man in his own image and likeness". With these words (cf. Gen. 1:26) the Synod bishops provided the point of departure for the foundation of marriage, for "created in this image (of the triune God) man is called not to solitude but to a relationship of love"[66].

The person is called to love in their totality. On this same ground is situated human *sexuality*, whereby persons, as man and woman, relate to each other, not according to pure biological givens but as something which is based in the core of the human orientation of life. Sexuality is then realized in a truly human manner so long as it constitutes an integral part of love. Bodily self-giving must correspond with the gift of the total person. If it does not, it is considered a lie.

All cultures consider marriage as the unique place for the truly human realization of sexuality. Society recognizes marriage and the family as a guarantee of its own survival and by institutionalizing them, both are enriched with new dimensions.

2. *Theology of the sacrament of marriage* (*Propositions 9, 10 and 11*)

a. The creation of man in God's image gives special meaning to the mutual gift of man and woman. Indeed this meaning is directly related to that image in the following ways: the profound difference between the spouses which makes their union possible; the dialogue and indispensible exchange between persons who are different and yet fully equal; their community as well as fruitfulness. The eminence of married love is of such a nature that through it God wished to pass on His own covenantal love of which it would be, as it were, a reflection (Old Testament). The way in which God gives Himself in His Covenant is so total that Christ became man and took the human condition completely upon Himself except for sin (New Testament). By His own gift of self, all the way to His death on the cross, Christ became the model for man and woman, the Savior of marital love and all human love.

b. In his sacrificial love on the cross, Christ bound Himself to the Church as a bride such that He remains faithful to her until the end of time. In the Old Testament, marriage is already a sign which is taken

66. We call attention here to an echo of one of the principle points of the first encyclical of John-Paul II, *Redemptor hominis* (1979).

over as a sacred sign the New Testament and becomes a true sacrament in Christ's Church. Married love between baptized persons is the form in which interpersonal fruitfulness is to be lived out within the mystery of the death and resurrection of Christ, the foundation and model of such love and giving. Through revelation the already eminent reality of marriage acquires new richness and unexpected dimensions.

c. Consecrated virginity and celibacy for the Kingdom not only do not argue against this theology of marriage but they presume it and confirm it. Marriage and consecrated virginity are two ways of expressing the same mystical reality of God's covenant with His people.

3. *The role of woman* (*Propositions 15, 16 and 17*)

a. It is pointed out in Sacred Scripture that human dignity was bestowed equally upon man and woman such that in stating that God created the human person, it is affirmed, "male and female, He created them" (Gen. 1:27). Both have received from God the inalienable rights and responsibilities of the human person. In marriage their specific relation comes to the fore in a special way which is completely personal, open to development and grounded in their mutual love and reciprocal gift. As equal, they partake in God's creative power. Mary, honored as the Mother of God by the Church, is called the new Eve and presented as the model of redeemed woman.

b. The moral criterion for authenticity in marital and familial relationships resides in promoting the dignity and vocation of the individual persons who come to self-fulfillment through their gift of self. In striving toward the promotion of woman's rights, the equality of the marital role (especially within the home) with public functions and other professions (outside the home) should be recognized.

A new theology of work is desirable to explain the meaning of work in the Christian life and to set out its relation to the family. The Church can be a help to society by examining the value of work in the home and of bringing up the children. Access to public roles must be equal for women as for men. On the other hand, women should not be forced to seek work outside of the home because of economic conditions. In her own life the Church should promote the equality of the rights and dignity of women as much as possible.

c. The last Proposition in this series contains a strong attack against all forms of prostitution and against pornography because it is offensive to the dignity of woman. (We also find here the reference to prostitution in developing countries disguised as "tourism".)

B. Pressing Pastoral Problems

1. *Pastoral demands with respect to faith and sacrament*

a. *Introductory background*

During the course of the 1980 Synod a difference of opinion became evident between the representatives of the deductive method of thinking and the defenders of a more inductive approach. This discussion has come to the fore in every Synod with continuing intensity. One immediately thinks of the same question with respect to the final document for the 1974 Synod on evangelization. The majority of bishops rejected the text in their final vote precisely because of this problem: the draft of the text, which was drawn up at that time under the responsibility of Cardinal Wojtyla, was rejected as deductive and abstract, while another, earlier, work document, which was more inductive and more representative of the interventions of the majority, was considered unacceptable by the leaders of the Synod and was therefore not presented to the Synod as a draft text. The three Propositions concerning the meaning of faith must be understood against this background.

At the end of the synodal meeting the bishops were generally not unsatisfied with the text of these Propositions. Many positively valued the general spirit in which the Propositions were drawn up. In their eyes that spirit was particularly evident in the beginning of this document, namely Proposition 2-7.

1) *The* sensus fidei (*Propositions 2-4*)

The Synod takes as its point of departure that a great deal of attention must be given to the *sensus fidei*, the appreciation of the faith among the faithful. This meant that ecclesial authority should not put forth an abstract and ready made doctrine for which the hierarchy alone would be responsible as teaching authority. On the contrary, the majority of the 1980 Synod bishops were of the opinion that they should propose a text that proceeded from a real understanding of the faithful's living of the faith and their existential experience.

This is schematically indicated in the general approach of Prop. 2 which characteristically sets out from a quotation from *Lumen Gentium*, 35: "...also by the laity whom he established as witnesses and provided with the appreciation of the faith and the grace of the word so that the power of the Gospel may shine out in daily family and social life".

Proposition 3 follows the same line: the appreciation of the faith makes itself most evident when "the right rule of development is followed", that is, when it preserves and clarifies the organic structure and inner relations of truths in correspondence with the sacred mysteries.

This is in conformity with the faith during all times and among all believers.

Proposition 4 closes the development with an application: with respect to questions about the family, the appreciation of the faith is especially dependent upon christian families through whom the sacrament of marriage is realized and expressed through the experience of faith. It is the task of the teaching authority of the Church to encourage this appreciation and to interpret it in an authentic manner.

2) *The signs of the times (Propositions 5-6)*

A second requirement touches upon the discernment of the *signs of the times* and their interpretation in the context of God's holy plan. This was dealt with in Props. 5 & 6. The criteria which are provided are: the continuity of the history of salvation as revealed in the Old and New Testaments, the analogy of faith, the teaching role of the Church and the proper insights of human prudence.

Furthermore, there is a distinction made between the positive and the negative signs of the times. Some of these signs are positive. They demonstrate on different levels the presence and work of God. Such signs are: concern for the freedom of the person, the quality of marital relationships, the promotion of the dignity of woman, responsible parenthood, greater concern for the education of children, mutual assistance between families, a keener notion of the ecclesial vocation of the family, and the concept of responsibility, especially with respect to achieving justice. there are also negative signs which flow not from the presence of God in history but from the opposition of sin (sinful resistence): human defection from God, the breakdown of cultures and values, the situation of poverty and misery of families brought about by unjust structures, and the growing numbers of divorce and abortion.

The Church does not remain suspended above history but is completely inserted into the human world as it evolves. She must distinguish between the positive and negative signs. In the period of rapid sociological and cultural change to which mankind is today subjected, marriage and family life are also subject to rapid changes. The Synod of Bishops intended that the Church take account of this new culture and evangelize it from the very beginning. It is the particular responsibility of the local churches to work for the development of new interpresonal communities so that the family can find its firm foundation in the new societies which are evolving.

b. *Toward a coherent pedagogy*

We will deal with three Propositions under this heading which do not occur together in the final text but which can logically be understood as dealing with the same topic: the law of gradualness (Prop. 7), education in sexuality (Prop. 28) and the need for marriage preparation (Prop. 35).

1) *The law of gradualness (Proposition 7)*

In Proposition 7 we find another requirement — the third up to this point — which is here presented to moral theologians: the expectation that theology will accept a *processus dynamicus* (progressive development) and integrate the concept into its methodology. In order to shed light on this notion, the authors propose that Christian life cannot be reduced to a simple dilemma between everything and nothing.

Conversion takes place through progressive stages. It is a dynamic process which begins with the love of God, is inspired by the Holy Spirit, and leads us to following Christ and the revelation of the Paschal Mystery. It slowly moves toward the integration of God's gifts and the demands of His absolute love into the entire personal and social life of the human person. Peoples and civilizations, as well as individuals, must patiently be guided toward a fuller understanding of this mystery and toward a fuller integration of it in their lives and behavior. Therefore, there is a need for pedagogical-pastoral guidance.

It is important to note here that the bishops of the 1980 Synod attempted to apply this law of gradualness to other proposals. Both with respect to the indissolubility of marriage (Prop. 13-14) and the teaching about the regulation of fertility according to HV (Prop. 21-25), the Synod tried to follow this line of reasoning: first, by repeating the principle in each respect; then, by recognizing that in concrete situations pastors are sometimes faced with insolvable problems; and finally, by striving to work toward a certain openness toward the law of gradualness in those pastoral situations. Whether or not and to what extent this approach is clearly expressed in the final version of the Propositions remains a question to which we will have to return later.

2) *Education in sexuality (Proposition 28)*

Proposition 28 sets forth from the idea that the family as a community of love and life is the eminent place for learning how to give of oneself. If this education is to be genuinely human, then it must take place in the context of the unifying bond of body and spirit in which human sexuality finds its deepest meaning, namely its appropriateness as a sign of self-giving which reflects the plan of the Creator. Thus, education in sexuality and affectiveness should take place in the context of the family and formal education in the schools should only fulfill a subsidiary role.

3) *The need for marriage preparation* (*Proposition 35*)

The pastoral approach to marriage preparation is placed in the same context in a special way. The goal is the prevention of marital failure and irregular situations as much as possible. The preparation for familial and social responsibilities must develop as a dynamic process. In this context, Proposition 35 makes a distinction between *remote* preparation, which begins in the bosom of the family, *proximate* preparation, carried out in the context of the development of faith and the integration of sexual relations into the sacramental bond, and *immediate* preparation. The last is in service to those who are engaged but especially for those who have special needs in respect to the understanding and practice of the faith.

This proposal calls upon bishops' conferences and dioceses to develop norms for pastoral guidance in these matters with respect to the content, length and method of such programs. The Proposition puts forth an express concern which was repeated many times and in many contexts during the Synod.

c. *The relation between faith and sacrament* (*Proposition 12*)

The discussions about the relationship between faith and the sacrament that took place during the 1980 Synod were much broader and involved than one might expect after a first reading of Prop. 12. In the above section we dealt with the need to handle problems in respect to the understanding and practice of the faith in the context of marriage preparation programs. This section deals with the difficult problem of "marginal-believers" who request a church wedding.

Both rigorism and laxism need to be avoided: a weak faith must be strengthened by every possible means, according to Prop. 12. A dynamic catechesis and an appropraite marriage preparation program can contribute to the couple's advancement in the faith. But the bishops went even further: they explicitly request that a fundamental study be initiated to investigate the idea whether the presumption of the existence of a valid sacrament between baptized persons can apply to those who have lost the faith. It is recognized that such a study can have both pastoral and juridical consequences. Even more specifically, it is suggested that a study be undertaken to determine the pastoral criteria for discerning the faith of the engaged couple and further explicitating the meaning of the intention "to do what the Church does" with respect to faith.

Commentary on Proposition 12

Over the past years, very serious discussions have been devoted to the subject matter of what was now Proposition 12 by the International Theological Commission (ITC). In this connection it is pertinent to take account of a report of those discussions (1975-1977: dealing as well with the subject of the following Propositions, on indissolubility) issued by the ITC on the different doctrinal aspects of christian marriage[67]. In the commentary on the Commission's proposals 2.3 and 2.4 dealing with "baptism, actual faith, intention, sacramental marriage"[68], Prof. Delhaye notes that the ITC had long discussions on the topics which evolved into the formulation of two questions:

1) When and in what manner can one come to know whether a young man and woman who request a Church marraige are truly believers or have lost the faith?

2) May one, as a number of authors have suggested, contend (assert) that where there is no faith there is no marriage, or on the contrary, may one presume a certain automatism: since the individuals have been baptized the only possibility is a sacramental marriage?

It is necessary to distinguish different cases. Some engaged couples seek a church ceremony only for conventional or family reasons while they remain personally indifferent or even hostile to the faith. In this case one would be speaking of a true sham. The absence of intention and faith would render the marriage invalid. However, another case would be when the couple is undoubtedly open to further education in the faith and there is an opportunity for catechesis.

According to Prof. Delhaye, general secretary of the group, the ITC sought to find a middle road: neither the fact of baptism in itself nor the absence of faith can serve as the only principles upon which a solution can be based, the first leading to a kind of automatism and the second calling into question the reality of the sacrament itself. The key is to be found in the question of intention. In order for a valid marriage to be possible, both baptism and explicit faith are necessary, for both together provide the ground upon which the intention is formed for grafting a human marriage onto the paschal love of Christ[69].

Not everyone who consulted the proposals of the ITC was convinced that this ecclesial commission of advisors had reached a true middle ground. Members of the Congregation for the Faith were of the opinion

---

67. This report appeared as *Problèmes doctrinaux du mariage chrétien*, Louvain-la-Neuve, 1979, and included a preface by Card. Ratzinger and an introduction by P. Delhaye.

68. The text of proposal 2.3 is not very distant from the Synod's Prop. 12. We give the following example from the book cited above, p. 70 (emphasis added). "... au fond des choses, l'intention véritable naît et se nourrit d'une foi vivante. Là donc où l'on ne perçoit aucune trace de la foi comme telle (au sens du terme "croyance", disposition à croire) ni aucun désir de la grâce et du salut, la question se pose de savoir, au plan des faits, si l'intention générale et vraiment sacramentelle, dont nous venons de parler, est présente ou non, et si le mariage est validement contracté ou non. La foi personnelle des contractants ne constitue pas, on l'a noté, la sacramentabilité du mariage, mais *l'absence de foi personnelle compromet la validité du sacrement*".

69. *Problèmes doctrinaux du mariage chrétien*, pp. 73-74.

that the proposal went too far and was at variance with currently accepted norms. In the eyes of the Congregation, baptized persons who refuse to participate in a Church marriage are living in concubinage. In contrast, other commentators on the ITC report believed that the commission had not gone far enough and had insufficiently dealt with the situation of "marginal-believers" who marry outside the Church. This was the position of Father Y. Congar in a note published after the appearance of the ITC report[70].

It is certain that the conclusion that the ITC had reached in Rome, in the given circumstances, is not to be underestimated: its report had accepted the premise that a marriage entered into by "marginal believers" outside the Church had a completely different meaning than simple concubinage. This had certainly progressed beyond the classical view of the matter. Furthermore, it is equally certain that the results of this commission's work did have a certain influence in the 1980 Synod and that its fruits had not been lost. The ITC's proposals had been discussed more than once in the language groups and was expressly mentioned in public session[71].

2. *The indissolubility of marriage*

The concrete difficulties which had been presented in the pastoral care of the divorced-remarried, the numbers of which have been increasing in many countries, led the Synod into some of the most soul-searching discussions. It is true that the principle of the indissolubility of marriage was never called into question, but it is equally observable that there were real attempts made to achieve a certain flexibility with respect to the "reception" of divorced persons in the Church.

a. *Basic orientation (Proposition 13)*

As a fundamental beginning, the principle of indissolubility was reaffirmed by the Synod and the basis for this principle was dealt with. Indissolubility rests upon the personal and total self-giving of the spouses in such a way that this becomes the fruit and sign of God's irreversible love for His People (cf. Old Testament) and of Christ's faithfulness to His Church (cf. New Testament). This gift present in the sacrament is both a call and a task.

There are many married persons whose lives testify to this indissolubility, including those who, despite the fact that they have been deserted by their spouse, have not attempted a new marriage and thus give to the

70. Y. CONGAR, *La Commission Théologique Internationale (déc. 1977) et le Canon 1012*, in *Revue des sciences philosophiques et théologiques* 65 (1981) 295-298.

71. In section IV above, we have already noted the contribution of Bishop Duchêne who supported the ITC's report. Cf. *supra*, p. 98.

world an authentic witness of faithfulness which today it needs so much. In connection with the same subject matter, it is suggested that the bishops' conferences give more consideration to an appropriate program of marriage preparation.

b. *The problems of the divorced-remarried (Proposition 14)*

Because the Church was instituted to lead all persons, and especially the baptized, to salvation, she may not neglect those who, although they are still under the bond of sacramental marriage after a (civil) divorce, attempt to enter into a second marital union. The Church will always do her utmost to provide the means to salvation for all those to whom she is in service. With respect to those who are divorced and who have remarried, pastors should be able to distinguish between different situations.

1) There are those who have been the victim of the breakdown of their first marriage, despite their attempt to save it.

2) There are others who have destroyed a valid marriage through their own serious fault.

3) There are still others who were convinced of the invalidity of a first marriage and enter into a second one for the sake of providing an atmosphere for the upbringing of their children.

Both pastors and the community of the faithful are encouraged to help these divorced persons and to take special care that they, as baptized, can and should participate in the life of the Chruch.

On the other hand, basing itself on Scripture, the Synod reaffirmed that the divorced-remarried could not be admitted to the eucharist because their life situation contradicts the indissoluble convenant of love between Christ and His Church. This refusal is also supported on the grounds of pastoral prudence. Furthermore, absolution can only be given in the sacrament of penance when, after having demonstrated their repentance, they "establish a way of life which is not in contradiction with the sacrament of marriage". In such a manner the Church attempts to remain faithful to Christ and merciful to her children, especially those innocent ones who have been deserted by their lawful husband or wife.

Finally, the Synod declared its wish that a new and deeper study be initiated into the pastoral care of these faithful, "taking account of the practices of the Eastern Churches", so that pastoral kindness can be brought more clearly to the fore.

Commentary on Propositions 13 and 14

The admittance to the eucharist of divorced-remarried persons who wish to participate in the life of the Church remained the most sensitive point for pastors and for the exchange of ideas that took place at the

Synod. It is common knowledge that the numbers of persons concerned in this is continuously growing: in France and other European countries there are groups of divorced-remarried people and in the U.S.A. many of these groups are organized.

During the discussions of October 1980, nothing was said about the admittance to the sacraments being demanded as a right. There was concern that the Church would become more open to the many who had been victims of a divorce and who, in a spirit of repentance, sought a better reception in the Church.

In one of the French language groups, Archbishop Danneels made a distinction between four sorts of cases:

1) when it is rather certain that a first marriage was invalid, despite the fact that it never had been (nor probably ever could be) declared as such;

2) when a second marriage caused no public scandal;

3) when the remarried do not wish a second marriage to be contested because of their concern for their children; and

4) when it is a question of those who were victims of the divorce which they had initialy resisted and in which they were not personally guilty.

The first paragraph of Prop. 14 clearly deals with the third and fourth cases. The next to last paragraph appears to point to the fourth case with the phrase "especially those innocent ones who have been deserted". The addition of the phrase introduced by "especially" in the final version of the Proposition may be read to imply that there are other categories besides these who are innocent. One could also question whether the paragraph dealing with those who "establish a way of life which is not in contradiction with the sacrament of marriage" might signal a reference to the second case: causing no public scandal.

The last paragraph about the wish for a new and deeper study "taking into account the practices of the Eastern Churches" is the result of a softening of the original suggestion for this text — presented in the Synod speeches and in at least one of the small groups — that is not fully explained. Originally, this was a request for an official study commission to be set up in order to investigate the teaching and practice of the Eastern Churches with respect to divorce and the validity of a second, non-sacramental, marriage that exists in their tradition.

Nevertheless, the 1980 Synod demonstrated that among the bishops there was a willingness to be open to a wider reception into the Church for remarried persons who had been the victim and not the cause of a divorce. These were respected by many of the bishops especially when the validity of the first marriage was not certain, when the upbringing of children must be taken into account, and when there would be no question of "public scandal". From the text of the Propositions, it seems that in the end their pastoral orientation could not win out or that their intention was not considered practicable.

3. *Inculturation and the diversity of cultural values (Proposition 18)*

Since the 1974 Synod, dedicated to evangelization, there has been no theme that has been closer to the heart of the bishops, especially those of the young churches, and prompted more movement than the specific subject of inculturation. When the balance of the 1980 Synod is finally calculated it will probably be this type of proposal that will be considered to characterize the general trend that reflected this particular gathering.

While retaining the principle of the unity and consistency of the cultural values of peoples with the Gospel of Jesus Christ, and while retaining the principle of the community of the universal Church, the Synod formulated a twofold request: first, that the bishops' conferences should apply themselves to a study of those elements of their indigenous cultures which have a bearing upon marriage and the family with the view of reaching a true inculturation of the christian faith; and secondly, that with these perspectives the local churches and the bishops' conferences should be recognized as possessing the necessary competence with respect to concrete value judgments and the working out of norms for the celebration and validity of marriage.

4. *The regulation of fertility and* Humanae vitae

Predictably, another of the burning issues to be faced by the 1980 Synod was the series of questions surrounding HV. Not that the declarations of this encyclical were ever called into question — a kind of self-imposed monitoring took care of that — but there certainly was no way to prevent attempts to "re-read" the text of 1968. The major trends with respect to the regulation of fertility, which had already become evident at an earlier time, concerned the tension between a "pastoral conservatism" and an "authoritarian conservatism", and these were not absent in the development of the Synod.

In retrospect, it might have been more appropriate to nuance what some called a "pastoral conservatism" with the name of "spiritual conservatism". Regardless of this, the attempt to bridge the gap between the "pastoral" and the "authoritarian" went forward. However, because the margin of negotiations (to use political terminology) had been so narrow, the pastoral re-reading of HV did not succeed very well, at least when understood from a reading of the final version of the Propositions which we will now discuss. It would also be possible to speak of a certain "anti-climax" in the whole affair when we read the closing Homily of John-Paul II, but we will for the time being leave this out of our consideration.

a. *Broadening the notion of fertility (Proposition 20)*

In the first proposal found in the section dealing with the transmission of life, the meaning of fruitfulness itself is said to be understood as touching upon more than merely physical life. The fruitfulness of conjugal love incorporates as well supernatural, moral and spiritual goods. It is an intrinsic part of the vocation of marriage that the couple share their goods with their children, the Church and the world. This observation is fully in comformity with the general thematic trend of the Synod.

b. *Protection of the dignity of marriage (Proposition 21)*

Protecting the dignity of marriage and the transmission of human life — created in the image and likeness of God — is part of the special mission of the Church. Is this sense both Vatican II and HV have been prophetic messages for our time. The Synod gave its definitive endorsement to the message that marital love must remain open to the possibility of new life. Specific mention is made here of HV, 11 with reference to HV, 9 and 12.

c. *Confirmation and elucidation of HV (Proposition 23)*

A consciousness of the complex problems with which married couples are faced today and of serious demographic pressures is said to once again confirm the importance of the authentic teaching of the Church put forth in Vatican II and HV. In order that this teaching can be better understood and accepted in wider circles, the Synod draws attention to the address of Paul VI: "(this encyclical) clarifies a fundamental chapter in the personal, married, family and social life of human beings, but it is not a complete treatment of the human person and marriage, of the family and moral life; this is an immense field to which the Church's magisterium could and perhaps should return in order to offer a fuller, more organic and synthetic explanation" (31 July 1968).

On the basis of this perspective the Synod invites theologians to join forces with the teaching authority of the hierarchy to shed light upon the biblical foundations and personalist arguments of this teaching. The intention should be to make the teaching clearer, to make it more accessible to all people of good will, and to deepen understanding of it.

d. *The law of gradualness in the application of HV (Proposition 24)*

The bishops of the Synod declared that they were aware of the numerous married couples who, despite their good will, feel incapable of strictly following the moral norms set forth by the Church because of their own weakness or because of objective difficulties. In the pastoral care of the married, pastors should continually keep in mind the law of gradualness in connection with the teaching of the Church. A pedagogical approach will always strive to help couples clearly recognize the teaching of HV as a norm in the exercise of their sexual lives. Joined with this should always be a sense of constancy and patience, courage and humility in the complete trust of God's mercifulness.

This pedagogy involves the whole of married life. The duty to transmit life should form a part of and find its scope in a global vision of married, family and social life, as well as in a vision of the total christian life which cannot lead to the resurrection except through the way of the cross. This communitarian approach demands sensitivity, information and an appropriate preparation for priests, religious and laypersons who work in the field of pastoral care, especially when one considers that this educational process must lead couples on a human and spiritual journey, involving an appreciation of the concept of sin and the desire to follow the law not simply as an ideal for the future, as well as the ministry of reconciliation. In following the law of gradualness neither the priest nor the couple should fall into a kind of false dichotomy between teaching and pastoral care, but they should seek the way to a complete and mature faith, with the same patience with which the Lord seeks us.

Commentary on Proposition 24

The concept of gradualness which is set forth in this Proposition is less of a way out of the difficulty than the creation of a labyrinth surrounding a solution. This is one of the most difficult texts coming from the 1980 Synod for the simple reason that, to put it mildly, it was the product of compromise.

It is no secret that the content of this Proposition was meant to be used for a broadening of the applicability of HV. However, the attempt suffered from so many precautions that in fact the final version fell back into a kind of juxtaposition of opposing tendencies (which would later be sorted out in the Pope's commentary on the law of gradualness.). The intention here had been a double one: to make room for a pastoral form of gradualness for couples who found it difficult to follow HV, and at the same time to avoid in any way giving the impression that the teaching of the encyclical was being set aside.

In a text that had once again to repeat the validity of HV, an attempt had been made to find a new terminology for dealing with the matter. It reflected a feasible notion of gradualness while precluding any form of laxism. The concept of gradualness had to be protected from being interpreted as setting up a false dichotomy. The difficulties involved in this formulation are again evident in the interpretation it received in John-Paul's commentary. One can presume that the Pope had followed the evolution of this Proposition very carefully and felt that the new use of terminology needed to be somehow clarified.

Something else which belongs not to the area of presumption but to that of certainty is the fact that at the last moment there was an intervention by the Pope to change the very last sentence of the first paragraph from *sunt* to *sentiunt* out of fear that there would be any misunderstanding: married couples are *not* incapable of following the moral norms of the Church, although they may very well *feel* incapable of doing so. The use of the word *sunt* could appear to justify the incapacity while *sentiunt* placed it back into the subjective realm. It is then pointed out that God would not place an unbearable burden on one's shoulders[72]. Yet one could also wonder whether the use of the word *sentiunt* really functions to balance what were pointed out to be the "objective difficulties" that were in the minds of more than one prudent Synod bishop.

What is also beyond doubt is that the introduction of the word *sentiunt* was influenced by the Latin language group. Indeed in the course of their discussions it was recalled that Jansenius was condemned for holding that some laws of God are simply beyond the power of men of good will to fulfill. The justification for the change which was put forth by Card. Ratzinger in general session was based upon the need to avoid any danger of Jansenism.

e. The natural methods for regulating fertility (Proposition 25)

The last Proposition of this series on the transmission of life dealt with the need for disseminating information and promoting programs of instruction in the "natural and scientifically established methods of regulating fertility", especially among the poor. This is said to be in keeping with true educational formation that respects the human person.

5. Economic and political pressure for limiting population

The bishops of the young churches had clearly let their voice be heard in the 1980 Synod with respect to regulating births. They lodged a protest that was much more far reaching than the mere attack on the so-called politics of birth control which were being forced upon the poorer countries. Their plea was a direct attack on every method of controlling births — including abortion and sterilization — which had been forced upon their people either by their own governments or by international organizations. Also dealt with here in a very detailed fashion were families "in special circumstances": those of migrants in general and guest-workers in particular. Of the three Propositions which treat this aspect, 31-33, we will summarize only the first.

---

72. This change which took place at the last moment *in aula* and which had to be written into the text that had been distributed was missed in more than one published version. The texts which appeared in *Archief* and in *Documentation Catholique* both translate *sunt*.

a. *The anti-life mentality (Proposition 22)*

This Proposition signals various forms of a threatening anti-life mentality. While many persons are anxious about the future and have doubts about the vocation to transmit human life, there are others who consider themselves as the exclusive beneficiaries of technology and who "shut out others to whom they export large quantities of contraceptives". Even the demographic studies of ecologists and futurologists are said to practice a kind of scare tactics when they exaggerate the threat posed by population increase. Nevertheless, with the conviction that all human life, even that of the weak, is a gift from God, the Church, against all pessimism and egoism, will use all her power to defend human life against the threatening dangers of contraception, sterilization, abortion and euthanasia. On the same basis, she condemns all attempts to bring pressure upon persons for these purposes by government authorities, including those which take place on the international level.

b. *Families in special circumstances (Proposition 31)*

There are numerous families who are being forced to live in very difficult circumstances because of emigration and exile, as well as alcoholism, drug-abuse, social injustice, etc. We cannot be satisfied with efforts that treat only the symptoms of these problems but all our capacities must be aimed at getting to their causes. To this end, social consciousness must be awakened and work toward changes in cultural, economic and social structures.

C. Principle Themes of the Agenda

It is something of a paradox that the 1980 Synod devoted more time to dealing with what were considered to be pressing problems that it did to the principle themes which had been placed upon the official agenda. It can be noted from the content and frequency of the bishops' interventions that the official themes were dealt with somewhat reluctantly. Nevertheless, these themes still played a considerable role in the final text of a number of Propositions.

It is possible to make a distinction between the way the Synod was dealing with questions with regard to family and those surrounding marriage. Those who represented the greatest amount of openness toward specifically marriage questions were the bishops from Europe and North-America (with respect to the basis for contraception, the study of the divorced-remarried and the relation between faith and sacrament) and those from Africa (with respect to inculturation and the question of polygamy). Those who showed more concern for questions with respect to the family were especially the Latin American bishops, such as the representatives from Brazil who critically reacted to the unrealistic, ideal images and functions that some of those present attempted to ascribe to the family. Others warned that the position of the Church ran the risk of co-opting the family and using it in certain perspectives; in many of the worst conditions it is not the family which must transform society but the society itself which must be changed in the first place in order to make normal family life possible.

In dealing with the official themes of the Synod, which touched upon the special functions of the family, it appears that few bishops had great interest in discussing the "roles" of the family. The bishops as a whole had little to say about the "office" of the family in the strict meaning of that term. This remarkable reservation can be ascribed to several causes: some bishops feared misusing the family; they could have been anxious about respecting the traditions of the Orthodox Churches which have never applied priestly terminology to the family; in general, many wished to avoid falling into a certain romanticism which would have done violence to the daily reality of family life[73].

1. The educative role of the family

a. Family as domestic church (Proposition 26)

The participation of the family in the work of creation and redemption which belongs to the vocation of married couples lays the foundation for the family's task of raising children. Therefore, the family is called together as a domestic church (*ecclesia domestica*). The responsibility for raising children belongs first to parents and forms the first duty of their "ministry" in marriage.

Parents educate their children in many ways: through the witness of their lives, the atmosphere of responsibility in the home, an appropriate transmission of the christian faith, fostering relationships of trust among each other, the gradual development of children's participation in the Church and in civil society, the formation of conscience, and prudent assistance in the choice of their vocation.

b. The bearer of the Gospel (Proposition 27)

The educative mission of the family is elevated by the sacrament of marriage to a true ministry by which the Gospel is passed on and shown forth. Each member of the family evangelizes and in turn is evangelized.

73. Cf. E. FRANCHINI, *op. cit.*, pp. 483-484.

By initiating their children step by step into the body of Christ — namely the eucharistic and ecclesial body — parents become generators not merely of physical life but also of that life which is renewed by the Holy Spirit. To this end a catechism for the family would be very helpful.

c. *Parents and the christian communities (Proposition 29)*

The renewal of Catholic schools should receive special attention from the parents of pupils and for the institution of an integrated program of education in society. The right of parents to choose a type of education that responds to their faith must be safeguarded in every way. Both the Church and the state must create and support institutions and educative programs which are required by the family. Those who are in charge of schools should remember that God made parents the principle educators of their children.

In schools where anti-christian ideologies are taught, families should join together in order to stand by their children with all their power and help prevent the loss of their faith.

2. *The social and cultural role of the family (Proposition 30)*

Some of the principle points of this theme are enumerated here following the numbers assigned in the Proposition itself.

1. Because the family forms the first cell of society to which it is bound in a vital and organic way, it must stand open to other families and communities so that it may care not only for itself but also for others in order to create a civilization of love.
2. The principle task of the entire family is situated in collaboration to build up the world so that human life in the truest sense can be made possible.
3. The family is the vehicle of humanization and personalization which enjoys the greatest power in preserving and passing on cultural values.
4. Interpersonal relationships in the family bring about the disposition which leads to the creation and growth of true dialogue with and respect for other persons.
5. The habit and practice of participation in community and the attitude of solidarity with others is learned in the family which forms the foundation for community living.
   (...)
10. The special role of the family in fulfilling its socio-political function must be sought primarily in the promotion of ethical convictions and relationships which make possible political decisions leading toward greater justice and ordered social living in which it will be possible

for persons to live in accordance with their dignity as children of God.

11. Relations between the state and the family should be governed by the principle of subsidiarity so that the state does not invade the intimacy of the family (sterilization, abortion, contraception, etc) and even more so that the family might be supported in fulfilling its proper tasks.

12. Christian families can also work toward a new international order, especially by joining together in special associations which promote love, truth, justice and freedom.

Commentary on Proposition 30

It appears to us that the principle theme of the 1980 Synod originally proposed for its agenda by John-Paul II is to be found in this Proposition. The two basic ideas of this theme are here in a nutshell, especially in the first three paragraphs: the family is the basic cell of society and, the building up of the world, and the preservation and transmission of cultural values, are the principle task of the family. The social function of the family as it is here described proceeds up to and includes a political education which children receive in the family leading to the promotion of justice and social order.

Before the final version of this text was drawn up and approved, it did not escape some critical observations in the general meetings. Some bishops had doubts that the family could function as the basic cell of society. There were also voices heard regarding the idea of the political function of the family as utopian, while others were denying the desirability of that function.

3. The apostolic mission

a. The apostolic role of the family (Proposition 34)

The future of evangelization is largely dependent upon the domestic church (John-Paul II, 28 Feb. 1979). The apostolic mission of the family is founded upon baptism and receives new strength through the sacramental grace of marriage to pass on the faith and to form and sanctify contemporary society according to the plan of God. The family must form children to live so that they fulfill each of their tasks in a way that corresponds to the vocation which they have received from God. The family that is open to transcendent values, that stands joyfully at the service of others, faithfully fulfilling its duties and being conscious of its participation in the mystery of the cross of Christ, is the first and best school for the vocation to a consecrated life. (...) The necessary vocation of the family to evangelize can be excellently and efficiently fulfilled in apostolic movements. These movements should be established in connection with the Church community on the diocesan and parish level to insure that they will fulfill their rask of proclaiming the Gospel and transmitting christian teaching. (...) The role of the priest is an essential part of the Church's service to the married and the family. He bears responsibility as much with respect to personal aspects as to those of a liturgical, social and moral nature. It is his duty to support the family in the midst of difficulty and anxiety, and, intimately bound up with the members of the family, he should help them to examine their life in the light of the Gospel. This bond will be of benefit to the priest as well as to the family when the families to whom he lends support will strengthen him and in turn give support to his vocation.

Commentary on Proposition 34

Closely tied to the previous thought that the family can be considered the basic cell of society, we come to the second aspect of the official principle theme, namely that in the future a great portion of the work of evangelization will depend upon the domestic church. In other words, the family is put forth as the most primary given of the Church for the future of our uncertain times. The parallel lines are here drawn.

It is particularly significant that the last minute amendments (and thus those proposed between the final votes on the texts of the Propositions) were concerned with the mission of families as basic communities of the Church closely tied to the framework of the Church as institution and, as it were, remaining limited. The intended amendments on the one hand included the terms "on the diocesan and parish level" with respect to the action of family apostolic movements, and on the other, dealt with the task of the priest and his special responsibilities for marital and family life.

b. *Family associations (Proposition 39)*

Family groups which are today being set up in many places provide the faithful with a feeling of solidarity that will help them to lead their lives according to the inspiration of the Gospel and the faith of the Church. They can help in the formation of consciences in the direction of christian values rather than that of public opinion. They can strengthen families in their responsibilities with respect to others and to society.

Therefore, the Synod affirms the priceless value of spiritual groups or associations which attempt to promote the christian life of married couples and of the family, not that these should separate their members from the rest of the faithful but so as to make them the "light" and the "yeast" of all families.

4. *Spirituality of the family*

a. *The first school of spirituality (Proposition 36)*

The spirituality of the family flows from the theology of the family. In a single word it is founded upon God's love for us and on the Gospel command to love one another. The family as domestic church, as a community of love and faith, is responsible for the lives of its members and their spirituality.

The family is the first school of doctrine, of spirituality and of the apostolate as was clearly pointed out in the documents of the last Council. Through the recognition of the dignity of the family—caught up in the love and call of God — the circumstances of daily life will form each person's responsibilities for this love and call. By their response, the family will be enlightened in their spirituality in its elements of creation, covenant, cross, resurrection, sign and eschatology.

b. *The means for promoting family spirituality (Proposition 37)*

Because the atmosphere, place and time for a true family spirituality is very often missing, some advantageous conditions should be promoted. For instance, there are changes necessary in mentality and in structures that will be beneficial to spirituality and to pastoral action. (...) Among the means which can be helpful toward this end, the following points should be mentioned: the faithful fulfillment of specific family duties, prayer that takes place in the family as such including the reading of scripture and preparation for the sacraments, the maintenance of popular forms of devotion, and the participation of the family as family in community celebrations, especially during the prominent liturgical seasons (Advent, Christmas, Lent, Holy Week, etc) and during special familial events.

c. *The formation of conscience (Proposition 38)*

Finally, the family is the preeminent place in which the human person comes to the experience of conscience: coming to know oneself in relation to others and ultimately to God. Such a conscience, born of love and solidarity, leads to holiness and is the beginning of the way toward a truly mature conscience. The necessary conditions for the formation of conscience are that it be an organic part of education in the faith and at the same time part of the overall education that takes place between spouses and their children.

Faith itself opens the way to insights into social justice and into all communitarian virtues. Indeed, in the family that forms the domestic church all members are brought together in the understanding that they cannot experience belief in the one God, the Father of all, in Christ and in the Holy Spirit unless they are joined together with all persons who seek truth, love and justice. (...) Conscience must be developed in all dimensions if it is to be enlightened by faith, brought to maturity and made capable of discernment.

5. *The rights of the family*

In the previous Propositions an emphasis has repeatedly been placed on the necessity for protecting the family against extreme dangers such as "intruders". We recall a few of the examples given.

— When public authorities impose methods of limiting births, this constitutes an assault against human dignity and against justice (Prop. 22).
— The school, the media and the climate of life which contribute to the formation of children should be controlled by parents (Prop. 26,3).
— It can happen that schools form part of a wrong or dangerous sexual education (Prop. 28).
— There are anti-christian ideologies taught in some schools which threaten the family (Prop. 29).
— One should not accept any state intervention in the intimate life of the family (Prop. 30).
— There are ideologies which breed division and which enter the home through the mass media (Prop. 33).

This context underscores the importance of the need for an official confirmation of the rights of the family. Representatives of the young churches, among others those from African countries, placed a great deal of weight in such a charter. Such a declaration could provide some protection against certain forms of dominant power exercised by the "clan" in Africa and against the common law which largely determines existing norms.

a. *Announcement of the charter (Proposition 42)*

This Proposition explicitates the wish of the Synod that the Holy See will work on "a bill of rights for the family" and will present it to the United Nations. As foundation for this declaration, two principles are set forth: that the family is the basic cell of society and is more fundamental than the state or any other group; and that the state is obliged to recognize the family in its laws, to protect it and to support it. Then, fourteen different rights are summarized headed by the right of the family to exist and to grow as a family; that is, the right of every person, especially of the poor, to establish a family and to support it with the appropriate means.

b. *A pastoral directory (Proposition 43)*

The last Proposition summarizes some general principles for the development of pastoral directories. These touch upon pastoral situations which were dealt with by the bishops, but only in rather vague terms. Because of the lack of time, the Synod did not go further than these generalities. However, basing itself on the observation of a wide diversity of unique situations throughout the world, the Synod could do no more than present the general principles, on the basis of which each bishops' conference should draw up its own pastoral directory for the family to be applied in a suitable manner to the different situations.

Such a directory would include: teaching on the sacrament of marriage and on the christian family; principles for marriage preparation; instructions for the celebration of marriage; guiding principles for pastoral care and action; elements of family spirituality; and principles for the catechesis of children. All of this should take into account the role of the family in the work of evangelization.

PART THREE

A PROVISIONAL ASSESSMENT OF THE SYNOD

VII. The Closing Homily of Pope John-Paul II

After the frankness of the first week of the Synod, followed by the lively exchange of ideas in the discussion groups, and after the tension to put together an acceptable series of Propositions, the closing Homily of Pope John-Paul II was expectedly listened to with feelings of both hope and apprehension. In the given situation, it does not appear unfair to say that the ultimate response to the papal homily was one of disenchantment. To explain this, however, we must look at the speech against the background of the events which we have described in the foregoing sections.

The first cause of this feeling undoubtedly rests in the procedure which was followed. The text of the Propositions had been handled with the strictest secrecy. It was not supposed to be made available to the public. Yet, in the course of his Homily, the Pope delivered some sharp criticisms of some of the most specific and essential sections of those Propositions. This was a rather uncollegial manner of approach and it made more than a few bishops uncomfortable.

The opening of the Homily was general in nature. After expressing his general appreciation for the accomplishments of the just ended Synod, and having thanked all those who gave their services for the event, the Pope underscored the importance of prayer during the Synod and the richness of its contributions whether in the interventions, the reports, or the suggestions that had been made. There were two pivotal ideas that, according to John-Paul II, came to occupy a central place: faithfulness to the plan of God with respect to the family and pastoral solicitude which is characterized by charitable love and by respect for the human person both in their "being" and in their "living". Among all the questions that were handled, he said, the bishops were sensitive to particular problems in which they realized and interpreted the expectations of many married couples and families. The Pope also expressed the opinion that these questions should be kept in mind and given the special attention indicated for them during the Synod. After this general overview, the attention of the audience naturally turned to the reception that these central questions of the Synod's work might receive from the Pope.

A. The Issues Addressed

Four "achievements" of the Propositions which the majority of the bishops attending the Synod felt to be of essential importance were explicitly touched upon by John-Paul II.

1. *The pastoral care of the divorced-remarried*

After having called to mind the wish of the Synod bishops to help the divorced-remarried and not to consider these persons as cut off from the Church — that by virtue of their baptism, such persons could and should participate in the life of the Church through prayer, hearing the Word, attending the liturgy and promoting works of charity and justice — the Pope nonetheless underscored the fact that the sacraments of penance and the eucharist would only be open to such persons "when they seriously open themselves to a way of life which is not opposed to the indissolubility of marriage", namely, "the obligation to take on a life of total continence ... and to avoid giving scandal". The last part of this symbolized a clear break from the more dynamic openness by which the majority of Synod bishops expected the possibility of reconciliation through the sacrament of penance "if these persons sincerely regret violating the sign of the covenant and faithfulness of Christ and open themselves to a way of living that is not in contradiction with the sacrament of marriage" (Prop. 14,d). Judgment about the criteria for this "way of life" had been left to the circumstances of time and place and the wisdom of the local bishop. The reduction of this "way of live" exclusively to the area of the sexual relationship of the remarried amounted to a hollowing out of the bishops' intention.

In the same Prop. 14, a further distinction was made with respect to those innocent partners who had been abandoned by their lawful spouse, and further study was requested which take into account the practices of the Eastern Churches. The contribution of these two essential elements found no place in the closing Homily.

2. *The transmission of life*

After having once again confirmed the value of HV and at the same time brought to mind the speech of Paul VI who recognized that his encyclical could and should be explained in "a more organic and synthetic way" by the magisterium (31 July 1968), the majority of Synod bishops invited theologians to join forces with the hierarchical teaching authority in order to bring to light in a better way the biblical foundations and personalist reasons for this teaching. In this way they should strive that, in the context of "a more organic and synthetic explanation", this teaching of the Church on a fundamental chapter in human life would be made more accessible to all persons of good will, and that its understanding would be made continuously deeper so that the command of God would be more fulfilled for the salvation of persons and the praise of the Creator (Prop. 23). In his Homily, the Pope took this proposal over and recommended its content. (The Latin text which appeared in the *Osservatore Romano* on 26 October 1980 inexplicably included quotation marks around the word "*personalisticae*", giving it a somewhat relative character).

3. *The law of gradualness*

Less positive was the manner of dealing with the concept of a *processus dynamicus*. The Propositions train of thought set out from three demands in its opening section: the *sensus fidei*, the "signs of the times" and the need for dynamic progression. This last concept was described as the law of gradualness which, as already mentioned, played a principle role in repeatedly making it possible for the Synod to exhibit a certain openness on pastoral grounds. This also had an influence with respect to the living out of conjugal morality according to the norms of HV.

John-Paul II, however, had a somewhat different opinion on the matter. In his Homily he made it very clear that the "law of gradualness" cannot be equated with a "gradualness of law", as if there were different levels or forms of divine commandments for different persons and situations. This somewhat disapproving interpretation of one of the main points of the Synod's Propositions was not very encouraging to the bishops.

4. *The need for inculturation*

The need for inculturation had become one of the principle themes of discussion during the course of the Synod. In his closing Homily, John-Paul II made a number of the bishops happy in taking over an important part of their Prop. 18 and expressing his approval. "Above all, the Synod Fathers recognized that within the boarders of marriage and the family an immense area lies open for theological and pastoral investigation so that the application of the gospel message can be better promoted in the context of each people and so that the way in which it is brought into agreement with the customs, the excellent values, and the meaning of life and the specific inner inspiration of each human culture can be understood"[74].

This reference, however, was coupled with a double limitation to which the audience was not insensitive. First, the episcopal conferences were not mentioned even though they had twice been put forth in the

74. The translation here is based upon the text as it was published in *Archief van de Kerken* 36 (1981) c. 142.

Proposition as the principle agents of this process of inculturation, especially with respect to their competence for the working out of norms for the celebration of the sacrament. Secondly, conformity with "the principle of community with the universal Church", which had been understood in the Proposition, was significantly narrowed by a papal reference to the union of the local bishops with "the See of the Holy Father which according to LG, 13 holds the position of leadership over the entire community of love". These limitations must have been especially attended to by the young churches which had insisted in the first place on the need for working out the inculturation of christian marriage[75].

Of the four "accomplishments" of the Synod that were addressed in the Pope's closing Homily, there were two cases of rather negative reaction, the divorced-remarried and the law of gradualness, one, on the transmission of life, signifying general agreement, while the fourth, on inculturation, was positively evaluated but at the same time subject to limitation[76].

B. The Issues Not Addressed

The papal Homily on the closing day of the Synod was a further cause for disenchantment in that it remained silent about a number of meaningful Propositions. Three central pastoral questions that received a good deal of time and attention from the majority of the bishops did not enter into this papal consideration. Indeed, John-Paul II did take care to mention that there were other questions raised by the Synod other than those that he addressed. He also admitted that these other questions should not be considered of lesser importance. However, this general reference was not sufficient to do away with a feeling of disillusionment on the part of many bishops since they considered these problems to be essential in dealing with their pastoral situations. There are three issues in particular among the Synod's "achievements" that seemed to have deserved some attention.

1. *The relation between faith and sacrament*

Twice in Prop. 12 the Synod drew attention to the need to investigate the manner in which the faith of the engaged, as a conscious and personal realization of their baptismal vocation, would be necessary for the

75. From comments of the bishops after the closing of the Synod, if is also evident that many leaders from the young churches were disappointed with these limitations.

76. It will perhaps strike some readers that an important point was not touched upon here in any detail at all, namely that of the dignity and role of women. It is true that John-Paul II did not avoid dealing with this question, but it is just as true that the social role of women who work outside the home was looked upon with a more conservative vision.

validity of sacramental marriage. The same Proposition suggests that the new code of canon law take this question into consideration. In the minds of the bishops, this was far more than an academic question for it dealt directly with a problem of pastoral care which was daily being confronted with life in a secularized society. There was a definite note of urgency in this question as it was discussed in the synodal meetings.

2. *Mixed marriages*

With regard to the question of mixed marriage, a topic which had repeatedly come to the fore even in earlier synodal meetings, the 1980 Synod undoubtedly opened new perspectives. One of these was to view mixed marriage as supportive of the process of evangelization and thus worthy of more positive evaluation. The bishops' suggestions, therefore, requested a review of the existing legislation "so that the episcopal conferences would have greater power in determining the norms for such marriages" (Prop. 19,b).

3. *Conjugal morality and the renewal of spirituality*

In the minds of a number of bishops, the need to renew marital spirituality became a principle theme of the Synod. In discussing questions in connection with HV and the serious difficulties involved in living according to that teaching, a real tendency developed to deal with the problem of spirituality. The bishops declared that a deepening of spirituality would help families in regard to those moral pressures within which they found themselves. This conviction came forth in various Propositions, among others especially in Prop. 36.

This rather brief summary of the synodal suggestions which were or were not mentioned in the Pope's closing Homily is in no way intended to be a complete inventory. At the end of the Homily, the Pope brought forth the obligation of truth, saying that "no one can practice love other than in the truth". He said further that this principle should be applied to the life of every family, and no less to the life and work of pastors who are at the service of families. It was inevitable that the conclusions of this theme would strike some of the Synod bishops as a kind of warning.

To better understand the final impression of disenchantment, one must take into consideration the difficult circumstances in which the final text of the Propositions had been drawn up and the frustrating way in which the Synod itself was forced to include a significant number of limitations in its suggestions in order to make that text "acceptable". When such an already restricted final text was again subject to further limitations in the papal commentary, it is hard to characterize that event as anything other than an anti-climax.

VIII. The Usefulness and Uselessness of the Synod of Bishops

At the beginning of his pontificate, John-Paul II many times emphasized his resolve, in being "faithful to the light of the Council" (17
Octobre 1978), to promote collegiality and to that end to bring appropriate structures into existence which might be partly new, partly
determined by contemporary needs. "In this connection we would first
point to the Synod of Bishops that, with great spirit, Paul VI had already
set up before the end of the Council"[77]. When Bishop L. Rubin, then still
Secretary General of the Synod of Bishops, held a press conference in
June 1979 to announce the preparatory work for the 1980 Synod, he
underlined the resolution of the new Pope now more than ever to appeal
to the Synod because of his own special interest for collegiality[78].

In light of these remarks, after the close of the 1980 Synod, which was
the first that took place during this new pontificate, the question of
evaluating that episcopal gathering quite naturally presents itself. We
have already drawn attention to the general atmosphere of disenchantment that characterized the closing of the Synod. In the second part of
this work, which is dedicated to an examination of documentation
including the "apostolic exhortation" of John-Paul II, it will be more
clearly evident that this text, *Familiaris consortio*, perhaps raises more
questions than it answers with respect to the Synod. An analysis of that
papal exhortation, delivered as an official response to the 1980 meeting,
thus begs the question of the usefulness or uselessness of the institution
of the Synod of Bishops in general.

A. An Inadequate Procedure

Since its first institution in October 1967, the Synod of Bishops has
been the continuous object of criticism. It is remarkable enough that
resolutions have again and again been made to improve the procedure
which is followed, while it is also noteworthy that those resolutions
having again been made in 1980 were, again as in the past, all but
forgotten.

When the newly instituted Concilium of the Bishops' Synod held its
first meeting in May 1970 to prepare for the 1971 gathering, it was
insisted upon that the Synod should have enough time and opportunity
for properly studying the amendments for their proposed text, for
bringing the definitive version of the final text to completion, and for

77. *Archief van de Kerken* 33 (1978) c. 1099.
78. Cf. *Le Monde*, 22 June 1979.

giving a full account of the results of the work of amendment and of the voting before the Synod came to a close. It was well known that all these concrete points were the result of a reaction to the end of the 1969 Synod that led to a general feeling of dissatisfaction. This was typified by the comments of Card. Marty at the time[79].

One of the small discussion groups of the 1971 Synod devoted an entire meeting to the question of synodal procedure. The first of ten proposals that resulted from this episcopal study stated that the bishops did not clearly understand what had been expected of them. At the conclusion of the 1971 Synod, a certain feeling of dissatisfaction still remained about the way in which the Synod itself is organized. No one less than Card. Luciani, then Patriarch of Venice and later to become Pope John-Paul I, expressed this feeling in an interview with the newspaper *Avvenire*[80]. One could even speculate that Paul VI himself, in his closing Homily to the 1971 Synod, was also looking for suggestions: "It will be our personal concern to make the working of the Synod more effective in the future. If it appears to you that some of the rules by which the meeting operates are not appropriate, we request that you make your thoughts known to the Secretariate for the Synod".

After having positively evaluated the general results of the 1971 Synod as a renewed expression of collegiality, Card. Luciani had no hesitation in pointing out faults of procedure such as the unnecessarily frequent repetition of standpoints and the timidity of the leadership in restraining this out of fear of being accused of limiting freedom of expression. The Patriarch of Venice had made some specific suggestions for improvement: the basic documents should be sent to the episcopal conferences sufficiently ahead of time, the suggestions that are returned from the different conferences should be clearly coordinated, summarized and put at the disposal of the Synod fathers; the actual discussions should be limited to a few well defined points; the number of speeches in the general sessions should be limited; and the small discussion groups should be given more time and freedom.

The Synod of 1974, which was devoted to the single topic of evangelization, was an especially lively event. Nevertheless, after the general discussions, the extraordinary vitality exhibited by the young churches, and the fruitfulness of their contributions, the leadership of the Synod was unsuccessful in guiding the development of a final text capable of winning approval from the majority of bishops. After the close of this Synod, there were again critical remarks about the pro-

79. Card. Marty's commentaries about the 1969 Synod and about the meeting of this council can be found in *The Catholic Herald* (15 May 1970), *La Croix* (14 June 1970), *Le Monde* (19 June 1970), *The National Catholic Reporter* (10 July 1970) and *The Tablet* (25 July 1970).

80. Cf. *L'Avvenire* (11 December 1971) and later, *Osservatore Romano* 118 (2 September 1978) and *Rheinischer Merkur* 33 (15 September 1978).

cedure of events and a feeling among some participants that they had not achieved their purpose and were returning home "with empty hands". Others were of the opinion that the production of a final text was not an essential task of the Synod. In any case, many had come away with the expectation that the procedure should be reviewed and made more efficient for the next gathering.

During the preparations for the 1977 Synod, it appears that neither the critical observations nor the earlier expectations with respect to synodal procedure would bring about much result. An expression of the many discussions that had taken place can be found in an article by Philippe Delhaye, Secretary General of the International Theological Commission. Under the title "Résultats et prospectives du Synod des Evêques"[81], Delhaye defended the opinion that a Synod was not the same as a council and should thus avoid producing detailed texts in imitation of Vatican II. Above all, he wrote, a consultative Synod should not be confused with a legislative assembly[82]. To improve the synodal procedure, Delhaye offered a few suggestions: more insistence upon the rotation of representatives that the episcopal conferences send to the Synod, a larger share of the time for the exchange of ideas in the *circuli minores*, regulation to prevent the repetition of ideas in the general sessions, and the establishment of commissions under the authority of the Synod Secretariate to deal with the submitted amendments in an efficient manner.

Nevertheless, as mentioned, the 1977 Synod took place without any statutes having been changed. Yet, by this time, it had become an assumption that the Synod would no longer attempt to draw up and approve a final text. At the same time, only one "special secretary" was installed instead of two to prevent a repetition of the dramatic tension that took place in 1974. This was the only official change implemented in the 1977 meeting. These aspects were naturally not substantial enough to bring about more efficiency or to restore the self-confidence of the Synod.

According to G. Caprile, who might be considered an official chronicler of the Synod, we are given to understand that the Concilium of the Synod Secretariate, at its meeting in May 1978, expressed the wish that the statutes of the meeting be reviewed. Bishop Rubin, then Secretary General of the Synod of Bishops, announced that Paul VI had allowed for *explicationes* for some of the articles of the General Statutes so that a complete revision would not be necessary at that time. The Concilium then decided to gather together all the earlier and new suggestions to

---

81. *Osservatore Romano* (French ed.) 28 (9 August 1977). It can be noted here that P. Delhaye was involved with the ultimate attempts to draft a final text for the 1974 Synod.
82. Bishop A.-L. Descamps, who worked with others on the draft of a final text in 1974, defended similar ideas during a press conference held on 31 October 1974 in Brussels.

make them available for review at some later time. The suggestions of this Concilium touched upon the distribution of the preparatory documents, a way in which the opinions of minorities could be expressed, the manner of interventions in general session, the way of dealing with suggested amendments, the nomination and tasks of the press secretary, etc[83].

In his introductory overview for the 1980 gathering, the new Secretary General, Bishop Tomko, once again delivered a report on the question of the revision of the statutes. Since 1971, he said, the Concilium had received and studied numerous proposals for a review of many points of the often criticized procedure. But it seemed that Paul VI had refused to allow for the implementation of these proposals, having preferred to wait some time longer before this was done. In his conclusion, Bishop Tomko let it be known that a dossier containing all the proposals (from 1971 to 1980) had been made ready for study but that this could only take place when the present Pope, John-Paul II, gave the order to do so.

B. A Meaningful Enrichment

Every gathering of the Synod from 1969 to 1980 suffered from the problem of serious organizational faults. Nevertheless, we must state that these shortcomings, which have marred the formal development of the Synod as a process, still have not prevented fruitful results having been achieved over and over again. In other words, the inadequate functioning has in fact always been coupled with a meaningful enrichment[84]. It is of essential importance, therefore, that we do not neglect that enrichment, blinded as it were by a preoccupation with the faults of the formal process.

The Synod of 1969 constituted a privileged moment in which Church leaders had the opportunity to undertake a critical evaluation of the method of applying the accomplishments of Vatican II. This collective examination of conscience took place in the context of investigating how collegiality could be exercised, namely, under two aspects: with respect to appreciating the place and the value of the local church and to addressing the notion of collegiality in a new, more international dimension. Even though the inertia of the procedure itself had hindered the clear explicitation of these questions at the time, it is still apparent that the theme of the local church was brought forth in a whole series of significant interventions. The other gain of the 1969 meeting can be

83. Cf. G. CAPRILE, *op. cit.*, p. 26.
84. A more detailed treatment of this theme can be found in J. GROOTAERS, *Les synodes des évêques de 1969 et de 1974: fonctionnement défectueux et résultats significatifs*, in *Les Églises après Vatican II — dynamisme et prospective* Paris, 1981, pp. 303-328.

found in the contributions of the representatives of the non-Western episcopal conferences. These bishops were seeking more collegiality with the older christian churches so that the relation between all the local churches could henceforth be understood in the spirit of fraternal solidarity. Essential to this are the relations between the "rich countries" and the "poor churches" that must work together on an equal footing. African, Latin American and East European representatives echoed the same objections in emphasizing that "collegiality" could also be understood as the concrete experience of *communio*, namely, the idea of the close relationship between all the local churches.

When, in 1974, the vast majority of bishops rejected the final text that had been proposed, the failure in the formal process of the Synod was even more striking than that of earlier meetings. Yet this gathering had a great deal more to offer than that simple, negative aspect of its final accounting. In fact, in the post-conciliar development of the Catholic Church, the 1974 Synod signified a definite change in direction. What we find there is a spiritual and pastoral process of maturation in which the representatives of the young churches worked toward the acceptance of a more dynamic concept of the demands of evangelization. This effectively led to a raising of consciousness with respect to future possibilities that would have to be paired with a certain ecclesial process of emancipation. The result had gone contrary to all expectations and centered upon a number of agenda points from the non-Western perspective achieving priority: "frontier evangelization", the function of the local church in missionary work, the special role of the basic communities, and the value of popular religiosity. There were also important themes, which Vatican II had dealt with both *ad intra* and *ad extra* and with which everyone was already very familiar, that surprisingly received a new elucidation in 1974 because they were taken up in this renewed perspective. These themes were now considered from the point of view of the young churches and took on a more future oriented vision.

In light of these fundamental reorientations, the assessment of the 1974 Synod cannot be based upon its failure to produce a final text but rather must be judged on the basis of the unexpected impetus it gave to further Church renewal. With this perspective we should draw attention to the remarks of Archbishop J.G. Rakotondravahatra (Madagascar), made in the name of many African episcopal representatives. "For the first time we have had the opportunity to say what we think; we have had the right to explain our problems, our desires, eventually our disagreements. We have seen that the majority of our colleagues think in the same way. The Holy Father has heard all of this. Why should we attempt to hand over to him all the richness of these exchanges in the form of some impoverished texts?"

The study of the two Synods that we have specifically singled out, 1969 and 1974, makes it possible to appreciate the development of concepts that came about in the concrete attempts to live out the notion of collegiality in the years following the promulgation of *Lumen gentium*. The meaning of the Synod as institution has not subsequently been left behind. The "concrete experience" of synodal gatherings does indeed signify clear limitations. However, the Synod has made no clear progress as an organ of collegiality and has given no concrete form to the process of ecclesial renewal; there was neither doctrinal nor procedural progress. Nevertheless, from the viewpoint of the local churches, as a process of raising consciousness for greater solidarity, and as a forum for a communal confrontation with new situations, the experience of the bishops in Synod has led to a meaningful process of enrichment.

IX. Final Thoughts on the Synod on Marriage and the Family

In the end, we come to the question of evaluating the 1980 Synod. It is, of course, evident that it is still too early to think of a balance sheet in terms of gains and losses. Yet it is possible to attempt to make a few observations on the 1980 event from the point of view of considering the inadequacy of its procedure and the meaningfulness of its accomplishments.

A. The Procedure

1. *Specific characteristics of the 1980 Synod*

It is obvious that the 1980 Synod must be situated and judged in the line of development coming forth from the earlier episcopal gatherings. But it is also important to be attentive to the specific characteristics of this meeting itself. We will suggest some of these in the following points.

a. First, we must take into account the personality of John-Paul II, who apparently had a greater influence on the Synod than did Paul VI. The first General Synod of the new Pope was devoted to a single topic, one in which he himself had a particular interest[85]. This was not necessarily a windfall for the Synod bishops, particularly since it appears that in October 1980 the new Pope was no longer defending the same position that he evidently held in Milan in June 1978.

One must also not forget that Card. Wojtyla had also had a great deal more synodal experience than his predecessor. Not only had he been associated with the Synod since its very inception and actively taken part in the meetings since 1969, but during the last years he had also played a leading role in the process. Along with this, we must also remember the 1978 conclave that chose Card. Wojtyla as Pope: under the influence of this conclave we find John-Paul II clearly dedicating his efforts to a reconfirmation of a specific "Catholic identity" that symbolized the return to a more solid "scale of values" felt to be needed in a world of change.

---

85. As a member of the Pontifical Commission set up to deal with conjugal morality (birth control in particular), the then Archbishop of Cracow had submitted a written contribution (1966) that apparently carried a great deal of weight in the eyes of Paul VI. A few months before his election as Bishop of Rome, Card. Wojtyla delivered a key speech at a meeting sponsored by the International Confederation of Christian Family Movements, in Milan, in which he called for a rereading of the encyclical H.V. in a wider context.

The numerous speeches delivered by the Pope in the months before the Synod on the Family took place may well have limited the freedom of expression for a number of bishops who took part in that event. During the Synod itself, there were also some rumours of a few incidents in which representative bishops were discretely advised to be more moderate, the "retraction" of Card. Quinn possibly being one case where this came into public view. Lastly, it is clear that a number of themes closely associated with the thought of John-Paul II, which we have heard in Puebla, in *Redemptor hominis* and in various speeches, had a significant influence in the texts of the Synod.

b. There were other forms of pressure and a certain limitation on the freedom of expression, not the least of which was a kind of self-censorship exercised by the bishops themselves, that naturally would be very difficult to document in a specific way. Nonetheless, there were also the pressures which were experienced when influential curial members seemed to take a certain offensive, such as Card. Felici's comments following the addresses of the North American bishops and Card. Knox on the issue of the relation between faith and sacrament, a topic about which Bishop Duchêne still had a word of reply [86]. Finally, there was the pressure coming from the particular atmosphere created in the "academic sessions" made up of several interventions from medical doctors and *auditores* and of the particular concerns of the "Comitato per la Famiglia", all of which appealed to the bishops on behalf of the "natural methods" which were put forth as the only salvific solution possible to the question of limiting births.

c. There were other striking factors which can be pointed out from the beginning of the general meeting. The Pope's opening Homily did not give a clear, leading mandate that defined that task set out for the Synod. Also missing were the panoramic views or *conspectus* dedicated to an overall description of the situation of the world Church and to the specific situations of the Church by continent. These had been a characteristic of the opening phases of the earlier Synods, especially typical being that of 1974, and had served to provide a very important source of information for outlining the main issues to be discussed. As a result, there was a very weak accounting of the critical reactions to the preparatory documents

---

86. The rather pointed words of reply given by Bishop Dechêne (St. Claude, France) were a good example of the fact that the pastors did not intend simply to be "taught lessons" by the officials of the curia: "Je remercie la Congrégation pour les Sacrements et le Culte Divin des réponses qu'elle nous a rappelées (...). Ces réponses, il est vrai, nous sont connues: elles sont classiques. Elles ne résolvent cependant pas les problèmes des pasteurs ni des baptisés mal croyants ou non croyants et ne garantissent pas l'authenticité de la réception du sacrement". Cf. P. GAUDET, *Synode des Evêques, 1980, La Famille*, Paris, 1981, p. 240. In the course of 1981, Card. Knox was appointed as President of the new Pontifical Commission for the Family.

from the local churches and thus an even weaker echo allowed to be heard from the "basis".

d. Meanwhile, there was another specifically significant factor at work in the 1980 Synod. We must also take into account the HV crisis that overshadowed this meeting. As has already been mentioned, a certain dissatisfaction with the apparent indecision of Paul VI on conjugal morality had an influence on the papal conclaves of 1978. While it had been expected by some bishops that there would be a certain moderation in the official teaching in the years following the encyclical, the events of the conclaves, as well as a careful analysis of the nature of new episcopal appointments contradicted those expectations. On the other hand, from the very beginning the young churches had given HV a political reading that was completely different from the Western interpretation. The influence of this reading was not only continually present but in recent years had actually increased.

e. Another aspect of this Synod in particular was the greater closedness surrounding its procedure than any of the earlier meetings. The direction given to the process and the divisions of labor were of such a nature that the bishops had very little contact among themselves and were practically cut off from the observers and from the world outside. The flow of information was also much below standard in 1980. During the most crucial phase, namely the task of working out the suggestions in the Propositions, there was not a single press release issued for five days. On several occasions, the fatal result was a one-sided image of the events presented in the media.

The strict secrecy surrounding the 43 final Propositions was without precedent and did not avoid a certain boomerang-effect: some bishops returned home without having a true final text from the Synod in which they had taken part. Since the Propositions were not to be made publicly available, both the media and public opinion focused attention on the closing "Message" of the Synod which was not representative of the meeting and with which most of the bishops did not identify. Even the final reading of the "Message" missed a usual polite applause from those present.

Added to this is the manner in which John-Paul brought the month long meeting to a close. In his closing Homily, the Pope addressed the bishops' Propositons, delivering critical remarks in public on a document that was supposedly intended to be kept secret. All these factors were compounded by fragmentary and isolated leaks concerning the Propositions that led to a number of misleading commentaries.

f. Finally, compared with all the earlier meetings, the 1980 Synod exhibited the narrowest exercise of "collegiality" and the poorest connection with the local churches. Just at the point when one of the most general topics was being dealt with, "The Role of the Family in the Modern World", we find an absence of lay representation that aggravated the situation. The actual exclusion of laypersons was colored over by the appointment of a hand picked delegation of agreeable participants about whom no one had any illusions. This was also the first Synod in which the bishops had neither the theoretical nor practical possibility of being advised by their own *periti*. Because of the closedness of the procedure, only the ten, officially appointed, *periti* could take part in actual events. These chosen experts were not at the service of the bishops but worked exclusively for Card. Ratzinger, the *Relator* of the general meeting, and Bishop Lozano Barragàn, the Special Secretary.

Therefore, behind the façade of deliberation and dialogue, all the conditions were fulfilled to limit this Synod to a monologue. To some extent, however, with the limited resources they had available and despite the difficult conditions under which their work had been divided, the bishops were still capable of drawing up a series of suggestions that expressed the pastoral needs that were close to their hearts.

2. Disillusionment and criticism

The unrealized expectations of the 1980 Synod could best be measured by the critical judgment of its participants. These expressions can be found in the evaluations that took place in two meetings of the Synod itself as well as in subsequent remarks by individual bishops.

During the Synod's own evaluative discussions on 23 and 24 October — about which there were no formal accounts released — one general complaint of the bishops touched upon the lack of continuity between the different phases of the meeting. The broad richness of discussions that took place during the first two weeks was not felt to be reflected in the final texts. Cards. Lorscheider (Brazil) and Zoungrana (Upper Volta) had proposed that the Propositions and the Message be discussed in general session as well as in the language groups. It appeared, however, that Card. Ratzinger was against this suggestion.

With respect to the amendments or *modi* that had been submitted after the first vote taken on the Propositions, Card. Hume expressed the opinion that it also would have been better to discuss these in general session. The process of handling the *modi* was considered inadequate in many quarters. In contrast with the conciliar procedure in which there was a formal explanation presented for handling the amendments that was discussed and voted upon in general session, the members of the 1980 Synod were kept in the dark about the amendment process and had no opportunity to express themselves on its outcome. The suggestion of Archbishop Martini to postpone the final work until after a recess of six months was not well received by the bishops from the Third World.

In regard to the statements of individual bishops, it is noteworthy that many bishops, among them Carter (Canada), Datubara (Indonesia) and Cordeiro (Pakistan), insisted upon the publication of a final text in a language that would be understandable for everyone. On the eve of the Synod's close, Card. Carter stated in the presence of journalists that, "We had supposed that the experiment of the Synod would carry on the type of work accomplished at the Council, but in its present form the Synod is a disappointment"[87]. Card. Enrique y Tarancón (Spain) publically lamented the majority decision to close the Synod without having produced any true final text and merely to hand over to the Pope an incomplete dossier[88]. At a press conference held on the night before the meeting ended, Bishop Ernst (The Netherlands) expressed his regret that the actual contributions of the Synod's leaders were not reflected in the final texts[89]. The lack of control exercised by the general gathering over the whole process of dealing with amendments in the final text was a frequently heard complaint.

More important and substantial were the post-synodal statements of Bishop A. Kaseba, chairman of the bishops' conference of Zaïre, made to a meeting of "Missio" in Aachen, West Germany. In responding to the question of why the results of the Synod had disappointed him, the bishop responded with three reasons: "First, the World Church and the Holy See should have explicitly recognized our efforts to confirm a truly local church", including an Africanization of the christian message; "Our second request was the recognition of our responsibility for everything that concerns inculturation. In other words, we must decentralize ecclesial competence, especially in respect to inculturation", ... "Our third request was the need to deepen theological research in Africa with the purpose of coming to a better understanding of the plan of God. Such an investigation is needed so that people will not be burdened any more than what may be necessary according to the will of God"[90]. These statements by Bishop Kaseba could be summed up in the concept of a need for the Africanization of the pastoral care of marriage.

There were a number of observers who had anticipated a kind of "objective" alliance to develop between the conservative powers from the Roman curia on the one hand and the bishops from the Third World on the other, with the result that the representatives of Western christianity would find themselves in a certain isolation. This could lead to the formation of a common "anti-Western front" with respect to the main lines of Church teaching in conjugal morality. Already during the Synod,

87. Reported by J. P. MANIGNE, *art. cit.*, p. 38.
88. Cf. E. FRANCHINI, *art. cit.*, p. 479, n. 1.
89. Cf. *Archief van de Kerken* 36 (1981) c. 130.
90. Cf. *Dem Menschen nicht unnötige Lasten aufbürden*, in *Katholische Nachrichten Agentur* 11 (3 April 1981) 2.

some "influential voices" from the Third World reacted against this attempt. The interventions of Cards. Lorscheider (Brazil) and Zoungrana (Upper Volta) and of Bishops Iteka (Tanzania) and Fernandez (India) sought to analyze this connection. At the end of the Synod it appears even clearer that the alliance was nothing more than a pure image. After the closing Homily of John-Paul II, there was little doubt that the expectations of the young churches with respect to inculturation and ecclesial autonomy would not be realized.

B. A Meaningful Enrichment

For some, it will surely sound paradoxical to speak about a meaningful enrichment in connection with the 1980 Synod. Yet it is our conviction that a process of maturation has affected the bishops of the world in respect to questions concerning marriage and the family that is attributable to the formation of opinion taking place because of that Synod. This is irrespective of both the Propositions and the apostolic exhortation which constitute the official results of the gathering.

It is clearly evident that the cultural diversity that characterizes the experience of marriage and family formation in the *oikumene*, the whole of the "inhabited world", has hardly ever been so well articulated as it was through the contributions of the local churches (first week) and during the exchange of ideas in the smaller groups (second week). As has been said repeatedly, amidst all human experience that the Church designates as sacramental, there is none more rooted in the cultural identity of peoples than marriage. Thus, the remarkable intervention of Card. Razafirmahatratra (Madagascar) can be seen as a summary of the requests of the African bishops that christian marriage finally be rooted in specific cultural traditions and in the common experience of Black Africa. Inculturation demands dealing with serious tensions between anthropological, socio-cultural and theological reflections. In the name of the episcopal conference of Madagascar, the speaker underscored three factors which are of decisive importance in harmonizing christian marriage with the experience of marriage in African cultural tradition: the importance of progeny in the ratification of traditional marriage, the fact that marriage is a bond between two extended families, and the manner in which the establishment of marriage takes a period of time. Finally, the Cardinal put forth the recommendation of his episcopal conference: "May the next Synod of Bishops — or the next Synod — take inculturation as its principle theme"[91].

It would also be appropriate at this point to recall the Brazilian bishops' indictment of social structures that make marriage impossible

91. The complete text can be found in J. PONTIN (ed.), *Aujourd'hui la famille*, pp. 92-95.

for masses of poor people and their rejection of the description of the family as the basic cell of society as a false romanticism. But the experience of marriage in a social context which is more typical of the older churches belongs just as realistically to the cultural diversity of the *oikumene*. This was certainly not forgotten in the Synod and was unequivocally one of the factors to be taken into account. If the young churches made an appeal for an appropriate inculturation, the representatives of the older sectors of christianity were not doing anything very different when they referred to the widespread use of contraception as part of the contemporary lifestyle and when they spoke of the growing numbers of baptized but non-believing persons who were content with civil marriage and valued it as something more than concubinage[92]. If openness to the socio-cultural context is positively valued, it will have to be valid in all directions and for all parts of the world. This is a clear gain of the Synod on marriage and the family.

But there is another aspect of the many sided issue of inculturation that should be pointed out. The change of accent that took place during the episcopal meeting with respect to the family being the principle theme should also be considered positively. As was pointed out earlier, the original intention of John-Paul II sought to give particular attention to the function of the family in a social order that was was caught up in a crisis situation. It was the bishops who brought forth the pastoral needs of marriage and the family, those with which they were being confronted daily, and who changed the general direction of the Synod in the process. In the same line, the majority of bishops went even one step further, in fact they requested that pastoral concerns should be given priority in ecclesial law and in doctrinal theorizing. It should thus be considered a further positive result that most of the bishops present strove to situate the larger problems within a proper (pastoral) scale of priorities[93].

It was also no small progression to demand that pastoral perspectives be given priority: thus the primary value of spirituality was underscored instead of normativity. Connected with this was the concern of many participants for a renewal of moral theology based upon the givens of the experience of married couples. Thus, Archbishop Danneels (Belgium) drew attention to the fact that the roots of the contemporary crisis are found not in immorality but in anxiety. Many people today fear the future with the result that parenthood, faithfulness and love itself have entered into a crisis.

---

92. Before leaving Rome, the French bishops at the Synod released a statement that emphasized their continued interest in the "burning issues" of the Synod. Referring to one of these, namely the marriage of marginal believers, they expressed their conviction that "Le Synode a posé là, vigoureusement, une question qui ne pourra pas rester sans réponse". Cf. *Osservatore Romano* (French ed.) 31 (4 Nov. 1980), p. 7.

   93. Cf. E. FRANCHINI, *art. cit.*, pp. 479 & 484.

In the course of his remarkable press conference, Archbishop Martini spoke of the need to choose a way that would be biblical, prophetic and personalist, because christianity, which is a spirit rather than a law, will not allow itself to be confined by normativity but rather should be directed toward the proclamation of values[94]. In almost all of the discussion groups, the renewal of moral theology was brought up in the sense of a more positive reorientation and as a spiritual mandate. Most of the bishops rejected the position of the "classical" perspectives that coupled the notions of the absoluteness of the law and the christian ideal with the greatest mercifulness toward sinners. The real question was why and how to practice mercifulness without it leading to a true schizophrenia between the goals to be reached and the possibility of realizing them. This gap was described by Bishop Jullien (France) as a "dangerous lacuna"[95]. In this perspective, the majority of bishops repeatedly expressed their preference for a further investigation into the organic totality of the *message* in the light of *experience* (including the experience of the Eastern Churches). The tendencies implicit in this kind of investigation were concretely embodied in two areas: the judgment on contraception and the pastoral care of the divorced-remarried.

It cannot be denied that the official procedure of the Synod resulted in the loss of much, if not most, of the priceless contributions of the local churches and the tendencies to initiate renewal in moral theology. Still, it is our conviction that the message was not wasted on the majority of participants and that this formation of consensus will have lasting value for the representatives of the World Church[96].

C. An Unsolved Ecclesiological Problem

We need to go deeper than the expectations and frustrations that were expressed in respect to the procedure and results of the institution of the Synod. At the root of this malaise lies the uncertainty of the episcopacy about the very foundations of the Synod itself and the precise function to which it is directed. The institution and the statutes of the Synod of Bishops are tightly bound up with the new ecclesiology of Vatican II and

94. *Ibid.*, p. 479.

95. In his intervention of 14 October, Bishop Jullien expressed the opinion that there was still a gap between the Church's response to the question of regulating fertility and the justification of that response: a "dangerous no-man's-land" between formal principles and practical attitudes.

96. It is regrettable that these contributions not only have been neglected by the official leadership of the Synod but also in most private publications dealing with the event. Most reports on the Synod are concerned with the obstacles encountered by the bishops, the expected results and the missed chances. Few have been sufficiently attentive to the contributions of the local churches or brought out the full significance of that phenomenon.

with the endeavor of giving institutional form to the collegiality of bishops.

Nevertheless, it is well known that the divergent conceptions of the bishops of the Second Vatican Council with respect to the precise meaning of collegiality led to some compromised passages in *Lumen gentium*, and later in the additional *Nota Praevia*, that were capable of winning the necessary majority of votes but which mortgaged the constitution with a resultant ambiguity. The history of the Synod's coming into being must be understood against the background of these endeavors and this ambiguity.

A decisive contribution to the image of the Synod of Bishops can be seen as coming forth during the time of Vatican II in the speeches of Patriarch Maximos IV (6 November 1963) and Card. Lecaros (8 November 1963). They expressed themselves at the time in favor of a commission of representative bishops dedicated to becoming "a true holy college". But the conciliar discussions of November 1963 did not appear capable of articularing a clear notion of what might be expected. In the *motu proprio* of 15 September 1965 that officially established the institution of the Synod, it was not explicitly stated that this was aimed at giving form to "collegiality". The text rather refers both to primacy and to the "bond" between the bishops and the pope. In his commentary, Card. Marella called the synod "a sign" of collegiality but not an expression of collegiality in the doctrinal meaning of the word, such as that which takes place in a general council.

The conciliar decree *Christus Dominus* that deals with the office of the bishops in the Church, states in paragraph 5 that, "Bishops from various parts of the world... will render especially helpful assistance to the supreme pastor of the Church in a council to be known by the proper name of Synod of Bishops. Since it will be acting in the name of the entire Catholic episcopate, it will at the same time demonstrate that all the bishops in hierarchical communion share in the responsibility for the universal Church"[97].

Whatever the weal and woe of the renewal of ecclesiology might have been during and after the last council, on the eve of the 1969 Synod (which would be expressly devoted to the lived experience of collegiality) there existed on all sides a renewed interest in the real meaning of the

---

97. In his commentary on this passage, W. ONCLIN, in *La charge pastorale des évêques* (Unam Sanctam, 74), Paris, 1969, 87-101, p. 94, offered the following thoughts. "Destiné à apporter une aide efficace au Pasteur suprême dans le gouvernement de l'Église, ce synode n'est pas à strictement parler un organe du collège des évêques, apte à poser au nom du collège des actes de nature collégiale. Il est plutôt un organe de pouvoir qu'exerce le Souverain Pontife, qu'il est appelé à assister dans l'accomplissement de sa tâche propre de chef du collège. Néanmoins ce synode, composé d'evêques choises dans l'episcopat universel, est le signe manifeste de la sollicitude de tous les évêques vis-à-vis de l'Église tout entière et de leur responsabilité à l'égard de l'Église universelle".

Synod. The open exchange of views on this issue served as a proof of the extent to which notions about the Synod remained alive among ecclesiologists. At the opening session of the 1969 meeting Paul VI delivered an initial speech that awakened a great deal of expectation for those who wished for a better translation of the notion of collegiality in ecclesiastical institutions. Among other things, the Pope declared, "When the Council, therefore, expressed its basic spirit, that the bishops are the rightful successors of the Apostles and that they form a special college, chosen and brought into life by Christ, it again seems good to take up the work and the idea of *collegial character* as having particular reference to the college of bishops"[98]. But despite this impressive speech, from which we have taken only one short quote, there was no definitive solution in sight.

In the years that followed the 1969 Synod, it seems very evident that the ecclesial-theological situation of the Synod remains unclear and that this lack of clarity continues to influence the post-conciliar institution of the Synod[99]. It is truly a question of the *unsolved ecclesiological problem of Vatican II* as it has been summarized in the title of an article by Yves Congar[100].

Without falling into a simplistic optimism, it is nonetheless sure that we can still search for future opportunities for the Synod of Bishops. It appears to us that in the coming decades the Synod can come to maturity if a certain number of conditions are fulfilled. There is first the condition that its doctrinal foundation should finally receive a much broader base in the line of an ecclesiology of *communio*. Then there is the condition that the Synod should develop a more precise consciousness of the real demands that are placed upon it by such an ecclesiology. Finally, there is the condition that the institutional means, which should be made available to the world episcopacy, will be more in accord with the conscious, lived experience of collegiality.

In a word, the Synod of Bishops will find the true meaning of its existence and fully exercise its function only when the "ecclesiological problem" of the post-Vatican II era has been solved.

---

98. Cf. *Katholiek Archief* 24 (1969) c. 1048.

99. A typical example of this lack of clarity was expressed at the end of the 1971 Synod. Just two days before the close of this meeting, it was impressed upon the bishops that they were not called together in the first place to produce a document either for the world or for the Church as a whole. It was then suggested that they were only expected to offer advice for the pope. This unexpected clarification resulted in the already prepared text being completely changed in orientation at the eleventh hour. Cf. P. HEBBLETHWAITE, *The Future of the Synod*, in *The Month* 223 (1972) 3-8.

100. Cf. Y. CONGAR, *Un problème ecclésiologique non résolu: le rapport entre le pouvoir papal et le pouvoir épiscopal*, in *La Croix* (19 Sept. 1969) 1-3.

AN ANALYSIS OF THE MAJOR TEXTS OF THE SYNOD

by

Joseph A. Selling

I. GENERAL INTRODUCTION

A. The Theological Background

The Fifth General Synod of Bishops, held at Rome from 26 September to 25 October 1980, should not be looked upon as having occurred in a vacuum. This can be taken in at least three senses, the last of which will be the main concern of the present study. The first sense would situate the Synod as the culmination of a process which took place over a year and a half prior to the actual meeting of bishops in Rome. In preparation for that event, the General Secretariate for the Synod drew up a document known as the *Lineamenta* in March 1979 and sent it to all the bishops of the world for their study and response[1]. After receiving and studying the bishops' reactions to the *Lineamenta*, the Secretariate proposed another document, known as the *Instrumentum laboris*, in June 1980 which would serve as a vehicle for discussion at the synodal meeting itself[2]. While all this was going on, a number of national and regional bishops' conferences organized local synods, conventions or surveys in order to collect information and raise awareness of the topic to be discussed at the Roman Synod, namely "The Role of the Christian Family in the Modern World"[3]. Thus, while subscribing neither to a so-called democratic process nor to a simplistic notion of consensus, one

1. *De muneribus Familiae Christianae in mundo hodierno (ad usum conferentiarum episcopalium)*, Vatican City, 1979, 50 pages. An English translation of this document can be found in *The Role of the Family in the Modern World*, in *Origins* 9 (1979) 113-128. The entire text of the *Lineamenta* will be designated *Lin.*

2. *De muneribus Familiae Christianae in mundo hodierno : Instrumentum laboris ad usum Sodalium Quinti Coetus Generalis*, Vatican City, 16 June 1980, 88 pages. Of the three parts of this text, only Part One, *De familiae statu in mundo hodierno*, par. 9-26, was published in English as *The 1980 Synod on the Family*, in *Origins* 10 (1980) 225-233. The Introduction to the text, par. 1-8, can be found at least in part in the marginal notes of the same text. The entire text of the *Instrumentum laboris* will be designated IL.

Both the *Lineamenta* and the *Instrumentum laboris* were published in their entirety in the appendices of G. CAPRILE, *Il Sinodo dei Vescovi: quinta Assemblea Generale (26 settembre-25 ottobre 1980)*, Rome, 1982. The texts published there even reproduce the indentical page format of the originals so that *Lineamenta*, pp. 3-45, are congruent with Caprile, pp. 615-657; *Instrumentum laboris*, pp. 3-83, are congruent with Caprile, pp. 658-738. The appendices of that volume contain much valuable information, such as a list of all the bishops who attended the Synod (pp. 782-792). However, Caprile does not include the text of the 43 Propositions.

3. This is a general statement which must be taken broadly. Neither did every episcopal conference engage in public dialogue nor did those who searched out or created greater awareness on the topic do so in the same way. Nevertheless, it seems safe to say that the 206 bishops of the Fifth General Synod were better informed on the topic to be discussed from a pastoral point of view than in previous Synods.

can characterize the 1980 Synod as the coming together of bishops from all over the world representing their local churches and attempting to reflect upon the teaching of the Catholic Church on this vital topic.

The second and much weaker sense of seeing the Synod as only one part of a much larger historical process is the claim made by Pope John-Paul II that the 1980 discussion on the family should be seen in the context of the previous Synods of 1971, 1974 and 1977, the topics of which respectively were priesthood and world justice, evangelization and catechesis[4]. Though one can see the connection retrospectively, there was no direct attempt to structure the 1980 Synod as a logical progression emanating from the previous discussions. The synodal process itself is not a uniform or even consistent institution in the Church and resembles more of a phenomenon in search of identity[5]. Since Vatican II, the bishops and the Church have been trying to understand concepts like collegiality and consensus, themselves hardly new or untraditional, and to construct a process for working those ideas out in a more or less formal manner. It appears fair to say that each of the five General Synods, and especially the Extraordinary Synod of 1969 on authority, were unique events only loosely connected through their titles, membership and place of occurrence[6].

The third and theologically much more significant historical context for the 1980 Synod is the entire tradition of the Church's teaching on marriage and the family, primarily that of the last one hundred years and especially the fifteen years of what some call the post-conciliar era. The teaching of the Second Vatican Council, "On Fostering the Dignity of Marriage and the Family", in *Gaudium et spes*, Part II, Chapter I, can be seen as a climax in the historical process of a theological evolution[7]. That

4. Cf. John-Paul II, *Closing Homily to the Synod*, par. 5, in *Origins* 10 (1980) 325-329, p. 327; and the apostolic exhortation *Familiaris consortio*, par. 2, in *AAS* 74 (1982) 81-191, p. 82 and in *Origins* 11 (1981) 437-468, p. 439. The text of *Familiaris consortio* will be designated FC.

5. The Synod was set up as an institution by Pope Paul VI in his motu proprio *Apostolica sollicitudo*, 15 Sept. 1965; cf. *AAS* 57 (1965) 775-780. The motu proprio, which was revised by an ordo of 8 Dec. 1966 by Card. Cicogniani, then Secretary of State, and revised again on 19 June 1967 (cf. G.H. WILLIAMS, *The Mind of John-Paul II: Origins of his Thought and Action*, New York, 1981), put forth the mechanics for an ordinary and an extraordinary (1969) Synod but did not go further in elaboration upon the event itself. The Synod was set up to be a continuous process in the post-conciliar period for implementing and applying the decisions of the Second Vatican Council, especially in their pastoral aspects.

6. An interesting re-reading of post-conciliar events up to 1979 can be found in J. GROOTAERS, *De onverwachte wending*, Beveren-Melsele, 1981. This text has been translated into French and Italian (see Bibliography).

7. *The Pastoral Constitution on the Church in the Modern World, Gaudium et spes*, Part II, Chapter I, par. 47-52, taken from W. M. ABBOTT (ed.), *The Documents of Vatican II*, New York, 1966. The official, Latin text of this document found in *AAS* 58 (1966) 1025-1115, pp. 1066-1074, should be taken to be the primary source since translations can differ

climax did not occur overnight or unexpectedly, as it were, but can be traced to the seminal elements present in papal teaching on marriage since Leo XIII's *Arcanum divinae sapientiae* (10 February 1880).

The encyclical of Leo XIII on christian marriage can be said to be the first specific papal document to teach in that area. Much like his famous *Rerum novarum* (15 May 1891) which "began" the elaboration of the Church's social teaching as such, *Arcanum* was a statement about marriage emanating from a traditional and predictable world view and dealing with problems specific to the Western European world at the time. Similar to the development of social doctrine as well, is the fact that progress beyond this point was slow and at first almost imperceptible. The next major step would take place only fifty years later with the issue of Pope Pius XI's *Casti connubii* (31 December 1930) [8].

It is possible, though hardly a consensus opinion, to consider *Casti connubii* as an encyclical written to celebrate the fiftieth anniversary of *Arcanum*. It is more accurate to say that this document was written in direct response to the Lambeth Conference of 1930 in which the Anglican bishops allowed, however cautiously, for the use of some contraceptive practices as a means of achieving responsible parenthood [9]. Pius XI rejected that position in the strongest of terms and referred to the use of contraception as "grave sin". However, in order to substantiate his position, the Pope took pains to elaborate what he considered to be the entirety of the Roman Catholic teaching on marriage [10]. The resultant synthesis can be said to be the departure point for understanding the Church's teaching and it is from this period that we begin to see further evolution in the theology of marriage and the moral evaluation of conjugal activity.

considerably. Cf. J. SELLING, *Re-reading Gaudium et spes on Marriage and the Family*, in *Louvain Studies* 8 (1980) 82-94. The text of *Gaudium et spes* will be designated GS.

8. *AAS* 22 (1930) 539-592.

9. Cf. A. DE WOLF, *Lambeth 1930 over huwelijk en contraceptiva*, in *ETL* 48 (1972) 509-541.

10. The teaching of Pius XI in *Casti connubii* is not without its own ambiguity. While the encyclical recounts the doctrine of Augustine, it inadvertently contained two passages which call into question the hierarchy of the ends of marriage:

This (conjugal faith), however, which is most aptly called by St. Augustine the "faith of chastity" blooms more freely, more beautifully and more nobley, when rooted in the more excellent soil; the love of husband and wife which prevades all the duties of married life and holds pride of place in Christian marriage. (*AAS*, pp. 547-548)
This mutual inward molding of a husband and wife, this determined effort to perfect each other can, in a very real sense, be said to be the chief reason and purpose of matrimony, provided martimony be looked at not in the restricted sense as instituted for the proper conception and education of the child, but more widely as the blending of life as a whole and the mutual interchange of sharing thereof. (*AAS*, pp. 548-549)

Cf. J. SELLING, *A Closer Look at the Text of Gaudium et spes on Marriage and the Family*, in *Bijdragen* 43 (1982) 30-48, pp. 43-35.

The fifty years between *Casti connubii* and the 1980 Synod can be broken into four periods. The first of these extends from 1930 to 1951, the year of Pope Pius XII's famous *Address to the Midwives*[11]. During this period, a fundamental questioning took place with respect to the doctrine of the hierarchy of the ends of marriage. Whereas Pius XI, in Part I of *Casti connubii*, simply repeated the Augustinian doctrine on the ends of marriage, Pius XII, in admitting the licitness of periodic continence "for serious reasons", effectively weakened the old natural law approach to conjugal morality and unknowingly highlighted a basic ambiguity in the traditional teaching[12]. On the one hand, it was admitted that not only was procreation unnecessary to justify the pursuit of sexual intercourse in marriage but also that this traditional "primary end" of marriage could be intentionally *excluded*, even from the whole of married life, for serious reasons. On the other hand, this effective demotion of the importance of the procreative end in conjugal morality led to a greater emphasis on the so-called "secondary end" of promoting the conjugal relationship itself. Regardless of his repeated attempts to reiterate the traditional teaching, Pius XII had drawn attention to the inadequacy of the Augustinian doctrine. Marriage could no longer be explained simply in terms of natural law. Indeed a much more theological approach was necessary to deal with conjugal morality and especially to elaborate a more meaningful theology of marriage as a sacrament. While this need to rethink the whole of the Church's teaching on marriage lingered implicitly during the remainder of Pius XII's pontificate, it became a major issue in the work of the Second Vatican Council.

The second period in the evolution of the theology of marriage, therefore, is from 1951 to 1965, the year of the promulgation of *Gaudium et spes* (GS). With the doctrine of the hierarchy of ends at least implicitly placed in question, a search began to restate theological expression in more contemporary terms. The first place to look was the so-called "personalist" view of marriage which had already begun in the 1930's and centered around the controversial book of Dr. Herbert Doms[13]. While both Pius XI and XII rejected this "new" interpretation, its appeal was inevitable to the exponents of *aggiornamento*. Regardless of any speculations about natural law or "ontological" order, both faith and

11. *AAS* 53 (1951) 835-854.

12. Cf. J. SELLING, *Moral Teaching, Traditional Teaching and Humanae vitae*, in *Louvain Studies* 7 (1978) 24-44, pp. 34-37.

13. H. DOMS, *Du sens et de la fin du mariage*, Paris, 1937, was translated from the original, *Vom Sinn und Zweck der Ehe*, Breslau, 1935. This book cannot be taken as a manifesto or even an outline for the reflection upon marriage in the 1960's. In fact, some of the author's speculation is very conservative and traditionalist. What is more important, however, is the historical fact that a "personalist" school of thought was already substantially developing in the 1930's and was bound to have an impact upon theological consensus.

experience testified to the fact that the "essence" of marriage is an interpersonal relationship based upon (conjugal) love. This traditional yet ever new insight is the starting point for expressing the sacramentality of marriage in terms of the covenantal relation between God and His People, Christ and the Church. But the restatement found in GS could hardly be said to stop at the expression of sacramentality. The short, opening chapter of Part II of GS virtually redefined the whole of the Church's teaching on marriage and the family and, by implication, called into question the basis for the entirety of sexual as well as conjugal morality. Indeed the theological evolution which took place in the thirty-five years between *Casti connubii* and GS is undeniable[14]. It remains necessary, however, to explicitate the major points made in GS in order to appreciate what happened in the fifteen years to follow[15].

The principle points are:

1. the positive evaluation of human work in the world and the worthiness of human institutions;
2. the recognition of the plurality and worth of various forms of marriage and the family;
3. the use of biblical and theological language to describe marriage as a "covenant or irrevocable personal consent";
4. the relegation of the doctrine of the hierarchy of ends to a mere historical reference;
5. an understanding of God's creative intention (Providence) as dynamic mystery and not static natural law;
6. the conception of fidelity and lastingness as characteristics, not preconditions, of conjugal love in service to the family;
7. the analogy between divine and conjugal love as illustrative, not constitutive, of sacramentality;
8. the priority of speaking of conjugal love over procreation in marriage;

---

14. Cf. L. JANSSENS, *Chasteté conjugale selon l'encyclique Casti connubii et suivant la Constitution pastorale Gaudium et spes*, in *ETL* 42 (1966) 513-554.

15. Commentaries on GS,47-52 are multiple and of various quality. First, there are those which are very close to the original such as B. HÄRING's commentary in H. VORGRIMLER (ed.), *Commentary on the Documents of Vatican II*, vol. 5, New York, 1969, 225-245. Accompanying these, there are more technical issues treated in single articles such as V. HEYLEN, *La Note 14 dans la Constitution pastorale, Gaudium et spes, P. II, Ch. 1, N. 14*, in *ETL* 42 (1966) 555-566. Then there are those contributions which were occasioned by the controversy over *Humanae vitae* such as P. DELHAYE, *L'encyclique Humanae vitae et l'enseignement de Vatican II sur le mariage et la famille (Gaudium et spes)*, in *Bijdragen* 29 (1968) 351-368; and the contrasting point of view in P. FELICI, *Della Costituzione pastorale 'Gaudium et spes' alla enciclica paolina 'Humanae vitae'*, in *Osservatore Romano* 108 (10 Oct. 1968) 3. This last article is the second of a three part series appearing in the *Osservatore Romano* on 7 Sept., 10 and 19 Oct. 1968.

9. the omission of procreation in the discussion of conjugal love and the evaluation of sexual acts as expressive of love, noble and worthy in themselves;

10. the restatement of chastity as a life task related to conjugal love and not purely a sexual criterion;

11. seeing procreation as a gift and the crown of both conjugal love and marriage and not the purpose, end or justification of sexual relations;

12. the exercise of responsible parenthood is based upon a mutual, contextualized decision of the spouses in conscience and should be considered independently from the technical execution of that decision;

13. in making conscience decisions in the sight of God, a couple should be attentive to the teaching of the Church as it interprets divine law in light of the gospel;

14. the recognition of the possibility of a real conflict in harmonizing the demands of responsible parenthood with the safeguarding of conjugal love;

15. a clear distinction between dishonorable solutions to the problem of exercising responsible parenthood and the regulation of procreative potential;

16. the affirmation of the specificity of human sexuality and a rejection of biological norms governing sexual activity;

17. the objective criteria for making responsible moral decisions with respect to determining and directing human activity are based upon "the nature of the human person and their acts";

18. the teaching of the Magisterium with respect to contraception prior to the Pastoral Constitution was in a state of doubt and remained an open question;

19. the social dimensions of marriage and the family must be appreciated and there is a genuine need to protect and promote this institution in ways which are socially, culturally and spiritually appropriate;

20. the equality of man and woman based upon their dignity as persons created in the image of God.

From this point on, one could say that theological reflection upon the role and meaning of marriage and the family would never be the same[16].

The third phase in the historical evolution is the shortest, lasting less than three years, and was almost entirely concerned with the specific question of the means for regulating fertility in light of post-Vatican II theology. During this period we find the work of the Pontifical Birth Control Commission (PBCC)[17] and the personal struggle of Pope

16. For a fuller explanation and sometimes needed justification see J. SELLING, *Twenty Significant Points in the Theology of Marriage and the Family Present in the Teaching of Gaudium et spes*, in *Bijdragen* 42 (1981) 412-441.

17. The term we are using here, PBCC, is based upon a popularized name for what was actually known as the "Commission for the Study of Population, Family and Births". The

Paul VI to deal with the issue and finally publish his encyclical *Humanae vitae*[18]. In one way this can be looked upon as the first step in the post-Vatican II era to deal with the changes which had taken place in the Church's teaching in this area. But such an evaluation would be unfair and historically shortsighted. It was too soon. The teaching of the Council had not yet had time to ferment or come to fruition. Although the influence of the elements of renewal played an important role in mitigating the papal teaching on contraception, Paul VI could not accept some of the changes in ideas which were taking place. In the end he took a "safe" position[19], giving honorary credit to the teaching of his predecessors Pius XI and XII, and in his own way marking progress in the evolution by avoiding the condemnations of the former and broadly interpreting the teaching of the latter. There is substantially nothing new in HV, but there were unmistakable, reactionary reminiscences.

To understand what is meant here we must pause in this development to give an account of a little known but important event. At the end of November 1965, during the final redaction of the text of GS, four *modi* (suggestions) were submitted to the Mixed Commission for GS by the then Vatican Secretary of State, Card. Cicognani. These *modi* did not come through the regular channels but were in the end treated in the same way as all the other written suggestions submitted by the council fathers. They were acknowledged to emanate from the papal office but their exact authorship has never been revealed[20]. It has been speculated that they were drawn up by a "minority" group of theologians, but they amost certainly had the sponsorship of Pope Paul VI. In any case, the style and the significance of the four *modi* would resurface at a later historical time. An echo of the thought contained in them has already been detected in the papal encyclical of 1968 and has been documented[21]. Our own purpose here is to bring forth the ideas found in the four

history of this changing group, as well as the commission(s) for GS, can be found in J. GROOTAERS, *Histoire de deux commissions: éléments d'information, points de repère*, in H. et L. BEULENS-GIJSEN et J. GROOTAERS, *Mariage catholique et contraception*, Paris, 1968, 140-272.

18. *AAS* 60 (1968) 481-503. The encyclical *Humanae vitae* will be designated HV.

19. This is discussed more fully in J. SELLING, *Moral Teaching*, pp. 40-44.

20. Neither the existence nor substance of the four papal *modi* are a matter of hearsay, but can be documented. Cf. art. cit. by Heylen and Delhaye above in n. 15. The *Expensio modorum* for GS, Part II, 3 Dec. 1965, which deals with the final text and explains how all the last suggestions were handled by the Mixed Commission, can be found in the *Acta Synodalia Sacrosancti Concilii Oecumenici Vaticani II*, IV, VII (Vatican City, 1978), 470-509. It states, "In Expensione Modorum sub numeris 5, 71, 98, et 107, Commissio Generalis Mixta sedule et reverenter ratione habuit consiliorum Summi Pontificis, quae ei, mediante E. mo Cardinali a Secretaria Status, transmissa fuerunt" (p. 509).

21. Delhaye, art. cit., has treated the issue at length and suggested that the Mixed Commission achieved "balance" in dealing with the *modi* such that different points of view were represented in the text of GS. In fact, while various perspectives are recognized ("non

suggestions in order to consider their possible role in the 1980 Synod and its documents.

The four *modi* were reactions to the draft text of GS, dated 14 November 1965, and the page and line numbers contained therein refer to the original copy of that draft. They were[22]:

1. Pag. 5, lin. 22: Artes Anticonceptionales debent habere mentionem simul cum referentia ad Casti Connubii, ita ut textus jam legatur: "siquidem polygamia, divortii lue, amore sic dicto libero *artibus* anti-conceptionalibus, aliisve *deformationibus* obscurantur". Cfr. Pius XI, Litt. Encycl. *Casti Connubii*: AAS 22 (1930) pp. 559 et 560. Denz. 2239-2240 (3716-3717).
2. Pag. 8, lin. 11: Omittatur verbum "etiam", atque brevis haec enuntiatio in extremam periodum addatur, ad. lin. 13: "Filli [sic] sunt praestantissimum matrimonii donum et ad ipsorum parentum bonum maxime conferunt".
3. Pag. 9, lin. 28-29: Haec dicantur: "Quibus principiis *innixi (docemus)* filiis Ecclesiae in procreatione regulanda vias inire *non licere*, quae a Magisterio *improbatae sunt vel improbentur*", vel: "Quibus principiis, *innixis*, filiis Ecclesiae in procreatione regulanda vias inire *non licet*, quae a Magisterio *improbatae sunt vel improbentur*". Praetera in adnotatione de duobus praestantissimis de hac materia documentis mentio flat [sic], scilicet: de Encyclicis Litteris "Casti Connubii", AAS 22 (1930). Cfr. locos in Denz. Schon. 3726-3718 [sic]; ac de oratione a Pio XII ad obstretrices habita: AAS 43 (1951).
4. Pag. 9, lin. 15: Haec addantur: "...non posse, sed ad difficultates superandos omnino requii ut coniuges castitatem conjugalem sincero animo colant".

The method which was used to handle the *modi* and the final decision as to their incorporation into the text has been documented in the *Expensio modorum* (EM). However, because the four were treated as any other of the suggestions submitted, the EM does not specifically single them out or give the precise source in its exposition. The content is present there, but it must be searched for. Obviously, when one knows the original text of the papal *modi* their isolation is much easier. For purposes which will be relevant to our future exposition, we will give a brief description of how the Commission dealt with the *modi*. More detailed accounts can be found in the sources given.

---

posthabitis ceteris matrimonii finibus"), the theology of marriage presented in GS is consistent and clearly different from that suggested in the four *modi*.

22. Cf. J. GROOTAERS, *Histoire de deux commissions*, pp. 175-176; and V. HEYLEN, *art. cit.*, p. 560, who also gives the text of *modus* 3 listed here.

1. The attempt to introduce into GS, 47 a condemnation of "contraceptive practices" as being one of the threats against conjugal love (after listing "excessive self-love and the worship of pleasure") was rejected for two reasons. First, the use of such broad terminology would imply a condemnation of the use of periodic continence. Secondly, it had been decided that the council document would not concretely address the moral evaluation of any methods for regulating fertility. That question was left open for the further investigation of the PBCC. The resulting compromise was the cause for the present text listing "illicit practices against generation" (*illicitis usibus contra generationem*) as something which "profanes conjugal love". The meaning of this phrase is intentioally vague but the commentary clearly points out that "contraceptive practices" were not under discussion at this point. Note also that the suggested footnote was not included. Therefore, it seems appropriate to read this phrase as meaning any unwarrented attack on human life from its very beginning (cf. GS, 51), especially abortion which the Council considered incompatible with the true meaning of conjugal love.

2. With respect to the use of the word "also" (*etiam*) in the opening sentence of GS, 50, the Commission agreed to let it drop. At the same time, however, they introduced a phrase to the effect that speaking about procreation was "not making the other purposes of matrimony of less account" (*non posthabitis ceteris matrimonii finibus*). The sentence to be introduced as second for the paragraph was accepted but introduced with the word "therefore" (*sane*) which considerably weakened the impact of the repetition. A good understanding of this *modus* and its response will prevent one from making the mistake of thinking that the use of the phrase "purposes of matrimony" (*matrimonii finibus*) was indicative of the fact that the Council was still thinking in terms of the traditionalist doctrine of the "ends of marriage" or the "ends of sexual intercourse". Ironically, the use of the word *fines* here serves to prevent the thought from falling back into that doctrine and erases any notion of the conciliar teaching implying a hierarchy of ends.

3. The two parts of this *modus*, concerning the main paragraph of GS, 51, were dealt with very carefully. The first, dealing with the expansion of an already existing sentence, was found very much wanting. At the end of the sentence, with respect to "methods which the Magisterium finds blameworthy", the change in the verb (*improbantur*) was rejected because both suggestions were unacceptable. The use of the perfect tense (*improbatae sunt*) would imply a literal repetition of all previous teaching, including that against the practice of periodic continence as well as the condemnations which were felt to be still open to question (hence the existence of the PBCC). The use of a subjunctive mood (*improbentur*) would result in an entirely speculative statement

reducing magisterial teaching to the level of mere opinion. Then, while retaining this original subordinate verb, the suggested change in the main idea, strengthening the prohibition from "should not use" or "should avoid" (*ne vias ineant*) to "may not use" (eventually: *vias inire non licet*), was accepted but balanced with a further specification of the scope of magisterial teaching, already found in GS, 50, to be limited to some connection with interpreting Scripture[23].

The second part of this *modus* includes a suggested footnote on the teachings of Popes Pius XI and XII condemning contraception. The resulting addition came to be the famous footnote 14 of GS, 51[24]. The Commission accepted the note from the *modus* which would serve historical purposes. But it went further in order to bring to light the real contemporary situation. Thus, it added a reference to the speech of Pope Paul VI on 23 June 1964 in which he officially announced the existence of the PBCC and expressed the opinion that the former teachings would not change "at least so long as we do not feel obliged in conscience to change them"[25]. Following these references there appear two sentences. The first notes the handing over of this specific question to the Pontifical Commission for further study and defers the final solution to the Pope himself. The second states that "With the doctrine of the Magisterium in this state, this holy Synod does not intend to propose immediately concrete solutions"[26]. It is clear that the perspective present in the

23. GS,50, in teaching about responsible parenthood as the moral decision whether or not to engage in (further) procreation, had advised that *one* of the sources to which Catholics should pay particular attention is the Magisterium "as it interprets divine law in the light of the gospel". That is, the primary source of inspiration is the divine law, not "natural law", the notion of which was entirely avoided in the text. Curiously, with respect to the text in question here, the EM (at 107, pp. 38-39 in the original) almost seems to contradict itself in the commentary for GS,51. At one point, 107, c, six bishops had suggested that the reference to the Magisterium be qualified once again with the words "which attends to the interpretation of divine law (*"quod Legem divinam interpretari curat"*). In response, 107, R, c, this suggestion is rejected on the grounds that "such a repetition does not seem necessary". At the same place, however, in 107, e, which suggests *"vias inire non licet"* or *"vias inire non possunt"* and evidently represents the text of the papal *modus*, the response, 107, R, e, simply cites the amended sentence as it now stands — along with the repetition of the qualification on magisterial authority which had just been rejected. It appears undoubtable that EM, 107, e was a later addition caused by response to the third *modus* from the papal office. The apparent contradiction was allowed to stand as it was.

24. Cf. V. HEYLEN, *art. cit.*

25. Cf. W. H. SHANNON, *The Lively Debate: Response to Humanae Vitae*, New York, 1970, p. 13.

26. We reproduce the exact text of the official footnote here in full:

"Cf. Pius XI, Litt. Encyl. *Casti Connubii*: A.A.S., 22 (1930), pp. 559-561: DENZ. 2239-2241 (3316-3318); Pius XII, *Allocutio Conventui Unionis Italicae inter Obstetrices*, 29 oct. 1951: A.A.S., 43 (1951), pp. 835-854; Paulus VI, *Allocutio ad E. mos Patres Purpuratos*, 23 inunii 1964: A.A.S., 56 (1964), pp. 581-589. Quaedam quaestiones quae aliis ac diligentioribus investigationibus indigent, iussu Summi Pontificis, Commissioni pro studio

conciliar teaching considered the issue of methods for regulating fertility to be an open question.

4. The introduction of the need for chastity after the observation that "a true contradiction cannot exist between the divine laws pertaining to the transmission of life and those pertaining to the fostering of authentic conjugal love", could have been misread as applying to some rules or divine laws governing sexual behavior in marriage. However, GS, 49 had already put forth a notion of chastity which was dynamic, oriented to the full integration of life in the conjugal relationship, and not restricted to mere sexual-genital behavior. Therefore, while the observation was accepted, it was placed much later in the section, after the observation that "in determining a moral way of acting, spouses must base their decisions on objective criteria, based upon the nature of the human person and their acts, which will preserve the full sense of mutual self-bestowal and human procreation". This task — of aligning particular decisions with an entire conjugal life — could not be accomplished unless the virtue of chastity is sincerely practiced. In this context the nature of the virtue is rightly restored: it is an attitude which accomplishes a reasonable regulation of human activity according to the norm of a fully integrated life-task. It is not reducible to a specific rule for sexual behavior.

In summary of this brief excursus on the four papal *modi*, we can see that at the last minute there was an attempt to introduce a pattern of thought into GS, 47-52 which was ultimately considered to be incompatible with the theology contained in that document as it evolved through the work of Vatican II. In the end, the conciliar document maintained its integrity. But as we shall see, the ideas and those who formulated them would not be lost in history. The first three *modi*, which were changed or altered beyond recognition in GS, implicitly resurfaced in HV and might be traceable to the influence of those representing the "minority" opinion. The fourth received less attention in 1968, but it came to be a misunderstood presupposition at the end of the next decade. It is necessary to remember the events of 1965 in order to understand those of 1980. But first we must return to the historical development leading up to the Synod.

The final redaction of HV can be said to be the result of a struggle between two schools of thought on the theology of marriage and the

populationis, familiae et natalitatis traditae sunt, ut postquam illa munus suum expleverit, S. Pontifex iudicium ferat. Sic stante doctrina Magisterii, S. Synodus solutiones concretas immediate proponere non intendit".

Note that in the opening words of the last sentence there is no comma between *Sic* and *stante*. A last minute attempt to insert a comma here, which would have changed the meaning of the sentence entirely, was stopped through the extreme care which was used to insure that the integrity of the footnote would remain (cf. HEYLEN, *art. cit.*, p. 564).

family and conjugal morality[27]. The encyclical itself, however, rather than being a first step in post-Vatican II renewal as mentioned above, is better seen as the real demise of pre-conciliar thinking. The reactions to HV were overwhelming and, while a certain authority-oriented submission led to an endorsement of its teaching[28], the majority of reactions interpreted, mitigated and, occasionally, completely rejected its conclusions and presuppositions. It is virtually a foregone conclusion that the encyclical has had little if any impact upon the life of the average Catholic in reaching decisions as to the methods for regulating fertility. If anything, the teaching of HV on contraception and sterilization has hightened anxiety among loyal Catholics in that their decisions in conscience differ from the advice given by Pope Paul VI; it has not, however, substantially altered those decisions or enhanced the credibility of the Magisterium in the areas of sexual or conjugal morality. What it did do was to underscore the inadequacy of that teaching not only in the Western, North-Atlantic world but especially in the wider and more populous regions of the Third World[29].

27. Cf. *Postkonziliare Hintergrund einer Enzyklika*, in *Herder Korrespondenz* 22 (1968) 525-536.

28. The implication here is not simply that some accept(ed) HV because it is a papal encyclical, but goes further. One major reason why HV was not strongly rejected in the Third World was because the document was given a "political reading". That is, the "authoritative character" of a papal encyclical could be used to enhance the observation that birth control and contraception were preoccupations of the North Atlantic World, while the moral questions envisioned by the Third World were concerned with the causes, means and results of overpopulation and its control in a social context. In standing up to political forces, which sometimes attempted to violate freedom of conscience and impose programs of family planning and contraception/sterilization, the bishops needed every support possible. Endorsement of HV then was an appeal to one more authoritative support. Cf. J. GROOTAERS, *Humanae vitae et les réactions dans les pays du Tiers Monde*, in *Pour relire Humanae vitae*, Gembroux, 1970, 51-66.

29. To say, as above, that HV was convenient for a "political reading" in the Third World is not the same as saying that its conclusions were morally acceptable. The encyclical could be used to refute "simplistic solutions" to population problems, like widescale sterilization or imposed family planning programs, but it provided no practical solutions for what in reality is an extremely complex phenomenon. The appeal to men of science and the recommendation of periodic continence, a "solution" which will reach frenetic proportions in the 1970's under the sponsorship of Natural Family Planning, is in fact, no solution, or at least one which reflects moral, sociological, and cultural ignorance.

As for the inadequacy of the moral reasoning in HV, this observation should be balanced with an appreciation for the probable reasons why Paul VI wrote and published the encyclical as it is. As already mentioned, and understandable in light of his previous encyclical *Populorum progressio* (1967), Pope Paul had a global picture of the problematic which precluded any simplistic solution. Further, the Pope could not bring himself to speak in such a way as could be interpreted as an endorsement or permission to use contraception. This was caused by the failure to distinguish between moral and pre-moral (ontic) statements. It was further complicated by HV,17's consequentialistic reasoning, the unspoken premise of which is that admission of non-procreative oriented sexual behavior would lead to the breakdown of all sexual morality. This observation is essentially correct

In the broad lines of historical theology, then, HV could be said to represent the end of an era. However, it was not the end of a certain, "minority" school of thought. Those who were responsible for attempting to alter the conciliar teaching and who very nearly caused an ecclesial crisis by supporting the view that *Casti connubii* and HV were solemn, even infallible, teaching were very much convinced of their position. Whether or not this school constitutes a "minority" of theological opinion, it cannot be doubted that their interpretation of the conciliar documents and their argument that HV is fully consistent with GS on these issues has remained a dominant view in some circles. At the risk of being too general, this school of thought might be referred to as "essentialist", holding that moral principles in the area of sexual ethics rest upon the essence of human nature, the purposes of marriage and the structure of the sexual act. Another view, which an apparent "majority" of moral theologians believe formed the inspiration of the theology of GS, might be called "personalist", although interpretations of that word vary rather widely. Obviously, "minority" and "majority" statistics prove little or nothing in determining any given argument.

Coming to the fourth period of this fifty year evolution, we can observe a concerted effort to interpret conciliar teaching in the area of sexual and conjugal morality within a certain "essentialist" perspective. The best example of this trend was the publication of the "Declaration on Certain Questions concerning Sexual Ethics" by the Sacred Congregation for the Doctrine of the Faith (1975)[30]. This document, along with the same Congregation's response to the American episcopate on the issue of sterilization[31], should be read against the background of GS. In paragraph 5 it is asserted that the Council "took particular care to expound the principles and criteria which concern human sexuality in marriage, and which are based upon the finality of the specific function of sexuality". Many would disagree that this is what the Council had taught. There is certainly no reference whatsoever in GS to the "finality of the specific function of sexuality". The use of this phrase is characteristic of essentialist thinking and the argumentation used has often been said to be equivalent to the use of a biological norm in sexual morality[32]. That norm contains a certain attractiveness for moral

but hardly relevant. Finally, of course, there was the authority issue. If Pius XI and XII had condemned contraception, would not its acceptance amount to saying they had been in error?

30. *Declaratio de quibusdam quaestionibus ad sexualem ethicam spectantibus*, sometimes referred to as *Persona humana*, dated 29 Dec. 1975.

31. *Documentum circa sterilizationem in nosocomiis catholicis (Responsa ad quaesita Conferentiae episcopalis Americae septentrionalis)*, Vatican, 1975. Cf. R.A. CcCORMICK, *Sterilization and Theological Method*, in *Theological Studies* 37 (1976) 471-477.

32. Greater theological nuance would call for recognizing the implicit presence of the biological norm in HV as well. This can be substantiated by a demonstration of the priority

reasoning, for it can easily be applied to a broad spectrum of questions including pre-marital sex, homosexual acts and masturbation (Cf. *Persona humana*, 7, 8, & 9 respectively).

It could not and should not be presumed, however, that the resurrection of this thought pattern was a premeditated attempt to undo the accomplishment of Vatican II and rewrite the teaching of GS. We would prefer to think that it grew out of a misunderstanding of that teaching and the assumption that nothing had changed since the pontificate of Pius XII. What occurred was that the practitioners of essentialist theology simply read GS in a very specific way. It appeared to them that if the essentialist approach were abandoned, the implications would be tremendous. Without natural law thinking (the biological norm) the traditional arguments against non-marital and non-coital sexual behavior would collapse. Indeed, this logical reasoning is correct, but a mistake was made in not recognizing that what was called for was not the reinforcement of the traditional answers, but the building of a new sexual and conjugal morality that no longer rested solely upon the biological finality of the sexual faculty. There are many theologians who are in agreement with this assessment and who have already begun to develop a new consensus[33]. Nonetheless, our concern here is for the fourth phase in the theological evolution, namely the functional misunderstanding of

given to "biological processes" (HV,10). But the norm itself is restated under a new name which we will call the "two aspect theory". Briefly, "this doctrine rests upon the indissoluble connection, instituted by God and against which man is not permitted to intervene by his own initiative, between the unitive meaning (*significationem*) and the procreative meaning, both of which are present in the conjugal act" (HV,12). Note that this teaching applies to sexual acts and not marriage as such, that it represents a different approach than that of CC by placing the "end of conjugal fidelity" on an equal footing with the "end of procreation", and that it remains essentially pre-conciliar in assuming that a procreative meaning (*significationem*) is always present. This begs the question, of course, why this meaning can be present in intercourse which is "naturally" infertile while it disappears if the infertility is intentional. The sole answer is that the "procreative meaning" is synonymous with complete, unhindered, heterosexual intercourse resulting in vaginal insemination. The norm of biological function could hardly be more obvious.

33. This new consensus is evident in the recognition of the fact that the teaching of HV does not rest upon convincing arguments. The bishops of the 1980 Synod were keenly aware of this fact and even implicitly aware that the entire theology of marriage needed restatement. Denying this would, of itself, render much of the synodal discussion superfluous.

Some representatives of a different moral approach in this area are: A. GUINDON, *The Sexual Language: An Essay in Moral Theology*, Ottawa, 1976; or, more popularly, A. KOSNIK and others, *Human Sexuality: New Directions in Catholic Thought*, London, 1977. The second of these received a very unfavorable review from the already mentioned Roman Congregation. Cf. *Morality in Sexual Matters: Observations of the Sacred Congregation for the Doctrine of the Faith on the Book 'Human Sexuality'* (*July 13, 1979*), in *The Pope Speaks* 25 (1980) 97-102; and J. SELLING, *A Closer Look at the Text of Gaudium et spes*, pp. 31-39.

the teaching of GS and the attempt to interpret that document in the line of pre-conciliar thought.

Taking HV as a starting point, and the evident need to defend its teaching, essentialism became more and more characteristic of official pronouncements in this area. This does not necessarily apply to the position of Paul VI who appeared satisfied to let the contraception issue stand as it was[34]. Then, in 1978, after the tenth anniversary of the encyclical, Karol Wojtyla, himself the author of a book on love and sexuality[35], became Pope John-Paul II. There was an expectation that a new pope would begin a new era and the evolution in conjugal and sexual morality would move further. However, the thought of John-Paul II appears to be more favorable to the essentialist interpretation of the conciliar texts and his own form of "personalism" lies closer to the pre-conciliar idea of human nature. This would become clear in his regular audiences which became more and more devoted to the topics of marriage, family and sexuality as the time for the Synod drew closer.

Meanwhile, the implications of post-conciliar reflection began to raise new problems. For one, the emphasis upon marriage as an interpersonal relationship began to take effect in the tribunals. A greater number of annulments were being granted, or at least publicized, on the grounds of the inability to contract a really meaningful relationship. This was alarming to Rome. Then, difficult questions about the relationship between faith and marriage as a sacrament began to lead to alternative pastoral practice for those who were baptized but non-practicing Catholics[36]. This inevitably led to a questioning of the meaning of sacramentality itself and the ability to legislate in the matter[37]. Marital indisssolubility had become a controverted issue.

These developments must be coupled with the growing voice of the bishops of the Third World and an increasing awareness of their own particular pastoral problems. Simmering below the Western preoccupation with divorce, contraception, and alternative life-styles, is the issue

34. It seems rather clear that Paul VI recognized the social dimensions of the "birth control issue". While his attitude was pastoral with respect to the contraception question, he envisioned his encyclical HV to be "a defense of human life", a critique of modern man's tendency to impose technological solutions on human problems. Paul VI is more likely to be remembered for HV, while his most important teaching was on social issues.

35. K. WOJTYLA, *Amour et Responsibilité: étude de morale sexuelle*, Paris, 1965. This is a translation of the Polish original *Miłość i odpowiedzialność*, Cracou, 1962.

36. Cf. J. SCHMEISER, *Marriage: New Developments in the Diocese of Autun, France*, in *Église et Théologie* 10 (1979) 369-385.

37. One need only think of the process of revising the Code of Canon Law. Cf. T. GREEN, *The Revised Schema De Matrimonio: Text and Reflections*, in *The Jurist* 40 (1980) 57-127. As for the competence to legislate, cf. S.J. KELLEHER, *Divorce and Remarriage for Catholics? A Proposal for Reform of the Church's Law on Divorce and Remarriage*, Garden City (New York), 1973; and L.G. WRENN, *Marriage — Indissoluble or Fragile?*, in L.G. WRENN (ed.), *Divorce and Remarriage in the Catholic Church*, New York, 1973, 134-149.

of the very nature and theology of marriage and the family itself. The phenomenon of polygamy had been inadequately handled; sexual morality was seen to be irrelevant in situations of social oppression[38]; and the family was under pressure from external, social forces which made the pronouncements of the Magisterium appear idealistic and unrelated to real situations. These pastoral problems needed immediate attention. The question was whether they would be approached as real problems or simply treated with formulae derived from traditional natural law thinking.

Extrinsically, the tendency toward essentialist thinking in official pronouncements was supported by the growth of the Natural Family Planning (NFP) movement[39]. This movement is dedicated to teaching various methods for predicting the fertility phase of the menstrual cycle, especially that developed by the two Australian doctors, the Billings, and asserting that periodic continence is the only morally acceptable method of regulating human fertility. Its appeal to a large number of couples (primarily in the West) is probably attributable to the fact that it promotes conjugal dialogue in sexual matters and allays anxiety for Catholics who have been unable to come to terms with the papal condemnation of contraception. Some would add to this the observation that NFP has developed a naturalistic and/or "ecologically sound" solution to the problem of controlling fertility, but such an argument is

---

38. J. L. SEGUNDO, *A Theology for Artisans of a New Humanity*, v. 5: *Evolution and Guilt*, New York, 1974, is quoted extensively by M. MOHS and P. TURBES MOHS, *A Word from the Home Front: Conscience — with Compassion*, in D. DOHERTY (ed.), *Dimensions of "Human Sexuality"*, Garden City (New York), 1979, 149-169. Two of the passages quoted, pp. 156-158, state:

"Consider the great physical and psychic pressure that sexuality exerts directly on the individual and then consider the general situation of most people on a continent such as Latin America. For the vast majority of the people, sexual pleasure is the only pleasure possible for them. It is the only one compatible with their economic status. It is the only one cheap enough for people who have been deprived of the economic resources to afford others ...

The sexual part of what is called Christian morality has a debilitating impact on overall Christian praxis as well. Man's outlook on sexual matters is in large measure a solitary affair, particularly in the light of the surrounding eroticism of society. Now if his eternal destiny is constantly at stake in his attitude toward sexuality, then Christ's single commandment to love one another must drop into the background and suffer severe distortion. The Christian moral life is an eminently social one designed to create solidarity in society. But it is now devalued and turned into an individual struggle to preserve one's chastity. It is as if chastity were something valid for its own sake instead of being meant to serve the social morality of Christianity. Paul's description of this social morality is completely opposed to the morality currently practiced by average Christians: 'The person who loves his brother has fulfilled the whole of the law'".

39. The primary organ for this movement is *The International Review of Natural Family Planning*, published by the Human Life Center, St. John's University, Collegeville, Minnesota, since 1977.

not only naive[40], it is morally inferior in that it is built upon the presupposition that the means justifies the end. Close attention to NFP proselytizing reveals that virtually no mention is made of attitude, intention or the question of motivation with respect to practicing responsible parenthood. Instead, it is easy to assume that as long as one is not using contraception everything is fine from a moral point of view.

The growth of NFP can hardly be isolated from the mutual support which it enjoys with the Roman Catholic Church. While the movement provides justification for the continued insistence on the "ban on contraception" being taught by hierarchical authority, the Church has given a forum for the movement, baptizing its principles, as it were, and recognizing its leaders. At a conference held in Milan 1978 to celebrate the tenth anniversary of HV, representatives of the movement were prominent and influential[41]. At the 1980 Synod, the exclusive list of 43 "auditores" included the doctors Billings as well as other advocates of NFP, while no dissenting opinion was represented[42]. While much can be said for the "natural" methods of regulating fertility, the movement supporting these methods has grown into an ideological campaign and taken on unproportionate importance. A deeper analysis of its premises and its effects would reveal a situation which would be highly questionable, especially from the pre-conciliar perspective of sexual morality[43].

40. Naturalism is not necessarily equivalent to ecology. The former would presume that natural forces are sufficient to promote human values. In this line of thought, the most natural means of controlling population growth are disease, famine, war and a high infant mortality rate. Informed ecological thinking, however, recognizes that humans have and will continue to intervene in "natural" life cycles and so must take the responsibility and initiative to minimalize the damage done and to compensate for long and short term consequences. Human intervention in sanitation, health care and nutrition lead to an at least temprary acceleration of population growth. The hazards this contains must therefore be countered by regulating human fertility so that a balance is maintained between the size of a population and the *available* resources for sustaining and promoting human life.

41. The conference was held 21-25 June 1978. Cf. A. McCORMACK, *Humanae vitae Today*, in *The Tablet* 232 (1978) 674-676. The two keynote speakers at the conference were G. Martelet and Card. K. Wojtyla.

42. Drs. John and Evelyn Billings were received by the Pope in private audience on 9 Oct. 1980. Cf. *Attività della Santa Sede nel 1980*, Vatican City 1981, p. 600.

43. Cf. J. MARSHALL, *NFP: The Facts*, in *The Tablet* 234 (1980) 1197-1198. The subject of this article is part of the growing debate on whether NFP is really effective as a means of regulating population growth. While its advocates claim that their methods are better than 95 % effective, their statistics are restricted to those who "follow the rules". Contrarily, one can ask about the effectiveness rate with respect to the entire group of people who have been exposed to and taught the NFP techniques. The dominant fact is that NFP is a method highly reliant upon "motivational factors", probably the single most important aspect in establishing the effectiveness of any method for regulating fertility.

However, a more controversial issue is mentioned only in passing here, namely that a survey of couples in England using NFP revealed that 45 % were using alternate forms of sexual expression during the calculated fertile period. One wonders what the essentialist approach to sexual ethics would think if it were realized that more and more people

All this said about the issue of regulating fertility, however, should not distract us from the wider developments which had been going on. That single issue is hardly of utmost importance, though it has served as a focal point for understanding the broader problematic. What is at issue is the whole of the theology of marriage and the family and the subsequent implications for conjugal and sexual morality. Indeed, every issue touching upon human sexuality, including celibacy and the roles of women in the Church, has been building to a crisis since Vatican II. The 1980 Synod was seen as a possible forum for resolving some of the tensions and making progress on applying the theology of the Council, the *raison d'être* for the synodal process itself. And so it is to that event that we must now turn our attention. This will be done by operating from the perspective of the conciliar legacy.

B. The Pre-synodal Process

In 1967, with the restructing of the curia and the occurence of the First General Synod, Paul VI filled the office of the Secretary General of the Synod of Bishops. The first person to hold this office was Wladyslaw Rubin, auxiliary bishop of Gniezno, Poland, appointed on 23 February 1967 (1967:1426)[44]. The nature of the office is basically coordinative and

practicing periodic "continence" were engaging in manual and oral genital stimulation. One indication can be found in J. F. HARVEY, *Expressing Marital Love during the Fertile Phase*, in *The International Review of Natural Family Planning* 5 (1981) 203-220. The author, in dealing frankly with sexual and genital stimulation, asserts that incomplete (without orgasm) sexual acts "should not be a proximate cause of masturbation". He then explains this in the following way: "By 'proximate' is meant that in the majority of situations where certain kinds of stimuli have been present, masturbation has occurred. If love-making has only *rarely* led to masturbation, the causal relationship is called 'remote'" (pp. 205-206). Now up to this point, the author is sufficiently orthodox, allowing for occasional "accidents" caused only "remotely" (and hence presumably inculpable). But he takes his casuistry a step further and justifies even "proximate" causation.

Even in situations where there may be proximate danger of proceeding to involuntary masturbation, spouses may engage in such imperfect acts provided they have a sufficient reason for so doing. But what constitutes "sufficient reason"? It includes the disire to express mutual love, the willingness to comply with the desires of the other spouse, a need to be held by the other spouse, the relief of tension — and so on. *It would be rare that some good reason would not be present*, and the married persons themselves should make the decision about its sufficiency. (p. 206, emphasis added)

And so we have the incredible paradox: contracepted sexual intercourse is sinful, but placing oneself in the proximate danger (where in the *majority* of situations masturbation occurs) of non-coital orgasm is permitted for a "sufficient reason" which only rarely would not be present. This form of reasoning is not only an insult to intelligence, but it supports the age old dualism of mind and body when it goes further to speak of "involuntary orgasm" or "ejaculation without giving consent". The position is absurd and underscores everything that is bad in traditionalist sexual morality.

44. The numbers which are given here in parentheses refer to the *Attività della Santa Sede nel 1967* [-1981]. The first number refers to the year of the volume, the second, separated by a colon, to the page number(s).

is meant to serve the workings of the Concilium, a committee of 15 members whose task it is to prepare the work for the tri-annual Synod of Bishops. The Concilium consists of 12 members elected at the end of each Synod and three additional members appointed by the pope, to work on the next general gathering. Thus, the membership of the Concilium can change every three years, but reelection or re-appointment is possible[45]. The General Secretary also has three or four "officials" to aid in his daily work, and the necessary contact with the other members of the curia.

On 21 and 24 October 1977 the assembled Synod elected the twelve members of the Concilium and on 25 October Pope Paul VI appointed the other three members[46]. The first recorded meeting of this Concilium was held 16-18 May 1978 and the principle order of business was to discuss possible topics for the future Synod. A subsequent letter was drawn up and sent to the Pope containing the various suggestions. It was indicated after this letter of 19 May that a reply would be given in October of that year (1978:744). One of the suggested topics was the theology of marriage and the family, a subject that the bishops of many countries had wanted to see discussed but which Paul VI had been reluctant to bring out into the open since the HV event. In any case, the Pope died soon afterwards and, after the brief pontificate of John-Paul I, Karol Wojtyla was elected Pope on 16 October 1978. Having been a member of the Concilium for seven years, John-Paul II was quite familiar with its processes and its proposals for the 1980 Synod.

The nature of the Concilium is such that the majority of its members are pastorally active bishops who remain for the most part in their dioceses and only rarely gather in Rome. Consequently, much of the work is carried by the Secretary General, his staff, and the various committees of "experts" who very often go unnamed. In the case of the

45. Karol Wojtyla had been associated with the Synod ever since its inception. While he had been designated a member in 1967 he chose not to attend as a form of protest against the fact that the primate of Poland, Card. Wyszynski, had not been granted permission to leave the country. In 1969 Paul VI appointed Wojtyla to the Extraordinary Synod. The Polish Cardinal was then elected to the Concilium in 1971 and was reelected in 1974 and 1977. He resigned this post upon his election to the papacy in 1978. (Cf. G. H. WILLIAMS, *op. cit.*, pp. 221-227).

46. On 21 October, elected by a clear majority were (1977: 721): Card. Aloisio Lorscheider (Fortaleza) and Archbishop Joseph Bernardin (Cincinnati). On 24 October, elected with a relative majority were (1977: 721): for Africa: Card. Hyancinthe Thiandoum (Dakar), Card. Maurice Otunga (Nairobi), and Archbishop Denis Hurley (Durban); for America: Bishop Gerald Emmet Carter (London); for Asia, Australia and Oceania: Card. Joseph Cordeiro (Karachi), Card. James Sin (Manila) and Bishop Patrick D'Souza (Varanasi); for Europe: Archbishop Roger Etchegaray (Marseille), Card. Joseph Höffner (Cologne) and Card. Karol Wojtyla (Cracou). On 25 October, Paul VI appointed (1977: 428, 722): Card. Pericles Felici (Rome), Card. Raul Primatesta (Cordoba) and Archbishop Maxim Hermaniuk (Winnipeg).

Concilium for the 1980 Synod, one member, Card. Felici, was a resident of Rome and could presumably play a more active role in events[47].

On 16 November 1978 there was a meeting of a certain "committee of experts" for presenting topics to be discussed at the Synod (1979:1245). The next day, 17 November, the Pope had a private audience with, among others, the Secretary General, Bishop Rubin, during which he approved the plans to designate "The Role of the Christian Family" for the 1980 Synod (1978:379, 745). Subsequent to that meeting as well, Bishop Rubin communicated in a letter of 22 November to Card. George Basil Hume (Westminster) that the Pope wished to nominate him to take the now vacant place on the Concilium (1979:1245).

The second meeting of the Concilium took place on 12-16 December 1978 under the presidency of Card. Höffner and the direction of Bishop Rubin. Its work consisted in dealing with the proposals for the *Lineamenta (Lin)* for the coming Synod. On the closing day the Pope addressed the Concilium, giving public approval for the topic, "The Role of the Christian Family in the Modern World", and for the preparatory work (1979:437, 1245). At this point it appears that a preliminary text for the *Lin* was in existence even though the Concilium itself had only one meeting on the specific issue. That text was divided into three parts (present situation, doctrine, and role of the christian family) and each of the parts was then handed over to "an expert" for further work (1979:1245). Within a month, 8-10 January 1979, there was another meeting of the "committee of experts" held at the Secretary General in which the "observations of the Concilium" were discussed (1979:1246). One has the impression that the previous meeting of the Concilium was devoted more to the evaluation of an existing text than the composition of the *Lin* from beginning to end. In any case it was this "committee" who formulated the final text and sent it to the Pope for approval (*Ibid.*).

This first series of events raises the question of the authorship of the *Lin* for the 1980 Synod. While the Concilium was definitely consulted, the real work of composition appears to have fallen into the hands of

47. Cardinal Pericles Felici is a well known figure. His many roles put him in an excellent position to exert great influence on the events leading up to the 1980 Synod. After having been Secretary General of Vatican II, he was made a Cardinal on 11 June 1967. That same year, he was named President of the Pontifical Commission for the Interpretation of the Decrees of Vatican II and President of the Pontifical Commission for the Revision of Canon Law. In 1977, he was appointed Prefect of the Apostolic Signatura, the highest court in the Church. At the time of his death in 1981, he was a member of the Congregations for the Doctrine of the Faith, for Bishops, for Sacraments and Worship, for the Cause of Saints, and the Pontifical Commission for the Revision of Eastern Canon Law. Besides these roles, he was also in charge of the Archives of Vatican II, a member of the Committee for the Public Affairs of the Church, on the Administration of the Patrimony of the Holy See, and a member of the Tribunal for the city of the Vatican. Cf. *Annuario Pontificio per l'anno 1981*, pp. 1007, 1009, 1012, 1019, 1044, 1051, 1071, 1074, 1077, 1099, 1111, 1175.

someone else. We will see in our analysis of the text itself that a discernible theological perspective emerges, one which is indicative of essentialist theology.

Presumably with the text of the *Lin* approved by John-Paul II, Bishop Rubin, in a letter of 27 March 1979, transmitted to the leaders of the hierarchy[48] the decision of the Pope to designate the theme for the Synod of 1980. The text of the *Lin* was promised in a subsequent communication which took place on 14 May 1979 and all concerned parties were requested to submit their reactions to the *Lin* before 1 December 1979 (1979:1246). The first stage of the synodal preparatory process had been completed.

On 26 May it was made known that the Secretary General of the Synod, Bishop Rubin, would be elevated to the College of Cardinals. Before he left his post, however, it was Bishop Rubin who introduced the *Lin* to the world at a press conference held on 19 June (1979:1247)[49]. The consistory for the cardinalate was held on 30 June 1979 and two weeks later Bishop Rubin resigned his post[50]. The same day, 14 July 1979, Josef Tomko was nominated Secretary General for the Synod of Bishops (1979:1247; 1979:696 gives the date of his nomination as 1 July

48. The "leaders of the hierarchy" include the patriarchs of the Eastern Churches, the metropolitans "extra patriarchatus", the presidents of episcopal conferences, the cardinals of the "Dicasteri" of the Roman curia and the president of the Union of Superiors General.

49. The text of Bishop Rubin's remarks can be found in *Osservatore Romano* 20 June 1979. After the presentation, "various questions" on the *Lin* were answered by Mons. Edmond Farhet, an "officialis" for the Secretariate. Mons. Farhat had begun work in the curia under the Cong. for the Doctrine of the Faith in 1965-1970. He has been an "officialis" at the Sec. Gen. of the Synod since 1971. His role in the development of texts is not clear, though his task at the press conference would indicate close familiarity with its content.

50. The Secretary General of the Synod is a post normally held by a bishop. Card. Rubin's resignation therefore was a matter of protocal and not the end of a career. That career was indeed a long one. Wladyslaw Rubin (Born 1917) was ordained a priest four months before Karol Wojtyla, in June 1946. Eventually he was appointed rector of the Polish College in Rome where he served as host to a number of Polish bishops during the whole of the council (Cf. G.H. WILLIAMS, *op. cit.*, p. 165). He was consecrated a bishop in 1964 and became Secretary General of the Synod of Bishops in 1967. Apparently he also functioned as "deputy and delegate respectively of the Primate of Poland for Poles in the Diaspora" (WILLIAMS, p. 235), a position which again brought him close to the future pope. In 1979, besides having already been a member of the Pontifical Commission for the Interpretation of the Decrees of Vatican II (1 Sept. 67) and what appears to have been a temporary appointment as counselor for the Cong. for the Bishops (1 Mar. 1978), after becoming a cardinal he was named a member of the Cong. for the Doctrine of the Faith (24 Mar. 1979) and of the Cong. for the Cause of Saints (24 Sept. 1979). He received his chief function as Prefect of the Cong. for the Eastern Churches (27 June 1980) and his name is also listed as member of the Apostolic Signatura, Secretariate for Christian Unity and the Pont. Comm. for the Revision of Eastern Canon Law. Cf. *Annuario* for 1981, pp. 993, 1009, 1015, 1044, 1051, 1056, 1074, 1077. Finally, Card. Rubin was one of the three papal appointments to the Concilium for the 1983 Synod (*Attività*, 1980: 1147).

1979). This Czechoslovakian member of the curia[51] was not unfamiliar with the issues facing the 1980 Synod. In fact, he had been a special secretary in the first Synod (1967) for the consideration of the issue of mixed marriages (1979:1247). His appointment as Secretary General took effect on 1 Aug. 1979. On 1 Sept. he sent a letter to all the bishops inviting them to send their responses to the *Lin* before 10 Oct., seven weeks before the date set by Bishop Rubin. Mons. Tomko was consecrated a bishop on 15 Sept. 1979 (1979:1247).

The work for the second preparatory stage was now underway with the gathering of the episcopal responses to the *Lin*. On 25 Sept. Bishop Tomko sent a letter to the heads of the Sacred Congregations which might have an interest in the discussions at the Synod. He solicited their observations on the *Lin* to be submitted before 15 Oct. During the month of November (1979) it was reported that "The Secretary General went forth with the preparation of the 'Lineamenta', based upon the observations received in order to submit it for the approval of the Holy Father" (1979:1248)[52]. This chronicle appears to be at fault for the *Lin* had long been prepared, sent out and reacted to. What is probably intended in the text is the preparation of the *Instrumentum laboris* (IL), though it remains a question how that document could be drawn up without the personal collaboration of the Concilium[53].

51. Joseph Tomko is first listed in *Annuario* in 1963 as working on a commission for the censure of books for the Cong. for the Doctrine of the Faith (Holy Office). He remained at that Congregation in various capacities up to 1974 when he became associated with the Committee on the Family and then an undersecretary for the Cong. of Bishops (1975). He was also a member of a subcommission for the Propagation of the Faith and Mission (1976). Subsequent to his assumption of the post of Sec. Gen. of the Synod of Bishops he became a member of the Pont. Comm. for the Interpretation of the Decrees of Vatican II and a counselor for the Cong. for the Bishops.

52. "La Segretaria Generale, nel mese di novembre, procedeva alla preparazione dei, 'Lineamenta', in base alle osservazioni ricevute, da sottoporre poi all'approvazione del Santo Padre".

53. It is possible that the text in fact is not at fault. If we interpret "the preparation of the *Lineamenta*" to mean that the document to be drawn up, the IL, was merely an "expansion" of the *Lin*, then there is no error. But according to this interpretation, the preparatory process for the Synod is not a two-phase project but only a single, continuous one. If that is true there would be no need to distinguish the two documents — which in the case for the 1980 Synod is more or less theologically true. The implications here are significant.

Considering the IL as a simple "extension" of the *Lin* means that the documents are fundamentally the same. Considering further that they both emanate from the same sources, namely those from which the Secretary General draws information and the ultimate text itself, the "committee of experts", the lines of similarity are clear. In this case, the Concilium would function very much like a rubber stamp and an administrative appendage, having little or no control over the content of the documents. Even further removed would be all the bishops, both those who would be members of the Synod itself and all those who would take part in "reacting to" the *Lin*. Since their reactions would have to be made to fit into the framework of the already existing *Lin*, their contributions could

In the beginning of 1980, during the meeting of the "Particular Synod" of the Dutch Bishops, it was decided to form a Study Commission for the preparation of the IL. This Commission consisted of four members: Javier Lozano Barragàn, Auxiliary Bishop of Mexico, who would later be designated "Special Secretary" of the 1980 Synod (1980:1143); Mons. James T. McHugh, member of the Pontifical Committee for the Laity and the Commission for the Family; Karol Meissner, a Benedictine from the monastary of Lubin (Poland); and Guido Gatti, Professor at the Pont. Univ. of the Salesians (1980:1142). This Commission prepared a text for the IL in three parts: descriptive, doctrinal and pastoral.

The Concilium then met under the auspices of the Secretary General from 18-23 Feb. 1980. The greater part of their work was dedicated to "preparing" the IL. The last day of their meeting took place at the

be seen as having little effect. Putting it into the simplest words possible, the "participation" of the world episcopate in the preparation for this Synod was rather marginal.

While we admit to the possibility that this observation is highly speculative, it is based not only on an interpretation of one small sentence in the *Attività*, but also on an analysis of the pre- and post-synodal documents to which we will shortly proceed. We will find a consistent influence of a single, essentialist theological perspective throughout those texts. Finally, the observation appears to be substantiated by the *Lin* for the 1983 Synod which puts forth its aims in number 3:

To better achieve the purpose of the Synod of Bishops, it is already an established practice to precede a synodal assembly with a two-stage preparation. In the first stage *the general secretariat of the synod prepares a brief document, the lineamenta* (outlines) of the theme, to stimulate reflection in the local chruches to receive information, advice and *useful* suggestions for the future synodal discussion; to provoke as soon as possible a movement of spirits and of prayer which disposes souls to the metanoia which is at the root of the synodal theme.

On the basis of the reflections, information and suggestions which the episcopal conferences and other organs will collect and send to the general secretariat of the synod, there is prepared at a later date a more extensive *instrumentum laboris* (working document) of the synod.

The *lineamenta*, therefore, are not a scheme or project of a future synodal document and have no pretense to completeness or perfection. *They are provisional in character and limited, and thus it would be useless to make a critique of them or to attempt to perfect the text.* It is important, however, to avail of them insofar as they are useful to the purpose. Intentionally they remain at the generic and allusive level, leaving space for the more detailed and concrete considerations which will be put forward as experiences of faith and life in the ecclesial communities. In the replies account is to be taken of the fact that *the Synod of Bishops follows pastoral aims, based, however, on a solid doctrinal foundation.*

Finally, it is to be noted that the consultation that the *lineamenta* intend to promote is without limits and not reserved. The episcopal conferences, who are obviously the first and authoritative recipients, have complete freedom of action within the sphere of the chosen theme. (emphasis added)

Cf. *Reconciliation and Penance in the Mission of the Church*, in *Origins* 11 (1982) 565-580, p. 567. Note that there is absolutely no mention made of the Concilium. The "solid doctrinal foundation" is presumed to exist in the document and be the responsibility of its authors; the episcopal responsibility appears to be limited to "experience of faith and life in the ecclesial communities". Lastly, the designation of the Synod being directed to "pastoral aims", unlike the presuppositions behind Vatican II that saw pastoral and doctrinal as inseparable, appears to draw a sharp distinction with the doctrinal aspects which remains in Roman hands.

Apostolic Palace, during which the Pope congratulated them for their work and contributions (1980:1142). The definitive text of the IL, however, apparently needed more work, at least in the form of translation, for it was not ready until June of that year. After having received approval from the Pope for the final draft, the text was sent to the bishops along with their invitations for attending the Synod (1980:1143). The text of the IL is dated 16 June 1980. The second phase of the preparatory work had now been completed. The following day, 17 June, in a letter to the Secretariate of State, John-Paul II nominated Card. Joseph Ratzinger of Munich as *Relator* of the Synod[54] and Bishop Lozano Barragàn as "Special Secretary". There followed the nomination of a Presidential Delegation (13 Sept.) consisting of Cardinals Primatesta (Cordoba), Picachy (Calcutta) and Gantin (member of "Justitia et pax" and "Cor Unum"), as well as the ten "Special Auditors of the Secretary", the "Commission for Controversies", the "Committee for Information", and the 43 "Auditors" who would attend the Synod. The General Assembly was solemnly opened on 26 Sept. 1980.

---

54. The *"Relator"* is overall in charge of the actual synodal meeting and directs its activities as well as presenting its theological and pastoral framework. Card. Wojtyla was *"Relator"* for the 1974 Synod on Evangelization (Cf. G.H. WILLIAMS, *op. cit.*, p. 236).

II. THE LINEAMENTA

The first preparatory document for the 1980 Synod was the *Lineamenta* (*Lin*) of March 1979. The official Latin text is 50 pages long, including 4 pages of index. As mentioned earlier, after a brief introduction it contains three parts: situating the problems, doctrinal issues, and the role(s) of the christian family. The sections or paragraphs are not numbered sequentially as has become standard practice in most official documents (including the *Lin* for the 1983 Synod). Rather, in the Introduction and Part One we find sections, I-III, further divided into paragraphs with arabic numbers. Parts Two and Three each have three "chapters" divided into sections, I, II, etc., further divided into paragraphs. Each of the three Parts is followed by questions. By far the most important text is that of Part II on doctrinal questions. Our commentary will follow the order of the text.

The Introduction sets forth the reason, the meaning and the division of the theme. The choice of topic is said to be in response to numerous requests and an attempt is made to justify this choice being in continuity with the previous Synods. One interesting aspect of the Introduction is a precursory definition of the family which is said to be understood in various senses, one wide and one narrow. The text continues, "The family coming from a marriage can mean the *partnership* of one man and one woman bound together indissolubly by conjugal love in accordance with the order laid down by God. This family is in the strictest sense ordained, as we shall relate, both for mutual help and community of life and for procreation"[55]. Prescinding from the fact that the second thought expressed is already an expansion of the first, we find here one of the presuppositions upon which the theology of these documents will be built. An "order established by God" (*ordinem a Deo statutum*) will eventually evolve into "God's will" or intention (*intentio Dei*) here and in the *Instrumentum laboris*, and be complete in *Familiaris consortio* as the "Plan of God" (*consilium Dei*). In the work of the Synod itself, this notion will carry less importance, but the theological school which will be responsible for official documents will capitalize on the idea.

The *Lin* has been criticized for being traditionalist in ethical matters

---

55. Familia procedens ex matrimonio potest significare *communitatem* unius viri uniusque mulieris indissolubiliter amore coniugali coniunctorum iuxta ordinem a Deo statutum. Haec familia in sensu strictissimo ordinatur, ut dicemus, tum ad adiutorium commune et ad communitatem vitae, tum ad procreationem.
The English text used for this document is that taken from *Origins*, unless otherwise specified. This definition will be repeated verbatim in IL,7 where it will be more clearly classified as a definition in the "strict sense".

and "very old-fashioned in its sociology"[56]. This observation can be documented by the text, but its causes run far deeper. In contrast to the conciliar momentum for a dynamic outlook, the theology here is static and represents an outdated view of natural law, though that specific terminology is prudently avoided. The authors apparently envision an *essentialist order* of created reality complete down to the last detail and imposed upon humankind regardless of the experience of human persons in their historical and cultural pluriformity. This "order" is untouchable and humankind can only submit to its demands without question. The leap which is subsequently made from factual observation to ethical normativity is not new. It was present in HV as well, extending from the structure of marriage (HV, 8)[57] to conjugal behavior (HV, 10)[58], both of which are said to be based upon an "objective moral order established by God" (*HV, 10: ad ordinem moralem, quem obiectum vocant, a Deoque statutum*). No responsible member of the Church would deny some form of objectivity in ethics, but the idea of a pre-ordained moral order which specifies human activity down to the slightest detail does not leave much room for human freedom or the dynamic character of God's creative activity. Such an outlook is the principle characteristic of the Introduction of the *Lin*.

A. Describing the Situation

Part One of the *Lin* is the so-called descriptive part and attempts to set out what the author(s) consider to be "The Situation of the Family in the Modern World". It begins with a short preamble that specifies the time under consideration, namely the fifteen years which have passed since Vatican II. That period, it is said, has been marked by profound change with two principle characteristics: the radical change in the way of thinking by society and the rapidity of the process of change[59]. While

---

56. S. O'RIORDAN, *The Synod on the Family, 1980*, in *The Furrow* 31 (1980) 759-777, pp. 760-761.

57. Tantum igitur abest, ut matrimonium e casu quodam vel e caeco naturalium virium cursu nascatur, ut reapse illud sapienter providenterque Creator Deus ea mente instituerit, ut in hominibus *suum* amoris *consilium* efficeret. (emphasis added)

58. Ex quo fit, ut in tradendae vitae munere iis (coniugiis) integrum non sit, se arbitrata suo genere, quasi ipsis liceat vias honestas, quas sequantur, modo omnino proprio ac libero definire; cum contra, opera sua ad *consilium Dei Creatoris* accomodare teneantur, quod hinc *ipsa matrimonii eiusque actuum natura* exprimit, hinc constans Ecclesiae doctrina declarat. (emphasis added)
Contrast this with the standards provided in GS,51: morales indoles rationis agendi ... objectivis criteriis, *ex personae eiusdemque actuum natura* desumptis, debet. (emphasis added)

59. Quindecim iam anni elapsi sunt postquam Concilium Vaticanum II, ... Haec periodus quindecim annorum mutationem profundam Ecclesiae et mundi cognovit, quae

recognizing that there are a plurality of factors at work in different parts of the world, the *Lin* will single out what it considers to be the most important.

Two of the three sections of Part One are overwhelmingly negative in describing the contemporary situation. Section I is indeed positive, but what is written there is basically a repetition of the thought found in GS and does not address itself to the present situation as the document purported it would do. Sections II and III, on the other hand, do address the situation of the family and are very negative in content and style. The two sections concern respectively the "changing role of the family in modern society" and some "special difficulties" facing the christian family in particular. What we find there is a list of problems faced by the institution of marriage, the family and society in general: divorce, "attempted" second unions, trial marriage, illegitimate pregnancy, transitory premarital relationships, ambiguity toward the good of procreation, increasing number of abortions, an uncertain situation of women in society and a decrease in maternal care for children, depressing economic and social factors and increasing materialism among the "affluent", a breakdown in parent-child relationships, and modern theories of "self-determination" because of which some parents allow their children to be led astray. As for the "special difficulties" facing christians there are: religious pluralism threatening the purity of Catholic positions on doctrine and morals, a rejection of magisterial teaching especially in the area of sexuality, legal and educational institutions imposing themselves on Catholics and leading to "the progressive disintegration of the concept and the institution of marriage", and, probably most fundamental of all, the "lack of a clear concept of the sacrality and the sacramentality of marriage". The last observation is extended to an increase in non-church weddings, the attempt to contract marriage without faith, and an insufficient catechesis on marriage. As for the problem of defining sacramentality, the *Lin* contents itself to say that it is based upon the Christ-Church covenantal relation. We will return to this topic further on in this work[60].

quidem duplici praesertim nota signata est, radicali nempe mutatione ipsius modi cogitandi ex parte societatis et ipsa velocitate processus mutationis.

It might be pointed out that this document was prepared only thirteen years after the close of the Council. A mere two year difference is no reason to quibble, but one could ask whether the author(s) somehow envisioned this document to be a schema for the outcome of the Synod, despite statements to the contrary. A simple use of the future perfect tense could have avoided the impression. See above, n. 53.

60. GS,48 had invoked the traditional understanding of the covenant between God and His People, Christ and the Church, in order to shed light on the mystery of love and conjugal love in particular. It is not said, however, that the covenantal love relationship is *constitutive* of sacramentality, although a number of contemporary commentators attempt to read this into the document. The problem of defining sacramentality with respect to marriage cannot be solved until one confronts the fundamental notion of sacrament in

Reading Part One of the *Lin*, then, one gets the overall impression that marriage, the family, and even the moral fabric of society are falling apart. If indeed this description of things is accurate, we must ask ourselves how one can respond to such a situation. To pick just one example, if divorce is rampant and persons have lost a sense of continuous fidelity and life-long commitment, is it not time for the Church to raise her voice and once again clearly proclaim the doctrine of the indissolubility of marriage? What should the bishops, as individuals or as a group, say in addressing this set of circumstances? The answers are all too clear.

The first and ultimately continuing criticism of this document and the one to follow (IL) is the impression given that rather than outlining topics for discussion or really seeking the advice and contributions of the bishops throughout the world, the author(s) had provided the questions which would be addressed and constructed a framework within which the answers should be given. This is what the bishops would be up against during the Synod. We will see that most of them resisted these restrictions and managed to make their contributions despite opposition. Nevertheless, the bishops themselves would not have the last word.

It appears that an alternative method could have been used. To use the one example of the increasing occurrence and widespread legalization of divorce, one could have simply discussed the factual observation of "marital breakdown". Rather than saying divorce is on the increase and how do we stop it, one could observe that life-long marital commitment is becoming harder to achieve and that the institution of indissoluble marriage is becoming destabilized. This approach, although it remains the observation of what we can still call a negative situation, has the potential to invite inquiry into the causes for the situation itself. Why is there an increase in marital breakdown? Is it because persons today are weaker and have an insufficient sense of commitment, or because they lack the supportive structures of social institutions which prohibit divorce thus making separation and remarriage "easier"? These would seem to be the presuppositions of the *Lin*. Or, is there a greater incidence of marital breakdown because persons have higher expectations of what marriage and commitment might be and might contribute to their lives? Have marital expectations become unrealistic, even romantic? Or, have they become more "person oriented" and demanding in calling for "mutual self-bestowal" and "increasing advancement of their own perfection, as well as their mutual sanctification" (GS, 48)?

One possible explanation why the *Lin* speaks of divorce, etc. only as

---

general, especially in light of the theology of Vatican II, its insistence on the ecclesiological dimensions of sacrament, and the logical conclusions which must follow upon that reflection. The preparatory documents for the Synod exhibit little or no appreciation for that fundamental renewal in sacramentology.

threat to the reality of marriage, instead of opening questions for inquiry, is because the notion of marriage operative in these documents is different from that which is experienced by millions of married persons and reflected upon by theologians. Namely, as a datum of experience, marriage is viewed by most people as a human relationship in and of itself; it is a relationship, the meaning of which for baptized Catholics would also be (called) a sacrament. For the author(s) of the Lin, we will see that "marriage" is an ontological reality which comes into existence as a result of the human commitment to the relationship. This ontological reality in and of itself is the only area of inquiry within their perspective. Once the ontological reality comes into existence, the activity or experience of the persons involved ceases to have any real significance. Thus, all these threats against marriage are threats against that ontological reality which of its very nature cannot "break down". It would have been impossible for the author(s) of this document to use the term "marital breakdown" because essentialist and ontological realities do not do such things. There was a fundamental difference between the notions which inspired this document and the way it would be read by many of the bishops, not to mention the vast majority of the laity and theologians who attempted to reflect upon it.

Nevertheless, from the perspective of those who considered the phenomenon of divorce from the experiential and not the ontological point of view, there is yet another problem which the latter mentality would be incapable of comprehending. Addressing the "problem of divorce" one also gets the impression of something evil which intervenes in people's lives from outside and destroys what would otherwise be a stable union. No one would disagree that divorce "as intervention" is unjust to at least one, if not both, of the parties involved. Further, divorce as "social institution" undermines the stability of the family and society as a whole. But does not this attitude presume that the legal possibility of divorce itself is an attack on what would otherwise be a positive, value-oriented social context in which marriage is healthy, sacred and well-functioning? Is it not pertinent to ask whether or not this is the case? It would become clear in the discussions of the bishops at the Synod that divorce as such is not as fundamental a problem as establishing marital and familial stability in the first place. In many situations the legal possibility of divorce is largely irrelevant because there are social and economic circumstances which militate against the very possibility of entering into a stable, indissoluble union. The form of the question with respect to divorce betrayed the Western, North Atlantic preoccupations of the Church in Rome. There would be some improvement of this perspective as the discussions proceeded. But the statement of the question(s) for response in Part One of the Lin in some sense preempted serious discussion of the issues, at least for the bishops from the North Atlantic world who, despite their concern for the problems of the universal Church, nevertheless were facing a severe pastoral urgency in their own dioceses[61].

B. The Doctrinal and Pastoral Outline

The second part of the *Lin* addresses "Doctrinal Questions on Marriage and the Family". There are three chapters, on fundamental principles, on the intention of God as Creator of the conjugal community and His work as Redeemer. The entirety of this doctrinal development covers only thirteen pages in the original text[62].

Chapter One addresses two types of fundamental principles: on the role and mission of the Magisterium to teach in this area and on the meaning of marriage and family as covenants. The first, on the role of the Magisterium with respect to conjugal matters and in particular the sacramentality of that covenant, is most interesting. It is proposed that the Magisterium has a competence for all aspects of the conjugal and familial covenants. The pastoral care of souls which is the responsibility of the Magisterium is said to be based upon reflection on the "Intention of God as Creator and Redeemer", but no further explanation is given. In what follows it appears that the primary source for this reflection is the natural law and not divine revelation[63].

---

61. The statement of the questions for response here refers to the whole of Part One in describing the "existing situation". They are not simply the "questions" which came at the end of Part One. These were two:
1. What should be said about the situation of the family in the various regions with reference to pastoral attention?
2. Are there other questions to be considered with respect to the theme for this synod?

Seen from the mentality which was responsible for the *Lin*, the first question merely seems to be looking for more problems. The second gives the impression that one or two details may have been missed by the *Lin* which could foreseeably be brought to the attention of the Concilium; otherwise the document appears content with its own formulation of the situation, asking only for additional questions which might have been overlooked.

62. Original text, pp. 13-25; *Origins*, pp. 118-123.

63. Post examen factorum et evolutionis culturalis, Pastores Ecclesiae volunt suae responsabilitati, per curam animarum aptam et authenticam satisfacere. Ad hanc pastoralem curam instituendam continuandamque, iuvat recolere quae sit intentio Dei Creatoris et Redemptoris circa vitam coniugalem et familiarem.

In addressing the *Responsabilitas Magisterii* the question of competence is implied insofar as determining "authentic teaching". The question must be recognized as a controverted one, although there is no such hint given in the *Lin*. Even Pope Paul VI in HV attempted to state magisterial competence in this area, though he failed to prove his case. Very few members of the Church doubt the competence of the Church to *legislate* with respect to marriage, but not a few have doubts about the Magisterium's authority in "natural law".

Marriage and the family are distinguished as covenants based upon love and an affection of the will[64] or upon the bond of blood which is completed by love. The family enfolds many human aspects, but all of these are recognized to be indicative of the presence of God[65]. Therefore, the responsibility of the Magisterium is presumed to extend to these "human aspects". The following paragraph attempts to summarize the basis for this competence with a series of five references and quotations from Vatican II. The first sentence is a paraphrase which notes the compatibility of Christocentric and human aspects of marriage and the family[66]. The second sentence is a quote from the same document but from a different and earlier place which deals with the independence of the temporal order and its relation to the ultimate destination in Christ[67]. This is a fine quote for recognizing the rightful autonomy of "earthly things" and "their own intrinsic strength and excellence", but it has little to do with marriage or the family and even less to do with the competence of the Magisterium to speak in those areas. The next sentence contains two references to the text of GS, 36 on the "Rightful Independence of Earthly Affairs"[68]. Again, there is no reference there to the competence of the Magisterium. On the contrary, the point of the section is the distinguishability of faith and science which are not in conflict but which complement each other. Finally, a long sentence just before the conclusion of the paragraph gives the impression that the text quoted establishes a conciliar endorsement for the competence of the Magisterium in the area of marriage[69]. Reading the quotation in context

64. "Matrimonii ligamen fundatur in amore et in 'voluntatis affectu'". Reference is given here to GS,49, the text of which reads, "Ille autem amor, utpote eminenter humanus, cum a persona in personam voluntatis affectu dirigatur ..." The difference here is perhaps slight, but one may pose the question whether or not there is a real distinction between the essence of love and the manner in which it is incarnated in a personal relationship. If the *bond* of marriage is founded upon a disposition (*voluntatis affectu*), how does one establish the presence of the disposition or posit its unbreakableness?

65. Here follows the quotation of the last sentence of GS,48 which, in its own context, is descriptive and not definitional in nature, and which is directed to the christian family and not simply the married couple.

66. Aspectus Christocentricus familiae et matrimonii non nocet aspectui humano ipsius. Reference is made to *Apostolicam actuositatem*, the "Decree on the Laity", 11.

67. Etenim "... destinatio (rerum ad Christum) non modo non privat ordinem temporalem sua autonomia, suis propriis finibus, legibus, subsidiis, momento pro hominum bono, sed potius perficit in sua vi et praestantia propria simulque adaequat integrae vocationi hominis super terram".
The quotation is taken from *Apostolicam actuositatem*, 7.

68. "Iusta rerum terrenarum autonomia" non tollit necessitatem procedendi iuxta normas morales nec referentiam ad Creatoris voluntatem.
Note the absence of quotation marks around the words *Creatoris voluntatem*. Some translations provide the marks which accent the key function of this concept. One could validly ask whether the theology of the *Lin* is "voluntaristic".

69. Etiam sub aspectu temporali, nec matrimonium, nec familia possunt excludi a responsabilitate Pastorum Ecclesiae de quibus Decr. *Apostolicam actuositatem* aiebat: "Ad

one is struck by the absence of any such connection. The affirmation present there is directed to science and technology and remains on the level of general principles.

The second subdivision of section one of this chapter discussed the "special responsibility of the Magisterium" with respect to marriage as sacrament. It is noted that as sacrament the marital covenant embraces more than that which is "purely human". But again, in denying a misuse of the so-called "pretense of absolute freedom", a claim is made for "the Church's teaching about her mission and her authority"[70]. The first two references given here, LG, 22 & 25, are texts about the hierarchical structure of the Church, in particular the role of the bishops. Nothing is said about the competence of the Church to speak in the area of conjugal morality. The last reference given, to HV, 4, does indeed touch upon this assertion, but that particular paragraph of the encyclical primarily addressed the issue of natural law and itself is not beyond question[71]. Following this there are two quotes and references to the apostolic nature of the Magisterium[72]. Consulting the context of the suggested texts we find the divine mandate to preserve and preach the gospel. There is no reference to specific teaching nor to the elaboration of the meaning of sacrament[73]. The section ends with a call to the christian family to

pastores spectat principia circa finem creationis et usum mundi clare enuntiare, auxilia moralia et spiritualia praestare, ut ordo rerum temporalium in Christo instauretur". Reference is to number 7 of the decree.

70. Et quoad hoc punctum, cum autonomia humana ultra fas praetendatur falsa specie libertatis absolutae contra Christum et Ecclesiam, iuvat recolere doctrinam Ecclesiae circa suam missionem et auctoritatem. Reference is given to LG,22 & 25 and HV,4.

71. HV,4 is directly addressed to the competence of the Magisterium. Of the three short paragraphs found there, the first two concern teaching authority and the "natural (moral) law". Only the last refers to "a coherent teaching concerning both the nature of marriage (*matrimonii natura*) and the correct use of conjugal rights (*coniugum iurium usu*) and the duties of husband and wife (*de ipsorum officiis*)". Reference here is given to a number of sources all of which *presume* this competence and exercise it. No nuance is given to *how* the teaching is exercised or the independent worth of each source. In fact, the content of the sources cited is evidence of the evolutionary aspect of that teaching.

72. Apostoli sunt in doctrina Christi "in quo summi Dei tota revelatio consummatur". "Quod vero ab Apostolis traditum est, ea omnia complectitur quae ad Populi Dei vitam sancte ducendam fidemque augendam conferent sicque Ecclesia, in sua doctrina, vita et cultu, perpetuat cunctisque generationibus transmittit omne quod ipsa est, omne quod credit".
Reference is given to the "Dogmatic Constitution on Divine Revelation", *Dei verbum*, 7 & 8 respectively.

73. It is far more interesting to continue with this quotation as it appears in the original, *Dei verbum*, 8: "This tradition which comes from the apostles develops in the Church with the help of the Holy Spirit. For there is a growth in the understanding of the realities and the words which have been handed down. This happens through the contemplation and study made by believers, who treasure these things in their hearts (cf. Lk. 2:19,51), through the intimate understanding of spiritual things they experience, and through the preaching of those who have received through episcopal succession the sure gift of truth. For, as the

give service and assistance not only for itself but "for all people of good will". There follows a quote from GS, 42 to this effect, but the context again reveals an anomaly. The original speaks of the "christian family" but in the sense of the "family as the sons of God". The quotation used is ironically the closest thing to speaking about the mission of the Church as a whole that one can find in the entire first part of this chapter. But, because it is taken out of context, like many of the other references given, the implied interpretation is different from its original meaning.

In summary, this commentary on the first part of Chapter One is perhaps longer than the text under discussion precisely because it has sought to investigate the historico-theological assertions which have been made. That investigation reveals that despite the good will of the *Lin* in this section, it failed to substantiate the presumption it had put forth. The argumentation is weak and it appears that the claims made here will eventually be left behind. When we read the *Instrumentum laboris*, we will see no attempt to repeat the assertion of magisterial competence in the specifics of conjugal morality.

The second section of the first chapter deals with "Marriage and Family as Covenants". It begins by emphasizing the importance of human relationships, basing itself on GS, 23 ff. Certainly, GS had a great deal to say about the social nature of persons, but it never went quite so far as to use the terminology we find here (*indolem ontologicam et psychologicam humanum*) because Vat. II did not operate out of an essentialist perspective. Nonetheless, the *Lin* states that "keeping relationships and commitments" demands two things: psychological maturity and a consideration of others. The second is said to be best exemplified by an increase in "parents responsibility" toward their children (*incrementum "responsabilitatis parentum" erga liberos*). No one will argue with this observation, but an objection can be made to the use of terms.

"Responsible parenthood" is a key phrase utilized by contemporary theology which takes its meaning from GS, 50. In dealing with the decision to procreate and thus exercise their mission of being cooperators in the love of God, spouses are urged to act in a responsible manner. That is, when determining the extent to which they will realize their procreative potential,

---

centuries succeed one another, the Church constantly moves forward toward the fullness of divine truth until the words of God reach their complete fulfillment in her."

Notice that the original text accents first the experience of the faith by believers and does not concentrate upon the role of the Magisterium. Secondly, it underscores development in doctrine and is forward oriented rather than being "traditionalist" by basing all its teaching on what has already been said in a previous age. Reading these references in context sometimes leads to a very different impression than that given by the simple quotation of a single phrase or sentence.

With docile reverence toward God, they will come to the right decision by common counsel and effort. They will thoughtfully take into account both their own welfare and that of their children, those already born and those which may be foreseen. For this accounting they will reckon with both the material and spiritual conditions of the times as well as of their state in life. Finally, they will consult the interests of the family group, of the temporal society, and of the Church herself. The parents themselves should ultimately make this judgment, in the sight of God. (GS, 50)

In reading the *Lin*, one wonders what happened to this teaching. Two of the places where the document uses the words "responsibility of parents" are in reference to parental care or education[74]. It has little to do with the conciliar idea. The point being made by the *Lin* is a valid one, but it is obvious that the document has redefined a pre-existing phrase and managed to eliminate the concept for which it was a representation. We will see in the *Lin*'s discussion of fecundity that the concept simply disappeared.

Following this we find a discussion of the marriage covenant proper. It is stated that this covenant is foreseen in the bond that flows from sexuality which is called a good, and, although "disturbed by sin", is a place where grace abounds. Then, "as is obvious, this force is not the whole of marriage and family life: it must be controlled and directed by a rational will and by grace so that the covenant between the man and the woman 'far excels mere erotic inclination'"[75]. There is a references given here to GS, 49 in which we find a teaching about conjugal love and not about sexuality per se. It is taught in the whole of GS, 49, on conjugal love, that sexuality is one part of marital love; it is one form of expression. Marital sexuality is not distinguished from "erotic inclination" which itself is good and part of human sexuality, but only from *mere* erotic inclination which is not informed by love. The difference is a loving relationship, not "a rational will".

The last part of this section deals with the "human and divine dimensions of the marriage covenant". The union of marriage is said to be total, that is, including body and spirit, going beyond the couple themselves "because from that union will be born children"[76]. The future sense of the verb is, to say the least, presumptuous. Nevertheless, the entire point of this paragraph is the unbreakableness of the bond of marriage. Reference is made to the traditional source of the relationship

74. The term also occurs in Part III, Ch. I, sect. I, nr. 2, p. 29. A third use, in Part III, Ch. II, sect. III, nr. 4, will be treated separately.

75. Ut patet, haec vis non constituit totam vitam matrimonialem et familiarem: dirigi et temperari debet a rationali voluntate, a gratia, ita ut foedus inter virum et mulierem "longe ... exsuperat meram eroticam inclinationem" et sit vere commutatio affectuum, opinionum, voluntatum.

76. Immo transcendit duas peraonal quae sese dant et accipiunt quia ex ea unione nascituri sunt filii et filiae qui indissolubiliter uniuntur parentibus ligamine sanguinis.

between God and His People, Christ and the Church. We will return to this point shortly. For now we simply want to draw attention to the repetition of what is becoming a familiar category, namely, "what is in question here is no symbolism or allegory but an ontological reality and a communion and loving union between God and human beings"[77]. We will see the notion repeated in Chapter Three.

In the second Chapter of Part Two we find the core of the *Lin*'s doctrine, "The Intention of God the Creator Regarding the Marriage and Family Partnership". There are four parts, the construction of which gives us the beginning — and the end — of the document's reflection. The first is pivotal for it is here we find the connection between what is presumed to be "God's Intention" and human reality. It is stated that the former is an aid (*manuductio*) to understanding the latter. There is no appreciation for the fact that one comes to know the former only through first knowing the latter, and that considerable care must be taken to avoid the danger of ideology and the naturalistic fallacy.

The point of departure chosen is the opening of GS, 48, the council's own doctrinal teaching on marriage.

The intimate partnership of married life and love *has been established by the creator* and qualified by his laws. It is rooted in the conjugal covenant of irrevocable personal consent. Hence, by that human act by which spouses mutually bestow themselves and accept each other, *an institution arises which, by divine will, is a lasting one* even in the eyes of society. For the good of the spouses and their offspring as well as of society, this sacred bond does not depend on human decisions alone. For God himself is the author of matrimony, endowed as it is with various benefits and purposes[78].

There are a few curious things about this quotation. First, the emphasis has been added to the original text. This can be granted if one is attempting to make a valid point. But in this case, the point made serves as a kind of reductionism that masks the true meaning of conciliar theology. It is indisputable that the Council taught that the marital covenant owes its existence to God, who is its Author. But this is said in a way that is neither naturalistic nor structural. The *Lin* appears to be saying that marriage as we know it today is the exact form, right down to the smallest detail, that was determined by God. Providence and the divine will are being equivocated with legislative intention. The conciliar text also demonstrates a concern for contemporary terminology and ethical insight. In saying that "this sacred bond does not depend on human decisions alone", GS underscores the fact that the relationship

77. Hic non agitur de symbolismo vel de allegoria sed de realitate ontologica et de communione et unione amoris Dei cum hominibus.

78. The Latin text in the *Lin* is the same as that in GS, *AAS* 58 (1966), p. 1067, but the original contains no italics. The English version, however, appears to come from an already existing translation, probably Abbott, and contains at least one fault: the conjugal covenant is equivalent to (*seu*) and not dependent upon ("of") the irrevocable consent.

spoken of is a real and continuing one which does not have to be "remade" by repeated decisions. The Lin contents itself with talking about a bond which is "ontological".

Another question which can be asked is why the text stops where it does. The original Latin text places a semicolon here and then goes on to specify what is meant. But the original text also has a footnote at this point which recounts some historical teachings on the "goods and purposes" of marriage. The text of the footnote itself is an issue of some controversy[79] and the text in question has been used by the Vatican to claim that GS upholds the doctrine of the hierarchy of the ends of marriage[80]. The first half of this third (Latin) sentence in GS, 48 has become a *crux interpretum* for the whole of the conciliar teaching on marriage. It is evident which interpretation is favored by the author(s) of the *Lin*.

The following paragraph contains four references (no quotations) which finally get down to the intended teaching. An astute observer will recognize where the text is going by reading the first few words. The key word is "meaning" (*significationem*), which is the contemporary ter-minology for the Vatican's doctrine of the purposes or ends of marriage. We refer to this as the "two aspect theory" and its development can be directly traced to HV.

The point to be raised here is an understanding of the human reality which is marriage. It appeared that the whole of that reality would be addressed. But it becomes clear in this first section that the emphasis is upon procreation. The "meaning" of marriage and the family is said to be drawn from four sources. The first is the Council. Reference is given to GS, 50 which is about "the fruitfulness of marriage" or its fecundity. The reference should have been to GS, 48 if the whole of marriage was to be addressed. The second reference is the Word of the Lord in the Gospel (Mt. 19: 4-6; Mk. 10: 6-9), parallel texts which recount the words of Gen. 1: 27; 2: 24 and 5: 2 on persons being created male and female, in the image of God, and being joined "two in one flesh". Third is the traditional reference to Eph. 5: 30-31 which again refers back to Gen. 2: 24. All these things are summed up in a fourth reference, this time to Gen. 1: 26 on God making man in His own image. The commentary on these texts is curious.

In these texts are seen the riches, the wisdom and the goodness of God the creator, who at one and the same time took care of the intersubjectivity or permanent complementary union of man and woman and of the procreation of offspring and the wonderful suitability of the married couple for this purpose[81].

79. Cf. J. SELLING, *A Closer Look at the Text of Gaudium et spes*.
80. *Ibid.*, p. 33.
81. In his textibus apparent divitiae, sapientia necnon bonitas Dei Creatoris qui simul

None of the scriptural texts noted even mentions procreation. In fact, a case can be made for these texts substantiating the belief that human sexuality has a goal or purpose all of its own, without necessarily having to be connected to procreation. God created persons in a manner which was complementary — humankind was created a relational being. Yet the *Lin* tells us in the third paragraph that these "two aspects" are also present in contemporary teaching, and goes on to list GS and HV together as if one could not make a differentiation. The chapter then turns to an elaboration of each "aspect" separately.

The "personalist aspect" begins with a repetition of the texts of Gen. 1:27; 2:24 and this time adding 2:23 on man and woman being of the same bones and flesh. The union of man and woman is said to be the work of the Lord himself, from which is concluded "what therefore God has joined together, let no man put asunder" (Mt. 19: 6; cf. 1 Cor. 7: 10, which should have included verse 11). The commentary goes on to speak of conjugal love in a very positive way. A final note warns against "fear of sexual life which is not to be confused with the need for discipline, the sense of responsibility or the awareness of one's duties to God and human beings"[82]. In keeping with the above mentioned need for "rational will" to govern sexual behavior, one would expect the notion of "discipline" to creep up eventually. But what is the meaning of the "duties" which are spoken of here? We will find out under the heading of "chastity" in marriage.

The "fecundity aspect" is now addressed in section III of this chapter and it is said to "widen" the personalist aspect[83]. Reading the *Lin* one gets the impression that all the effort that GS put into avoiding the notion that conjugal love only comes to "completion" when there is procreation and subsequently that there are two types of marriage, the childless one being deficient, has been lost. Nowhere in this document does an appreciation of the non-procreative union come to light. Instead, the text continues with a quote from GS, 50. This, too, is an interesting quotation.

> Children are really — as *Gaudium et spes* says — the supreme gift of marriage, and they contribute very substantially to the welfare of their parents. God himself who said, "It is not good that man should be alone" (Gen. 2:18)... blessed male and female, saying: "Be fruitful and multiply" (Gen. 1:28).

curavit de intersubiectivitate, de unione complementaria permanenti viri et mulieris deque procreatione prolis et mirabili aptitudine coniugum ad eamdem.

82. Non est confundendus timor erga vitam sexualem cum necessitate disciplinae, sensu responsabilitatum, conscientia officiorum erga Dominum et personas humanas.

83. Aspectus personalisticus matrimonii amplior adhuc fit cum, per benedictionem Dei Creatoris, amor coniugum ducit ad procreationem et ad educationem novarum personarum humanarum.

We have noted above that this was the place for a papal *modus*[84]. The quotation here begins with the papal insertion and avoids the original first sentence of GS, 50. That sentence had predicated "procreation and education" to the entire project of "marriage and conjugal love" which was consistent with the theology of that document. The second sentence restricts it to marriage. Then, where the break appears (...) we see that the quote leaves out "and 'who made man from the beginning male and female' (Mt. 19:4), wished to share with man a certain special participation in His own creative work. Thus He..." Why is it missing? The absence reduces the scriptural foundation for appreciating the relational value of human sexual differentiation and gives the impression that the entire purpose of creating "male and female" is solely to allow for procreation. Furthermore, by leaving out the quote from Mt. 19:4 (cf. Gen 1:27) and the Council's explanation, the text in the *Lin* gives the impression that God, "wishing that man should not be alone", granted the power to procreate. Clearly, GS, 50 preserves the meaning of Genesis: so that man should not be alone, He created humankind in two sexes, i.e., as a relational being. Then, and only then, after the "purpose" of sexual differentiation had been fulfilled (marriage *and conjugal love*) and a relationship exists, there comes the *added* dimension of cooperating in the work of the Creator to "be fruitful and multiply". In this sense, GS had respected the real "personalist aspect" of the male-female relation enunciated in Genesis. This intimate closeness of man and woman could also be substantiated by reference to Gen 2:23 ("bone of my bones" which GS included in nr. 49 on conjugal love, cf. note 10 in that text). But even this is thwarted and forced to fit into a meaning proposed in the *Lin*. The reference to Gen 2:23 occurs twice in this chapter: in the opening lines of the section on the "personalist aspect" where it appears to retain its meaning and in the closing lines of the section on the "fecundity aspect" where it is interpreted that *children* are the bone of bones and flesh of flesh. Taking all these factors together it is clear that the *Lin* was using its own interpretation of both scripture and GS to "construct" its argument — an argument which is not substantiated by the sources.

Lest there be any doubt of what has been implied, the *Lin* goes on to explain that the "gift of God" and "conjugal duty" rest in this: "the beginning of human history and the possibility of dominating the whole of the earth"[85], in short, procreation. The next paragraph needs to be quoted in full.

Although a regulation of births can be opportune and licit (21), this cannot be secured while forgetting what was said by the Second Vatican Council: "Relying

---

84. Cf. *supra*, pp. 186-187.
85. In hoc verbo inveniuntur et donum Dei et officium coniugum: in hoc stat initium historiae humanae et possibilitas dominandi totam terram.

on these principles, the sons and daughters of the Church may not undertake methods of regulating procreation that are found blameworthy by the teaching authority of the church in its unfolding of God's law". (22) Such methods were again found blameworthy not long afterward in the encyclical *Humanae vitae*[86].

First there is the notion of birth regulation being "opportune and licit". The reference given at this point is Pius XII's "Address to the Midwives" (1951). One wonders if this is the best that could have been done. What happened to the teaching of GS on responsible parenthood? Surely that was a much fuller expression about "opportuneness" than Pius XII's "serious reasons". Obviously, the point to be singled out here is the former Pope's condemnation of contraception — something GS failed to include because it considered the question in a state of doubt. Then comes the famous dictum of GS, 51 which is also the place of a papal *modus*. In the original, "relying on these principles" is very clear: there are real conflict situations in which the couple must preserve both the value and dignity of life, even from conception, as well as their relationship by not breaking off conjugal intimacy; in dealing with human sexuality, one should not be reduced to the application of mere "biological norms"; rather, the criteria to be used in making moral decisions is to be based "on the nature of the human person and their acts". When we read the phrase here, all that information is absent. Are the implied "principles" to be relied upon those of Pius XII? Next comes the quotation of the conciliar text itself. It should be recalled that the papal *modus* suggested the change of the subordinate verb from *improbantur* to *improbatae sunt vel improbentur*. The first, perfect tense, and the second, subjunctive form of the verb were rejected and the original present indicative was maintained. But when we read the Latin version of the *Lin* we see the reappearance of *improbentur*. One might like to say that this was a typographical error. This might be an acceptable explanation if it happened only once. We will see that it recurrs in IL, 65. Finally, to erase any doubt about the intended meaning, the last sentence tells us that HV has once again reiterated the teaching condemning contraception. The implication seems to be that nothing had changed between 1951 and 1968.

With the problematic of the moral evaluation of various methods for controlling or limiting fertility now presumably out of the way, the section on the aspect of fecundity returns to its basic premise. "The logical normal evolution of married love itself leads husband and wife to procreate new human beings"[87]. This will remain a central phrase, for it

86. Si aliqua regulatio nativitatum opportuna et licita esse potest haec non potest obtineri obliviscendo verba Vaticani Secundi: "Filiis Ecclesiae, his principiis innixis, in procreatione regulanda, vias inire non licet, quae Magisterio, in divina lege explicanda, improbentur". Quod nuper denuo factum est in Litteris Encyclicis *Humanae vitae*.

87. Ipsa logica et normalis evolutio amoris coniugalis ducit coniuges ad procreationem novarum personarum humanarum.

will reappear, along with the quote to follow, in IL, 63. One does not doubt the "logic" of the statement, but one could have serious questions about its relevance. What is "normal" for one couple in one situation may be very abnormal for another. Even if one could agree with the interpretation of "statistical normality" this would not account for the derivation of a moral norm. Objective facticity does not lead to a moral precept, unless of course one chooses static natural law thinking as their point of departure.

This opening sentence is followed by a quote from GS, 50 which directly follows the quote given in truncated form in the first paragraph of the section. In the original conciliar text, this sentence had two meanings, both of which are lost here. First, the phrase "while not making the other purposes of matrimony of less account" was introduced to balance the papal intervention in this text and guard against a traditionalist interpretation of the doctrine of the hierarchy of ends of marriage. The second was to define the acceptance of the vocation and mission to procreate *and educate* children as a voluntary decision to "cooperate with the love of the creator and savior". That mission is offered to married persons and its acceptance would be further spelled out in GS, 50 in terms of the teaching on "responsible parenthood". The way in which the statement appears here, out of context and following the introductory, naturalistic theory of human procreation as a "logical normal evolution", amounts to a reinterpretation of the conciliar teaching. Unless one returns to the original document and reads the teaching in its entirety, its meaning could be lost or at least obscured.

The fourth paragraph of this section demonstrates that long before 1979 there were already various ways of interpreting conciliar documents. The extensive quote given from HV, 8 repeats an interpretation of GS that already had been present in the encyclical in 1968:

Marriage, then, is far from being the effect of chance or the result of the blind evolution of natural forces. It is in reality the wise and provident institution of God the creator, whose purpose was to effect in man his loving design. As a consequence, husband and wife, through that mutual gift of themselves that is specific and exclusive to them alone, develop that union of two persons in which they perfect each other, cooperating with God in the generation and upbringing of new lives[88].

---

88. Tantum igitur abest, ut matrimonium e casu quodam vel e caeco naturalium virium cursu nascatur, ut reapse illud sapienter providenterque Creator Deus ea mente instituerit, ut in hominibus suum amoris consilium efficeret. Quocirca per mutuam sui donationem, quae ipsorum propria est et exclusoria, coniuges illam persequuntur personarum communionem, qua se invicem perficiant, ut ad novorum viventium procreationem et educationem cum Deo operam socient. (HV,8; *Lin*, p. 20, separates *quocirca* into two words)

The text of HV here does not give any reference to GS, but the parallel text would necessarily have to be GS, 48 on the doctrinal teaching on marriage. Consulting that text we see that nowhere is the identification made between "the *institution* of marriage and the family" and the fact that God is its ultimate author. GS says that God is the author of *marriage*: the conjugal relationship. The function of the word "institution" in the whole of GS refers to the product of the work of human society. Institutions are human realities and although their meaning and foundation *may* be traced to the divine plan of the Creator (there are unjust, as well as just, institutions which obviously should not be traced to the divine plan) their actual structure is recognized to be historical and in constant need of reevaluation and development. Then, in saying that "marriage is far from being the effect of chance or the result of the blind evolution of natural forces", HV had set up a kind of "straw man". There is no responsible person who asserts that it is purely the result of chance, for marriage and family life develop in ways which are adapted to their social milieu and must be appropriate to the realization of their goals. Nor is it fair to attribute its development to the "blind evolution of natural forces". This statement prejudices the issue. There are "natural forces" at work here, but their evolution is not literally "blind". Rather, as GS well understood, there is a *historicity* of the institution of marriage and family, the same historicity which shapes and molds culture itself and makes human institutions efficient transmitters of the values which form the "patrimony of each human community" (GS, 53).

Further, consulting the Latin text we see that the English translation left out a very important word: *ut*. The original was evident in its intent. The last phrase was a purpose clause and the entire statement says that "husband and wife develop their union *so that* they can cooperate with God in the procreation and education of children". Thus the original (Latin) version of the *Lin* is consistent in its message: there may be a so-called "personalist aspect" to the marital relationship, but that "aspect" is clearly in service to the "fecundity aspect". The teaching of the *Lin* had effectively returned to the doctrine of the hierarchy of the ends of marriage, regardless of its appropriation of some of the "new" vocabulary.

The last paragraph of section III simply reiterates this reinterpretation of the scriptural and conciliar teaching. Section IV brings together the various elements for a statement of its basic presuppositions, the "two aspect theory". The title of this section is "The Two Aspects are Inseparable". It reads as follows:

The inseparability of these two significances (*significationum*) of married life is taught in an especially clear way in the encyclical *Humanae vitae* published by Pope Paul VI of blessed memory. After recalling the intimate connection between the two finalities (*finalitates*), the pope writes: "This particular doctrine, (often) expounded by the teaching authority of the church, ('') is based on the inseparable connection, established by God and not breakable by man on his own initiative, between the unitive significance and the procreative significance inherent, both of them, in the marriage act. ('') The reason is that the fundamental nature of the marriage act, while uniting husband and wife in the closest intimacy, also renders them capable of generating new life — and this as a result of laws written into the actual nature of man and woman. And, if each of these essential qualities, the unitive and the procreative, is preserved, the use of marriage fully retains its sense of true mutual love and its ordination to the supreme responsibility of parenthood to which man is called. We believe that our contemporaries are particularly capable of seeing this teaching is in harmony with human reason''. (parentheses added)[89].

This section consists basically in a quotation of the whole of HV, 12. In a way this is logical because the *Lin* is fundamentally a repetition of that encyclical, adding on a few more interpretations of Scripture and GS to substantiate its case. But there is a problem in that the *Lin* simply takes over the text of the encyclical without realizing the inherent weakness of that doctrine. For one, Paul VI had obscured the controversy over the doctrine of the ends of marriage by using a new (cf. GS) word: *significationes*. Thus the shift from the "primary-secondary" doctrine to what we call the "two aspect theory". In the former there is a clear hierarchy; in the latter there is no evident hierarchy but the "inseparability" factor functions just as well. The doctrine itself is deficient because it begs the question how the "procreative meaning" is present in non-fertile intercourse. It begs a more subtle question in respect to the implication that *nothing* can be done to break this connection by man's own initiative. Does this include the intentional manipulation of fertility via a program of periodic continence? The intended meaning of the statement is clear, contraception may not be used. But it would be unwise to ignore the other possible meaning which itself would stand in contradiction to the acceptance of controlling fertility by "natural means".

Then, there is a slip of the pen in referring to the two "finalities", a word which should have been avoided if one were attempting to move away from the biological norm for sexual morality. Evidently, no such attempt was made. This is no surprise since HV itself is a restatement of that biologism. Furthermore, the doctrine given here, the "two aspect theory" is very often misunderstood. A careful examination of the text

89. The Latin text provided by the *Lin* is the same as that of HV,12 with two exceptions. The *Lin* leaves out the word "often" (*saepe*) from the first sentence of the quote. Perhaps this is closer to the truth than was HV because the Church indeed has *not* "often" taught this doctrine. The so-called "unitive meaning" of marital intercourse has only recently been discovered by the magisterial teaching on conjugal morality. Secondly, for some unknown reason the *Lin* introduces extra quotation marks which give the impression that there is a break in the text: "Huiusmodi doctrina, quae ab Ecclesiae Magisterio (saepe) exposita est" ... "Etenim propter intimam suam rationem ..."

reveals that HV, 12 is not speaking of the "aspects of marriage" but rather of sexual intercourse. The meanings are present "in the marriage act". The reason is based upon the "fundamental nature of the marriage act", which in turn is based upon the "laws written into the actual (biological?) nature of man and woman". And following the doctrine, "the use of marriage" (a traditional euphemism for sexual intercourse) retains its full sense, "its ordination to the supreme *responsibility of parenthood* to which man is called". Note that one does not have a calling to *responsible parenthood* but rather to the responsibility (in the original, more clearly, "duty", *munus*) *of* or *to* parenthood. Note especially that the "use of marriage" has an ordination to "love and the duty of parenthood". Since it is intercourse which is being spoken of, one can only posit procreation as its duty (*munus*). Even the traditional doctrine was always careful to stipulate procreation *and education* as an end of *marriage*. Finally, the last sentence on the rationality of this doctrine is presumed to be acceptable to all persons. Obviously we find ourselves begging one more question: then why do many reasonable persons not accept the doctrine?

Here ends the basic doctrine on marriage. It is pre-conciliar and essentialistic, built upon a specific interpretation of documents about which there is hardly universal agreement. As a final note, we could say that this chapter never attains to the meaning of its title. Although there is an obvious example of the *Lin*'s doctrine of marriage, the notion of "Family Partnership" is hardly touched upon except under the presupposition that procreation is a "duty" and necessary part of the conjugal relation. Nothing is said about the relationship between parents and children themselves, much less about the "Intention of God the Creator regarding Family Partnership". In fact, the very notion of "God's creative intention" has nothing to do with His moral will, His creative activity as continuous, or what we would call His Providence. All it means in the theology present here is natural law.

The third chapter of the doctrinal Part II is devoted to "The Intention and Work of God the Redeemer". It has, again, four sections, the last of which has two subdivisions. The first section begins the chapter with the so-called "wide definition" of family, namely that all of mankind can be spoken of as the "family of God". At first this is spoken of broadly in that the New Covenant encompasses all of mankind, "whether Jew or Gentile" in a paraphrase of St. Paul's writings on the "mystery" of Christ which establishes the covenant between all persons[90]. Then the depar-

---

90. A footnote given here (n. 27) lists the references as Rom. 16:25-26; Eph. 3:3-10 and Col. 1:26. But no reference is given to the text recalling that all persons who have faith are sons of God and "there is neither Jew nor Greek ..." (Gal. 3:28), even though the image is used in the text of the *Lin*. Indeed the omission was perhaps intentional for a full quotation of this text, "... neither slave nor free, neither male nor female; for you are all one in Christ

ture point is narrowed down to the specifically christian family as those who are members of Christ's Church. Quoting *Lumen gentium* (LG), 1 on the Church, it is said "by her relationship with Christ, the Church is a kind of sacrament or sign and means of intimate union with God and of the unity of all mankind". The Church is a "kind' of" sacrament, as Christ Himself is a "kind of" sacrament of God. Then, one of the images said to represent the Church is "the family". From this is drawn the conclusion that family as such — now in its narrow sense as family unit — is also a "kind of" sacrament.

The images here are rich and point to a renewed form of sacramentology which is typical of the theology of Vatican II. But here is where the appropriation of that sacramentology ends and the words are used to fit the theology of the *Lin*. The second section begins with a subtle shift from speaking of the meaning of "family" to "Inserting the Marriage of Christians into the Mystery of Christ". Again, the document, supposedly dedicated to the role of the christian family, reduces its thought to the meaning of christian marriage. It begins by stating that persons share in the "sacrament or mystery" of Christ through the special sacraments, the first of which is baptism. Another of these is marriage, or the "effective communion of Christian married people". One is tempted to stop here and investigate the meaning of the word "effective": does an ineffective union, one in which there is no real "covenantal relationship" in the full sense, disqualify the union from being sacramental? Such a line of reasoning, however, does not come into the scope of the document's reflection, primarily because "marriage" is still looked upon as a singular event, isolated in time and totally encompassed within the external moment when vows are exchanged in the public forum. The text continues:

A new covenant, a new union "in Christ" takes the place of the purely human covenant, elevating married love to the firmness of the charity of Christ without any suppression of its human specificity. This covenant is assumed in the covenant of the love between Christ and the Church, not merely psychologically but ontologically as is taught by the letter to the Ephesians[91].

One wonders exactly what is meant here. The "union in Christ" *takes the place of (locum sumit)* the "purely" human covenant, yet it does not suppress its human specificity. Are there two covenants here or one? The second sentence appears to answer the question by returning to the "ontological" language of the *Lin* itself. The establishment of the

Jesus", might prove to be an embarassment to the theology of the author(s) of the *Lin* who evidently holds to a fundamental distinction between male and female.

91. Foedus novum, unio nova "in Christo" locum sumit foederis pure humani, extollens amorem coniugalem usque ad firmitatem caritatis Christi sine ulla detractione (*suppression*) suae specificitatis humanae. Hoc foedus assumitur in foedere amoris Christi et Ecclesiae, non tantum psychologice sed ontologice, ut docet ipsa epistola ad Ephesios.

marriage — that instant of verbalization frozen in time forever — is the essence of the "covenant" which is here called (and reduces the meaning of) "sacrament". Everything is presumed. Because the marriage is entered into "in Christ" it *will be* efficacious, it *will be* total and faithful, it *will be* lasting.

The problems of this text are complicated by the fact that there is a certain lack of attention to detail. As an example, we draw attention to a footnoted reference, presumably testifying to the ontological reality of the marital covenant "assumed in the covenant of the love between Christ and the Church". Returning to the source (Eph. 5:25), one reads, "Husbands, love your wives, as Christ loved the church and gave himself up for her". Does the *Lin* intend to imply that there is a direct parallel between marriage and the Christ-Church relationship in which the man is "head" of his wife as Christ is the head of the Church (Eph. 5:23)[92] and the women is "subject to her husband" as the Church is subject to Christ (Eph. 5:22)? This was the interpretation of Pius XI in *Casti connubii*. The correct reference should probably have been to Eph. 5:32, "This is a great mystery, and I mean in reference to Christ and the church", which in fact appears in the following paragraph of the *Lin*. We should point out that that reference is here immediately followed by a repetition of the interpersonal communion being "the example and *ontological* foundation for a new kind of lawful union of wife and husband".

Rather than exegete every phrase of the rest of this section we should concentrate on the attempted parallel of the Christ-Church relationship to establish the sacramentality of marital union via an interpretation of Paul's letter to the Ephesians. To begin, the text of St. Paul is not as simple as it first appears. The very first verse of the pericope is a problem. Does 5:21, "Be subject to one another out of reverence for Christ", belong to the pericope which goes before on the relations of christians in general, or does it belong to the sayings on marriage as texts in translation usually structure it? There is no conclusive evidence for either possibility. It would seem that if the entirety of the text, disregarding chapter and verse designations, is taken into account then we should interpret this verse as applying to the relations between christians, between married persons, between children and parents, and between slaves and their masters. In this thinking, the marital relationship is only one of many examples to illustrate the sacramental character of the "great mystery" of the Christ-Church relation. In attempting to use this analogy there should be no more emphasis on the "absoluteness" of

92. The text immediately following the quote given above reads as follows: "Mysterium" (seu sacramentum) Christi, enim praesentatur ut manifestatio amoris sponsi erga Ecclesiam suam. Christus praesentatur ut "Caput Ecclesiae, ipse Salvator corporis" (Eph. 5,23).

Paul's notion of marriage than there is on his notion of the relation between slaves and masters — except for the fact that *all* these human relations should be lived out in a specifically christian way, namely, as symbols of Christ's love for us. Taking Paul's analogy literally, if masters treated their slaves as Christ treats the Church, it would result in a social revolution that would ultimately abolish slavery, presuming of course that Christ established His Church in freedom and called it to responsibility.

Turning to the pericope itself, 5:23-33, there is another question as to whether Paul is using the phenomenon of marriage to teach us something about the Church or is he using the Church to say something about marriage? The *Lin*, following an essentialist interpretation, opts for the second possibility while another interpretation of the text could argue to the first one just as validly, if not more so. The reasons for accepting the first are twofold. First, there is verse 32, "This is a great mystery, and I mean in reference to Christ and the church". Paul does not specifically say that the marital relationship is a "mystery". Secondly, the notion of using marriage as an analogy in Scripture is not an invention of St. Paul. The Old Testament often referred to the same analogy but in a curious way. The examples given are for the most part concerned with marital infidelity: whereas a wife (God's People) very often proves herself to be unfaithful to her part of a mutual commitment, the loving husband (God) not only remains ever faithful but in His "kindness and mercy" never ceases to forgive the erring spouse. It is typical of Scripture to use common examples to teach great truths, whereas it is common of some schools of interpretation to use great truths in order to impose precepts upon daily life experiences.

Finally, to complete the picture, it is necessary to follow through the general theme of our entire analysis and consult the teaching of the Council on this matter. It is interesting that this particular, and one might say crucial, section of the *Lin* makes no reference to conciliar documents. Had the Council spoken of this matter or used the same analogy? The logical place to look is GS, 48 on the doctrinal understanding of marriage. There we find that the Council, in speaking of conjugal love, teaches that "Christ the Lord abundantly blessed this many-faceted love, welling up as it does from the fountain of divine love and structured as it is on the model of His union with the Church". What is said here is that all human love has its origin in and is a reflection of divine love, for God, who is love, is the source of all things. This is not to say that human love is divine, which would boarder on the idolatrous. Rather it is an attempt to trace conjugal love to its source in the hope of revealing everything that it can be and eventually be capable of realizing. The specifically christian contribution to this meditation is that God's love for His People and Christ's love for the Church reveal a model in the covenant of absolute fidelity. This is the goal to be achieved, the ideal to be striven for. Its nurture and the intentional commitment to its realization provides the grounds for the Church to speak of its sacramentality: the human reality of the marital covenant is both sign and reality of the presence of God.

It would be more accurate to say that GS invokes the analogy of divine love in order to come to a better understanding of conjugal love. That analogy is *illustrative* of what is commonly referred to as the sacramentality of marriage, namely that an event which both signifies and effects the presence of God (grace) is sacramental; some of those events are especially singled out as specific sacraments. In other words, all human relationships which genuinely live out the essence of the christian message are sacramental because they evoke and are a sign of the real presence of God ("where two or three are gathered together in my name, there I am in their midst", Mt. 18:20). When the marital covenant is taken on in the light of the gospel message, we call it a sacrament. Where persons involve themselves in a total and lasting commitment in a specifically christian way, they reflect the faithful commitment of God to His People. This phenomenon is also present in what is called the sacrament of "Holy Orders". One may wonder why the same type of commitment, especially when accompanied by vows of poverty, celibacy and obedience, cannot always be called "sacrament".

The idea of singling out marriage as such a specific type of relationship that it can be called a sacrament can be substantiated by referring to the analogy with divine love (God-People, Christ-Church). But the analogy is not *constitutive* of the sacrament itself. We must be careful of working in the right direction in order to apply the analogy. We do not start with divine love and then say that this human love relationship must be, in its very essence, exactly the same. That would amount to saying that human persons were capable of exercising divine love in an absolute way. Rather, we must work in the opposite direction. Starting with the experience of human love we seek to analyze it to find whether this phenomenon can truly be spoken of in terms of being "sacramental". We find that immature love, such as that of children, is not a proper vehicle for making this statement. Further, even mature love, which is not specifically christian and does not aspire to be representative of God's presence, is certainly good but not yet capable of being called "sacramental". Only that type of love relationship which is mature and responsible, which truly wills the good of the other in its self-giving, which is committed to being faithful and lasting, and which is lived out in the name of Christ, can truly be called "sacramental". This relationship, which is an ongoing project in the process of realization, and not simply the isolated moment of exchanging vows verbally and publicly is so special in the eyes of the Church that it is defined as a sacrament, a specific phenomenon which signifies and really effects the loving and faithful presence of God. If the relationship, *qua* relationship, does not accomplish these things, how is it possible to call it a sacrament?

The text of the *Lin* reverses this order and considers the invocation of the word sacrament as "imposing" characteristics on the love relationship which may in fact never have been or are not present. It even goes so far as to refer to Christ's love for the Church as "conjugal". Is it not curious that Christ's love is called "conjugal" only in this context? The appropriation of the adjective is in truth unnecessary and amounts to "reading something into" an interpretation (which is superfluous) so that the idea can later be used as a justification for a statement which was intended in the first place. In any case, the citation of Christ's love being "conjugal" is clearly put forth for a very specific reason (cf. also, *Familiaris consortio*, 37).

The third section of this chapter, on "Perfecting Married Love through the Will for Definitive Self-Giving", is largely a watered down version of what has been expressed better elsewhere (GS, 48-49). The point of the section is more accurately a reiteration of the doctrine on the indissolubility of the "permanent sacrament" of marriage. A major problem here is the absence of discussion about the fact that this relationship and this self-giving is supposed to be *mutual* and reciprocal. The document here is dealing with a very individualistic notion of sacramental creation. One could even characterize it as stoic.

Coming to the final section of this document upon which we will give any substantial commentary, section IV of Chapter III, Part II is dedicated to "The Asceticism of Conjugal Fidelity and Chastity". It has two subdivisions, the first dealing with the "asceticism of conjugal fidelity"[93] and the recognition that although "indissolubility is a precept of the Lord and a consequence of the insertion of human love into the charity of Christ", it must still be worked out by the spouses themselves. This, it is said,

requires generosity, an open mind, continual attentiveness to the other, mutual respect, self-denial and forgetfulness of offenses or defects. Married life is the way in which the daily duties and tasks, the sorrows and inevitable hurts, and the ordinary and religious acts of the domestic church show that, in this also, "everything works for good with those who love God" (Rom. 8,28).

It is doubtful that many persons would argue with these elegant thoughts. It is equally doubtful that many persons would not look upon them as idealistic. While they serve to explicitate a list of "ideals" for christian life, they hardly reflect reality, especially in light of social,

---

93. The title of the first subdivision is *Ascesis fidelitatis coniugalis*, inaccurately represented in translation which included "chastity", the treatment of which comes only in the second subdivision.

economic, political and religious structures which militate against their realization. Without wishing to question the role of "ideals" in teaching and exhortation, we could point out that if the *Lin* was really aimed at addressing the situation of marriage and the family in the world, it should have been more honest about the gap between ideals and their engagement.

The second subdivision then deals with "conjugal chastity". It is clear that by "chastity" here is meant the anachronistic notion of "control over sexual desire and behavior". As noted above, GS had put forth a more dynamic idea of virtue, especially the one being dealt with here. The *Lin* relies, instead, upon the teachings of St. Paul with respect to the sacredness of the body as "sanctified by the Holy Spirit" and possessing "the gift and the fruit of the Spirit of the Lord". No one will disagree with Paul's teaching, as long as it is accurately represented without prejudice, i.e. allowing for varying interpretations. But a closer examination of the texts to which reference is made raises the question of their relevance. The first, 1 Tim. 4:1-4, is indeed a representation of Paul's doctrine on the goodness of created things[94]. The *Lin* then asks what Paul "asks for here and in the other exhortations that he addresses to christian married people"? Unfortunately, no such "exhortations addressed to married christians" are given by the *Lin*. Instead, we find two more references, one on the body being a temple of the Holy Spirit[95] and another on the gifts and fruits of the Spirit[96]. The conclusion then drawn, supposedly from Paul's writing, is that spouses should be aware of their sanctification by the Spirit "so that all their conjugal acts, even the more intimate ones, are inspired by the couple's vocation, which is both God-given and fully human, and not by the impulse of unbridled disordered passion"[97].

We would have to agree that all conjugal acts — here including *all* acts and not just the sexual ones — should be guided by the total life task of the marital project which could also be called the couple's vocation. But

---

94. I Tim. 4:1-4: "Now the Spirit expressly says that in later times some will depart from the faith by giving heed to deceitful spirits and doctrines of deamons, through the pretensions of liars whose consciences are seared, who forbid marriage and enjoin abstinence from foods which God created to be received with thanksgiving by those who believe and know the truth. For everything created by God is good, and nothing is to be rejected if it is received with thanksgiving: (v. 5: for then it is consecrated by the word of God and prayer)".

95. 1 Cor. 6:19: "Do you not know that your body is a temple of the Holy Spirit, within you, which you have from God? You are not your own".

96. Gal. 5:22-23: "But the fruit of the Spirit is love, joy, peace, patience, kindness, goodness, faithfulness, gentleness, self-control; against such there is no law".

97. Optat ut coniuges conscii sint sanctificationis sui corporis per Spiritum Sanctum et praesentiae in eis doni et fructus Spiritus Domini, ita ut omnes actus coniugales etiam intimiores inspirentur vocatione tum divina tum plene humana coniugum, non autem impulsione passionis effrenatae et immoderatae.

we would also ask what the opposite of this would be? The *Lin* opposes "acts inspired by the couple's vocation" to acts inspired "by the impulse of unbridled disordered passion". When does passion become "unbridled" and "disordered"? Passion itself, and the acts which it might inspire, can be totally incorporated into the marital vocation. Indeed, if it is not, the notion of marriage would be entirely spiritualistic. Therefore, unbridledness and disorderedness have to do with passionate acts which are not appropriate expressions of conjugal love. The actual structure of the passionate acts, stated in a purely descriptive way, are in themselves neutral. Their appropriateness can be judged according to how well they realize and serve the marital project, in other words, their goal and intentional purpose.

The meaning of the text of the *Lin* here, however, appears to have something else in mind. There is a latent notion that passionate — or what is obviously meant here: sexual — acts must be "controlled" and "ordered in a right manner". Along with this control and ordering, one comes to the accomplishment of "virtue". The virtue of chastity primarily has to do with specific acts. The way in which they are to be ordered is spelled out later, in the pastoral Part III.

In Part III, Ch. II, section III, on "Issues of Today", the fourth subdivision singles out "Married Love and Chastity". The text is very brief.

The importance for the attainment of holiness of the expressions of *married love*, veneration for the virtue of chastity and the progressive education of husband and wife for the observance of the ethical order as regards the honorable performance of the generative role (*munus*) in the present chircumstances of society — what is today called "responsible parenthood"[98].

There are four major concepts present in this statement of "an issue", all of which are meant to be an explanation of the "holiness of the expressions of *married love*". They are: "veneration for the virtue of chastity" which is clearly act-centered in dealing with the *expressions* and not the project of married love; a restatement of the essentialist ethical order which must be "observed" because it rests entirely outside of and is imposed upon the person; the conclusions of that ethical order which specify "the honorable performance of the generative role in the present circumstances of society"; and lastly, the very specific notion of "responsible parenthood" which is totally dependent upon the concepts enunciated above.

It appears that the meaning of this text is oriented to that observance of an ethical order which results in rules governing the proper use of the

---

98. De momento quod in assecutione sanctitatis habent expressiones propriae *amoris coniugalis*, cultus virtutis castitatis et educatio progressiva coniugum ut ordinem ethicum observent quod attinet ad honestam perfunctionem muneris generandi, pro hodiernis societatis adiunctis, quod hodie dicitur "paternitas responsabilis".

sexual faculty and respect for its finalities, namely the two aspect theory of human sexuality. Following that ethical order, one achieves "chastity" by exercising the expressions of married love in a way that is "ordered", i.e. to the finalities. The condemnation of contraception is implicit in the statement. The mechanistic notion of chastity is more clear. But the most disturbing thing about the statement is its interpretation of the doctrine of "responsible parenthood".

As mentioned above, the *Lin* usually interprets responsible parenthood as the responsibility of parents towards educating their chrildren. GS had put forth the doctrine with respect to the decision whether or not to take on the task of procreating and educating children, and it might be added, prior to and independent from any means which might be chosen to realize that decision. In this text we see the definition of responsible parenthood limited to the "education of husband and wife for the observance of the ethical order as regards the honorable performance of the generative role in the present circumstances of society", in other words, not using contraception. In short, chastity remains a mechanistic, act-centered concept aimed at exercising control over the sexual faculty by means of the rational will which observes an objective moral order. There is no hint of the integrative function of virtue but only a repetition of the textbook ideal of practicing self-discipline and control.

At this point we will end our commentary on the *Lin*[99]. The central part of that document is its "doctrinal" teaching, putting forth the theology of marriage and the family which will inform everything else which is said. The third part, for instance, on "The Roles of the Christian Family", consists of three chapters on "The Upbringing of Children and the Handing on of Faith, Preserving Spiritual Values and Sanctifying its Members, and Fostering and Animating Social Life" respectively. The view presented here is idealistic, namely in keeping with the notions present in Part II that presume a just society, smooth family and marital relationships, and a real potentiality for acting in a free and democratic manner toward the whole of society. This freedom, however, is not extended to one's membership in the Church, for all initiatives taken by parents are qualified as having to come under the supervision of the Church or a pastor. The one improvement of this Part over the others is that there is finally an emphasis upon the family as such, although on a few occasions the discussion turns back to that of marriage alone, especially in Chapter Two.

99. As a postscript to Part II we find the questions for response of the bishops. These are two: 1. Does this setting forth of doctrine answer well enough the pastoral needs of today? Should something else be added? 2. In view of pastoral experience, what points of doctrine should be stressed nowadays? How can and should this be done?

Notice, once again, that the "doctrinal" content of what is said is presumed to be complete and the only point of inquiry here is a possibility for additions or emphasis. There is no inquiry on the doctrine itself.

To summarize the content of the *Lin* as a document for proposing discussion on the topic of marriage and the family, we find a rather closed and very limited perspective on the issues to be dealt with in the post-conciliar era. There is little or no appreciation for the renewed and highly nuanced theology of GS. Finally, there is even less evidence that "marriage and the family in the modern world" was being consulted and taken as a starting point. Rather, the document concentrates on its "doctrinal teaching" which was constructed in such a way as to provide all the answers to questions which never seem to be properly raised[100]. Rather than being an outline of points for discussion, it appears to be more of a blueprint for the Synod's confirmation.

100. We have already mentioned that the "situation of marriage and the family" in Part I was almost entirely negative and painted a picture of extreme crisis. In Part III, the actual role of the christian family is described in terms of a stable, idealistic situation which has little to do with reality. No one disagrees, for instance, that parents should educate their children religiously and socially; but it was an expectation that the Synod would address the problem of how to achive that goal in light of the contemporary situation.

III. THE INSTRUMENTUM LABORIS

The second preparatory document for the 1980 Synod, IL, was issued on 16 June 1980. It is longer than the *Lin*, consisting of 88 pages, 4 of which list the contents, and 95 sequentially numbered sections. Like the *Lin*, after a brief Introduction (1-8), it consists of three parts: "The Situation of the Family in the World" (9-26); "God's Plan for the Contemporary Family" (27-50); and "Pastoral Problems" (51-95). From the very beginning, IL, 1, the text insists that this document is proposed only as a vehicle for "meditation and discussion" during the Synod itself and not a schema for the outcome of that meeting. By its nature and content, the IL is a transitory document. It is much more developed than the *Lin*, but it is still not worthy to be called synodal in any sense because its presuppositions are still those of only one school of thought.

The *Lin* had been reacted to and criticized for being very Western in its inspiration, too preoccupied with problems instead of their causes, and looking at marriage and the family individualistically and from the inside out instead of from a more social perspective. Some of those shortcomings have been corrected in the IL which showed signs of a broadening outlook. This can probably be attributed to the reactions to the *Lin* coming from the bishops during the previous year (1979). But the overall vision of the document is still not integrated. It operates out of the same theological perspective as the *Lin*, often repeating ideas and even exact words which were in the earlier text [101]. At the same time there is a slight shift in structure. Whereas the *Lin* had concentrated most of its substance in Part II, on doctrinal teaching, the IL has been expanded to give some answers to "Pastoral Problems", Part III. Nonetheless, this remains a change in style, for the basic approach is the same in both documents.

A. The Situation

The description of the contemporary situation of the family given in the first part of the IL is something of an improvement over the previous document but remains essentially negative. In what appears to be the result of direct influence of episcopal reactions to the *Lin*, the first section (IL, 10-15) concentrates more upon factors affecting the family and making it difficult for marriage and family structure to develop, especially in conditions of social and economic deprivation. This attention to objective factors was very much wanting in the *Lin*, but its inclusion here

---

101. Some of these have already been mentioned such as the definition of family in the Introduction to the *Lin* and in IL,7.

is at most passing. It will not play as major a role as many would have liked in the rest of the IL. For that matter, neither would attention to detail. IL, 15, on human sexuality, for instance, repeats the *Lin*'s practice of quoting or referring to texts, especially those of Vat. II, in a somewhat dubious manner. It is said here that, "Indeed the Second Vatican Council remarks that the sexual act is the one vehicle of conjugal love that 'is able to endow the expressions of body and soul with a particular dignity and to ennoble them as being special elements and signs of conjugal friendship' "[102]. If we return to GS, 49 from which this statement is taken we find that the quotation is correct but that the subject of the sentence is "conjugal love" and not the sexual act as the Latin text of IL seems to imply. Further on in the same number there is another reference to conciliar teaching which recommended that children "be given a positive and prudent sexual education as they grow up"[103]. This is hardly objectionable, but the same paragraph goes on to put a label on this which is drawn not from the council but from HV, namely that it would "bring about 'a state of things ... which favors the cultivation of chastity'"[104]. "Chastity" is once again linked to sexual regulation whereas the conciliar notion of it being a life project, here pertaining to the whole of married life, is completely lost.

The second section of this first Part then singles out four "aspects of contemporary life" which are said to challenge both "christian principles and the teaching of the Church". The four are familiar: non-marital unions, the transmission of life, divorce and abortion (IL, 16-19). But we do find a slight nuance in the way in which the topics are presented. There is the acknowledgement of different types of "cases" with respect to these phenomena. There are social conditions, customs, etc. which are recognized as having a role in the formation of "extramarital unions". The IL even goes so far as to admit that "not all unions contracted outside of matrimony signify an outright denial of the good points of christian marriage, those consisting in unity, fidelity, permanence, procreation". While this can be viewed as a rather "open statement" we should also be aware that it simultaneously provides us with what is the operative definition of "marriage": the characteristics of both conjugal love and marriage mentioned by GS, 49 and 50 now applied to marriage directly.

---

102. Ipsum Concilium Vaticanum Secundum animadvertit opus sexuale esse unam amoris coniugalis rationem quae "corporis animique expressiones peculiari dignitate ditare easque tamquam elementa ac signa specialia coniugalis amicitiae nobilitare valet".
The translation for Part One of the IL is taken from *Origins, art. cit.*, but does not contain the paragraph numbers; cf. p. 229. To my knowledge the remainder of that document has not been published in English.

103. Reference is made to the "Declaration on Christian Education", *Gravissimum educationis*, 1.

104. Reference is made to HV,22.

While these "good points of christian marriage" seem neutral enough, what we are encountering here is a nascent idea which will play a role in the outcome of the Synod. HV, 9 had described conjugal love as "fully human, total, faithful and exclusive, and open to procreation". It had further, in footnote 8, ascribed these ideas to GS, 50. Consulting that document we find that only the procreative aspect is discussed at that point in connection with *both* conjugal love and marriage, while the first three "characteristics" are found in GS, 49 — where no mention of procreation is made at all in the discussion of conjugal love alone. There was a significant nuance in the conciliar teaching. Conjugal love, in and of itself, is properly human, total, faithful and exclusive. It need not be "open to procreation" to be valid, fulfilling and a suitable basis for building a marital covenant. For one, procreation is not always possible; for another, there may be an indication that procration should be avoided. In accordance with traditional insights the Council taught that the childless marriage is no less a marriage or sacrament than one in which procreation has been realized. Nonetheless, HV had sought some form of justification for positing the necessity of procreative "openness" and thus ascribed that opennes to conjugal love, as one of its "characteristics". In doing so it lost the nuance present in GS, 49 and inaccurately attributed the teaching to GS, 50. This change had been picked up in the IL, 16. It would reappear again in Proposition 21 and FC, 29 & 50.

As for the problem of the transmission of life itself, a new element has been introduced which also will be highlighted during the Synod. Going beyond the private ethical issue of the methods for regulating fertility, the paragraph begins with the problem of government intervention in the conscience decisions of couples with respect to the size of their family. Referring to *Populorum progressio*, 37 there is an indication that this one issue will be handled in a more global way than it was in the past. Unfortunately, however, the text ultimately reverts back to the "private" issue of method which it promises to explain further on in Parts II and III. At this point there is already an endorsement of the so-called "natural" methods of family planning.

Discussion of the last two subjects, divorce and abortion, appears to deal more with the legal aspects — permission, changing laws — than the moral issues. The laws have made both easier, it is said, which is interpreted as a cause and effect relation leading to an increased occurrence of these phenomena. While the parallel cannot be denied, one wonders what form of solution is envisioned in the IL. Will it be a simple matter of recreating stricter laws? Then, there is an interesting precision in regard to abortion in the text here which reiterates the Church's doctrine condemning any form of *direct* destruction of the life of the fetus. That precision, viewed from the area of contemporary moral theology, should be appreciated for introducing more complexity and questions into the issue than it does solutions. However, it is doubtful that this was the intention of the IL at this point.

Section Three, on the Catholic family in the world today, brings this first Part to a close. It is rather different than the earlier document and even sounds a positive note in appreciating some of the progress which has been made in family life and spirituality. Nonetheless, there are negative elements to be found. These occur under the heading of "pluralism in religious matters", specifically in that type of pluralism which is said to be within the Church herself (IL, 22). On the one hand, this is said to come from theological renewal and greater attention to biblical theology; on the other,

the plurality arises as much as anything from rejection of or dissension from the teaching of the magisterium, especially in the domain of sexual morality. This plunges Catholics into much confusion which, in the first place, affects families which see their religious heritage openly impugned or impaired. It even poses great difficulties to the bishops who, together with the Roman pontiff, are "authentic teachers, that is, teachers endowed with the authority of Christ who preach to the people assigned to them the faith which is to be believed and to be put into practice"[105].

From the very beginning, then, it becomes clear that the IL will tolerate no dissent on the issues of sexual and conjugal morality. Any existing dissent is held to be threatening not only for christian families but even to bishops. Such a statement does not seem appropriate for a document which is supposed to stimulate "meditation and discussion". One might even venture to describe the outlook as "closed". Unfortunately, the issue has become closed not through an evaluation of any of the moral argumentation but purely on the grounds that differing opinions constitute dissent from the teaching of the Magisterium.

B. The Doctrine

The title of the second part of the IL is "God's Plan (*Proposito*) for the Contemporary Family". This signals the operative theological perspective that from the beginning God laid out a plan or design for the way

---

105. ... verum eadem pluralitas oritur pariter ex reiectione vel dissensione a magisterii doctrina, praesertim in provincia moralitatis sexualis. Id Catholicis magnam parit confusionem et in primis eorum familiis quae vident hereditatem suam religiosam foris impugnatam intus infirmatam. Infert etiam graves difficultates Episcopis qui una cum Romano Pontifice sunt "doctores authentici seu auctoritate Christi praediti, qui populo sibi commisso fidem credendam et moribus applicandam praedicant".
The reference for the quotation is given as LG, 25. Note that nowhere does the quote refer to the *content* of that faith which is to be believed and practiced. Fuller reading of LG,25 reveals a very close connection with scripture with respect to this content and a relative silence about those things outside the deposit of revelation.

things should be (natural law). The guideline is given in the opening paragraph, IL, 27.

Matrimony, from which the family proceeds is a special covenant which takes its origin from the Creator, and as a covenant of familial love is raised to a sacrament by Christ[106].

The covenantal aspect of marriage, as irrevocable personal consent in GS, 48 is extended to the whole of the family which is inextricably linked to marriage as such. This serves to insure that marriage can never be spoken of without including procreation, but it fails to make the distinctions present in GS, 48 and 50 which view that possibility as flowing from marriage and conjugal love in a responsible manner.

The doctrinal part of the IL is divided into six unnumbered sections, each having three to five subdivisions (a, b, c, etc.). They are: I. Marriage as Covenant (28-31); II. Marriage as Sacrament (32-34); III. The Institution and Experience of Marriage and the Family (35-39); IV. The Source of Grace and Holiness (40-42); V. Communal and Participatory Relations in the Family (43-47); and VI. The Role of Familial Evangelization (48-50).

I, a (IL, 28 & 29) bases the marital covenant in creation. It begins with the scriptural and conciliar perspective that the human person was created as a relational being. This is colored with the vocabulary also present in the *Lin*: the relation pertains to "the ontological and psychological nature of man". Of all relations, that between a man and woman is "privileged", it is exclusive and definitive[107]. This is already foreseen in the nature of sexuality itself, and is substantiated by a quote from Gen. 1: 26-27, 31. The text goes on to extol the complementarity of the sexes almost to the point of exaggeration. It climaxes with the idea that "this is the spousal meaning of the body in Revelation"[108].

Having situated the perspective, IL, 29 now makes its major point; "The duality of the sexes is given in service to fecundity", and follows this with the quote from Gen. 1:28, "Increase and multiply and fill the earth". Thus from the beginning God created an exclusive relation between one man and one woman which is called the "reality of the ontological union of love" (*realitas communionis ontologicae amoris*). Again, this structure is elaborated with a repetition of the words of the *Lin* that "the logical and normal evolution of conjugal love ... is effected

106. ... matrimonium ex quo familia procedit est speciale foedus quod a Creatore originem trahit et up foedus familiare amoris assumitur a Christo ut Sacramentum.

107. Sane, relationes cum aliis et cum altero non sunt minoris momenti vel tantum opportunae, sed pertinent ad indolem ontologicam et psychologicam hominum. Inter omnes has relationes longe excellit status amoris "privilegiatus", exclusivus et difinitivus inter virum et feminam in martimonio.

108. Haec est significatio sponsalis corporis in Revelatione.
Reference is given here to a talk of John-Paul II, 9 Jan. 1980. (Cf. FC,37)

in procreation", and followed by the quote of the second sentence of GS, 50 — the result of the papal *modus* which has already been elaborated[109].

The two other divisions of this first section attempt to substantiate these notions with reference to covenant in scripture (IL, 30: Marriage as Covenant) and to the Trinity (IL, 31). The first attempts to build a case for indissolubility based upon God's image as Father (Lk. 15:12; Eph. 3:15) and Pope John-Paul's comment that "in His intimate mystery God is not alone but a family"[110]. The images used here are abstractly theological, but insufficient care has been taken to preserve their reduction to literal interpretation. We have already mentioned that insights and analogies must be respected in their context. The essentialist thinking of this document takes a particular view of divine mysteries and gives the impression that human persons can perfectly imitate the example of divine love. It is as if human life can simply be manipulated to follow a blueprint established at creation.

The ideas proposed here form a preparation for section II on Marriage as Sacrament. That development covers: a. sacramentality (32), b. the true meaning of conjugal love (33), and c. the faith required to receive the sacrament of marriage (34). As for sacramentality, the same argument as that found in the *Lin* is repeated with the same scriptural proof-texting and is elaborated with the addition of membership in the Mystical Body of Christ. At the risk of our own repetition we simply ask whether the New Testament images are analogously meant to give an insight into the divine mystery, or if this is being reversed and an ontological, essentialist view is being superimposed upon human reality? The vocabulary of a "unitive and fecund mystery of love"[111] appears to be used carelessly and in order to fit pre-ordained purposes. It is not human experience which is being allowed to open the way toward the mystery of love, but an already presupposed understanding of divine love (of Christ for the Church) which is being used as a measure for human experience. One might validly ask whether this is the purpose of theological reflection.

Perhaps theological abstraction would be a better characterization for the thoughts present here, for it sometimes leads to a functional

---

109. Ipsa evolutio logica et normalis amoris coniugalis, excludendo revera solitudinem, efficit maximam donationem mutuam coniugum in procreatione et educatione novarum personarum humanarum; uti Constitutio *Gaudium et spes* iterum dicit, "filii sane sunt praestantissimum matrimonii donum et ad ipsorum parentum bonum maxime conferunt". Cf. *supra*, p. 187. The same phrase will again be repeated in Part III, IL,63, on procreation.

110. Deus "in suo intimiore mysterio non est solitudo sed familia".
The comment was made in a homily in Puebla, 28 Jan. 1979.

111. Iuxta Paulum coniuges christiani non tantum imago sunt unionis Christi et Ecclesiae, non tantum illam significant, sed etiam participes sunt eius unitatis fecundique amoris mysterii, quod extat inter Christum et Ecclesiam. Coniugium christianum non solum est signum, sed via quoque sanctificationis, et hoc sacramentum appellamus.

blindness about the richness of human experience itself. When II, b (IL, 33) addresses the "true meaning of conjugal love", it is observed that "this love also leads to an attitude of sacrifice which differs from the type of love among the pagans"[112]. To caricature the latter as simple egoism might be an attempt to describe "christian" love more clearly, but it simultaneously ignores the fact that God as source of all love is manifest in every truly loving human relationship. The perspective used here is hardly ecumenical and could very well have the result of creating divisions in the "unity of mankind".

Thirdly, the discussion on sacramentality recognizes what apparently had been the result of episcopal reaction, namely the question of faith as prerequisite for reception (IL, 34). After a very brief quote from the conciliar "Constitution on Sacred Liturgy" to the effect that the sacraments "not only presuppose faith, but by words and deeds also nourish, strengthen and express it"[113], there is some discussion of sacramental dispensation being a form of evangelization. This is fruitful thinking, but does it answer the question? The later part of this section comes close to addressing the issue by falling back upon the distinction between validity and fruitfulness of a sacrament, usually applied to baptism. But how does this apply to the acts of supposedly mature adults? The only answer which directly touches the issue of personal faith is formulated along the lines of the spouses being the ministers of the sacrament itself and as such, validity is established "as long as they have the intention of doing what Christ and the Church do"[114]. So long as there is no positive exclusionary act of rejecting the gift of Christ and an at least minimal attitude of receiving the sacrament, there appears to be no problem here. In one sense, this is a very pastoral approach to what in reality is an extremely complex problem. However, it does not address, for instance, the question whether a valid marriage can exist which is not sacramental, or not a sacrament in the strict sense. In the end, we see a real issue being forced into the confines of an existing theology, which is rather mechanistic in its view of sacraments, and not a theological reflection upon human experience and genuine pastoral problems.

The third section of Part II is the longest and treats "The Institution and Experience of Marriage and the Family". It begins with an elaboration upon the "nuptial covenant and institution" (IL, 35) which is based upon mutual consent to a unified, singular and indissoluble union.

---

112. Hic etiam amor ad sacrificium dispositus conicitur, qui a proprio amore paganorum.

113. *Sacrosanctum concilium*, 59.

114. Circa *fidem personalem* futurorum coniugum memorandum est ipsos sacramentum matrimonii adire sive qua ministros celebrationis eiusdem, sive qua subiecta nata recipere gratiam Christi Iesu. Pro quanto sunt *ministri*, sponsi valide matrimonium celebrant si habent intentionem faciendi id quod faciunt Christus et Ecclesia.

"Through the sexual aspect (inclination) they mutually give themselves to the witness of intimate love and the generation of new life which is the sign and fruit of mutual love"[115]. It has already been observed how the "gift and crown" of procreation (GS) has been recast into the "sign and fruit of love", something to the detriment of the childless marriage. This particular text uses the procreative aspect to posit the inseparability of the personal and the social aspects of "the bond". Using a quote of the first three (Latin) sentences of GS, 48, the IL calls attention to "internal laws" governing marriage which were posited by the Creator. These, it is said, are to be protected by normative ecclesial and civil legislation which will guard that inseparability. Therefore, any attempt at marriage as "experimental" or "without written witness" must be condemned because it violates the institution.

Having posited the institution, III, b (IL, 36) attempts to describe "The Responsibility of Spouses in the Familial Institution". This is simplified to a single aspect, procreation and education of children. The text uses two quotes from GS:

"By their very nature, the institution of matrimony itself and conjugal love are ordained for the procreation and education of children and find in them their ultimate crown". In transmitting new life spouses will be prepared "to cooperate with the love of the Creator and Savior, who through them will enlarge and enrich His own family day by day".

Both these quotes have been taken out of context. The first comes at the end of the doctrinal development present in GS, 48 and the second comes in the highly nuanced treatment of marital fecundity in GS, 50. The passages have left out the phrase "while not making the other ends of marriage of lesser account" which was meant to balance the papal *modus* in the conciliar teaching. That balance is not maintained here.

Next, III, c attempts to set out the doctrine of "responsible parenthood". Instead of simply quoting the teaching which is found in GS, 50, IL, 37 gives a precis of that text and leaves out the conclusion that "the parents themselves should ultimately make this judgment in the sight of God". Furthermore, whereas GS had taught this as a value judgment, a decision in conscience which is independent from any technical question about the method for carrying out that decision, the IL immediately moves to that aspect. As if to put words into the mouths of the bishops before they even come together, the text suggests that:

The Synod reminds the faithful to manifest religious obedience toward the authentic teaching enunciated by the Church and to follow those objective criteria, which are based upon the nature of the human person and (the nature of?) their acts and "which preserve the full sense of mutual self-giving and human

---

115. Sexuali propensione se mutuo donant ad testificandum intimum amorem et ad novam vitam gignendam, quae est signum et fructus mutui amoris.

procreation in the context of true love, which cannot be achieved unless the virtue of conjugal chastity is sincerely practiced". (parenthesis added)[116]

Besides the incorporation of both conscience decisions and method of execution in the same text, this sentence exhibits a couple other peculiarities. By jumping from GS, 50 to 51, the whole notion of real *conflict* which had originally bridged the two sections is missing. This was a major fault in the logic of HV. Then, the text of GS, 51 has been changed. Instead of quoting *ex personae eiusdemque actuum natura*, we find *ex natura personae huiusque actuum*. The *ex...natura* enclosure has been broken and the change of *eiusdem* could very easily be read to see two separate categories here: the nature of persons and the nature of their acts, an idea specifically avoided in GS[117]. Lastly, it is perhaps pertinent to draw attention to the fact that the reference to chastity was the result of a compromise for another papal *modus*. It does not refer to the "integral sense ... of human procreation" as meaning that "each act of marriage must be open to procreation". Read in its proper context, the "integral sense" refers back to the notion of responsible parenthood, and "chastity" has nothing to do with the mere integrity of the sexual act.

If the implications of this text were not clear enough, they would be spelled out in Part III. In the meantime, two more sub-divisions, on abortion and social responsibility (IL, 38 & 39) end the section. The first calls attention to the sacredness of life and the need for public authority to protect it. The second reflects the teaching of GS, 52 on the family being the basic cell of society. The family and society are interdependent and should work toward their mutual benefit. These are certainly good thoughts, but their idealism would cause great discussion during the Synod itself.

Section IV on the "Source of Grace and Holiness" has three sub-sections. That on sacramental grace (IL, 40) relies heavily upon the *participation* of the marital covenant in that of Christ and the Church. The second, on "spiritual fecundity" (IL, 41) is linked to living out the baptism of christians. It contains a passage on those who voluntarily remain celibate for the Kingdom, but says nothing on involuntary or

116. Synodus fideles admonet, ut religiosam oboedientiam erga authenticam doctrinam ab Ecclesia enuntiatam manifestent adque illa criteria obiectiva sequantur, quae ex natura personae huiusque actuum desumuntur et "quae integrum sensum mutuae donationis ac humanae procreationis in contextu veri amoris observant; quod fieri nequit nisi virtus castitatis coniugalis sincero animo colatur".

117. See the commentary on this text in the *Expensio modorum*, 104, R. c & f (p. 37; p. 502 in the *Acta Synodalia Sacrosancti Concilii Oecumenici Vaticani II*, v. 4, VII): "elementa ex utraque hac propositione retinendo, '*ex personae eiusdemque actuum natura desumptis*'; quibus verbis asseritur etiam actus diiudicandos esse non secundum aspectum merum biologicum, sed quatenus illi ad personam humanam integre et adaequate considerandam pertinent.

non-ministerial celibacy. It also refers to the childless marriage, which is an improvement upon the *Lin*. Such a couple is said to fulfill (*complent*) their mutual giving by continually offering themselves to God and the community and extending their own spirituality (*spiritualitatem propriam*) to others. This may have been an afterthought, for it is not integrated into the rest of the reflection on the meaning of marriage.

The final subdivision is on the family as "domestic church" (IL, 42), a concept taken from LG, 11. This contains a number of fine ideas including the notion of the ministry of the family, not only internally but also to the whole community. If the reflections present here would have been applied more globally, a different type of theology might have emerged. It did not. If we pass ahead to section six on "Evangelization" (IL, 48-50) we see that this role remains fundamentally domestic: it takes place within the confines of the family and is always subject to "pastors" who are the custodians of the deposit of faith. Any communitarian dimensions are limited to the witness value of family life and do not encompass recognizeable offices in the structure of the Church as such.

Section five treats "Communal and Participatory Relations in the Family". After a brief preamble (IL, 43), three aspects are dealt with. First, "Chastity and Conjugal Ascetism" (IL, 44) is similar to the perspective found in the *Lin*, stressing education and discipline and warning against "permissiveness". But there are a few positive notes on the progressive character of growth and the ultimate goal of self-giving. Had the notion of chastity in GS been preserved, that of the fulfillment of the marital life-project, this would have been present in the earlier document. As it is, the association of chastity with ascetism remains negative and based largely upon self-denial.

V, b on "Indissolubility and Unity in Marriage" (IL, 45) is probably the closest thing in the entire document that attempts to provide something of a broad outlook. The text argues that these notions make sense from different perspectives: the spouses experience the need for lastingness for the good of the union as well as for the children (cf. GS, 48); God is said to have intended this bond to be unbreakable from the act of creation; Christ has set forth the example of lasting union in his relationship with the Church (again, Eph. 5); and society has a stake in maintaining the stability of this institution for the common good. Ultimately, the lasting character of the marital relationship flows from the nature of the covenant itself. This is a dynamic process in continuous evolution which must be protected by faithfulness. No one would argue here, but again are we not presuming that the ideal of the covenantal relationship has been reached — or even aspired to — by all christians in all cultures? Does the model of personal (individual) covenant really fit every social and historical situation? Even if it might, has not the element of reciprocity been left to the side? When the marital covenant is entered into, it is a mutual undertaking. Humanly — and not divinely —

speaking, it is made "on condition" of the reciprocity. While all the arguments provided here are cogent in their own right, we must ask if they address the real situation of lived experience. The ideal of indissolubility may be reached by many, and it certainly should play a major role in the marital *intention* we would call specifically christian, but this does not diminish the reality of marital breakdown or the fact that some relationships called "marriage" are not even poor reflections of any type of covenant. Indeed, the "ideal" has been put forth, but little room is left for discussion.

Finally to be discussed from this Part II is the issue of the "Dignity of Woman" (IL, 47). The text here begins from a very good perspective. According to the creation accounts, *both* man and woman are created in the image of God. This argues for equal dignity upon which the covenant of marriage might be built. It is also insightfully pointed out that often marital problems are the result of not recognizing that equality. Thus, St. Paul is invoked as teaching that a man should be devoted to his wife as Christ is to the Church (Eph. 5:32)[118]. A further invocation is made of the Blessed Virgin Mary and the esteem she has received in the Church.

The text should probably have stopped here, but it goes on to address the so-called "woman's liberation movement". Although it is admitted that there can be very positive and even christian elements contained therein, the overall evaluation is not very satisfactory. A saving element is that it rightly criticizes a society which uses women and treats them as objects. But the only defense against this is a recognition of the proper dignity of the "feminine". One has visions here of a separate "feminine nature" particular to women and giving her a different type of personhood than that exhibited by her "masculine" counterpart. As long as the difference and distinction is used as the basis for argumentation in this complex issue, little progress will be made in asserting genuine equality. With all deference to Mary occupying a special place in Catholic tradition, one could seriously question the appropriateness of this unique model for addressing the problems of contemporary society. It is no wonder that the Synod and its aftermath contributed little to this vital issue. To touch upon a single key point, the place of woman in the Church itself is not even a topic of discussion in this document.

C. The Pastoral Aspects

The third part of the IL, on "Pastoral Problems", is the longest. It attempted to include all the dimensions of the broadest discussion on marriage and family life. There are eight numbered sections but we will

---

118. The reference here should probably have been 5:25 or 5:33. Eph. 5:32 is about the "great mystery — Christ and the Church".

not give a detailed discussion of all of them. Our interests lie in those elements which had been given special attention and had been going through transformation since the Council.

After a general introduction (IL, 51), Section I speaks of "The Role of the Family Effected in the Community of Persons" (IL, 52-55). The stress is placed on mutual help, not only within the family but also between families, especially in offering help to new marriages. There is also a critique of the consumer mentality which seeks its gratification in the things of this world. The call to recognize God as the ultimate end of humankind and to share goods with others is a most admirable teaching. A last paragraph links the consumer mentality to the increasing number of abortions.

Section II deals with "The Role of the Family in Sanctifying itself and the World" (IL, 56-61). It relies very much on scriptural and conciliar inspiration and presents a generally good, if idealistic, text. Again, discussion in the Synod itself would raise the issue of the ability to speak of sanctification before the establishment of stable and continuous family relations. This is a particular problem in the Third World where, despite the hardships and mitigating circumstances, new forms of ecclesiology are emerging. One of these forms has to do with the concept of the "basic communities" which in fact is named in the document (IL, 60). Unfortunately, the idea is merely mentioned in passing along with a number of (new) possibilities, none of which is given specific attention or real encouragement. Alternative ecclesiology did not come within the scope of the IL.

Section III now approaches a key issue, "The Role (Duty) of Solicitude toward Human Life" (IL, 62-67). It begins by noting that the family is the most apt, the privileged, place for the care of new life. Then (IL, 63), the first concern will be for following the "principles of generous responsible parenthood". Whether as reason or explanation, we then find the repetition of the phrase "the logical normal evolution of conjugal love leads spouses to procreation". This is the third time this phrase appears in the two documents. Here it is immediately followed by two quotes from GS, 50 which appear in reverse order.

"the true practice of conjugal love and the whole meaning of family life which results from it, while not making the other purposes of matrimony of less account, have this aim: that the couple be ready with stout hearts to cooperate with the love of the Creator and Savior, who through them will enlarge and enrich His own family day by day".

As was already said in the second part, "Marriage and conjugal love are by their nature ordained toward the begetting and educating of children. Children are really the supreme gift of marriage".

This time the first quote given includes the balancing phrase (*non posthabitis...*) missing in IL, 36. The invocation of what "was already said" refers to IL, 29, the other place of *ipsa evolutio logica et normalis...*, where we find the first sentence of GS, 50 to be absent. Only the second one, the result of the *modus*, given here in abbreviated form, is found in that previous text.

The regulation of births is then taken on under two headings, "The Problem" (IL, 64) and "The Christian Solution" (IL, 65-66). It begins,

> The role of transmitting life must be exercised in the family according to the principles and within the limits of generous responsible parenthood. That responsibility is to be understood either as positive in the sense of deciding to procreate children or as negative in the sense of limiting the number of children by licit means[119].

Now looking at this entire introduction to the issue (IL, 63-64), we find the invocation of responsible parenthood but the specifics of that doctrine are not given (cf. IL, 37). It is admitted that the decision can be either positive or negative, but there is no notion of *real conflict* experienced in coping with the decision to limit births. The exposition of the "problem" goes on to recognize the role played by demographic, economic and social factors. But then these are nearly dismissed by shifting to a concern over "the manipulation of public opinion on the true nature and genuine dimensions of this problem". The conscience issue is turned into a social issue, going so far as to recognize "the urgent necessity for a new international economic order".

Placing the problem in a social context is indeed a proper restoration of an often forgotten dimension. This will be reinforced in the Synod discussions by the bishops of the Third World. But it may be pertinent to introduce a critique of this approach. There are two issues to be dealt with here. The first is the question of responsible parenthood and the decision — ultimately taken by the spouses themselves, consulting all the available information (cf. GS, 50) — whether or not to procreate. This is a value decision. It calls for a prudent and generous attitude and the cultivation of a spirit of sacrifice. When that decision is negative, that no (further) procreation should take place, this should be respected as an exercise of responsibility and not pejoratively labeled or associated with a so-called "anti-life mentality". Furthermore, it should be recognized that although this decision "ultimately rests with the spouses", it is not entirely a private decision or one taken in isolation. There are external factors — social, political and especially economic — which influence the decisions of responsible parenthood and which are not under the control of the individual couple. These factors are the responsibility of

---

119. Munus vitae tradendae exerceri debet in familia secundum principia et intra limites generosae paternitatis responsabilis. Quae responsabilitas tum positive in sensu decisionis procreandi prolem, tum negative in sensu limitationis numeri filiorum mediis licitis intellegenda est.

the wider community, especially national and international authorities, who should work to improve conditions as much as possible to favor the support and stability of the family. However, despite the *need* to improve conditions, the actual decision making takes place in a given context. Decisions are made on the basis of actual conditions and not with respect to how things should be.

These two elements should not be put forth as antagonistic. One can simultaneously call and work for a change in conditions, yet advise others on how to deal with the existing situation. The question of an equitable distribution of resources is an urgent one, but the practical question is how to deal immediately with *available* resources. The two aspects are separate and should be kept apart to avoid rhetoric. That is something of what happened during the 1974 U.N. World Population Conference held at Bucharest. By confusing the two aspects one almost never arrives at a clear means of solution for either one. Nor is one disposed for dealing with the second issue.

After the first issue of a responsible decision has been dealt with, the second one presents itself, namely the technical question of how to execute whatever decision is taken. Here we should insist upon the term "regulation of fertility (or fecundity)" for at least two reasons. On the one hand, this may avoid the confusion introduced by such linguistically vague terms as birth control or family planning which can be interpreted as including the decision for abortion. The last is a completely separate issue which should be dealt with under the heading of justice and not just in connection with sexual morality. On the other hand, the regulation of fertility can be positive or limiting. The responsible decision to procreate may yet encounter technical problems which will have to be handled, perhaps even with "extraordinary means" such as the use of artificial insemination. The negative decision to prevent, limit or space conception is likewise a technical question which does not escape moral evaluation, yet it pales in significance when compared to the value decision of procreation itself.

Furthermore, the second issue has *its own* social dimension because of the need to respect freedom of conscience. Just as the first decision is ultimately a personal one for the spouses, so is the second. Without the most extreme situation threatening the common good in which the de facto non-limitation of procreation is placing the very survival of a population in jeopardy, it is almost impossible to justify government intervention in the application of programs for regulating fertility. Again, there is a rhetoric built up around this issue which misses the point. The imposition of "family planning" programs on a population or a segment thereof is a violation of the freedom of conscience. The moral question is one of justice, not sexual morality.

It has not been unknown for the complexity of these questions to be reduced to simple formulas. HV, 17 fell into this in its "evil consequences" argument, ruling out contraception because it "would be a dangerous weapon placed in the hands of public authority". It happened again in Bucharest in 1974 when the question of an equitable distribution of resources overshadowed the urgent needs of millions of people right here and now. We might even suspect that it happened at the Synod because one group of bishops was speaking about the private decision to use contraception and another was speaking of the social dimension of supporting the family and providing necessary resources. We may never know what happened in all the closed meetings in Rome during Oct. 1980. What we do know is that almost no one saw their expectations fulfilled. Perhaps this could be attributed to a poor formulation of the questions, the inability to separate questions which were related but independent, and the unwillingness of those who coordinated the various groups to achieve consensus. Below all these speculations remains a clear observation: an urgent concern for justice and the different social dimensions of the problems concerning the regulation of fertility can (be used to) obscure the relatively trivial question of "artificial birth control". Too frequently, when arguments are lacking to substantiate the technical question (artificial means), the social issue (freedom of conscience) is used, as here, to fill the gap.

Returning to the IL, the brief statement of the problem is followed by what is called the "Christian Solution" (IL, 65-66). Quite expectedly we see an immediate return to the technical question of the means employed for regulating fertility, here called the "regulation of births"[120]. This, it is said, cannot be done while forgetting the words of Vatican II:

Filiis ecclesiae, his principii innixis in procreatione regulanda, vias inire non licet, quae Magisterio, in divina lege explicanda, improbentur[121].

120. Consult what has been written in the text with regard to using appropriate vocabulary. Speaking about the regulation of "births" instead of fertility serves another purpose. There is a certain form of speaking that classifies the use of contraception or sterilization in and of itself as "anti-life". The argument suggests that everything can be thrown together and condemned in one package: contraception-sterilization-abortion-infanticide-euthansia-and so on. Thus, using a term like "regulating births" opens the way to this *non-sequitur* reasoning. This argument was not absent in the Synod. Whenever it appears it should be strongly objected to, for it is insensitive to the personal struggles in conscience of millions of people, not only Catholics. Morally aware persons can see the logic of regulating fertility in a responsible manner, but they object to being labeled "anti-life". Nor, sometimes, do they wish to put themselves forward as being "pro-life" because of the frequent rhetoric of certain pro-life groups. Confusing the issues of conception and birth (prenatal care) has done great damage to contemporary moral reasoning.

121. Besides the major fault of *improbentur*, we can also point out two minor differences between this text and that of GS,51: a comma is missing between *innixis* and *in procreatione*, and the preposition *a* is missing before *Magisterio*. Because these are similar faults present in the quotation in the *Lin* (the comma is present there), we can suppose either that this text is dependent upon the earlier one or that both were taken from a common source. In any case, neither quotation is accurate, which begs the question how such an important and controversial text could have been changed.

Again we find the rendition of this text closer to the papal *modus* than it is to GS (*improbentur*). And again we find the admonition that HV had reaffirmed the "traditional teaching", explaining it in a new light[122]. With the direction very clear, the document provides the statement for the Synod to make before discussion even begins, "The Synod most firmly believes this teaching to be more and more clear and convincing to minds through its subjection to better investigation". The doctrine is said to be "prophetic" because it serves the dignity of the human person in reverencing life at its very source[123].

Having accomplished its insistence upon reiteration of the teaching of Paul VI in HV, the IL now takes one step beyond in proposing and baptizing the so-called christian solution, namely the "natural methods". These are said to be disposed to promoting education and conjugal dialogue, in line with the objective moral order, helpful in achieving sexual discipline and generally opening the way to greater magnanimity in marital life. The text goes on to give some advice on how these methods can be promoted.

Eventually, both the Synod and John-Paul II would endorse these methods as the saving solution. Could we not ask, however, a solution to what? Does Natural Family Planning (NFP) really address the complexities of responsible parenthood — especially along with its far reaching social dimensions — or does it continue to propagate an individualistic, privatized concern over the integrity of sexual intercourse? Ultimately we must ask ourselves, is this really the issue with which we should be concerned? Even Pope Pius XII who was responsible for the Magisterium's endorsement of periodic continence saw that technical question as subordinate to the larger issues of motivation and doing one's part in propagating the human race and furthering the Kingdom of God[124]. We should be sensitive to the possibility that the "Catholic solution" of the 1950's might become the "Catholic ideology" of the 1980's. Most people are not concerned with the contraception

---

122. Quod nuper denuo factum est in Litteris Encyclicis *Humanae vitae*, saecularem Ecclesiae traditionem confirmantibus et nova luce explicantibus.

123. Synodus firmissime credit hanc doctrinam magis magisque clarescere atque mentes evincere quo melius investigationi subiiciatur. Iam hodie clarius vim suam propheticam ostendit: in dies enim evidentius fit quomodo personae humanae revera dignitas servari non possit nisi vitam inde ab ipsius scaturigine tuendo.

Again there is a linguistic trap here. Speaking of "life at its source" tends to equate conception with the process that leads to it. It is a simple fact that before sperm and ovum meet there is no separate human life involved. The words used here are reminiscent of the medieval notion that "wasting seed" or keeping sperm and ovum (then unknown) apart was equivalent to homicide.

124. Pius XII stated these concerns by changing the nature of the question itself from a moral one (manipulation of fertility) to a legal one (duty to procreate). In so doing he complicated the issue and at least temporarily stopped discussion on the question of "artificial means".

question and if the Church chooses to invest time, support and even resources in the NFP movement it will do little to advance the greater issues. Furthermore, the Magisterium's self-identification with this ideology presents an image of what it means to be "Catholic" that may very well obscure the gospel and present a barrier to active participation in the Church. "Natural" methods of regulating fertility are a viable option which may be beneficial for some couples, but insistence upon these methods as the only morally acceptable approach to the problem appears somewhat shortsighted.

In the following number, IL, 66, it is advised that priests and religious become more involved in these issues. However, anticipating that difficulties will be encountered, the IL suggests a text which was ultimately taken over in Prop. 24.

The Synod of Bishops is not unaware of the difficult and truly painful situation of many christian couples who, despite their sincere good will are unable to obey the moral norms taught by the Church because of their weakness and objective difficulties[125].

There follows a quote from HV, 29 advising married couples with difficulties "to have recourse frequently and with faith to the sacraments of Eucharist and Penance without ever allowing themselves to be disheartened by their weakness". Finally, there is a long quote from Paul VI's address to the "Equipes Notre-Dame" on 4 May 1970.

There are two curious things about this approach which deserve mention. First, there is a huge gap created between theoretical morality and daily living. The so-called objective moral order is presented as something more or less beyond the reach of many, if not most, married couples. In ascribing all failure to live up to these "moral norms taught by the Church" as due to weakness and conditions beyond one's control, an impression is created that one may as well give up trying[126]. We

125. Synodus Episcoporum non ignorat situationem valde difficilem et vere tormentosam tot christianorum coniugum qui, non obstante sincera voluntate, normas morales ab Ecclesia doctas adimplendo propter eorum infirmitatem et obiectivas difficultates ipsis oboediendo impares sunt.

It should also be noted that this text was not in the first draft of the Propositions but was a later addition.

126. It is one thing to say that christian married couples are unable to obey because of "objective difficulties" and quite another — as GS recognized — that moral decision making takes place precisely in the context of these difficulties which are *real*. The approach offered in the IL, which will return at the Synod, gives the impression that in face of the difficulties (i.e., real life) there is really no moral solution possible, or at least not one which can be called good or "obedient". The implications of this view are that persons *cannot* act morally and the only hope they have of doing so is to act in a way which ignores the real situation. In contrast, by admitting real conflict, GS taught that persons *can* act morally by confronting the real situation and taking the best, most responsible solution available. Those decisions are morally *good* and exhibit moral *strength*, not weakness. The difference in fundamental theologies could not be greater. The essentialist school protects a

might ask whether or not we are paying too high a price to prevent the Magisterium from having to reexamine its moral argumentation. The picture of an out-of-reach morality is hardly inspirational and does a great deal of damage to the more important social issues facing the modern world. It also reduces the image of the christian people to a mass of undisciplined and egotistical weaklings incapable of living up to moral standards. In her pastoral care, however, the Magisterium advises that there is still a means for forgiveness. And here is the second curiosity. Despite moral immaturity, even HV teaches that the way is always open to the sacraments. There is an incredible tolerance of recidivism implicit in this approach that undermines the very integrity of the moral teaching itself, not to mention the image of the sacraments. One gets the impression that there really is no consensus on just how serious this particular moral issue might be. This problem will emerge in the Synod in connection with the so-called "law of gradualism".

The final number of this section draws attention to the insight that biological generation is not the only form of being open to and caring for human life. The christian family is in a position to reach out to the poor, the orphaned, the handicapped, etc. This is a particularly good perspective which should probably have come at the opening of the section. Fortunately, the insight was not lost at the Synod.

Section IV of Part III is on education. The general principles put forth (IL, 68) envision the family as playing the central role and bearing primary responsibility. Much is drawn from the Council here, but the specifics are too broad for even this document to attempt to cover. Therefore, a good deal of this section is schematic. One section in particular, IL, 78, is on the instruments of social communication, an often neglected source of education but also of ideological propaganda. Much more should be said about this field because of its continually growing pervasiveness. The aspect of education is important so that one will know how to use the media as resource and how to critically discriminate its many messages.

Section V is on the social role of the family and again the text is limited to general principles and schematic ideas. In a way it appears facile to point out that problems like "peace, international justice and the liberation of peoples" are in need of urgent attention. But the fact that very little else can be said is, in some way at least, a recognition of human, political and cultural plurality. This is very close to what has been becoming characteristic of the Church's social teaching in general: referring the questions for discussion and resolution to the local level and the data from lived experience.

"morality" which has little to do with real life. The conciliar teaching promotes engagement in the real world and a willingness to make responsible decisions.

Two of the last three sections have a more direct connection with our topic[127]. Section VI (IL, 86-90) is on marriage preparation, something in which most pastoral ministry is already far ahead of official teaching. The perspective present here is more typical of the classicist world view and gives little credit to peoples' customs and local traditions. It is also skeptical of educational programs in the schools which are called "manipulative" when any mention is made of "family planning".

The next two numbers on the remote and immediate preparation for marriage are also brief. The notion of marriage as a significant moment in the lives of christians and an opportunity for "re-catechization" is recognized, but it appears that much more will have to be done in fundamental sacramentology before a clear set of guidelines can be formulated. Again, actual practice is very often far ahead of the vision offered here. The final part, on mixed marriages, relies heavily on Roman documents (a *motu proprio* of 1970) and demonstrates little appreciation for the complexity of the issue, its widespread practice, or the many opportunities it presents. It will become evident in discussion that the episcopal conferences desire and need much more autonomy in this area, particularly in countries in which Catholics form only a small minority.

The final section of the IL provides some "Remarks for Pastoral Practice in Some Difficult Cases", namely non-marital unions, (92-93), divorce (94) and the increasing number of abortions (95). These problems are ascribed to cultural change and civil practice. IL observes that the bishops at Vatican II urged an investigation and analysis of these things and that now the task of the Synod is to provide doctrinal and pastoral norms. Under the first heading (non-marital unions), it is further recognized that variant kinds of these unions are connected with social, religious, cultural and economic conditions. But then a good deal of these phenomena are reduced to what the IL calls privatized and subjectivistic attitudes. The two observations, about general conditions and subjective responses do not appear to contribute very much to understanding the issues involved. In IL, 93, it is prudently advised that patience and giving witness to the values of genuine christian marriage will be a fruitful resource. But neither is this explained nor does sufficient account appear to be taken of the possibility that the core of the problem may stem from a lack of positive experience in this area, either culturally or in that first experience of most persons with regard to marriage, that of their own parents.

The phenomena of "divorce, separation and second marital unions" are said to be dependent "without doubt" on the increasing laxity of civil legislation and on the "universal cultural condition of our time, satu-

---

127. Section VII (IL,91) is about the preparation of priests, etc. for their ministry to families.

rated by subjectivism and hedonism and no less a widespread ignorance about the true nature and effect of christian marriage". There is no room for admitting second marriages, even in the case of a good conscience, because of the danger of scandal. Although pastoral care is urged to encourage a spirit of penance for those who have attempted such unions, there is no question of their admission to the Eucharist before they regularize their situations.

The argumentation here could be characterized as "rigorist practice" without even the slightest hint of exceptional cases or making pastoral application. There is little evidence given for the reasons behind this position except a few scriptural quotations (1 Cor. 7:10-11; Mk. 10:1-12; Lk. 16:18; which do not even mention all of the possible sources, in particular leaving out the controversial "exception clauses" in Mt. 5:32 and 19:9) and a footnote reference to the Council of Trent, session XXIV, canon VII. Admittedly, the problem of divorce and remarriage is a preoccupation of the North Atlantic world, but that does not make it any less of a pastoral urgency. There has been a great deal of research and study on the issue because of that urgency but none of that is reflected in this document.

Finally we find a concern expressed for the increasing number of abortions. This is, without a doubt, a lamentable situation and most people are perplexed about what can be done about it. On the one hand, there is the legal issue. Most countries, including many so-called Catholic ones, have relaxed or even eliminated laws punishing abortion and thus made it easier to practice and procure. There is an experienced need to have some legislation to protect human life, even in its prenatal stages. But *what* legislation and *how* to achieve it in a pluralistic society are extremely difficult questions. On the other hand, regardless of legislation, the more important issue is the moral evaluation of abortion and its actual occurrence. Experience shows that legislation is not enough and that it can even make a bad situation worse.

The moral debate about abortion was developed neither here nor in the synodal discussions. The latter devoted a good deal of effort to the problem of programs of abortion being imposed upon large populations. The IL simply singles it out as a moral problem without much further comment. In one sense, this perspective is not altogether bad, especially considering the amount of regretable rhetoric that surrounds the issue of abortion in these times. It is admirable that the Church not become involved in that rhetoric. However, some guidance, particularly with respect to the legal aspects of the issue, would have been helpful. Also, it would appear most helpful to avoid the (again rhetorical) type of argumentation that postulates a logical connection between contraception — sterilization — abortion — euthanasia. Such *non sequitur* reasoning is not worthy of serious moral reflection, especially in Church documents.

D. Summary of the Pre-synodal Period in Light of the Council

In the months preceeding the Synod in 1980 the preparations continued to go on not just in Rome but also in dioceses and episcopal conferences throughout the world. There was at least some consolidation of the input which the representative bishops would be bringing to Rome in September of that year. However, it should be clear by now that those bishops would have to deal with a plan which had been laid out in the preparatory documents. Before we proceed to an analysis of what the Synod did or did not accomplish, it may be helpful to summarize the theological perspective of those documents in light of the theology of marriage and the family which had been set forth in the Second Vatican Council. As others have already sufficiently pointed out, some of the general ideas exhibited in these documents are rather essentialist. Whereas a word like "personalist" might be used, for instance, the notions behind that term are closer to traditional natural law thinking than to other contemporary insights. The vocabulary has also changed to some extent, substituting "God's plan" or intention or design for natural law, but the ideas have remained more or less the same. The resulting notion of marriage and the family is therefore also rather static and structured, arguing, as it were, from a pre-ordained order of things. The purpose of this summary is to demonstrate how these general impressions and remarks have been put forth by the documents.

To begin, the first contrast with conciliar thinking concerns the role of the Magisterium. This in itself is worthy of a full ecclesiological study in light of the theology of *Lumen gentium*. But we will not go into those explicit points here. The *Lin* had attempted to state the competence of the Magisterium in the area of marriage and family life but it was not very successful in doing so. The IL had avoided the issue and as a result the specific topic never came up at the Synod[128]. Nevertheless, both documents presume that competence and have an operative ecclesiology which situates the teaching function of the Church. That view is a highly structured, unquestionably hierarchical approach to ecclesiology which sees all truth and teaching emanating from the highest levels and then filtering down to the ordinary person. This is possible because of the

---

128. Although the competence of the Magisterium as such was not raised as a topic during the Synod, there was a parallel issue that was much discussed and had a bearing upon the presentation we are about to give. That issue had to do with theological method, the first point touched upon in the summarizing report of the *Relator*, Card. Ratzinger, on 6 October. Was the method to be used a deductive one, beginning with traditional principles, or an inductive one, basing itself in contemporary experience? The *Lin* and IL had used the former, but a significant number of bishops wanted to use the latter. We will see that the end result was split between the two. Cf. B. MARTHALER, *The Family in Global Perspective: Synod 1980*, in *The Living Light* 18 (1981) 57-74, pp. 69-70.

presumption that everything can be explained and dealt with by applying the single, essentialist model: truth exists in an ontological realm wherein one can discern the essence of things. That essentialism is then translated into contemporary language and dispensed to the bishops and the laity to solve their pastoral problems. This task is to some extent carried out by theologians who are considered "spokespersons" for the hierarchy. Theologians are supposed to be neither original thinkers nor critics and it appears that the principle source for their work should be the statements of the Magisterium. Hence, the severe critique of IL, 22 against dissenting voices. In the view present in the documents, all truth is ontological and purely objective. The reality of human experience is considered to be primarily subjective and must be made to fit the model which is being applied.

When we read GS in its entirety there appears to be a different impression created. Human experience is taken to be objective and itself a source of truth. This is evident in the positive evaluation of human work in the world and the resulting social institutions which develop in the process of building culture. Through culture, mankind works to humanize nature and, by both respecting and changing the givens of nature, to create a milieu which is conducive to the realization of human values. This process is historical and pluralistic in that at different times and places the adaptive procedures undertaken are suited to the needs and expectations of the human community and not the result of an imposed plan or model. Therefore, it was understood that not only the specific community but also the Church herself must attempt to discern truths within a given situation and allow culture to speak for itself, revealing the insights and values expressed in the order and laws of human institutions themselves. When the first specific topic is approached in Ch. 1 of Part II, marriage and the family are considered as given, and the role of the Magisterium is to collect and articulate those common elements which can be addressed from the insights of revelation and faith. Thus, for example, the Church recognizes that the growing contemporary emphasis upon the relational aspect of marital union which it calls "covenant" both reflects and helps us understand God's own covenantal relationship to His People. In fostering the analogy our experience can be enlightened by faith, the human reality is revealed to have many dimensions, and the loving and saving presence of God is made more evident for all to see. To "teach" in this perspective is to join with the community of humankind and to work together in discerning the great mysteries. The Church articulates these findings from a theological perspective, that is, in the light of revelation and faith.

In contrast to this experiential approach both the *Lin* and IL begin with the idea that from the beginning God created with a very specific plan in mind. This plan was realized in the construction of an ontological nature for human persons who would be relational. Human relations themselves would also follow an ontological design which would result in the procreation of new human persons. This was accomplished by the creation of sexual differentiation manifested in the sexual faculty which has its own purpose and finality. In light of these givens we find the meaning of marriage. Besides satisfying persons' relational needs, the total involvement of one person with another, spiritually, emotionally and bodily, also fulfills God's plan (the logical normal evolution) that procreation take place. The role that human persons play in this process is essentially passive, though there is the need to respond to duties. When procreation takes place, parents must act in a responsible manner, bringing up and educating the child which has been "given to them". Hence, "responsible parenthood".

This design of God, however, has been disturbed by sin. As a result, human sexuality tends to be disordered and sexual instincts have virtually taken on a life of their own. In order to restore the original plan, therefore, persons must practice self-discipline and control their sexual urges by means of their rational will, the pattern for which is explained in the laws and norms governing human sexuality. When this is accomplished, persons achieve chastity. Without the imposition of rational will, the sexual expression of conjugal love, passion, will become disordered and unbridled.

The possible desire or reasoned conclusion that procreation should not take place in the context of a given marital situation has nothing to do with God's plan, but rather is an exceptional event. The ideal, but unarticulated, response to the "indication" for non-procreation is the non-engagement in sexual acts (abstinence). However, since sexual intimacy can also be recognized as beneficial to the relationships of persons who do not yet have control over these instincts, non-procreative intercourse may also be pursued so long as nothing is done to insure that conception remains an impossibility.

As for marriage itself, it is interpreted from the Genesis account of creation that God intended this relationship to exist for two purposes. Conjugal *love* itself is procreative as well as relational. The former is present by virtue of laws and the finalites built into the sexual faculty. The latter is present because one takes the decision and publically declares to enter into a permanent relationship. Then, because this relationship built on love resembles the relationship God has with His People and Christ has with the Church, it is a sacrament. Also, because God's covenantal relationships are irrevocable and permanent, the human relationship which resembles them is indissoluble. The laws and regulations which are drawn from the model of divine love are applied literally to the human reality in such a way that even the Church herself is unable to provide for adaptation or reconciliation.

The christian family is also understood according to the model of the ideal People of God, all of whom individually exhibit and respond to nearly perfect, self-giving love. Despite difficult conditions, the family continuously testifies to divine love and is somehow seen more to be the agent of cultural change and value formation than its product. Little else is said except that the family needs protection against forces which appear bent upon its destruction. The model of the family is a monogamous union of man and woman surrounded by their children who form a close unit of divinely inspired love and are fully capable of living in such a way despite the conditions of local customs, social expectations or even detrimental factors from economic or political pressures.

Any human experiences which depart from the images presented in the *Lin* or IL are considered to be negative and detrimental. Alternative unions, divorce and second marriages are not only evil in themselves, they are a direct threat to the stability and sacredness of institutions which were divinely created. All these difficulties can be overcome simply by educating persons to the norms which the Church teaches, and perhaps by instituting stricter laws to prohibit deviations. Given the selfishness, hedonism and general permissiveness of the modern world, the necessary measures seem clear: to stamp out misbehavior while remaining patient with those who are weak or perhaps lacking in freedom because of conditions which are beyond their control.

It goes without saying that human persons have roles assigned to them by virtue of their sex, marital status or place in the family unit. These roles are the result of laws and norms which are contained in the essential moral order that governs the ontological structure. Morality is therefore *applied to* reality and not engaged in it. The task of the Magisterium is to teach the principles of that morality and perhaps show persons how it is to be applied. The role of the Synod is to confirm this teaching which is characterized as "constant". As envisioned by the preparatory documents, the purpose of the Synod is to "clarify" the norms taught by the Magisterium and demonstrate unity among the world episcopate. To facilitate this process, those documents not only provided the questions to be addressed but even sometimes suggested the answers which should be given. Ultimately, the questions are more subtle and more important than the answers, for they provide the framework within which the various "problems" would be viewed. Indeed, even calling something a "problem" is to prejudice the way in which it would be considered.

This characterization of the synodal preparatory work is vastly different from the vision which informed conciliar thinking. The approach of GS is basically experiential without loosing sight of the continuity in Church teaching about faith and revelation. Without being moralistic, the fathers of the council addressed contemporary problems with an image that was inspiring rather than dictatorial. They appealed to the consciences of persons and attempted to give guidance on how to approach the many issues facing marriage and family life. The morality presented there is engaged, starting with the givens of experience and the real human condition. It recognizes conflict as well as aspiration; it takes account of limitation as well as freedom; and it supports the christian vocation to live in and be the light of the world while it does not hesitate to warn against egoism, privatization or being content with the minimum. All this was said, of course, with the risk of knowing that the ideal would not or could not always be lived up to. The fact that reality did not always live up to our expectations or that not everyone would be, or would act in a way which was, morally mature and christian did not pose a threat to the Church. For as much as teaching and witnessing is the task of the Church, its role of mediation and reconciliation were never to be forgotten.

The vision presented at Vat. II was admittedly general and in need of being worked out and applied. The question is whether or not the Synod accomplished this task. The bishops who assembled in Rome in 1980 each came with their own agenda and expectations. To some extent they were limited by the framework presented in the preparatory documents even though these purported to be only vehicles for discussion. It does not appear unfair to say that the outlook present in those documents was limited to a particular interpretation of conciliar and post-conciliar texts and events. There was a certain contrast between the theology of marriage and the family presented in GS and the vision that was present in the *Lin* and IL. It remains to be seen how the bishops dealt with that contrast. The pre-synodal documents carried a certain amount of weight because of their official character. Nevertheless, the bishops who represented the universal Church were also operating under the influence and legacy of Vatican II. Even if they did not or could not articulate the theological expressions which that historic event contributed to the process of *aggiornamento*, they were participants in a process which owed its existence to the accomplishment of the Council. The spirit of renewal had been awakened and the need to carry it forward was indisputable if the Church was to continue to speak to the modern world. The Synod was dedicated to that task. We must now ask if or to what extent it accomplished its purpose.

Our manner of approach will not be to study the actual events of the 1980 Synod because this is the topic of another part of this work. Our own concentration will continue along the lines of an analysis of the documents. The most important document emanating from the Synod was the list of 43 "Propositions" submitted to the Pope for his consideration. These Propositions represent the findings of the synodal discussions and a significant amount of consensus among the bishops. We must determine what the content and meaning of that consensus might be.

Of lesser importance are the two closing statements of the Synod. The first, "The Message to Christian Families", was an extremely general statement authored by only a few bishops so that something could be presented to the Church at the end of that month long meeting. The second, the Pope's "Closing Homily", is slightly more important because it indicates John-Paul's attitude toward some key issues and foreshadows the document he would write in response to the Synod and publish one year later, the apostolic exhortation, *Familiaris consortio*. Already at the close of the Synod it was evident that some questions had been decided. This should come as no surprise because from the evidence of the preparatory documents it is clear that some issues were decided even before the Synod took place, at least in the minds of some.

IV. THE SYNODAL STATEMENTS

A. The Propositions in General

The last week of the synodal meeting was dedicated to bringing together the findings and suggestions of the bishops into some kind of list which could then be presented to Pope John-Paul II. This was no easy task, for in the general discussions and in the eleven language groups many topics were discussed and a number of different perspectives had emerged. The process by which the final text was drawn up is dealt with elsewhere in this work. The preliminary stages of that process will not concern us here except to point out that in the end there were two versions of the text of the Propositions. The first version (*textus prior*) was submitted to the biships on 20 October. The next day, a vote was taken and the bishops had the opportunity to make their objections and suggestions (*modi*) for revision of the text. These *modi* were handed over to a committee who where responsible for the final version (*textus emendatus*). That version was presented on 23 October and the final vote taken on the next day, the last working session of the Synod[129].

129. For a more detailed examination of the process of drawing up the Propositions, see Chapter Three in the first part of this book, especially *The Calendar from 14 to 24 October 1980*, p. 83. There is considerable confusion with respect to who was actually responsible for the various texts emanating from the Synod. T. J. REESE, *Reporting on The Synod*, in *America* 143 (1980) 407-411, p. 410, speculated that the committee in charge of dealing with the *modi* for the Propositions consisted of the same members who had drawn up the text in the first place and had drafted the "Message to Christian Families" as well. This is highly doubtful, however, because neithter are the styles of these documents very similar nor would such a procedure constitute a logical division of labor during the final working days of the Synod.

Form what we have been able to ascertain, the various workgroups were made up of different but sometimes overlaping members. *Origins* 10 (1980) 301 (marginal notes) gives the members for the committee in charge of the final "Message" as: Archbishop J. Bernardin (Cincinnati), Cardinal P. Zoungrana (Oougadougou), Carbinal A. Lorscheider (Fortaleza), Cardinal J. Cordeiro (Karachi) and Archbishop G. Danneels (Mechelen-Brussel). According to Grootaers (cf. *supra*, pp. 78-79), the committee for writing the Propositions was drawn from the representatives of the *circuli minores* and worked in collaboration with the *Relator* and the Special Secretary. It is the committee for incorporating the *modi* which remains a mystery. The official commentary on the incorporation of the bishops' suggestions on the *textus prior* is entitled, *Familiae Christianae in mundo hodierno: Elenchus Propositionum: exitus suffragationis cum expensione modorum propositionum*, Vatican City, 1980, 115 pages. This document lists a committee of five bishops: F. Arinze (Onitsha), S. Kocisco (Pittsburgh), J. Delicado Baeza (Valladolid), M. Revollo Bravo (New Pamplona) and P. D'Souza (Varanasi). However, it has been suggested that this group did little else than count the various votes. That suggestion is founded on good reason, since none of these bishops had any experience or particular, proven qualities for the type of work demanded for the *Expensio modorum* (EM). There were certainly other bishops present who were better qualified to do that

It is the final version of the Propositions which eventually found its way into print, despite the original intention that these remain "secret". It might be speculated that the text was readily available after the close of the Synod because of a certain dissatisfaction with the Pope's "Closing Homily" which apparently had passed judgment on some of the suggestions before they were studied. Nor was the bishops' own final "Message" completely satisfactory because it did not accurately reflect what had been put forth in the synodal discussions. The discrepency between what the bishops felt they had accomplished at the Synod and the image which was created by the published "Message" and the "Homily" may have been responsible for the text of the Propositions coming to light.

The final text of the Propositions itself does not always accurately reflect the thinking of the bishops as a whole. Because that text was not available until the last days of the Synod, because the changes introduced were not sufficiently explained, and because there was no time for further discussion or debate, the vote taken on the final version was the reflection of a "take it or leave it" situation. The vote itself, therefore, does not always reflect what the bishops may have thought of the text as amended.

To comprehend the Propositions it is necessary to consult the two, first and final, versions in their original (Latin) text. These were apparently published together, the first version on the left page, the final one on the right. Changes in the text are signaled by the use of italics in the final version or sometimes by leaving space where something had been omitted. For analysis both versions must be compared for, unlike the Council documents which went through many editions, each of which was accompanied by an explanation, we cannot presume that the final version was always closer to the intention of the bishops. In fact, it is the first version, the result of coordinating the suggestions of the different groups in the first place, that will give us an indication of the original

work. The question remains, who in fact dealt with all the *modi* and subsequently drew up the EM? There is no record or memory of any vote having been taken to elect members of that committee. Those members must have been appointed by those in charge of the Synod itself and were probably drawn from the group of "special advisors to the Special Secretary", sometimes referred to as *periti*.

Lack of further (verifiable) evidence has left this crucial stage of the Propositions' redaction history rather vague. Nevertheless, one thing is more or less certain with respect to the EM, namely that its content is not absolutely congruent with the (two) texts of the Propositions that we have at our disposal. On the one hand, references in the EM do not always correlate with our version of the *textus prior*. This is understandable, for our copy of the *textus prior* is evidently that published along with the final version in booklet form. Thus, page numbers would be different from the original version (20 Oct. 1980). On the other hand, however, a careful study of the EM and the *textus emendatus* together reveals that not everything admitted in the EM (as addition or omission) was incorporated into the text. We will signal these discrepencies in our own footnotes.

meaning. Until we know the full story of the redaction history, we will have to use both versions as the subject of analysis.

Like the preparatory documents, the text of the Propositions exhibits a certain structure, divided into three parts in its body but now having a fourth part as an appendix. But the content of these parts is rather original. The schema is as follows[130].

General Status of the Propositions   (1)
I. The Will of God Known by the Pilgrim People of God
   1. The *Sensus fidei*   (2-4)
   2. The Signs of the Times   (5-6)
   3. Gradualism   (7)
II. The Plan of God concerning the Family
   4. Anthropological and Theological Foundation of the Sacrament of Marriage   (8)
   5. Theology of the Sacrament of Marriage   (9-11)
   6. Faith and the Sacrament   (12)
   7. Indissolubility and the Problem of Divorce   (13-14)
   8. Woman and the Family   (15-17)
   9. Marriage in Ancient Cultural Customs and Christian Marriage   (18)
   10. Mixed Marriages   (19)
III. The Roles of the Family
   11. The Transmission and Safeguarding of Human Life   (20-25)
   12. The Role of Education   (26-29)
   13. The Social and Cultural Role of the Family   (30)
   14. Families in Special Circumstances   (31-33)
   15. The Apostolic Role of the Family   (34)
   16. Preparation for Marriage   (35)
   17. Family Spirituality   (36-38)
   18. Family Associations   (39)
   19. Extra Marital Relations   (40-41)

130. The translated text of the Propositions which we will be using for this commentary is that found in *The Tablet* 235 (1981) 116-118, 141-142 and 164-167. This version is the same as that published in the *National Catholic Reporter* in Nov. and Dec. 1980, reprinted there by permission. While that English text will be used as a reference for the reader, we will primarily be consulting the original Latin versions (*textus prior* and *textus emendatus*) as they were published together in the final days of the Synod. A better translation of the Propositions appears in Dutch in *Archief van de Kerken* 36 (1981) 199-226. This version not only contains the headings and titles for the 4 parts and 21 sections but also reduplicates all the italics used in the *textus emendatus* which supposedly signal differences between that text and the *textus prior*. A short introduction to the Dutch translation provides a chronology of events and states that there were approximately 800 *modi* submitted, only 144 of which affected the final version of the Propositions.

The schema presented here consists of our own translation of the original text of the final version of the Propositions (cf. Appendix). It differs from that found in the first part of this book (cf. *supra*, p. 131) provided by Grootaers. That schema is thematic and presents the Propositions as the end product of both the contributions of the bishops and a working out of the Synod's more or less official agenda. Our own schema merely represents the text of the Propositions as finally adopted. We will follow this formal outline in our own commentary.

Note that the subject matter is broken up into sequentially numbered sections. This will facilitate our commentary which will follow that numbering as well as give the relevant Proposition numbers. Note also that the plan of development is much more synodal than either the *Lin* or IL. Those documents had limited themselves to specific topics. The Propositions begin with the source for reflection, follow this with a general theology of marriage and the family and only then discuss specific areas of application. This approach is more conciliar in nature, beginning with general theological affirmations and not wishing to simply provide answers to specific problems.

A preliminary statement (Prop. 1) notes the purpose of the text but it also says that other things will be submitted to the Holy Father. That dossier contained the outlines (*Lin*) and the working document (IL) as well as the reports of the lauguage groups and the *relationes* of Card. Ratzinger. It has become customary in papal advisory bodies to submit complete dossiers to the pope at the end of their work. In this case, the compilation of the dossier was one more sign of the totally advisory function of the Synod of Bishops.

B. Part One: The Sources

The title of this Part is "The Will of God (*Voluntate Dei*) Known by the Pilgrim People of God" (Prop. 2-7). This is a rather excellent text which clearly reflects a conciliar manner of thought. It contains three sections which are completely new, i.e., they are not found in any of the preparatory documents. The first, on the *sensus fidei*, was virtually unknown by the authors of the *Lin* and the IL but it is not a surprising contribution from bishops who were using concepts taken from Vatican II. The first paragraph (Prop. 2) is the best. It begins with an immediate appeal to the *sensus fidei* experienced by the laity, the reference to the hierarchy being a later addition[131]. Here is the experiential approach, the spirit of the Council and the reason for the existence of the Synod. Naturally, this does not signify a simple "consensus" about particular issues (*sensus fidelium*) but rather a real *appreciation for the faith* as it is lived and experienced by *all* the faithful, hierarchy included.

131. Prop. 2 contains three additions and, in the English translation, an omission of a reference to LG,12 after *sensus fidei*. The first is to the hierarchy who also share this experience (non solum per Pastores sed ...), the second introducing the word *tantum* (as such) after the non-equation of the *sensus* with statistics (i.e., "the *sensus fidei* is not the result of opinion pools or statistics *as such*"), and the third spelling out the value of those (other) sources to be "a better investigation of the truth" (ad veritatem melius investigandam).

In a fundamental way, it is this perspective which was the major cause for tension at the Synod. The preparatory documents and those who represented the same thought see the whole process of theology and teaching as deductive. There was no room for experiential input. The bishops reversed this order at least in that they felt they had to understand what the experience was if they were going to address it. Those who had a more essentialist, and therefore deductive, perspective did not, and probably never would, volunteer the concept of the *sensus fidei* as a theological source. Its introduction came from the bishops.

The next two Propositions attempt to clarify this departure point by expanding on the ideas of development and universality. These characteristics are achieved through reasonableness and the criterion of faith itself which means a life not "according to the pattern of the world" but taking place in faith and within "the whole Church". With the *sensus fidei* as a starting point, it is mentioned in passing that "the hierarchical Magisterium is to foster this appreciation and authentically interpret it"[132]. It remains to be said how that *sensus* can be discerned.

The next section (Prop. 5 & 6) provides the means for that discernment by discussing the "Signs of the Times". This is no mere sociological survey but begins by specifying the ability to seek God's plan in every age; in other words, in continuity with the history of salvation which is revealed in scripture "in an outstanding way" (*eminentiori modo*, an addition). Attending to faith, the Magisterium and prudence (with an added reference to GS, 4, 11, 37), we can discern in our own age the meaning of God's plan. There are both positive and negative signs. The positive ones reveal the work of God through Christ and list a number of contemporary experiences, including the additions: families' mutual assistance and the transformation of unjust structures. There is a decidedly social dimension to the bishops' statements which intentionally avoided getting trapped in purely private issues. This is reinforced in the list of negative signs which do *not* reveal God's presence. Whereas the first draft had, just as the *Lin* and IL, rushed into the issues of divorce, abortion, etc., the amended version starts with "the poverty and misery brought on many families by unjust structures". It is also interesting to note that one of the signs listed is the "contraceptive mentality" and not simply "artificial contraception" in itself.

A third paragraph in Prop. 5 denies that history is deterministic (Hegel) and sees reality as a continuous tension between the two kinds of

132. Magisterii hierarchici est hanc sensus fovere et authentice interpretari. We wrote that the Synod did not address the role or competence of the Magisterium as such. The statement here is merely the last sentence of Prop. 4 which is closer to something being taken for granted than actually being the subject of discussion. The key issues here are the theological *sources*. The statement given evidently subordinates the Magisterium to the sources at its disposal.

signs which can only be discerned through love. This leads into Prop. 6 which concentrates upon the aspect of change. Again, like GS and unlike the *Lin* and IL, change is viewed not as threat but as challenge. While there is growth and plurality, both of which are evaluated positively, there is also the possibility of subjugating and diminishing marriage and family life, an addition which brought balance to the picture. This is followed by another addition on the task of the Church "to evangelize emerging culture from its beginning". There is no opposition here but a healthy appreciation for the "new kind of humanism" (GS, 7)[133] which is also a sign of the times. Finally, an appeal is made to consciences and a last, added sentence recognizes the positive influences families can contribute in creating structures of justice and love. Note the basic independence of culture which is part of this entire perspective.

The third and last section of Part I is on the sole topic of "Gradualism" (Prop. 7). This strange and unexpected aspect of Church teaching came to be a controversial subject in the Synod and its aftermath. The idea is said to have been introduced by Pedro Arrupe, then Superior General of the Jesuits[134]. Gradualism is by no means a new idea, having been part of traditional moral theology and having implicitly resurfaced immediately after HV as one of the mitigating interpretations of that teaching[135]. In short, it stands for the notion that conversion is a dynamic and "gradual" process which does not happen overnight. It depends on discernment and a growing willingness to be open to the mystery of Christ. The obvious conclusion is that not

133. The reference to a "new humanism" was probably ascribed to GS,7 because of the following remark that this can turn persons away from as well as toward God. The conciliar teaching at this point is concerned precisely with that issue. However, another reference could have been GS,55 which also mentions the "new humanism" but in a much more positive fashion: "one in which man is defined first of all by his responsibility toward his brothers and toward history". Perhaps it is more the "potentially atheistic" humanism which needs evangelization, but it appears better to single out the second definition of humanism (actually another aspect of the same reality) to maintain the positive orientation.

134. Cf. B. MARTHALER, *art. cit.*, p. 72.

135. The notion of "gradualism" as it will later be applied to the moral law is implicit in the interpretation of HV which views that encyclical as putting forth an "ideal" teaching. This is most clearly found in "The Statement of the Presidential Council of the Italian Bishops' Conference", issued 10 Sept. 1968. After mentioning that HV represents the teaching of an "ideal goal", the bishops state: "The Church, whose task it is to declare the total and perfect goodness, is not unaware that there are laws of growth in goodness, and at times one passes through stages still imperfect, although with the aim of loyally overcoming them in a constant effort toward the ideal". Cf. J. HORGAN (ed.), *Humanae Vitae and the Bishops*, Shannon, 1972, p. 68. The notion that HV represented the teaching of some form of an ideal is stated or implied in the statements of eleven groups of bishops: Austria, Brazil, C.E.L.A.M., Czechoslovakia, Italy, Poland, Portugal, Scandanavia, Spain, Switzerland, and the U.S.A. Not all these statements, however, consider the observation to mitigate that teaching significantly.

everyone is at the same stage of conversion, nor can persons be expected to be equally mature in their christian faith.

One gets the impression, especially from its place in the structure of the Propositions, that the bishops were making a general statement here about the Church and the role of the Synod in addressing modern man. This is a sound theological and pastoral perspective which could be applied to the Magisterium as well as to christians in general. Viewing itself as reflecting upon the signs of the times and being attentive to the *sensus fidei*, the Synod recognized that it, too, was going through a process of conversion. Unfortunately, the invocation of a certain "law of gradualism" will redirect this observation into a controversy over moral teaching in particular (cf. Prop. 24 and the reaction it received).

Returning to Prop. 7 itself, a few comments should be made on the text. The original simply noted that "injustice and sin permeate the structure of the world and must be fought by conversion". The corrected version is more social and theologically precise in saying that "injustice, which has its origins in personal and social sin, permeates the structure of this world, and should be continually fought by a conversion of the mind and heart, which will also lead to a transformation of structures". Then it is observed that "this conversion is given in stages (not "two stages" as in the English version). After describing that process (which, incidently, adds "pastoral" to educational guidance, both of which must be patient) it also adds the observation that "suffering and sacrifice will be part of this process" but these realities should not be "disturbing" to the believer.

Reviewing the whole of Part I we find an open and searching attitude characterizing the Propositions which flowed quite naturally from the many discussions which had taken place among the bishops. The theology is fundamentally conciliar and seeks dialogue with the world. Furthermore, as we will also find in Part II, the differences between the first and final versions represent some real improvements. They are more social minded and preserve a nuanced, positive theology.

C. Part Two: Theology of Marriage and the Family

The title of the second Part of the Propositions is "The Plan of God concerning the Family" (*De Proposito Dei circa Familias*). It has seven sections and is very general in nature. This might be called the "doctrinal part" in parallel with the earlier documents, but we will see that with one possible exception (the discussion on divorce) it does not attempt to answer questions in the same way as those texts. There is also a great deal more subtlety and precision in its theology.

A word on the title is appropriate at this point. The "Plan of God" is taken to be the starting point of this theology. This, as we have mentioned, was becoming a key phrase in the *Lin* and IL and will play a major role in FC. But the meaning implied here is quite different. Props. 5 and 6 had already used the phrase in discussing the "signs of the times". It is evident that those texts were not approaching reality with a pre-given notion but were urging investigation of contemporary phenomena in order to discern what that "plan" might be. The phrase will appear again in Prop. 13, c (where the term *consilium* is used) on marital indissolubility. There we find the observation that "Christ renews the primordial plan of God by helping human weakness with His grace". It also occurs in Prop. 34, a which is a precis of a statement of John-Paul II. Beyond these texts, however, no appeal is made to "God's plan". The notion, even in these texts, is not a starting point for deduction nor a model superimposed upon nature and culture. Creation is not looked upon as an historical event which gave the pattern for every aspect of reality to come. Rather, the idea of "God's plan" used here is dynamic. Its occurrence in the title of Part II should not prejudice our reading of the texts. Even though many of the same sources that we have already seen will be used, their interpretation will not always be the same. In the Propositions, "God's plan" has nothing to do with natural law.

Section 4, the first of Part II, includes one four paragraph Proposition (8)[136]. The English translation of the first paragraph is somewhat lacking, so we will give our own version.

God, who Himself exists as love, created persons in His own image and likeness (cf. Gen. 1:26f). Because He is love, He lives in three persons, that is, in relationships of self-giving, of receiving and reciprocating with each other, of mutual donation and cherishing. Created in this image man is also destined not to solitude but to a relationship of love[137]. However, because the person is an incarnate spirit, that is, a soul which is expressed in a body and a body which is informed by an immortal soul, he is called to love in this totality. Love pervades the body of the person and the body participates in spiritual love.

Ostensibly this is the same starting point of the IL, but the phrasing is more concise. The appeal to creation is not an analytic one, attempting to isolate principles for subsequent deduction, but rather a simple theological statement of belief. The knowledge of person created in God's image is as avaliable today, consulting the *sensus fidei* and the givens (signs) of our own times, and perhaps more so, than what can be found in a minute and artificial analysis of the story of adam and eve.

---

136. The title of Section 4 is the occasion of the first significant discrepancy between the EM and our version of the *textus emendatus*. EM, p. 24, nr. 6 admits a change in the title "De Fundamento Anthropologico et Theologico Sacramenti Matrimonii" omitting the word *Sacramenti*. It is, however, retained in the final version.

137. EM, p. 23, nr. 1 admits the addition *et communionis*, not found in the final version, after the word *amoris*. "Created in this image man is also destined not to solitude but to a relationship of love and communion". EM: "It perfects the text".

The entire image here is that of "person as a whole", an integrated being destined to find fulfillment in loving relationships. As integrated, the person *is* sexual. As noted in GS, 48 and 51, sexuality is not mere biology, it is not "added on" to the person, it is specifically human and an aspect of the original (and ongoing) creative intention. Thus, the first sentence of para. 3 in English is misleading when it says that "sexuality is part of the human person ..." A better translation is "because sexuality pertains to the very core of human existence ..."[138] There is no duality here. A person's sexuality is not something that one can choose to advert to or not. This is the presupposition behind the *Lin* and IL. Rather, all persons are sexual and must respond to and come to terms with their sexuality, whether this be through marriage, celibacy of something in between.

Again, in para. 2 we can improve on the translation which states that "sexuality is truly human ..." by more accurately rendering, "sexuality is realized in a truly human way when it becomes an integral part of love by which a man and woman give themselves to each other until death"[139]. It is not a question of whether sexuality is human — it is. The point is whether human sexuality is integrated into the whole life of the person. What is presented here, an integrated heterosexual relationship lasting throughout life, is considered the ideal, the most integrally human realization of sexuality. It could very well be observed that not all persons are capacitated to accomplish this ideal or have the opportunity for its realization. But that is another topic not dealt with in the Propositions.

What is observed is that in establishing a relationship which is destined to be total and integral, thus including sexual expression in its genital dimension as well, one must be open to the person adequately considered. One of the continuous dimensions of the person is their temporality and historicity. Therefore, to be totally involved is to have a relationship which also looks to the future. Anything less, where one or both of the parties does not have an honest assessment of the future dimension of the relationship, is dishonest because it does not deal with the whole meaning of the person. The Proposition assumes that responding to the temporal dimension demands a lasting relationship. We would have to classify this as an ideal as well, presuming capacity, opportunity and free choice. Obviously, the ideal is not always realized.

It is in the context of this ideal, total relationship where love "creates room for fidelity" (and we might add, *only* is this type of relationship),

138. Quia sexualitas ad nucleum existentiae hominis a Deo ad suam imaginem creati pertinet, matrimonium ut unicus locus eius (plenae) realisationis vere humanae in omnibus culturis ..." The addition of *plenae* was "admitted because it perfects the text" in EM, p. 23, nr. 4. It does not appear in the *textus emendatus*.

139. Sexualitas tunc modo vere humano realizatur, si pars integralis amoris fit, quo vir et mulier sese invicem usque ad mortem donant.

that love is *also* harmonious with *responsible* fecundity, which is said to be intrinsic to the love of man and woman. Attention should be paid to the careful choice of words here. Note the use of also (*etiam*) and recall the opening words of GS, 50 and the last minute attempt of a papal *modus* to change it. Note also that love as such is *not* open to procreation. But the *relationship* (here: "love which creates room for fidelity"; in GS, 50: "marriage and conjugal love") is consonant with responsible fecundity. Both words are important: responsible, because it assumes conscious decision; fecundity, because it deals with a human potential and not mere biological fertilization. It is admirable that the bishops expressed themselves so carefully.

Lastly, Prop. 8 speaks of the institution of marriage. It does *not* say that God created marriage as an institution. First, it is observed that all cultures see (the institution of) marriage as the most eminent of sacred things which gives a unique place for human sexual expression. "Marriage *is* (not "gives") the concrete and public form of that fidelity which human sexuality postulates (takes for granted) for the expression of fruitful love in itself". This is a simple statement of fact. The love relationship which is (possibly going to be) fecund is best expressed in a protected, institutionalized structure. Secondly, thus institution of marriage is clearly recognized to be the product of culture. It is not imposed upon culture but grows from it. Nor is there any pre-ordained structure presumed here. This is quite different from the earlier documents and resembles both conciliar thinking and the evident influence of bishops from pastoral situations outside the singular, nuclear family model of the North Atlantic world.

Our commentary on section 4 (Prop. 8) is perhaps long but is felt to be necessary to fully explain what is found there. The differences with the *Lin* and IL are striking once they are uncovered, and they continue on in the next section, 5, on "The Theology of the Sacrament" (Props. 9-11). One must read the text very carefully, remembering the expressions of the preparatory documents. In being attentive to the subtlety, one immediately sees that the Propositions preserve the notion of analogy present in Scripture. Beginning with the statement that the human person is created in God's image, we need "to probe more deeply the meaning of this mutual gift between man and woman". Everything is not decided from the beginning. The attitude of searching, of learning from experience, is fully operative here. The observations are then listed as: the differences which make union possible, the indispensable dialogue between individuals who are equal, and "their interpersonal communion as well as their fruitfulness". The last of these underwent an important change for the original version had the order reversed: "their fruitfulness as well as their communion". The priority is extremely significant, enough so that the bishops ordered it properly established and then added the reference to Gen. 1:26-28 which witnesses to the same priority.

Proposition 9,b[140] then states that indeed God willed conjugal love to be an expression of His own convenantal love[141]. But again through an addition the status of analogy is insisted upon (*in connubii figura*; cf. GS, 48). Also added are the Old Testament references, all of which deal with the infidelity of one spouse and the benevolent forgiveness of the other. While 9,c reiterates the continuity of God's love in the Christ event (incarnation), 9,d moves to the Christ-Church analogy which applies to conjugal love but also to *all* human love. In other words, christian love in and of itself is based upon the model of total self-giving. Conjugal love, when christian, is no different. We could easily say that all human love is sacramental.

Proposition 10 becomes more specific in speaking about marriage as a sacrament. It links this to the entire incarnation-redemption event which establishes the New Covenant. *In* the New Covenant, and not because of it, marriage is recognized as a sacred sign: a sacrament. The sign value is already present by virtue of the human marital relationship. This sign is given a special place in the life of the Church — it is not dependent upon the Church for its existence, but in union with Christ all christians and their activities are open to (being) events of grace: God's loving and saving presence. Thus, in what was an addition, the last sentence of para. 3 mentions the mutual sanctification which is occasioned by the love relationship (cf. GS,48). There is a dynamic present here: everything does not happen automatically. Para. 2 realistically points out that marriage is not equivalent to the Christ-Church mystery but is enriched by it. This happens in the same way that all relationships are influenced by one's christian belief and engagement in the "great mystery". These two Propositions, therefore, are much closer to GS,48 in their theology. There is no determinism, no automatic "filling up" of the human reality by "grace". The sacramentality presumed here is theologically rich and dynamic, going far beyond what the working document had proposed.

Section 5 does not stop here but goes on (Prop. 11) to discuss virginity (the Latin does not say "consecrated") and "celibacy for the Kingdom", (which was an addition) which are situated in the same theological perspective as marriage. That is, in keeping with section 4 where human sexuality is an integrated dimension of the whole person, the choice of how to live out that sexuality takes place for the christian in the context

140. The Latin text uses arabic numbers for designating subdivisions of a particular Proposition. We will maintain the use of letters, as in the English translation, for the purpose of clarity.

141. It may be important to underscore the relationship between God's *covenantal* love and the love upon which marriage is based. In reaction to the first text of the Propositions at least one bishop suggested that the word *sponsalis* be omitted as a description of God's love for His people. The EM, p. 27, nr. 8, admits this suggestion, but the final text retains the word. We will see that FC is equally generous with its use of metaphors in describing God's "conjugal" love.

of one's response to Christ. It is very keenly observed that where marriage and sexuality are not positively seen as gifts from God, there is no meaning in the choice for celibacy as a sign of the Kingdom[142]. "Marriage and virginity are two ways of expressing the same mystical reality, God's covenant with His People". This sentence is an addition, and a thankful one at that. There is absolutely no hierarchy here, no preference expressed, no value judgment made. In the conciliar mold the bishops have expressed a theology which had finally overcome the marriage-virginity dichotomy that the Western Church had inherited from many of the Latin Fathers. The perspective found in FC,16 will be somewhat different.

A final comment on Prop. 11 should take note of other changes which occur in the last two sentences. The first changed the very awkward original, "in their physical sterility they are fruitful ..." to "although physically infecund (i.e. not actualizing their potential fertility) the person is spiritually fruitful, the father and mother of many (i.e. not "family life" as in the English)". Then, the entire last sentence was also an addition. It specifically includes non-married persons who are not "celibate for the Kingdom" as a sign but who have accepted (come to terms with) their state and are thus living out their human sexuality.

This entire section represents a significant accomplishment. The bishops had gone beyond the pre-synodal outlines and expressed a contemporary theology. Its significance is even further enhanced when we realize what had not been said: the entire theology of marriage and conjugal love is developed without any reference to procreation[143]. The accomplishment of GS,49 had come to fruition.

Section 6 (Prop. 12) takes on the problematic of "Faith and the Sacrament". The very fact that this is a separate section testifies to the bishops' concern for a real pastoral problem. The *Lin* had nothing to say

---

142. By way of extraneous commentary we could characterize this approach as value oriented. Human sexuality and marriage are both goods (*bona*). When they are recognized as being in service to the person adequately considered, they may be called values. As a value, human sexuality needs to be integrated into the totality of one's life. Sacrificing that value — ignoring or denying one's sexuality — cannot be justified without (in this case, because it involves serious harm to human integration: a serious) proportionate reason. So, too, is marriage a value and worthy of pursuit. Sacrificing the value of marriage also demands a proportionate reason. In the case of celibacy for the Kingdom, the reason is the sign value of what one does. In the case of involuntary celibacy no sacrifice has been made, though one must still come to terms with its loss. When marriage is voluntarily given up or sacrificed, one should probably ask themself why, simply to be sensitive to their own priority of values.

143. Admittedly, we have drawn attention to the third observation made in Prop. 9, about "fruitfulness". But this is an observation and nothing more. It does not return in the discussion of conjugal love as basis for the theology of the sacrament. GS,48 had also mentioned fruitfulness but based its sacramentology on the love relationship. Thus, GS,49 on conjugal love never mentions procreation. Recall the absence of this distinction in the *Lin* and IL.

about the issue and IL,34 had brought it up, probably at the episcopal insistence, but handled it poorly. Now the bishops themselves turned their attention to the problem, not with the idea of giving a solution, but with the intention of exposing the issue in its complexity. It does this in five parts. The first paragraph begins with the reference to *Sacrosanctum concilium*, 59 (cf. IL,34). Then, whereas the original had simply stated that faith is necessary for validity, the bishops added, "That is why *we must investigate to what extent* the validity of this sacrament requires faith ..." This is the first of a number of questions the bishops will put and investigations they will call for in the Propositions. This should be expected because it is the very nature of the synodal process. The bishops did not gather together to give solutions to questions the complexity of which demanded careful study and research, meditation and prayer. They came to take stock of the contemporary life of the Church, its mission to its members and the world at large. They came to raise the questions and point out the present difficulties. Unfortunately, we will see that some of their questions are answered with a terse "judgment". Others will simply be ignored or the point of investigation will be dismissed. This first call for investigation will fall into the latter category (cf. FC,68).

Paragraph b then delineates the problem: the request for marriage may itself be a sign of faith, but it may also simply be a matter of custom which has little or nothing to do with faith. Paragraph c recognizes that there are different levels of maturity (cf. Prop. 7), that there is need for a minimal intention[144] and that approaching the sacrament is an opportune time for catechesis. This can be accomplished "with the community's help" (an addition once again restoring the theological perspective: sacraments are ecclesial, not individual, events) through programs of premarital education. The bishops prudently advise a middle course between rigorism and laxism. Evidently they believed this to be possible — an absolutist, essentialist, or legal mind would not.

Prop. 12,d is almost entirely the result of revision. The original said "more deeply to be investigated is the statement according to which for baptized persons (even those) who have lost the faith the matrimonial contract is totally identified with the sacrament of marriage. This will have juridical and pastoral consequences" (parenthesis added). The final

---

144. On the one hand, Prop. 12, c repeats the idea of IL,34 that there is a minimum of "doing what the Church does". On the other hand, the bishops saw that this begs the question: in the sacrament of marriage, what does the Church do? The attempted response turned out to be very theological: "the minimum intention of believing with the Church and its baptismal faith". In other words, to marry "in Christ" demands a faith in Christ: "where two or three are gathered together *in my name*, I am present" (grace). The insight is so simple we can call it obvious. Unfortunately, when seen from a juridical interpretation, the beauty of the simplicity remains hidden (IL).

version is much more explicit in its intention[145]. Similarly, para. e originally read "Again the special effects of unity and indissolubility are to be affirmed for the natural marital contract". The final version changed this to read simply "for natural marriage" (the English translation here being inaccurate), and then added the final sentence calling for the new code of canon law to take the entire Proposition into account. Prop. 12 had vertured upon new ground and opened many questions for further investigation. We will have to be attentive to the reception of the bishops' advice.

Section 7 (Props. 13-14), on indissolubility and divorce, went even further than the previous text because it refused to simply take over the essentialism of the *Lin* and IL. Again, there is linguistic and theological precision. Prop. 13,a begins with a simple declaration of belief in indissolubility. But note that the characteristic of lastingness is first posited only to christians, a self-restriction by the episcopal magisterium which realized the limits of its jurisdiction; and that there is no immediate invocation of the Christ-Church relationship. Apparently the bishops knew that a simple quotation of Eph. 5 or Mt. 19 would not be sufficient. However, they do not neglect the images or forget the *analogy* when in 13,b they write, "The indissolubility of marriage is rooted in and sustained by the personal, total donation of the spouses insofar as this is fruit, sign and consequence of the irreversible love of God for His People and the donation and faithfulness of Christ toward His Church". The text goes on to call this a "sacramental gift" which depends upon a responsible and free decision of the couple who make their promise specifically as christians. But we want to be attentive to the quote given here. To begin, we recall the respect that the bishops had for the use of the covenantal analogy. The marital relation is personal and total self-giving (understood: on a reciprocal basis in the case of marriage; the Latin does not include the word mutual) *insofar* as it resembles God's convenantal love. There is no automation here, no mechanistic notion that entering the union transforms a reality into something different than it was (cf. IL,28-34). Also, the choice of words is interesting. The human relation is "fruit, sign and consequence" of divine convenantal relations. These are words reserved for procreation in the earlier documents. Lastly, the indissolubility is "rooted in and sustained by" the marital relationship, based upon a responsible and free promise, and does not

145. The text of Prop. 12,d reads,

We must further investigate whether the statement that a valid marriage between baptized persons is always a sacrament is also applicable for those who have lost the faith. This will then entail juridical and pastoral consequences. Above all it must be investigated what the pastoral criteria might be for discerning the faith of the engaged couple and how much their intention of doing what the Church does more or less should include the minimal intention of believing with the Church as well.

emanate from something outside, imposed, as it were, upon the relationship.

In comparison with the suggestions they had been given (IL), the bishops did not do badly in representing the nuances of contemporary theological expression. After 13, c situates marriage once again in the New Covenant and observes that Christ's sacramental grace (presence) will help overcome human weakness, 13, d exhibits excellent pastoral sense in praising those who, despite difficulties, are living a life of witness to indissoluble love. They include here not only the married but also those who have been deserted by their spouse and yet remain faithful to their promise by not "attempting" a second marriage. The latter group could be considered heroic and the bishops call for the pastors and community to support them. In light of what has recently become a rather negativistic style in official teaching, it is again refreshing to hear the bishops utter a word of praise.

Prop. 13, e singles out a possible source of modern problems in calling for better premarital instruction. The final sentence, an addition, suggests that episcopal conferences introduce some form of betrothal ceremony to enhance the premarital decision-making process. This contains two important and even revolutionary ideas. First, it is the first hint of what will become a resounding theme of the Propositions: episcopal conferences need to exercise more autonomy and have this recognized by Rome (at least for legislative reasons). This is the only realistic way that pastors will be able to serve the particular needs of their own local church. Secondly, the suggesion of some form of betrothal ceremony is a very strong hint of what had become a controversial experiment in France with respect to Church marriages "in stages". The diocese of Autun, in response to the pastoral problem of those who were non-practicing or even non-believing "Catholics" requesting a Church wedding, initiated an experiment of "welcoming a (civil) marriage into the Church". This was not simply an attempt to recognize what was a marriage between non-participant but baptized persons, nor a form of simplistic accomodation. It was a program of catechesis whereby the occasion of marriage and the expressed desire to have this blessed by the Church presented an opportunity for re-initiation[146]. Although one can debate the pros and cons of this experiment, it was a concrete attempt to do something, taken on through local initiative in a responsible manner.

During the Synod, an intervention on 15 Oct. by Card. James Knox, then Prefect of the Cong. for Sacraments and Divine Worship, strongly objected to this practice in no uncertain terms. With clear reference to the Autun experiment he said,

---

146. Cf. *supra*, note 36, and J. A. SCHMEISER, *Marriage: New Alternatives*, in *Worship* 55 (1981) 23-34.

Therefore, every welcoming ceremony by which a priest or any other person in the name of the Church manifests approval is to be considered illicit. It is worse still if the invalidly united persons are approved in such a way as to give them some status within the Church, written in a register, with celebration and prayer in the name of the Christian community, like those who contract a valid marriage[147].

We are not postulating that in 13, e the bishops were underhandedly endorsing this specific experiment, but we cannot deny that they had something in mind with respect to responding to a specific pastoral problem. We have no idea what is meant by the suggestion of a "betrothal ceremony" and have the distinct impression that it was intentionally meant to be vague. In any case, we must admit the significance of the bishops' making this twofold suggestion. Again, we will have to be attentive to the (non)-reception of their advice.

Turning to the second aspect of this section, Prop. 14 is a long text meant to deal with the problem of divorce and remarriage. It is unrealistic to think that the Synod alone could have solved this problem. One group of bishops, those from North America in particular, wanted something said because of the urgent need in their pastoral domain. But there was no satisfactory "answer" forthcoming. The disappointment which was experienced at the end of the Synod, however, was occasioned not by the bishops' accomplishment but by the decision rendered by the Pope in his "Closing Homily". We will attend to that in due time. But at this point, especially now that the issue is no longer being spectacularized in the media, we should take a careful look at what the bishops said in Prop. 14.

The first paragraph was entirely reworked in the final version. Some initial changes expanded the Church's mission from "leading all the baptized" to "leading all people, especially the baptized to salvation". Then, in specifically addressing those who "have attempted to remarry", there is an openness exhibited by immediately invoking the Church's role of reconciliation. The rest of the paragraph is an addition to the original and clearly exhibits good pastoral sense.

But pastors should know that love obliges them to discern well among various categories. There are differences between those who really tried to save their first marriage but were unjustly deserted, and those who deliberately broke up their canonically valid marriage. There are others who have remarried for the sake of their children; some of them are subjectively certain in their consciences that their first marriage, now irreparably broken, was never valid in the first place.

One gets the distinct impression that the bishops wanted pastoral care to be geared to the real, distinguishable situations. This, of course, is

---

147. *Marriage Questions Addressed*, the text of Card. Knox's intervention, can be found in *Origins* 10 (1980) 315-317, here, p. 316.

completely new when we evaluate it in light of the IL. Considering the pre-synodal outlines, we should have more appreciation for what the bishops said. The next paragraph in particular, is, in comparison with the essentialist perspective, rather revolutionary.

Prop. 14, b can be seen as nothing less than a departure from tradition. In the not too distant past, Catholics who divorced were excommunicated; if they attempted remarriage they were considered public sinners and were to be shunned by the community. In a complete turnabout the bishops have literally thrown open the doors of the Church for those persons. "The Synod exhorts pastors and the whole community of the faithful to help divorced persons". They should be welcome in the Church, participate in its life, they should attend mass (this was an addition to the text which clarified any doubt as to what was meant), practice charity, justice, penance, and so on. They are encouraged to raise their children in the faith. In essence, divorced-remarried persons are to remain or become part of the living community.

Words can hardly express the significance of this paragraph. To begin, we recognize that traditional practice had always expected divorced persons to continue attending mass. However, here the bishops are clearly addressing the situation of *remarried* persons and encouraging them to be active members of the community. The refusal to shun divorced-remarried Catholics was a definite step forward, inspired by recognition of the fact that the Church is not a public judge but as representative of Christ must reconcile, heal, and continuously find means of reaching out to all persons. We can only hope that the bishops went home to their dioceses and preached this message to their communities. All persons, including the divorced and remarried, should be welcomed by the community and loved as Christ loves them.

There remains a stumbling block, however, a line which neither the bishops nor the Pope could cross in their official statements. The issue of remarried persons receiving the eucharist became the one aspect around which most of the controversy revolved. Prop. 14, c addresses this with predictable hesitation, but the arguments are poor. "This Synod reaffirms the Church practice, based on Sacred Scripture[148], of not admitting divorced and remarried persons to eucharistic communion". Two supportive arguments are given: that their state in life contradicts the indissoluble Christ-Church covenant which is signified and effected in the eucharist; and because of the problem of scandal (error and

---

148. The reference to Sacred Scripture here can be called into question. EM, p. 49, nr. 20, suggested that there was really no foundation for the reference, but the response rejects omitting it "because the discipline of the Church is really founded upon the teaching of Sacred Scripture on the indissolubility of marriage". On the same page, nr. 24 is simply said to be the same as nr. 20, but the response then states simply that "it is accepted" (*accipitur*). EM, p. 50, nr. 30, again simply accepts the suggested omission of reference to Scripture. Yet the *textus emendatus* retains the phrase.

confusion) for the rest of the faithful. The theologian is sensitive to
immediate questions: Where does scripture establish this practice? Is this
not a very prejudicial interpretation, the exact reference for which is not
even given? And what form of eucharistic theology is underlying this
proposal? Is there not also a contradiction between being a real part of
the living community and being barred from full participation? And
finally, does the burden of scandal rest on the shoulders of the individual
or does it not demand that the community itself needs education? While
a number of discussions have been occasioned by this standpoint, many
have forgotten that following it through, the progression of thought will
clearly expose its own inadequacies.

The next paragraph, 14, d, is less explicit than the Pope would be, but
the idea is clear. Remarried Catholics may receive absolution and the
eucharist when they "sincerely pledge themselves to a way of life that does
not contradict the indissolubility of the sacrament of marriage". The
vagueness of this statement could have been left as it is so that each
community and local church could interpret it to fit their needs and level
of maturity. Unfortunately, the papal "Homily" would become explicit
and once again invoke the traditional solution that there may be no
sexual relations in a second marriage. As long as there is no sexual
relationship, full participation with the community can be restored.
There is a well justified doubt that this is what the bishops intended.
Their concerns are valid for they had to responsibly consider whether or
not the Church as a whole was ready for such a drastic change in its
official practice. They decided that the time had not (yet?) come. But let
us not forget that in *exhorting* the Church to welcome remarried persons
back into the fold, they had laid the groundwork for that change.

We will briefly return to this issue later. For now, the last two
paragraphs of Prop. 14 must also be appreciated in themselves. Para. 14,
e returns to the theme that the Church should discriminate between
cases, with an addition singling out "especially the innocent ones who
were deserted by their spouse". The episcopal intention of 14, a on
different kinds of cases was explicitly repeated. Then, 14, f calls for "a
new and extensive study" in the area of pastoral care. In a rather subtle
but clear way, another fruitful idea is adopted by explicitly stating that,
"this study should take into account the practices of the Eastern
Churches"[149]. Unfortunately, this suggestion will eventually disappear
from view.

---

149. EM, p. 47, nr. 15, dealing with the first two sections of Prop. 14, contained the
suggestion that a *commission* be set up to study the authority of the Holy Father with
respect to marriage. The response accepted this suggestion and proposed the following
addition to the end of nr. 6 (14,f), therefore, following the text given here. "Synodus
proponit ut instituatur commissio quae ex episcopis et theologicis constituatur ad
investigandam potestatem sic dictam vicariam Summi Pontificis relate ad sacramentum
matrimonii".

Section 8 (Props. 15-17) represents another step forward taken by the bishops which addressed "Woman and the Family". The first Proposition clearly puts forth the equal human dignity of woman basing itself on Scripture (Gen. 1: 27), and especially the actions of Christ (LK. 8: 13; Jn. 20:11-18; Mt. 28: 10). In what was an addition, the bishops do not hesitate, as IL, 47 did, in quoting St. Paul that "there is neither male nor female..." (Gal 3:27-28). Finally, attention is drawn to Vatican II and a statement proposed from the Council for the Laity, Copenhagen 1980.

Prop. 16 then relates these teachings to marriage. Recognizing that in the past woman's role was largely restricted, there is a positive evaluation of modern movements which take a more open attitude toward domestic roles, recognize woman's dignity and equality both within the home and in work outside the home, and admit of the interchangability of roles between husband and wife. There is also a good corrective introduced that women should not be *forced* to work outside the home, nor should their status (originally: independence) be judged simply because of outside work. Whatever her chosen role or job, woman must be respected, first and especially by her husband if married. The Proposition ends with a call for furthering rather than denying woman's feminine characteristics and taking account of different customs and cultures. But this ending is preceded by another cautious but surprising call for the Church "to promote as much as possible in her own life equal rights and dignity". Like many other insights the bishops had put forth, this advice would not be influential.

The last Proposition of this section (17) is the direct result of socially minded bishops who warn about the concrete cases of exploiting women, especially in prostitution and slavery, but also by discrimination of every kind. A long addition to this exploitation exposure concerns the use of the tourist trade which very obviously came from specific bishops. Then there is a further explicit mention of women who are the victim of prejudice because of their state in life, childless women, widows, etc. The Proposition ends with one of only two condemnations found in the entire text and it is directed against "all attacks against the dignity of the human person". Again, the theology of Vatican II was clearly reflected in the Propositions.

We can expect that not everyone would be pleased with the Synod's position on woman's rights, some of that dissatisfaction being caused by what was John-Paul II's already rather well known position on the matter. But reading the Propositions on their own reveals a balanced perspective. We must not forget that the bishops were speaking in

---

This text does not appear in our version of the *textus emendatus*. At least that version includes the call for a study to be made, but the concrete suggestion for a commission would have been stronger.

context and charged with responsibility to the universal Church. In many parts of the world woman's social status is much below that sometimes strived for in the industrialized countries. The statements of the bishops here are soundly based in faith and theology. The implications and long range consequences of adopting these positions will again be revolutionary both for society and for the Church. In the meantime there was a prudential judgment not to interfere with, or worse attempt to dictate to, various cultures and traditional customs. The bishops were aware that evangelization was not equivalent to the superimposition of cultural values.

These thoughts are reflected once again in the last two sections of Part II. "Marriage in Ancient Cultural Customs and Christian Marriage" (Prop. 18) is a clear call for what is meant by the modern catchword: inculturation. The only change in this text was the addition of references to GS, 44 and *Ad gentes*, 15 & 22 to substantiate the position put forth. The text speaks for itself and is very conciliar. We will give no further comment except to note that there are two more specific requests for further study and episcopal autonomy[150]. We must not forget these when evaluating the later events.

Finally, Section 10 (Prop. 19, a-e) is on "Mixed Marriages" and again contributes information and reflection upon a topic which was beyond the comprehension of the older world. The bishops know how widespread and rapidly growing is the phenomenon and that it is entirely to be expected. They also know that there is little appreciation for this in some circles. Therefore, 19, b specifically calls for more autonomy for the local bishops' conferences in setting norms. In its final version the Proposition was amended to strengthen the intention of providing for baptism and the Catholic upbringing of the children. But another addition, "as far as possible", shows that the bishops were more keenly aware of the realities of these situations than those who had little or no experience. In general this is also a fine Proposition that offers encouragement and the will to move further in pastoral practice. It is clearly optimistic and sees potential in contemporary events rather than threat. The invocation of the ecumenical possibilities at the end, 19, e, is a good note on which to bring Part II to a close.

Considering the working scheme, the background, diversity and needs of the different bishops, the sense of pastoral urgency and responsibility to the universal Church, and most of all the influence of those who were officially responsible for preparing the synodal event, we can look with satisfaction at the first nineteen Propositions, Parts I and II of the document, and sense a real accomplishment on the part of the bishops.

---

150. The two requests are: studies by the episcopal conferences themselves in order to aid the process of inculturating the faith, and more faculties and autonomy for the local churches in adopting norms for marital celebration *and validity* to cultural customs.

Generally, both versions of the text are rather conciliar but there is definitely an improvement by the *modi* incorporated into the final version. The major lines of argumentation were already present, especially most of the studies called for and the assertion of more autonomy for the local Churches. If anything, the additions contributed clarity to what was a remarkable resurgence of conciliar theology by the episcopal magisterium. It can be postulated that this was due to the fact that pastoral advance in these areas was unalterable and could not be denied. We will see that this remains true for some of the later Propositions in Part III which dealt with what might be called general ideas and non-specific problems. But before those can be addressed, we must encounter the greatest controversy of all, the question of regulating fertility.

D. Part Three: The Pastoral Problems

This Part is on the various "Roles of the Family". With the general ideas and theology established, the document now turns to specifics. The nine sections and 22 Propositions make this the longest Part and, outside of the discussion on divorce and remarriage in Part II, some of the topics discussed make it also the most controversial part of the development.

It must be pointed out that up to this point alterations in the text have been basically synodal. That is, the *modi* which were incorporated did not draw upon the preparatory documents. Nor were they entirely predictable before the Synod took place. Many elements, especially those aimed at social justice, came to be expected when it was evident that a number of Third World bishops were speaking in unison, for perhaps the first time in the synodal process. Their contributions were a valuable asset and we expect will play a greater role in future Synods. However, the fact remains that because of the structure of the process of the Synod a good deal of tension is still present.

Section 11 on "The Transmission *and Safeguarding* (an addition) of Human Life" was the most controversial issue because it represented the problem of what had been a well known[151] teaching of the Magisterium

---

151. The high profile of the debate over contraception rests not simply on the HV event but on the fact that of all Church teaching, the area of sexual morality is probably the best known, having been preached and repeated in pulpits, confessionals, Catholic schools and wherever the clergy was expected to teach. Everyone *knew* what the Magisterium's position was. Therefore, when it became a question of whether that position could change, the primary issue was not always the moral teaching itself, but whether *any* change in the "strict reading" of the tradition would amount to an apparent admission of "error" on the part of earlier popes, especially Pius XI (1930) and Pius XII (1951). Pope Paul VI could not bring himself to "depart from the constant teaching of the Magisterium" (cf. HV,6), and Pope John-Paul II had been elected at least partially because of his position in this moral controversy.

Nevertheless, we should not neglect the significance of Pope Paul's position in HV,

that was not being followed in practice by huge portions of the faithful. The bishops were caught in between these two poles. But they also experienced another problem. Some bishops saw this as an essentially private moral issue on the level of human behavior. These were the representatives of the North Atlantic world, especially those from the English speaking countries. However, other bishops viewed the issue as a social one. They needed a weapon to fight against family planning programs being imposed upon people by public authorities. This latter group was hesitent to call the teaching into question. The resulting Propositions seemed to form a compromise. As we read through them we must be conscious of two things: the basic social mindedness of these Propositions, especially in the reading of the first version; and the nature and tone of the additions which were brought into the text, often without explanation. There are six Propositions.

Prop. 20 is a relatively brief introduction to the issue. It begins with the creation perspective, adds that God *established* (*constituit*: not institutionalized) marriage and "called men and women to a union of love in service to life"[152]. Then, echoing GS, 50, there is the idea that spouses *participate* in God's creative power in transmitting the gift of life. But the sentence is different from GS which spoke of participating in and being cooperators with the *love* of God (i.e. not "power"). It is also somewhat awkward in speaking about transmitting the gift of life, as if there were already a being present which may or may not receive the gift. The language may have been poetic but on such a sensitive topic more care should have been taken. Finally, there is the insight that this vocation is not restricted to physical procreation "but extends to supernatural, moral and spiritual fruits". This addition resembles what was already found in IL, 67.

Prop. 21 then puts forth the core of the position and needs to be quoted in full in order to explain some subtle changes.

Because conjugal love is a share in the mystery of God's life and love, the Church has a special role in protecting (and promoting) the dignity of marriage

especially in light of the well known character of the teaching itself. While his predecessors had condemned the use of artificial contraception in strong terms, Pope Paul took a very mild position. Knowing that he could never give unequivocal endorsement to artificial means for regulating fertility, at least because of the social consequences of doing so (cf. HV,17), the pontiff took a "safe" position and merely repeated the traditional observations. However, Paul VI never explicitly equates contraception or sterilization with (personal) sin, nor does he repeat the earlier condemnations. These observations may possibly be the most significant aspect of the teaching in HV, though they are hardly ever mentioned in commentaries.

152. The original had *in servitio vitae*, which use of the ablative denotes "in" or "among" as with a class of things. Thus, "a union which among many things is in the service of life". This was changed to *in servitum vitae*, which use of the accusative indicates "toward" or "for". Thus, "a union for the purpose of serving life". This is a minor change but it already indicates the mentality behind those who were altering the text.

and the transmission of human life created in God's image and likeness. Both the Second Vatican Council and the encyclical Humanae vitae spoke prophetically to our times, clearly affirming the Church's ancient but ever new teaching on marriage and the transmission of human life. This Synod, gathered in unity of faith with Peter's successor, firmly holds what was proposed by the second Vatican Council (cf. Gaudium et spes, 50) and afterwards in the encyclical Humanae vitae, especially the teaching that conjugal love must be fully human, (total), exclusive and open to new life (Humanae vitae, 11, cf. also 9 and 12).

The final version of Prop. 21 had omitted "and promoting" from the first sentence, perhaps so that the Synod could distance itself from the popular notion that the Church teaches that a couple should have many children. There are two other changes represented by what is emphasized in the text given here. The original had simply said that the Synod "firmly holds what was proposed by the second Vatican Council and the encyclical Humanae vitae, especially that conjugal love must be fully human, total, exclusive and open to new life (cf. Humanae vitae, 9 and 11)"[153]. Taken for what it is, this is a very general endorsement, very similar to many of the episcopal reactions to the HV event, that simply places the two documents side by side and implies that both must be read to comprehend the whole of Church teaching. However, an eventual change introduced a more specific idea. It is built upon the repetition of the idea found in IL, 16 (on the "good points of christian marriage") already inserted into the text: that conjugal love is fully human, total, exclusive and open to new life. As we have already pointed out, this would become the standard means for interpreting the teaching of HV, 9 which itself was an interpretation of GS. Note the progression.

Stage one:
GS, 49: conjugal love is eminently human, total, faithful and lasting
GS, 50: conjugal love and marriage are open to responsible parenthood

Stage two:
HV, 9: conjugal love is fully human, total, faithful and exclusive, and fecund
HV, 12: the two aspect theory applied to sexual intercourse

Stage three:
Lin, II, II, I-IV: two aspect theory, quotes HV, 12 in full

---

153. Haec Sacra Synodus ... firmiter tenet omnia quae in Concilio Vaticano II et in Encyclica Humanae vitae proponuntur et in specie quod amor coniugalis debet esse plene humanus, totalis, exclusivus et apertus ad novam vitam (cf. Humanae vitae 9 et 11).
There appears to be no reason why totalis was dropped from the final version. It could have been an oversight.

Stage four:
IL, 16: the good points of christian marriage: unity, fidelity, permanence and procreation
IL, 65: GS and HV contain the same doctrine

Stage five:
Prop. 21: Both GS and HV teach that conjugal love is fully human, total, exclusive and open to new life

Whereas GS, 49 and 50 carefully and intentionally distinguished these realities, HV, 9 puts them all together and inaccurately attributes the idea to GS, 50 alone. A change in Prop. 21 inserts the reference to GS, 50, which the bishops had not had in the original, that serves both to underscore the aspect of procreation and recall the interpretation found in HV, 9. To cement the idea we find the addition of the word "afterwards" (*postea*) which creates the impression that both documents say the same thing. They do not. Also, the original ended with a reference to HV, 9 and 11: the reinterpretation (HV, 9), and the need to respect sexual intercourse so that "each and every marriage act must remain open to the transmission of life" (HV, 11: *quilibet matrimonii usus ad vitam humanam procreandum per se destinatus*). A change places the reference to HV, 11 first and then adds HV, 9 also and HV, 12 on the two aspect theory. Reading Prop. 21 in its original form one finds a general statement which remains open to interpretation. Reading the amended form we see the influence of those who wrote the *Lin* and IL[154]. This will continue throughout section 11.

Prop. 22, in keeping with the bishops' generality, addresses the philosophical and theological question of attitude toward life. It is (was) a fine statement in its original form. But again interventions changed its tenor. In the middle of the first paragraph there is an addition, obviously inspired by IL, 64 which saw contemporary concern for demographic problems as equivalent to the "manipulation of public opinion", that accuses "demographers and futurologists" of practicing "scare tactics". Then, the whole second paragraph is an addition containing the misleading theory about all those things which are "anti-life".

The Church should clearly manifest this policy by promoting human life with every means and by defending it against those dangers — such as contraception,

154. These changes in the final text are the result of multiple *modi* ranging from the suggested quotation of HV to a reassertion of the concept of responsible parenthood. The debate was resolved in response to nrs. 22-28 (dealt with together, EM, p. 69) which accepts the citation of both Vatican II and HV and states, "although proximity in no way signifies being in the same line, for greater clarity, as some have proposed, *postea* (afterwards) is added after 'Vatican Council II' ". Therefore, although EM itself did not put forth the idea that the two teachings were equivalent, the resulting, compromised, text became part of the pattern of influence we are proposing in our commentary.

sterilization, abortion, euthanasia, and so on — that attack it at every stage and condition.

The bishops originally had not made this kind of simplistic generalization, putting everything together in one package so to speak and giving the (erroneous) impression that all four categories are equivalent or that there is some kind of progression from one to the other.

The last paragraph contains the second condemnation found in the Propositions and it was reserved for the interference of public authorities "circumscribing in any way the freedom of spouses to determine the number of their children". It goes on to condemn the *imposition* of contraception or sterilization (in the final version adding: or procured abortion) or the linking of these programs to economic aid. At first glance it appears that the bishops 1) were condemning contraception/sterilization in itself and 2) making the contraception-sterilization-procured abortion progression. But careful reading shows 1) that their entire concern here is the unjust use of government authority in violating freedom of conscience and 2) that the so-called progression of "birth control methods" was not their original idea. Again, by subtle change Prop. 22 in its final version is only a clouded resemblance of its original form.

Taking the first three Propositions of Section 11 in their original form, they could hardly be interpreted as an enthusiastic endorsement of HV. What they did contain was a clear manifestation of the "social reading" of that teaching and the care to place GS and HV side by side in order to see the whole picture. There was no rigorist insistence on one answer to a complicated question. When we approach Prop. 23, we again see an exposition of the contemporary problems married couples must face today (especially demographic ones) and the invocation of both Vatican II and HV as having addressed the issues [155]. Then there is a quotation of Paul VI's speech of 31 July 1968 on his just issued encyclical. The original quote had to do with problems still to be studied, a logical progression from the opening remarks of the Proposition. The final version expands the quote at its beginning to include the statement that HV "clarifies a fundamental chapter in the personal, married, family and social life of human beings". Originally the bishops wanted to use Paul VI's own words to show that many aspects of this issue still needed a great deal of investigation. The changed text made sure to quote the Pope as claiming that his teaching was really very lucid.

After the quotation the rest of this Proposition was completely reworked. The original version read:

---

155. The reference to Vatican II is an addition accepted without comment (EM, p. 74, nrs. 14-15). It is a fortunate restoration of a more comprehensive perspective.

Therefore, since this teaching of the Church is of greater importance for our times than in any preceding epoch, the Synod asks that the Magisterium might give it a "fuller, more organic and more synthetic explanation", which would shed light on the biblical foundations of this teaching, explain in detail its personalist reasons and situate it in the context of a better founded and more integrated exposition of human sexuality. In the investigation of this profound mystery of love and life, in which married persons should participate, the Church, in her pilgrim journey on this earth should proceed with humility so that she can more deeply penetrate the truth which has been handed down and convincingly expose it to many persons[156].

When we read the amended version we find: a call to theologians to be working side by side with the Magisterium (which is reminiscent of IL, 22 that virtually excoriated theologians for causing confusion among the faithful and making the work of the bishops difficult), a statement about the biblical and personalist foundations of the Church's teaching which needs only exposure and not establishment or explanation, a presumption that once exposed and made accessible to all the teaching would be convincing on its own, and an equivocation of the substance of the teaching with God's commandment (which needs to be more fully obeyed to attain salvation)[157]. The original version placed the burden of proof on the Magisterium, since it was evident that theologians had not or could not substantiate the main point of HV. The amended version considers it sufficient for the Magisterium to state the teaching while the task of theologians is to substantiate it.

Reviewing the two versions of Prop. 23 we find two entirely different ideas. The first had begun with a recognition of the many, complicated problems facing contemporary married couples, referred to GS, HV and Paul VI himself as addressing those problems, and then requested the Magisterium to reformulate its teaching on a much broader basis with the obvious understanding that it had more in mind than the controversy over contraception (HV,11: *quilibet matrimonii usus...*). The second

---

156. Cum igitur haec Ecclesiae doctrina maioris sit momenti nostris temporibus quam in qualibet epocha praecedenti, Synodus petit ut Magisterium faciat hanc "pleniorem, magis organicam, magis syntheticam expositionem", quae fundamenta biblica huius doctrinae in lucem ponat, rationes eius personalisticas enucleet ac in contextu fusioris et magis integratae expositionis de sexualitate humana sita sit. In investigatione profundiori huius mysterii amoris et vitae, prout a coniugibus participatur, Ecclesiam in terris peregrinantem humilitate procedere oportet, ut profundius paulatim veritatem traditam penetret eamque melius hominibus exponere valeat.

157. The amended text is the following: This Synod therefore invites theologians to join forces with the hierarchical magisterium to throw more light on the biblical foundations and the personalistic reasons behind this teaching. Let the purpose of this activity be, in the context of an "organic and synthetic explanation", to make church doctrine on this fundamental matter more accessible to all people of good will, to increase its understanding, and to ensure that God's command will be ever more fully obeyed to the salvation of human beings and the glory of the Creator.

version also begins with the recognition of the many complicated problems, then expands the quotation of Paul VI so as to draw attention to the teaching of HV itself, and goes on to rework the last sentences as a call for more substantiation on the contraception teaching itself. The original text of the bishops and the whole meaning of the Proposition had been changed to sound like a clear endorsement of the (papal) Magisterium's position on contraception. The fact that the final version of this text received only ten votes *non placet* is rather surprising.

Prop. 24 originally began with the notion of a "law of gradualism" which must be kept in mind in pastoral care. This idea remains but in the final version it is preceded by a verbatim quote from IL, 66 on the "difficult and really tormented situation of many christian couples" unable to "obey the moral norms taught by the Church because of their weakness and objective difficulties". Originally, the bishops had neither endorsed the "moral norms" nor made an appeal to "weakness" as a cause for disobedience. Whoever made the suggestion for change was also more closely affiliated with the IL than the vast majority of bishops who, in Parts I and II, had exhibited no slavish dependence on that document.

The so-called "law of gradualism" itself is now interpreted. Having invoked the idea in a very general fashion (Prop. 7) it is now applied to "an educational approach (that) will exhibit constancy no less than patience, courage, humility and complete confidence in God's mercy..." This is the original text. Another addition at this point strove to be more specific and again managed to work in a statement about the teaching of HV being "normative for the exercise of sexuality" and the need to "fulfill these norms". This was not the original intention of the bishops. The law of gradualism was not being applied to an eventual acceptance of *quilibet matrimonii usus...* but to the whole educational approach which was necessary for pastoral ministry. The precise meaning of this "educational approach" (education for what?) is explained in the next paragraph: it concerns *the whole of married life.* "The duty to transmit life should be integrated into an overall vision of conjugal, family and social life..." etc. What we find here is a reiteration of the doctrine of responsible parenthood, a call for sacrifice as part of this project which is also from GS, and the invocation of "the virtue of chastity" in a very nuanced way. "Continence", it is said, "which must be considered as a positive condition of the virtue of chastity *in sexual matters* is appropriate in its own way either for spouses or for persons who are not joined in matrimony" (emphasis added)[158]. Note that: 1) continence is mentioned as a manifestation of sacrifice, not in the context of "keeping

---

158. Continentia, quae considerari debet ut habitudo positiva virtutis castitatis in ambitu sexualitatis convenit suo modo sive coniugibus sive personis, quae non sunt matrimonio coniunctae.

the moral norms taught by the Church", 2) continence is not equivalent to chastity but a positive condition or aspect (*habitudo*, not *habitus*) of its practice, 3) chastity itself relates to continence when it is applied "in sexual matters" (i.e. the virtue of chastity is a much broader concept applying to the whole of married life), and 4) continence as a manifestation of chastity in sexual matters has different meanings for the married and the unmarried (which are prudently left unexplained).

The original Proposition was again very conciliar. The amendments have changed the tone entirely and give the impression that the whole point is an exhortation to follow the norms of HV. In a final remark about the process of growth and the educational approach, the original had reminded us that this would include "the consciousness of sin and ministry of reconciliation". Whoever was changing the text inserted between these two, "the desire to keep the law not just as an ideal for the future". The phrase serves two purposes: it insinuates that sin is the result of not keeping the law, and it specifies that the "law of gradualism" is not applied to the "moral norms" because these are in full force and do not operate as an "ideal".

There were more changes present in the rest of Proposition 25. The whole next paragraph, on the conjugal act involving free will, is an insertion. This idea is typical of a specific theological approach, namely that if one party insists on using contraception "against the will of the other", the offended partner is not guilty. We believe that the bishops themselves were not so juridical in their thought. At least they expressed nothing of that mentality in the rest of the original Propositions.

Following this addition is an original paragraph reminding us that there is no dichotomy between teaching and pastoral practice. If we return to Prop. 7 we can see exactly what the bishops meant: growing in the faith is not something that takes place overnight. It is this growth in faith which is the object of christian life, and the law of gradualism is something to be kept in mind by pastoral ministers who are, we should not forget, the subjects being addressed in this Proposition as it was originally written. However, this was not allowed to stand as it was, ending at this point, for one more addition again goes back to IL, 22 and warns priests that they must "agree among themselves so as not to cause crises of conscience for the faithful". The revised text puts forth a very clear idea about the role of priests, demanding absolute conformity to the Magisterium. One may wonder what the individual priest is supposed to do when he has his own "crisis of conscience"?

Bringing this section to a close, let us quote first the original version of Prop. 25 and then its amended form.

It is necessary that there be more profound investigation, an exchange of information and much stronger effort for a more widely spread education concerning scientifically established methods for the stable regulation of births which conform both with human dignity and with the moral teaching of the Church.

It is necessary that there be more profound investigation, an exchange of information and much more effort for education — which would especially be accessible to the poor — for more widely spreading scientifically established natural methods for the stable regulation of births which conform both to human dignity and indeed (*necnon*) with the teaching of the Church. For here it is a question of true education which respects the human person in all their dimensions.

Clearly the original put on an equal footing human dignity and the teaching of the Church (cf. GS, 51 and its ultimate moral criterion). It also assumed that information and education were enough for persons to reach their decisions (in conscience) whereas the later version calls for active spreading of the *natural* methods. The original had no such endorsement. The revision is reminiscent of IL, 65: "the christian solution".

In summary of Section 11, we cannot ignore the fact that the nature of the changes introduced is entirely different from the type of alteration present in the first 19 Propositions. The earlier texts had been broadened, nuanced and especially given a more social dimension by amendments which for the most part did not change the meaning of the original versions. We expect that these represented the introduction of episcopal *modi* which were in basic conformity with the spirit of the Synod that itself clearly reflected conciliar theology. That is, both versions were experientially oriented and very positive in their approach while exhibiting an attitude of searching and dialogue. In contrast, changes introduced into Props. 20-25 often changed the meaning of the texts and introduced ideas which were reasoned deductively from the pronouncements of the Magisterium. These reflected the attitudes and even sometimes the words of the IL that itself has already been shown to have misunderstood and/or reinterpreted the teaching of GS.

In its original version Section 11 does not enthusiastically endorse the teaching of HV. It resembles more the episcopal attitude of 1968-1969 which preferred to speak in generalities and let the moral argumentation of the encyclical stand or fall on its own. The single issue about which the bishops are clear was the injustice of government run programs of family planning that violated the individual couple's freedom of conscience and/or were linked to programs of economic aid. When we read the final version of these Propositions we get the impression of episcopal unity rallying around the papal Magisterium in defense of a doctrine which they were convinced was absolutely right. In light of the exposition we have just given on the difference between the two versions, it would be interesting to see the results of a new vote by the same bishops without the pressure of being the last working day of the 1980 Synod.

The nature of the remaining 18 Propositions more closely reflects that of the first 19. That means that the basic outlook is positive and informed by the spirit of the Council and that changes between the first and final versions are generally more broadening. The four Propositions of Section 12 on "The Role of Education" demonstrate this. Prop. 26 begins with a theological perspective. The family "is the domestic Church called together by *the Word of God, faith and* (added) the Sacrament of Baptism". It therefore functions, like the Church, as mother and teacher (*mater et magistra*). Subdivision b notes the task of education as flowing from the "goal of procreation" and belonging "inalienably" (*inalienable,* a change from *indelegabile*) to the family. Then, 26, c recalls the influence of school, the media and society, all of which the parents should strive to teach their children to use. It adds a reference to *Communio et progressio,* 64-70[159]. Fourthly, there is a list of suggestions on how to fulfill these tasks. The last two of which, on conscience and vocational choice, are additions[160].

Proposition 27 remained basically unchanged in its final version and addresses the catechesis of children. Through the sacramental aspect of marriage the educational mission is raised to the status of ministry. Parents are the first teachers and should be completely involved in the christian initiation of their children. Unlike IL, 48-50 the bishops apparently felt no need to remind parents that this whole process should come under the control of a "pastor". Like their brothers at Vatican II, they had a good deal of trust in parents.

Proposition 28 is about true education involving the whole of life. Paragraph a describes the family as a "community of love and life" and although one might expect these words to lead into the idea of procreation, they do not. Refreshingly, the bishops discuss the whole of life and the art of giving. Then 28, b speaks of sex education in a similar way, involving the whole person, and which takes place in the context of the family. There is one change here. In speaking of sex education programs in schools, it is said that the Church opposes programs which *frequently* are nothing more than an introduction to technique and pleasure. Obviously not all programs are, and in principle sex education in the schools is not opposed, as long as it observes the principle of subsidiarity and cooperation with parents. A final subdivision on chastity as a virtue of self-giving probably should have been corrected

159. *Communio et progressio* is a "Pastoral Instruction on the Means of Social Communication", issued on 29 Jan. 1975. Cf. A. FLANNERY (ed.), *Vatican Council II: The Conciliar and Post-Conciliar Documents,* Dublin, 1975, pp. 293-249.

160. There are two other changes in Prop. 26,d: nr. 3 changed "transmitting doctrine" to "transmitting the doctrines of christian faith"; nr. 4 ends with "not damaging parental authority". The mention of conscience in Prop. 26,d (6) as an amendment is important. The Synod dealt with conscience under the heading of Spirituality, which itself is somewhat significant. (See below, Prop. 38.)

because it mentions only consecrated virginity and marriage. Prop. 11 had introduced such an addition and its value here would have far outweighed any criticism of being repetitive[161]. The last Proposition (29) of this section is about Catholic schools and the freedom to an "education that matches religious belief". In the second part, through the addition of a couple phrases, it is noted that when this is not available families should join together to wisely "preserve young people's faith". Note that this does not call for an attack on government or a school system but does call for parental initiative. The tone of the Proposition is again very social and rather prudent about a delicate issue.

Section 13 on "The Social and Cultural Role of the Family" consists of one, long Proposition (30, a-1), of which e, f and g are additions. The text speaks for itself and is a catalogue of ideas which have been around since the Council. Of special mention is the social and communitarian aspect which "begins in the home" (an addition to 30, h). The mention of "sterilization, abortion, birth control and so on" in a parenthesis in 30, k should again be noted as a warning against government intervention and not judgments passed on these things in themselves.

Section 14 on "Families in Special Circumstances" (Props. 31-33) grew out of the same mentality as the previous section and gives long lists of all those situations which stand in urgent need. While Prop. 31 is very general, Prop. 32 concentrates on the families of migrants and Prop. 33 is on "politically divided families". The last is a clear reference to the Church and christian families in communist and totalitatian countries. However, a number of the ideas mentioned here can be applied very generally, such as the discrimination which should be exercised with respect to "guests" that enter the home through the media[162].

"The Apostolic Role of the Family" is the topic of Section 15 which is summarized by the word "evangelization" (cf. the 1974 Synod). This task begins with the children (Prop. 34, a), fosters vocations (34, b), and goes out to the rest of the world (34, c-f)[163]. The last two sub-divisions are additions: 39, g on the special role of the family in mission territories, and 34, h on the role of the priest. The last is put forth not as the controller or judge of the family's ministry but as a "support for families with difficulties and anxieties and a help for examining their lives in the

---

161. EM, p. 82, nr. 4: "Proponitur addictio horum verborum 'penitus excludere debet quamlibet relationem sexualem ante matrimonium' (2 Patres)". The simple response given was "Acceptatur". However, no such idea is present in the final version of Prop. 28. This is one more anomaly in the documents at our disposal.

162. EM, p. 95, nr. 1, suggests "Deleatur linea 9 (2 Patres)". The response, "Acceptatur" does not seem to have been followed in the final version of the text. The statement at issue deals with the relations between parents and children.

163. EM, p. 97, nr. 12, suggests: "Post n. 4 (here 34,d) addere vult mentionem facere de iuvenibus, qui Ecclesiae et societatis sunt spes (1 Pater)". The somewhat enthusiastic response, "Bene, acceptatur!" was apparently not followed, for the final text does not contain any expansion beyond the original version.

light of the Gospel". Note that the attitude of priest as "director" of the family (IL, 48-50) is completely absent here.

"The Preparation for Marriage" has already been mentioned as being generally further ahead in practice than in teaching and the bishops at the Synod, in Section 16 (Prop. 35), did not attempt to spell out how such programs should be run. On the contrary, they again call for greater autonomy in that bishops' conferences and dioceses should be responsible for the guidelines for such programs. What this Proposition does do, however, is to situate that preparation in the whole of christian life. It again invokes the idea of gradualism in the growth of faith. Marriage, and especially its aspect of sacramentality, is something that demands a living and ever deepening faith. One could say that "marriage preparation" is something that should not stop with the wedding ceremony. The preparatory process itself is called (in an addition) "a faith journey like the catechumenate". In a sense, facing the unfathomable mystery of faith in Christ, we are all catechumens throughout our lives. Marriage is just one more, enriching step in that journey.

Three more points can be made about this text. In both the first and final versions it is stated that the proximate preparation, among other things, should help the couple "make their sexual relationship an important part of their sacramental union". This observation even goes beyond GS — to work out that document's logical implication — in appreciation of the sexual dimension of the human relationship and ties it directly to *sacramental union*. This is the first time that the Church in official teaching has valued marital sexuality in such a completely positive way that it can be called sacramental. The bishops' perspective here is a clear endorsement of the "personalist" reading of GS.

The other two points involve changes in the final text. First, immediately after the sentence mentioned above, the bishops omitted a reference to preparation programs in the schools that was tied to another reference to sex education being the prerogative of parents[164]. Apparently one (non-opposing) reference to sex education was enough, and this one sounded rather negative at that. Finally, a last, added, sentence demonstrates good sense in advising that preparation programs should "not be a burden or obstacle for the engaged couple". The bishops were speaking with a pastoral voice.

Section 17 on "Family Spirituality" has three Propositions (36-38), the first of which has 6 parts (a-f) after a general introduction. That introduction is remarkable not only because it situates the issue in the theology of marriage and the family but also because it situates that theology itself.

---

164. No explanation — or even suggestion — for this omission can be found in EM.

The spirituality of the family flows from the theology of the family. In a word, it is founded on God's love for us and on the gospel command to love God and neighbor. It is a call to holiness, a divine invitation that expects a response. The family is the "domestic church". It is a community of love and faith. The family is responsible for family life and its spiritual quality.

Notice that there is no invocation of Genesis, no mechanistic idea that God created the "institution" or ordained it to function in a specific way. All those ideas of the *Lin* and IL have been left behind. In their place we find a contemporary, conciliar approach that takes the givens of experience seriously. Against a background of essentialist thinking which always viewed "marriage" as something manufactured in the grand design of creation and subsequently was imposed upon the man-woman relationship with attendant "rights and duties", the bishops speak of marriage as relation and draw our attention to the immediately obvious commandment to love. Marriage is a relationship between the closest of neighbors. Exactly as our love for fellow human beings, this does not entail possession or domination. Nor does it operate according to a pre-ordained scheme. It is a call, an invitation from God who is the informant of every loving human relationship.

Living out a love relationship is itself an occasion of grace and holiness. In the words of GS, 48, the spouses "increasingly advance their own perfection, as well as their mutual sanctification, and hence contribute jointly to the glory of God". But because the family is the domestic church (LG, 11), its function of sanctification does not end with the partners but extends to their children and eventually to all persons with whom the family has contact. The bishops specifically point to the "apostolic aspect of the laity" and signal LG, GS and *Apostolicam actuositatem* as evidence of their theological sources.

The third paragraph notes that "the *image of* (left out in translation) Christ's love for the Church strengthens and challenges families who endeavor to fulfill His commandment 'to love one another' ". Note that our own translation of the original reveals a distinct impression. The use of *analogy* for the Christ-Church relationship is again maintained by the bishops. There is no mechanistic sacramentality, the "image" is not forced upon the partnership, nor is there a cause and effect relation between God's invitation and challenge and the families who are attempting to live out this commandment to love. In the exercise of family spirituality the image remains complete and the divine mystery of love is reflected in the human project itself. Thus the bishops draw from salvation history and enumerate the aspects of this spirituality under the headings: a) creation, b) covenant, c) cross, d) resurrection and e) sign. The final version added a sixth aspect on this being an "eschatological spirituality". The one line comment on persons having eternal life is rather inadequate and shows a lack of care in responding to one *modus*[165]. Lastly, we can point out a change in the first sentence of sub-division b, on a spirituality of covenant. The original reflected the strange use of scripture found in the preparatory documents and read "The spouses become one flesh and so do parents with their children". The final version was careful to note that this too was "in an analogous sense".

Proposition 37 notes that for some families, especially those which are "incomplete", living out their spirituality may be difficult. Thus, they especially must be welcomed into and supported by the Church. Most of the text then lists various aids for spiritual life. The final version changes "the Most Holy Rosary" to "the marian Rosary", and adds the reference to popular piety, important family events, and the enthusiasm of the lay apostolate.

Proposition 38 is entirely devoted to the development of conscience. It is interesting to find this text here and not in Section 12 on "The Role of Education". Evidently the bishops shared the conciliar insight that a person's conscience is very much a part of their spirituality (GS, 16) and is primarily a faculty of discernment. It is not, as essentialism often says or implies, a kind of memory which is educated by teaching moral norms and serves simply to distinguish right and wrong. Furthermore, conscience is in a continuous state of development, open to moral and spiritual values which elucidate moral norms and obviously take precedence over them. All this depends upon faith and communication with others, especially those "who are seeking truth, love and justice". The entire development of these ideas is experiential. It is from human relationships that we are led to our relationship with The Other, with God. The perspective is totally different from that exhibited by the *Lin* and IL. It is informed by contemporary human sciences and is very conciliar in its approach. FC, we will see, hardly even alludes to these three Propositions.

Section 18 (Prop. 39) is a very brief text on "Family Associations" which may be a veiled reference to the "basic christian communities". In any case, it is too short to discern exactly what is meant except that the bishops did see value in families joining together to live out their christian lives and give mutual support. The most striking thing is that all this is said without specifically having to mention the clergy. The sentence which does not appear in the English translation reads, "Formative experience and daily customs connected with religion (i.e. 'family culture') should be transmitted through pastoral care".

The two Propositions (40-41) of Section 19 bring the main text to a close and address the delicate topic of "Extra Marital Relations". This is first about what was originally named "the phenomenon of persons

---

165. Even the suggestion was not adopted completely for it included a reference to Phil. 3:3,20-1. The text itself is more or less equivalent to the *modus*.

living together in a marriage which is called experimental", which the final version changed to "the phenomenon of persons living together in a union which is called 'experimental marriage'". Apparently, there was some concern about the words used possibly conferring some form of real status[166]. Nonetheless, the bishops proceeded in an open way and explicitly recognized that experience shows that some people see value in these relationships. However, they do not go so far as to give their approval. Concentrating on the aspect of being "experimental", they remind us that persons are not to be experimented with and by extension experimental relationships can be detrimental. Then they note that "in the light of *faith* the giving of one's body is a real and especially profound symbol of the whole person..." (emphasis added)[167]. Did the bishops wish to insinuate that this is not always so clear in human experience? Perhaps they felt that the issue was not as simple as it might first appear. In any case, the Proposition rather insightfully notes that this phenomenon will not (add: ordinarily) be changed without rethinking and redirecting the entire process of education in human relationships and sexuality. Therefore, they end by calling for a study of the phenomenon in all its aspects.

However, the section does not end with this, for Proposition 41 turns its attention to what was evidently considered to be a very different phenomenon, namely couples living together "without benefit of matrimony". The Latin text used the term "free unions" (*unionum s.d. liberarum*). It is immediately pointed out that "situations vary greatly". They can be the result of previous marital breakdown, political conviction or merely convenience. The Proposition rejects this primarily because it severely undermines faithfulness as an institutional value. It can also be detrimental to the children of such a union and, in words that are uncharacteristically judgmental such unions are said "to become a refuge for egoism". Nonetheless, it is advised that pastoral care not abandon these situations, nor that it attempt to convert them immediately. Rather, in displaying good sense once again the bishops advise that ways must be found for developing the "meaning of faithfulness more coherently in moral and religious instruction". Finally, in what is largely an addition, we again see the social consciousness of the bishops who distinguish yet another phenomenon which is the situation in which couples do not have the opportunity to embrace a marital union. All these factors, especially poverty and harmful social customs, should be overcome.

166. The change in the opening sentence of Prop. 40 was suggested by three bishops (EM, p. 109, nr. 4). The response of the redactor was, "Bene, admittitur".

167. EM, p. 109, nr. 1, admits the expansion of this sentence to read: "Sub luce fidei valent omnia quae de matrimonii sacramento dicta sunt; praeteria donatio corporis ..." This addition did not appear in the final version of the Propositions.

The two final Propositions (42 & 43) form an appendix to the text. The first suggests that a "Bill of Rights for the Family" be drawn up and presented by the Pope to the United Nations. The bishops' own suggested list was amended to give an explanation of the first proposal, directing it primarily to the poor, and the final version also saw the addition of proposals 8, 13 and 14[168]. Then, looking more internally for some aids to develop and help the pastoral ministry for families by the Church itself, Proposition 43 suggests the creation of pastoral directories and in a final paragraph gives some guidelines for their content. However, in recognition of the complexity and plurality of various pastoral situations, the expectation is that episcopal conferences will develop their own directories. A final addition explicitly states that these "should explain Church teaching and discipline in a manner suitable for diverse circumstances". In keeping with the continuous tenor of these Propositions and evidently a major emergent theme of the Synod itself, we find once more the episcopal call for recognition of greater local autonomy.

E. Summary and Reaction

In our commentary we have seen that the content of the Propositions in general is vastly different from the theological and pastoral ideas which were suggested to the bishops by the preparatory documents. The episcopal formulations are conciliar, experiential and theologically and pastorally positive. With the exception of Section 11 (Props. 20-25) the thought expressed in their text is consistent and exhibits a picture of the Church in service to humanity. Further, it is informed by a social consciousness in search of justice. It does not dwell on individual matters or privatized moral problems. Above all, the text is not judgmental. It is open to human experience and frequently calls for further investigation and study of particular issues. At the same time, in recognizing the diversity of pastoral situations, the bishops clearly call for more responsible autonomy for the local episcopal conferences. All these specific suggestions and explicit requests can be brought together in one list. The bishops request:

1. an investigation of the extent to which the validity of the sacrament of marriage requires faith (12, a)[169]
2. an investigation of the meaning of "sacrament" for baptized persons

---

168. EM, p. 113, nr. 6(a), also suggested adding "et veterorum parentum" to the end of proposal 7. Again, though the suggestion was admitted, the addition does not appear in the final text.

169. Numbers and letters in parentheses indicate the Proposition in which the request can be found.

who have lost the faith and the pastoral criteria for discerning the faith of an engaged couple (12, d)

3. that the revision of the code of canon law take account of the bishops' findings (12, e)

4. that episcopal conferences should introduce some form of betrothal ceremony (13, e)

5. a new and extensive study on pastoral care for the divorced and remarried, taking into account the practices of the Eastern Churches (14, f)

6. that the Church should promote as much as possible in her own life the equal rights and dignity of human persons (with a clear reference to women) (16)

7. that episcopal conferences should study the cultural elements of marriage as an aid to inculturation of the faith (18, a)

8. that local Churches should have faculties and more autonomy in adapting norms for marital celebration and validity to cultural customs (18, b)

9. more power for local episcopal conferences in setting norms for mixed marriages (19, b)

10. that the Magisterium reformulate the teaching of the Church on marriage and human sexuality, giving it a "fuller, more organic and more synthetic explanation" (23)

11. more profound investigation and educational programs to promote scientifically proven methods of regulating fertility (25)

12. that episcopal conferences and dioceses draw up guidelines for marriage preparation programs (35)

13. a study of the phenomena of experimental marriages including the psychological and sociological aspects (40)

14. autonomy for episcopal conferences to develop pastoral directories which explain Church teaching and discipline in a manner suitable to diverse (local) circumstances (43)

It is evident from this list and the Propositions themselves that the bishops at the 1980 Synod did not consider the many issues surrounding marriage and family life as having been solved. They did not give solutions to pastoral problems which they recognized to be complex and very often specific to local situations. In fact, they clearly state that most of the problems need much deeper investigation and ultimately should be handled on a local level. This even extends to profoundly theological issues like the validity of sacraments, divorce and remarriage and the entire process of marital preparation from the standpoint of faith. What the Synod signified, therefore, was to a good extent accomplished. The bishops had gathered together as representatives of the universal Church in order to take stock of the contemporary situation of marriage and family life, to specify issues which needed urgent attention, and to indicate the methods which should be used for dealing with those issues. In doing this the bishops exhibited a good understanding of conciliar ecclesiology and theology and insisted that the future project of addressing the issues more explicitly should be undertaken from the perspective of Vatican II.

There was, however, one issue which did not benefit from this accomplishment. That, of course, was the issue of regulating fertility. The original version of the Propositions (20-25) had more or less left this an open question and, very much like the bishops at Vatican II, indicated that serious doubt existed at least about the adequacy of the Magisterium's formulation of its teaching in this area. At the same time, the Synod placed a strong emphasis upon the social dimensions of the problem. Many bishops from the non-industrialized countries were relatively unconcerned about the moral issue from the individual (couple's) point of view but very insistent on warning against and even condemning government intervention in family life and the imposition of programs of family planning that emphasized contraception, sterilization and even procured abortion as means for regulating fertility. These are obviously an affront to freedom of conscience and a violation of justice.

At this point it might be advantageous to offer a few words of commentary on the *Expensio modorum* (EM) for the Propositions. As noted above (see our note 129) and as pointed out frequently in our commentary on the Propositions themselves, the EM itself does not completely or adequately explain the transition between the first and final versions of the episcopal text(s). While some errors can be understood because of the brevity of time during the final days of the Synod, a number of questions remain, especially with respect to Props. 20-25.

All the acknowledged changes introduced into the final version of the Propositions can theoretically be attributed to the various *modi* submitted by (unnamed) bishops. However, there appears to be no way of accounting for how the suggestions were processed. For one, an overwhelming majority of the *modi* were simply rejected, often without explanation. Then, there is no consistent method evident in the acceptance or the handling of those *modi* that were incorporated. In general, there appears to be a rather inconsistent method applied. Many of the original Propositions were improved and given more precision while the substance of thought remained unaltered. Others underwent subtle change that did have a bearing upon substance. We believe that this is particularly true of Section 11, on "The Transmission and Safeguarding of Human Life".

In order to deal with this problem we did a textual analysis of the EM concentrating upon the responses which were given to the various suggestions. The results of that analysis indicate that there were different redactors (or groups) at work for the *modi* to different Propositions. The types of responses given for the first 11 votes (*suffragationes*)[170] and Propositions were rather straight forward and simple. The basic vocabulary of judgment is (*non-*)*admittitur*, sometimes along with a few words of explanation, rarely longer than one line. The next set of responses, for votes 12-24 (Props. 12-17), are equally brief and straightforward. However, in this group the vocabulary has changed. (*Non-*)*admittitur* has completely disappeared and the previously unused words *reiicitur* and (*non-*)*accipitur* exclusively are given for judgment. The shift in vocabulary leads us to believe that there were different authors at work on these sections of the Propositions.

The next two votes (25 & 26 on Props. 18 & 19, Inculturation and Mixed Marriages, respectively) indicate another, though less clear, shift. For one, the responses become longer and more involved. For another, the vocabulary is diverse. Vote 25 includes (*non-*)*admittitur* (3 times), *reiicitur* (4 ×), (*non-*)*accipitur* (5 ×), and introduces a new word: (*non-*)*acceptatur* (5 ×). Vote 26 only uses (*non-*)*accipitur* and has a number of lengthly responses. The dominant vocabulary for the responses to *modi* in section 11 (Props. 20-25, votes 27-32) is (*non-*)*acceptatur*, though *reiicitur* occurs twice (for Prop. 20) and (*non-*)*accipitur* occurs five times each for Prop. 20 and 25. In this section we see the greatest number of extensive responses, utilizing none of the above mentioned vocabulary, as well as the occurrence (eight times) of a new word (*includi(un)tur*) which occurs nowhere else in the text of the EM and the use of which is sometimes associated with *acceptatur*, the word which made its appearance only in Vote 25 (Prop. 18).

The style of the remaining 18 votes (for Props. 26-43) contains a broad mixture of vocabulary, including a few novelties: *addatur* (twice already for responses to *modi* for Prop. 18, now in connection with Props. 26 & 41), (*non-*)*recipitur* (twice in connection with Prop. 31) and even *inseritur* (twice for Prop. 41). Also in these texts the word (*non-*)*admittitur* reappears and responses employing none of this key vocabulary are frequent.

Broadly speaking, then, we can discern different influences in the work of response to the *modi* for given Propositions. It is clear that the suggestions for Props. 12-17 were dealt with by a different (group of) redactor(s) than those who handled Props. 1-11 and that a third influence came into play from Prop. 18 onwards. The redactor(s) for Props. 1-11

170. Though there were 43 Propositions, there were 50 separate texts upon which votes were cast (*suffragationes*). The reason for this is that there was a separate vote on each of the five sections of Prop. 12,a-e (adding 4 votes) and four votes cast on Prop. 14 covering a-b, c, d-e and f (adding 3 votes). Both these Propositions addressed rather "delicate" issues: the relation between faith and the sacrament (12) and divorce and remarriage (14). The remaining Propositions were voted upon as a whole.

apparently were not involved in responding to *modi* for Props. 12-25 which included some of the most delicate and controversial topics. Finally, a departure from standardized responses (*admittitur, accipitur,* and so forth) that begins in dealing with Prop. 18 becomes typical in the section on "The Transmission and Safeguarding of Human Life" (Props. 20-25). Who the principle redactors were for each section is still unknown, but at least there is evidence that the committee in charge of dealing with the *modi* did not act as a whole or possibly did not even work together. Consequently there was an unevenness in the types of changes which were introduced into the final version of the Propositions. If there were more information available, we would be tempted to hypothesize that a definable (groups of) redactor(s) took particular interest in insuring that certain things were (not) said in the text of the Propositions. A comparison of the first and final versions of that text indicates that the strongest influence of this (group of) redactor(s) is present in Props. 20-25 and that the final version of this section was to some extent manipulated. In any case, we must now go further with our analysis and ask, what happened?

The propositions were not drawn up for the purpose of publication. However, the bishops followed what had become a custom in the synodal event and agreed that a committee should prepare a "Message" to be published at the end of the meeting[171]. "The Message to Christian Families"[172] went through a number of drafts because of dissatisfaction with the original proposal. It is a brief statement, not intended to fully reflect the discussions which had taken place at the Synod. Therefore, it cannot be read as truly representative of what had been accomplished. The text contains 21 numbered sections grouped under 6 headings[173].

171. Cf. supra, note 129 for the members of the committee.
172. The English text of the "Message" can be found in *Origins* 10 (1980) 321-325, and in *The Tablet* 234 (1980) 1078-1080.
173. The official headings (I-IV) and our own description of each numbered section (1-21) are as follows.

  I. *Introduction*
     1. General introduction, no solutions to complex questions
 II. *The Situation of Families today*
     2. Recognition of both good and difficult signs
     3. Much has been learned from culture but "God's plan" is normative
     4. Recognition of material and spiritual poverty and oppression
     5. Rejection of government intervention in family life
     6. Recalling our divine vocation as opposed to wealth, power and pleasure
III. *God's Plan for Marriage and the Family*
     7. Men and women participate in divine life and being
     8. Special role of family as domestic Church; mission of procreation; marriage is a sacrament
     9. Marriage is permanent, indissoluble and open to life
    10. Living christian marriage demands conversion
    11. Openness to pascal mystery indicates pain as well as joy; weakness should not discourage

One of the immediately striking characteristics of the "Message" is the frequent invocation of "God's plan" for marriage and the family. This key term became important in the *Lin* and IL. It was not significant in the Propositions. From this time forward, however, it will become central. Also, the meaning of the term itself reflects the thinking of IL. The explanation in Part III of the "Message" mentions creation in God's image (Gen. 1:26), the mission to procreate (Gen. 1:28) and the sacramentality of marriage (Eph. 5:22-32). The identification of conjugal love and procreation is cemented with an invocation of HV, 9 & 11. The ideas deduced from a set conception of the "plan" became normative while deviation from those norms is largely ascribed to weakness. Nevertheless, the norms are absolute and beyond question.

Both the tone and the text of the "Message" were closer to IL than to the Propositions. Section 20 contains the quote from IL, 66 (on not observing the moral norms taught by the Church because of weakness or difficulties) that had been forced into Prop. 24, and whereas Prop. 23 had quoted Paul VI's address of 31 July 1968, the "Message" quotes that of 4 May 1970 to the "Equipes de Notre Dame", which had also been quoted in IL, 66. The very last section is also reminiscent of the "divine plan" notion in claiming that "everything we have said about marriage and the family can be summed up in two words: love and life". Of course, the bishops know that everything is not as simple as that, but here we have a ready made (but not original) phrase to be picked up by the media. To some extent, it worked.

The simplicity of the catchphrase "love and life" should not preoccupy us because of the insignificant purpose of this document. Yet it does indicate the superficiality of the entire text. It was a press release and we should be aware of the nature of such things. But such an event does create an impact and media conscious persons should be sensitive to the image they create. Not only was the "love and life" theme indicative of a certain mode of thought, but the text as a whole perhaps inadvertently created another image. It has already been pointed out by others that a certain image of solidarity was created by the "Message". The bishops were speaking with one voice in union with the pope. But what were they saying? If one simply glances at the document, the eye could possibly fall upon the references which were provided. These tell us: that the "plan of God" is clearly outlined in Scripture; that HV, 9 & 11, as well as HV, 25, are an important source for Church teaching; and that the only thing worth mentioning from the Council is that GS, 52 spoke of the priest's ministry to the family. Certainly, the absence of more explicit conciliar teaching and references is surprising.

Of rather more significance, however, was Pope John-Paul's "Closing Homily" to the Synod, delivered, in Latin, during the closing liturgy of 25 October[174]. The text has eleven sections but is about the same length as the "Message". It also contains its own number of curious statements, such as thanking the bishops for their "sure and clear judgments" concerning doctrinal and pastoral questions, and attempts to create its own catchphrase with the words "doing the truth in charity". Certainly not to be considered in any way insignificant is the invocation of the "eternal plan of God", which the Pope (inaccurately) ascribes to the title of the first Proposition. This will be a continuing theme in the thought of John-Paul II. The "Homily" was taken as an occasion to address four of the topics which were discussed in the Synod and the Propositions. They were: the problem of divorce and remarriage (7), HV and the law of gradualism (8), inculturation (9), and the role of women (10). All four of these had been the subject of the bishops' call for further investigation or greater autonomy.

The first topic to be discussed was that of divorce and remarriage. The Pope could not deny the need to be more open and pastorally solicitous toward the remarried, and he repeated the bishops' call that they continue to be considered members of the community. He also said that the bishops once again affirmed the indissolubility of marriage, though he gave no allusion to their carefully worded remarks, and that they reaffirmed the Church's practice of not admitting such persons to the eucharist. However, he chose to be more explicit about the conditions for eventual reception of penance and the eucharist (cf. Prop. 14, d) by defining what he understood by "living in a manner which is not opposed to the indissolubility of marriage":

namely, when a man and woman in this situation, who cannot fulfill the obligation to separate, take on themselves the duty to live in complete conti-

---

174. Slightly different versions of the English text of the "Homily" can be found in *Origins* 10 (1980) 325-329, and *The Tablet* 234 (1980) 1080-1082. *The Tablet*'s version does not contain the Pope's appointment of his chosen representatives for the Concilium for the 1983 Synod. They are: Card. Rubin, Archbishop Tzadua (Addis Ababa) and Archbishop C. Martini (Milan). Archbishop Martini was very influential in creating the image of unison and solidarity at the Synod and went so far as to claim "unanimous and explicit acceptance of Pope Paul VI's encyclical Humanae vitae" at a press conference on 16 Oct. 1980. Cf. B. MARTHALAR, *art. cit.*, p. 71.

nence, that is by abstinence from acts in which only married couples may engage, and when they avoid giving scandal.

The traditional solution to this problem, about which the bishops had chosen to remain silent, is now stated. In his reaction, Pope John-Paul underscores the position that sexual intercourse is reserved strictly for valid marriage. Therefore, a man and woman who are living together but who are not "validly married" should not be having sexual relations if they desire or attempt to approach the sacraments. One might ask who should make this judgment? Does this put the person distributing the eucharist in the position of inquiring first whether a certain person who is known to be in a second conjugal union is having sexual relations? There is also the problem of how the community can respond. If remarried persons are really welcomed into the Church, participate actively in all of its life and become respected members of the community, what kind of eucharistic theology is responsible for barring these persons from receiving communion? As for the question whether these persons are remaining totally continent, a number of the faithful might simply wonder why this is so important. The position taken here inadvertently steps back into traditionalist theology which very much sexualized marriage, as if that aspect of the relationship were the most important part of conjugal life. In the minds of many, this is not the case.

The second point had to do with HV and the so-called law of gradualism (8). The Pope said that the bishops "openly confirmed the validity and clear truth of the prophetic message, profound in meaning and pertaining to today's conditions — contained in the encyclical letter *Humanae vitae*". No mention is made of the nuanced text or the very open discussions which took place during the Synod. Instead, the second version of Props. 20-25 is read literally, even down to placing the burden for explaining the doctrine on the shoulders of theologians who are therefore implicitly reminded to conform their thought to that of the (papal) Magisterium. Then, John-Paul addresses the application of the "moral norms" by again referring to two of the last minute insertions in Prop. 24: the idea that the law is not just an ideal for the future, and the problem of free will. The first, also quoting the bishops' own (actual) words on there being no dichotomy between doctrine and pastoral practice, is taken as an occasion to discuss "gradualism". The bishops themselves had put this forth in regard to the whole of christian life, especially in the experience of growth in faith (Prop. 7). Their invocation of a "law of gradualism" in Prop. 24 should have been read in that light. But the Pope was evidently fearful that this would be misinterpreted and thus makes his own distinction between the "law of gradualness" which is a valid insight for understanding a person's coming to discern moral norms and a "gradualism of law" which he rejects outright. In the mind of the Pope, there is one, certain, absolute and always binding moral law that takes precedence over everything else. Its content is evidently clearly spelled out in HV.

Then the "Homily" invokes the paragraph inserted into Prop. 24 on the conjugal act involving the free will of two persons. However, John-Paul goes further than the bishops' text in saying that,

if both spouses are not bound by the same religious insights[175], it will not be enough to accommodate oneself in a passive and easy manner to existing conditions but they must try, so that with patience and good will they might find a common willingness to be faithful to the duties of christian marriage.

Therefore, the "believing spouse" also has a duty to convert the other spouse to accept the teaching of the encyclical. In effect, by absolutizing the norms "taught by the Church", rigorously interpreting the "law of gradualism" and insisting that one cannot simply accommodate to the existing condition that one spouse does not believe or accept the teaching, John-Paul had closed every door for "interpreting" HV and once again made its teaching a criterion for orthodoxy and orthopraxis.

The third topic to be addressed in his "Homily" (9) was inculturation. Not only had a number of African bishops continually insisted upon the need for greater adaptation in teaching and practice, taking account of cultural customs and norms, but the whole Synod finally recognized this voice and allowed it to play a very important role in the Propositions. Examining the bishops' requests, we find not only the specific call for inculturation and adaptation (Props. 2, 4, 7, 8), but an equally significant voice calling for more autonomy for episcopal conferences in setting norms (Props. 8, 9, 12, 14). This had been a growing theme in the synodal process over the years and it would not appear unfair to emphasize its importance. The "Homily" itself takes note of this movement but places upon it a condition which from the beginning seems highly restrictive, namely "if (this inquiry) is instituted according to the principle of communion with the universal Church". In and of itself, there can be no objection to this comment. But the bishops had gathered in Synod, they had attempted to act in a way responsible to the universal Church, and there appeared to be no reason to doubt that their intentions would continue in the same direction. So what was the purpose of this condition? It will become clear later (FC) that in the mind of the Pope, appreciating the value of local customs and norms is one thing, but their value will always have to be judged according to a single, pre-existing norm.

175. One might ask what this phrase means. Is it possible that the teaching of HV only applies to Catholics? Such an interpretation would be untenable given the view of the absoluteness of this moral law. However, there is the recognition that not everyone accepts the teaching. One could validly inquire about the demand to respect freedom of conscience here. Are we reverting to the notion that only a "correct" conscience enjoys freedom?

Lastly, a few words were addressed to the topic of the role of women (10). We will quote the text in full.

In words both opportune and persuasive the Synod has spoken of women with reverence and a grateful spirit, especially of her dignity and vocation as a daughter of God, as a wife and as a mother. Therefore, it commendably asked that human society be so constituted that women not be forced to engage in external work, proper to a certain role or, as they say, profession, but rather so that the family might be able to live rightly, that the mother might devote herself fully to the family.

Strictly speaking, the Propositions did put forth the wish that a woman not be *forced* to work outside the home (Prop. 16). But the nuance and tenor of the entire development (Prop. 15-17) has been obscured. The Synod called for a reevaluation of domestic roles "whether it is done by husband or wife", and it had noted that the goal should be that "the distinction between different types of work and professions" disappears. The bishops even gave the conclusion that "it follows that woman's access to all public roles must be as open as it is for men". This does not mean that one social structure is superior to another. Women who pursue the domestic role are to be equally regarded as those whose professions take them outside the home.

In response to this, John-Paul II presumes that only when a woman is engaged "as wife and mother" can the family live "rightly". While this may represent one cultural ideal, it does not take account of the pastoral situations which were being addressed by the bishops. This would also involve the great deal of work that must be done to support the equal human dignity and rights of women. The Synod had been very explicit on society's discrimination against and exploitation of women. It had even gone so far as to condemn every attack on the dignity of the human person, with the clear implication that they were speaking of women in society in particular. Finally, the "Homily" does not mention the more delicate problem the bishops had indicated, namely that "the Church must promote as much as possible in her own life equal rights and dignity".

The "Closing Homily", in one sense, brought the 1980 Synod to a close. But it was not the last word on the subject of marriage and the family. On the one hand, there was still the official papal response which would react more specifically to the Propositions. On the other, there was the impact that the episcopal gathering would still have on the life of the Church. The Synod is a process. It is supposed to be an ongoing process of interpreting, implementing and continuously looking for a more profound understanding of the achievement of Vatican II. It is supposed to promote dialogue not only within the Church but with the whole of mankind. It is a means for bringing the givens of human experience to light in order that they can be dealt with in the contemporary life of the

Church. The bishops had made a sincere attempt to do all these things and exhibited a remarkable familiarity with the whole of conciliar theology, especially the theology of marriage and the family. They had shown courage in explicitly touching upon some of the most complex and controversial issues still to be worked out in light of that theology. What remained was for the episcopal "advice" to be considered. The papal response was expected in the form of a document similar to the exhortation in response to the 1977 Synod, *Catechesi tradendae*. Theoretically, this document would coherently present the findings of the Synod, give a papal response to the most pressing issues and, it was hoped, set up the mechanisms for carrying on the investigations and studies which the bishops felt were necessary or at least opportune. It appeared at the end of the Synod that these hopes were very bright. We must now turn to that papal document and read it in the light of what the bishops had accomplished.

We must also keep in mind that however the Pope chose to respond, he would have to do it in a particular way. Namely, in following the Synod's example or not, he would have to take some position on the theology of marriage and the family as developed in Vatican II. There were, and still are, different interpretations of that theology. The 1980 Synod was a kind of watershed for articulating those differences. Thus, in our commentary to follow, we should be aware that the analysis must relate both to the Synod of 1980 and the Synod of 1962-1965, the Second Vatican Council.

V. FAMILIARIS CONSORTIO

On 15 Dec. 1981 John-Paul II published his "Apostolic Exhortation on the Family", *Familiaris consortio* (FC)[176]. The document was officially dated 22 Nov. 1981 and might possibly have appeared even earlier had the Pope not suffered an attack on his life earlier in the year. Indeed 1981 had been a busy year for the Pope for he also published his third encyclical "On Human Work", *Laborem exercens*, on 15 September[177]. Thus, it might be surprising that FC could have been produced in such a relatively short time, especially considering its length. We will see, however, that with the sources readily at hand, this was not very difficult.

The apostolic exhortation is an extremely long document. The official Latin text in *AAS*, for instance, covers 111 pages and consists of more than 30,000 words. GS, the longest document of Vatican II, covered 91 pages in *AAS* and consisted of 23,335 words. GS, 47-52, on marriage and the family, was only 8 pages in length. FC itself is much too long to absorb in one reading and thus lends itself to a selective type of reading which should be avoided if the text is to be studied objectively. The length itself is a cause for many persons to avoid reading the document at all. Almost none of the laity would attempt it and even very few of the clergy would take the time to study its content. Instead, most persons would rely upon interpretations and selective commentaries presented in the media. This is unfortunate because the whole of the document must be analyzed in order to comprehend the papal thought, especially the presuppositions and frame of reference. We will attempt to present such a commentary, keeping in mind the relevant background material.

The language of the document also presents a certain problem. The first available text of FC was that published in modern languages. There is reason to think that the original was written in a modern language and only then translated into Latin. The "official" Latin version was not published in *AAS* until February the following year. In any case, a first comparison made between this document and others which preceded it was done via the English texts[178]. That comparison revealed a striking

176. The English translation used there is the official Vatican version, published in *Origins* 11 (1981) 437-468. The official text, found in *AAS* 74 (1982) 81-191, gives the date for the apostolic exhortation as 22 Nov. 1981. However, the text was not released to the world until 15 Dec. 1981.

177. Published in *Origins* 11 (1981) 225-244. The official date given is 14 Sept. 1981. This was the third encyclical of the Pope's three year pontificate.

178. The other documents include the texts of Vatican II, HV, the "Message", the Pope's own speeches, etc., most of which are given reference in footnotes. Use of the text of the Propositions is usually not credited. There are also a few places where the text of the IL has had significant influence, none of which explicitly refer to that document.

similarity between FC and much of the text of the Propositions. In fact,
no less than 15% of FC appeared to be taken directly from that synodal
text although neither quotation marks nor references were given.
Another 10% of FC consists of direct quotes from other sources. Thus,
approximately 25% of FC was material taken from elsewhere.

When the Latin version of FC appeared, a direct comparison with the
original text of the Propositions was possible. It revealed that most of the
similar texts were not quotations because of differences in word order
and vocabulary. However, if FC were written in a modern language on
the basis of a translation of the Propositions, and if it were only then
translated into Latin itself, this could explain the discrepancies. The
point to be made here is not that portions of the Propositions were taken
over in FC with or without credit. Rather, it is simply the observation
that the sometimes almost verbatim parallel between the two texts
reveals that Pope John-Paul II relied very heavily upon the Propositions
and very often took over their ideas directly[179] The ideas which he took
over point to continuity with the Synod. Other texts, which were
reworked, demonstrate the interpretation of the bishops' suggestions
that entered into the papal commentary. Perhaps most significant is that,
having established a very close usage of, if not dependence upon, the
texts of the Propositions, attention can be drawn to those portions of the
episcopal findings and requests which found no place in papal thought or
expression. We will return to these neglected texts after our commentary
on FC itself. For the time being, when we refer to taking over or using
the text of the Propositions, we do not necessarily imply direct quotation.
The language differences in themselves would make such a characterization impossible.

The structure of FC's 86 numbered sections, excluding the
Introduction (1-3) and Conclusion (86) , has four parts.

I. Bright Spots and Shadows for the Family Today (4-10)
II. The Plan of God for Marriage and the Family (11-16)
III. The Role of the Christian Family (17-64)
IV. Pastoral Care of the Family (65-85)

These divisions clearly reflect the scheme which had developed in most
all the documents studied so far. Part III is the longest and most explicit,
but the other Parts are equally important because they express the Pope's
attitude and provide some of his fundamentally operative concepts. The
dominant theme of the text is "The Plan of God", a phrase that,
excluding titles, appears in the text in one form or another at least 30
times. Every numbered section has a title in the modern language
versions but not in *AAS*. Part III has elaborate divisions and sub-

---

179. Approximately one half of the text of the Propositions appears in FC in one form
or another.

divisions. Part IV has 4 divisions. There are 183 footnotes covering a rather broad use of sources.

The Introduction (FC, 1-3) begins with a notation of the Church's mission to serve the family (1) and takes explicit recognition of the 1980 Synod (2), attempting to establish its continuity with the three preceding Synods (1971, 1974, 1977). John-Paul also explicitly mentions the Propositions which he says are to be entrusted to the Pontifical Council for the Family[180] "with instructions to study it so as to bring out every aspect of its rich content". Note that the Pope calls for studying the synodal text and not any new investigations for which the bishops had called. This section also mentions the Synod's request that the Pope act as spokesman for the Church, which request he characterizes as "unanimous" (*unanimi sententia*) despite the fact that Prop. 1 had 3 "no" votes and 8 abstentions.

A third section of the Introduction sets the theme for the work to come, "the plan of God for marriage and the family". This is said to be founded upon Scripture (Gen. 1-2; Eph. 5 and Mt. 19:4)[181] and it will be the source for understanding the family which "is the object of numerous forces that seek to destroy it or in some way deform it" at this moment in history. The method, then, will be deductive. The following Part I, therefore, on the givens of experience, will only be used to set the scene and not be considered any kind of a resource. The principles will be laid down in Part II, "The Plan of God", and the conclusions drawn out in Part III, "The Role of the Family". Part VI, on "Pastoral Care" will deal with some suggestions and problems.

A. Part One: The Situation

Typical for official Church documents is to begin with describing the situation to be addressed. FC is no exception and this first Part will go even further to address some specific topics raised in the Synod. The

180. The "Pontifical Council for the Family" is an organization set up by a motu proprio of John-Paul II on 9 May 1981. This Council supersedes the former "Committee on the Family" set up by Paul VI on 11 Jan 1973 as an outgrowth of the "Pontifical Council for the Laity". Therefore, it is not actually an entirely new organization. The President of the "new" Council is Card. James Knox, former prefect of the Sacred Cong. for Sacraments and Divine Worship, who delivered an intervention at the Synod (15 Oct.) severely criticizing any experiments for "welcoming" marriages into the Church. Card. Knox is also a member of numerous Vatican organizations.

181. The scriptural references refer to marriage and the family being willed in creation, ordained to fulfillment in Christ, and restored to its "beginning". FC,3 also refers to GS,47 twice, to the effect that marriage and the family need grace because of having been wounded by sin and that they are intimately tied to the well-being of society. GS,47 does mention threats and disfigurements as well as problems facing marriage and the family. It does not use the word sin.

opening section (FC, 4) states that we need understanding of the situation. He, and the Church, must address the situation itself because of the mission to evangelize. We also find here a recurrent theme in the Pope's thought: we must be wary of "facile solutions" to problems which are often presented through the means of social communication (media). Many of these solutions do not respect the dignity of the human person.

The following section (FC, 5) is about "Evangelical Discernment" and must be read as John-Paul's response to the Synod's notion of the *sensus fidei* (Props. 2-4). That term appears in this section as well as the same references to LG and even the same quote from LG, 35 which is given in Prop. 2. The third paragraph is strikingly similar to that Proposition. It carefully distinguishes between surveys as majority opinion, and truth which is known in conscience. This is followed by the task of the Magisterium which is to "examine and authoritatively judge" the expressions of faith[182]. Prop. 3 had simply said the task is to interpret the *sensus fidei*.

FC, 6 then comes to the development of the positive and negative signs affecting marriage and family life. The positive ones are put forth by rewording the text of Prop. 5. However, the negative signs are presented somewhat differently. While Prop. 5 had been amended to emphasize social structures, FC, 6 concentrates on the private dimension, beginning with "a mistaken theoretical and practical concept of the independence of the spouses in relation to each other". However, the conditions of the Third World are not neglected, especially in terms of being contrasted with the richer countries and their consumer mentality. The contrast between good and bad signs is then illuminated with an appeal to St. Augustine in distinguishing the love of God and the love of self (cf. Prop. 5).

The following sections appear to be very much the Pope's own thought. There is again the theme of the influence of the media as a negative aspect (FC, 7). This is followed by a list of particular problems which he says the Synod fathers stressed. While all of them can be found in the Propositions, the list more closely resembles the style of the IL. In any case, we then come to the beginning of the Pope's commentary on some issues touched upon at the Synod. FC, 8 is about the "Need for Wisdom" but its content is a development of thought on the "new humanism" (cf. Prop. 6). John-Paul emphasizes the danger of relying upon science and technology which are sometimes directed against, rather than being used in service to, the human person and moral values.

---

182. Two references are given here in note 14: LG,12 mentions that the Church has to judge the validity of extraordinary gifts; *Dei verbum*, 10 points to the need to protect the handing on of revelation. See Part II, Ch. I of the *Lin* in which it was also found that references given to Vat. II in order to substantiate the authority of the Magisterium usually have little to do with teaching in the area of conjugal morality.

The thought is a profound one, though somewhat negative when compared to the context of positively evaluating cultural values that was the topic of the Synod's invocation of humanism.

FC, 9 explicitly turns to the topic of "gradualism" which very much resembles the original ideas of Prop. 7. The process of conversion is a dynamic one and is necessary to overcome the injustice present in structures because of personal and social sin. This was the original context for discussing gradualism. It is followed by the closing section of Part I, FC, 10, directed to the specific topic of "inculturation". This had been put forth especially in Prop. 18 and had already been commented upon in the "Closing Homily" (9). That papal comment was speculated to have placed a condition on this process, namely that it "must be instituted according to the principle of communion with the universal Church". The same comment appears here and we even find a recognition of the need for further studies. However, while Prop. 18 had called for these to be initiated by the episcopal conferences, FC adds to this "and the appropriate departments of the Roman Curia". The addition can be read in two ways: either the final decisions must always be made by centralized authority, or the curia itself should be more open to cultural input. There is no mention of the very specific request by the bishops that episcopal conferences be granted faculties that "would allow cultural adaptation and the creation of norms dealing with the celebration of marriage and its validity" (cf. Prop. 18, b).

B. Part Two: The Plan of God

"The Plan of God for Marriage and the Family" is the keynote for the whole theology of FC and it is here laid out in explicit form. The opening section (FC, 11: "Man, the Image of God Who is Love") is virtually a rewording of Prop. 8 [183]. Most of the ideas found here are represented in the Pope's own words. This "translation" sometimes reveals a difference in perspective, especially toward the notion of "institution". In the Propositions, there is a reflection of the conciliar thought that marriage as relationship contains its own dynamic that is lived out according to cultural customs and values. Because of its importance, society "institutionalizes" marriage. However, the thought exhibited in FC considers marriage as an institution in itself which is then recognized by society. This presupposed a definitive form, specifically willed by God and knowable through an exegesis of Scripture. While it would be hard to take issue with this on the grounds of religious orthodoxy determined

---

183. An idea introduced in FC, 11 briefly mentions that the christian vocation is realized through marriage or virginity. This notion, found in Prop. 11, will be more explicitly treated in FC, 16.

by the (papal) Magisterium, the image of marriage which results has little
to do with the experience of cultural givens[184]. It appears that the Synod
and the Pope are approaching the fundamental concept in a very
different way. This will have an effect on subsequent methodology as
well as on the conclusions which are drawn.

The consequences of this observation are immediately evident in the
following two sections. FC, 12, on "Marriage and Communion Between
God and People", and FC, 13, on "Jesus Christ, Bridegroom of the
Church, and the Sacrament of Matrimony", should be read along with
Props. 9 and 10 which give "The Theology of the Sacrament of
Marriage". It has been observed that the Synod took care to maintain
the concept of analogy when addressing the sacramental aspect of
marriage. There is no simple reading of Scripture nor a mechanistic
superimposition of divine love onto human love. Reading FC, 12 and 13,
however, renders a different impression. The words are, in a sense,
beautiful and profound. But the way in which the concepts are used is
deductive. There is, indisputably, a metaphorical relation between divine
and spousal covenantal love. But one does not create the other. Rather,
the existence of a marital relationship between christians is recognized to
be sacramental when it concretizes a particular kind of (christian) love.
The human relationship, which according to GS, 48 and 49 *is* eminently
human, total, faithful and leading the spouses to lastingness, is a special
event which the ecclesial community celebrates as sacrament.

There are two aspects of marital sacramentality in FC that it might be
interesting to investigate. The first is that of reciprocity. Even the
scriptural passages to which reference is made[185] underscore the unique-
ness of divine love which is *not* reciprocated by Israel. Furthermore, the
idea of covenant evoked from Scripture here is not between equals, nor is
it consistently responded to by the recipients of God's initiative. The
New Covenant can be characterized in the same way. Thus, the theological notion of covenant in Scripture is a matter of initiative and response,
not simultaneous initiative. How, one may ask, is this to be applied to
marriage?

Anticipating an answer to the first question leads us to the second.
Namely, if reciprocity is presumed, one has already altered the analogy
and has a model whereby each spouse takes the part of God's initiative

184. FC,11 ends with the notion that the (known) structure of the institution of
marriage guarantees the ability to avoid "every form of subjectivism or relativism". No one
wants to argue in favor of subjectivism, but how is it possible to approach the givens of
experience without a healthy respect for "relativism"? In a sense, this is the core of the
problem. If everything were really so neat, either conforming to or measurable by a
predetermined pattern, what would be the purpose of discussion? Would we need the
Synod?

185. The scriptural references are more or less the same as those found in GS,48 and
Prop. 9.

and total self-giving. Undoubtedly, this is what John-Paul has in mind[186]. But is this not truly an ideal? How many concrete marital relationships are conceived or function according to this model? Furthermore, is this not itself very Western in mentality? Can it function in different cultural milieus, or should it?

Without questioning either the idealness of this model or its ultimate, universal applicability[187], we can ask if it is a good idea to make marriage itself function as the vehicle for the mystery of salvation in such a unique and absolute way. The text of FC tells us,

By virtue of the sacramentality of their marriage, spouses are bound to one another in the most profoundly indissoluble manner. Their belonging to each other is the real representation, by means of the sacramental sign, of the very relationship of Christ with the Church[188].

Why do marriage and the spouses' relationship have to carry the burden of representing the entire mystery? Of course, the same thing can and should be said about every sacrament. But the literal way in which it is here applied confuses what was pointed out earlier about the direction in which one can apply an analogy. Do we start with divine love and demand that human reality live up to its characteristics, or do we begin with the human reality and come to a better understanding of the divine mystery? The two directions will yield two, different sacramentologies. The deductive method used here is juridical in mentality rather than theological.

One more thing can be said about the comparison between the work of the Synod and FC at this point. In developing the notion of conjugal love as basic for the theology of marriage, both GS and Props. 9 and 10 were able to do so without including the aspect of procreation. FC, 13 is again

---

186. We should not forget that this vision is already different from the traditional and so-called constant teaching. Pius XI in CC draws an ambiguous picture which clearly exhibits elements of domination-subordination in the use of Eph. 5. Man, as Christ, is the head of the relationship; woman, as Church, must be subject to her husband. The intricacies of interpreting the covenantal model are much more complex than the Magisterium admits, especially in the Old Testament. Cf. D.J. McCarthy, *Old Testament Covenant: A Survey of Current Opinions*, Oxford, 1973.

187. Stress here should be placed upon the word "ultimate". FC evidently conceives the applicability of this model to be immediate and necessary. While we can question the validity of the theological presupposition no more than we can question the ultimate goal of christian marriage being monogamous, we should exercise care in not allowing those concepts to influence the work of evangelization. Even where a monogamous, mutual love relationship between equals is the operative model for explaining marriage, an absolute imposition of that model for determining marital validity would have severe consequences. This is the problem of confusing the theological with the juridical.

188. This text from FC,13 is followed by a phrase which either betrays a mentality or represents a poor choice of example. It reads: "Spouses are therefore the permanent reminder to the Church of what happened on the cross". Perhaps the invocation of joy (GS) would have been a more positive way of making the comparison.

different. Before completing the development, it brings in the idea that conjugal love is "open to fertility" and gives the expected reference to HV, 9. "In a word", the text goes on, "it is a question of the normal characteristics of all natural conjugal love..." (Cf. IL, 16: "the good points of christian marriage"; and IL, 29 and 63 as well as *Lin* Part II, Ch. II, on "the logical and normal evolution of conjugal love").

The thought is continued in a more explicit way because the next section, FC, 14, is on "Children, the Precious Gift of Marriage". Although the opening paragraph restores the conciliar insight that it is *both* marriage and conjugal love which are oriented to procreation and education, this is all once again placed under the heading of the "plan of God". The vocabulary that follows lies outside the conciliar genre and returns to the notion of the spouses "giving life to a human person" as if a being pre-existed their decision and actions. It follows with the idea that children are "a living and inseparable synthesis of their being a father and a mother". For one, this is a statement of the obvious: one does not become father or mother without having children. For another, it boarders on the romantic. Fortunately, the section ends with a few words for the childless couple. Of course, this is conceived solely in terms of "physical sterility". The idea that procreation may not be realized for other reasons, including the explicit decision by the couple, lies outside the consideration of the text as it attempts to describe the "plan of God".

After a few brief comments on "The Family, a Communion of Persons" (FC, 15) which uses the analogy of the whole christian family (the Church), FC, 16 turns to "Marriage and Virginity or Celibacy". The opening sentences are a precis of Prop. 11 and therefore contain some of the insights of that text. The end of the section will return to the style of precis, but not before a commentary is given. Beginning with a quote from St. John Chrysostom and climaxing with a reference to Pius XII[189], FC returns to the notion that celibacy for the kingdom is superior to marriage. Whereas most contemporary theology has attempted to overcome the dichotomy between marriage and celibacy, which inevitably leads to the establishment of a priority, the notion of comparison is reintroduced.

In summary, Part II has presented the fundamental concepts. There is a singular, pre-determined model of marriage and family life operative here from which will be deduced the answer to every question that will

189. The quote from Chrysostom is from *De Virginitate*, and the reference to Pius XII is *Sacra virginitatis* (1954). Between these, besides references to Mt. 22:30 and 1 Cor. 7:32-35 (would that it had been 1 Cor. 7:7: "I wish that all were as I myself am. But each has his own special gift from God, one of one kind and one of another."), there is a quotation from the conciliar "Decree on the Appropriate Renewal of the Religious Life", *Perfectae caritatis*, 12. Reading that text, as all the other conciliar teachings, reveals the same care to avoid dichotomizing and thus comparing celibacy and marriage that was found in the Synod.

present itself. The "normal characteristics" of the marital relationship give us a guide for establishing fidelity, indissolubility and fruitfulness. The covenant explains sacramentality. Divine love is the model for human love in a literal way. All that is left is the need to be specific and deduce exactly what this means. This will be done in the next Part.

C. Part Three: The Role of the Family

"The Role of the Christian Family" is the longest Part of FC. It is presented according to the following structure[190].

1. Forming a Community of Persons   (18-27)
2. Serving Life
   A. The Transmission of Life   (28-35)
   B. Education   (36-41)
3. Participating in the Development of Society   (42-48)
4. Sharing in the Life and Mission of the Church   (49-50)
   A. The Christian Family as a Believing and Evangelizing
      Community   (51-54)
   B. The Christian Family as a Community in Dialogue with God   (55-62)
   C. The Christian Family as a Community at the Service of Man   (63-64)

This structure is introduced with a separate section (FC, 17) that begins with the words, "The family finds in the plan of God the creator and redeemer not only its identity, what it is, but also its mission, what it can and should do". This is indicative of a deductive method. Everything that is necessary can be found if the family goes "back to the beginning". This is the source of "God's plan" and the words to describe what that plan might be are taken from GS, 48: "an intimate comminity of life and love"[191]. The conciliar text had specified that it is a community of *conjugal* love but FC apparently does not think that the specification is necessary. GS had also used this as a descriptive phrase whereas the present text is using it as a source for deduction. The difference may be one of interpretation, but if we stop to think of the marital covenant as a joining of two lives based upon love, we have an image of a specific kind of human relationship that can then be called sacrament. However, if we say that marriage must realize life and love, there is an impression of

190. The divisions and titles given here are taken from the (official) English version and do not appear in the Latin text. The numbers in parentheses represent the designated sections of the document which do appear in the Latin text. The fourfold division of Part III is attributed to an observation that "the recent synod emphasized four general tasks for the family" (FC,17). It is not clear what the source of this synodal intention might be. It does not reflect the structure of the Propositions. We expect that it is an interpretation.

191. Quoniam ex Dei consilio constituitur tamquam "intima communitas vitae et amoris" ... FC,17 (*AAS*, p. 100). Cf. GS,48: "Intima communitas vitae et amoris coniugalis" (*AAS*, 1966, p. 1067).

bringing something into existence which was not there previously. In other words, when there is a marriage, it must bring about love. When there is a marriage, it must bring about life. The implication is obvious.

The first aspect to be dealt with is that of love. This is put under the heading, "Forming a Community of Persons". It covers 10 sections in which the Pope's theology of marriage is put forth. After an introductory section in which love is described as being the principle, power and goal of the family which is a community of persons (FC, 18), we come to an exposé of the doctrine: unity or monogamy (19), indissolubility (20), communion (21), and the roles and rights of women (22-24), men (25), children (26) and the elderly (27). Some of these developments are rather original, especially the last three topics which deserved special mention. Before we come to these, however, there are a few crucial points to be discussed.

First is unity or monogamy. Taking Gen. 2:24 (cf. Mt. 19:6) as his starting point, John-Paul develops his image on the model of "two in one flesh". The "natural complementarity that exists between man and woman", the sexual bond, is the source of the marital union. The communion which results is said to be "the fruit and the sign of a profoundly human need" that the Lord then "confirms, purifies, elevates and leads to perfection through the sacrament of matrimony". Through the sacrament, the "Holy Spirit is poured out" and the result is a "new communion" which is described by shifting the image to the Church as "the indivisible mystical body of the Lord Jesus" (cf. IL, 32). What we find here is a distinct anthropology. All the elements fit together very neatly and serve a determined purpose. However, one might ask if the philosophical influences are not more dominant than the theological ones. What, for instance, is the "profoundly human need" to which marriage seems to be the answer? If this is universal, what impact will it have on celibacy? Would we not be justified in asking whether this thinking is also essentialistic? When the human bond is confirmed, purified and elevated to a sacrament, it not only is the recipient of grace but "the gift of the spirit is a commandment of life". One has images of the "ontological bond" sketched out for us in the IL. However, the point soon becomes clear. The whole development is aimed at establishing one idea:

Such a communion is radically contradicted by polygamy: this, in fact, directly negates the plan of God which was revealed from the beginning, because it is contrary to the equal personal dignity of men and women, who in matrimony give themselves with a love that is total and therefore unique and exclusive.

The anthropology present here is abstract. Its only cultural element rests in that it grows out of only one culture. The Western mentality will probably have no difficulty accepting it because the concept of "equal personal dignity" is usually defined in individualistic terms in Western culture. But is this a valid model to teach the universal Church? Even if one accepts the ideal of monogamy, is it valid to infer that a socio-cultural milieu which currently defines human dignity in non-individualistic terms and accepts conjugal union under different in-stitutionalized patterns "radically contradicts" marriage as a com-munion of love?

Even within a monogamous structure we could ask the meaning of emphasizing the man-woman relation to such an extent that it becomes not only exclusive but closed. The image presented here is that conjugal union is capable of answering all the profound needs of the person. A good deal of contemporary thought would seriously question that image. Monogamy itself takes place in a social context and does not consist simply in a union of one on one — "the couple". To say that it does is to exaggerate one aspect of the social phenomenon. The question to be asked is whether we should allow that exaggeration to function as the basis for establishing marital exclusivity.

FC, 20 then turns to the question of indissolubility. The text is basically an expansion of Prop. 13, a-d[192], most of which is repeated here in sometimes different and stronger words. The Church stands for marital indissolubility absolutely and without question. The basis for this, of course, is the definitive character of Christ's love for the Church. Again, no one disputes the image, but the imposition of the charac-teristics of divine love on human love appear to beg for some form of adjustment. For instance, in repeating the words of the Synod (which are here given credit), praise is given both to spouses who remain united despite difficulties and those who, abandoned by their spouse, do not attempt to enter a new union. These are said to need the support of the community, especially the latter group. Would it not be pertinent, however, to also ask how Christ himself would treat such persons? In the Synod's Propositions this statement of policy is immediately followed with a discussion of divorce and remarriage in which the bishops carefully distinguished between different types of "cases". That discus-sion does not appear in this document until the very end (FC, 84). Thus, the doctrinal point becomes radicalized by remaining isolated from the need for pastoral engagement. That engagement and the application of doctrine is what the Synod was all about. It has no influence, however, on these papal teachings (FC, 21).

After an exhortation on the meaning of communion for the whole family, the rights and role of women are taken up. This occurs in a broader context that will also comment upon the other members of the family. However, women are given much more attention. This is directly

192. Prop. 13,e, which called for better marriage preparation, is not repeated here. That text's suggestion for episcopal conferences to initiate some form of betrothal ceremony is not mentioned anywhere in FC.

parallel to the development found in Props. 15-17 and, in the beginning of FC, 22, mentioning his source, the Pope uses those texts very liberally. FC, 22 is a restatement of all the ideas in Prop. 15, and FC, 24 went on to add its own endorsement to the thoughts of Prop. 17. But the discussion present in Prop. 16, on the roles of women, is completely reworked. As was foreshadowed in his "Homily", John-Paul is definitely more in favor of married women remaining in the home. Again, no one will dispute the fact that women who do devote themselves full time to child care are performing a task and following a profession on an equal footing with other professions. However, this is not really the issue. There is a much deeper question of role identification and human classification which has always managed to keep women "in their place" and substantiate genuine discrimination and prejudice against them. The Synod appeared to be open to discussing this more fully — even with respect to the life of the Church. FC does not repeat that perspective. Unfortunately, the Pope's text will probably serve to close off any further discussion and set the Church back from what little progress had been made on the issue — at least officially.

In some contrast to this, FC, 25 shows a willingness to discuss man as husband and father. Despite the literal interpretation of Gen. 2:18, the text is a good critique of masculine roles, going so far as to mention "machismo" as "a wrong superiority of male prerogative which humiliates women and inhibits the development of healthy family relationships". We could only have wished that the discussion could have been broader and included the social and ecclesial dimensions of these very same role types. But such a fundamental approach is not envisioned in the document and it relies very heavily upon what are already widely accepted notions of role identification. Woman is wife and mother, and man is husband and father. Beyond this, there appears to be nothing to talk about.

The following two sections bring this first division of Part III to a close discussing children (FC, 26) and the elderly (FC, 27). Both are good texts and both include extensive quotes of John-Paul's earlier speeches. In one sense, they demonstrate how FC is more a combination of texts than an original document. It brought together many previous ideas into one place.

The second division of Part III is about "Serving Life". Following the classical model, it is further subdivided into procreation (28-35) and education (36-41). The parallel of the first part with the Propositions is direct, with the introduction of some extra material (FC, 32 & 33). That parallel is: FC, 28 — Prop. 20, 29-21, 30-22, 31-23, 34-24, and 35-25. In making the comparison we must remember that we are dealing with the amended text of the Propositions along with the subtle changes of meaning that were introduced. The papal texts, again, are not strict reproduction, but put the ideas in their own words.

FC, 28 begins and ends with a precis of Prop. 20. After invoking creation in God's image and likeness, the Proposition says that "God established marriage and called men and women to a union of love in the service of life". This line is reduced to the observation that God calls spouses "to a special sharing in His love..." and is immediately followed by "...and in His power as Creator and Father..." The absence of any mention of the conjugal union, which lends the "sharing in God's love" to the interpretation of being solely His creative love, is reminiscent of the *Lin*'s quotation of GS, 50 which also left out a phrase on the man-woman union being part of the creative intention[193]. There is also a repetition of the quote from Gen. 1:28, "be fruitful and multiply" that aids in constructing the impression that procreation is the main purpose of the creation of sexual differentiation. This is brought to a climax in the next paragraph.

Thus the fundamental task of the family is to serve life, to actualize in history the original blessing of the creator — that of transmitting by procreation the divine image from person to person[194].

As if the intent were not yet clear enough, the next paragraph opens with the idea very much present in the pre-synodal documents, but avoided by the bishops themselves, "Fecundity is the fruit and sign of conjugal love, the living testimony of the full reciprocal self-giving of the spouses". This is followed by a quote from GS, 50. FC, 28 ends with a precis of the Proposition noting that creativity is not simply biological.

The immediate impression one gets from this text is that of the primary end of marriage. The vocabulary is pre-conciliar: gift and crown has reverted back to fruit and sign of conjugal love. The quote from GS, 50 has been similarly used before (cf. IL, 63). It simply remains to be worked out specifically. This is done in FC, 29, the first half of which is a precis and the second half a quote from Prop. 21 in which, with the help of a small addition[195], signified the "endorsement" of HV as being in total continuity with GS. If the Propositions were unclear or even hesitent in that endorsement (at least in their original form), this reworking of the synodal text provides the clarity and eliminates the hesitency. To read FC's account of the matter is to get a very different impression than what actually happened at the Synod.

FC, 30 begins by admitting that the Church's teaching in this area is rather difficult to understand against the background of the con-

---

193. Cf. *supra*, pp. 215-216.

194. Princeps ergo familiae officium est vitae ipsius ministerium, progredientibus aetatibus pristinae Creatoris benedictionis impletio dum per generationem divina imago homini ab homine traditur. (*AAS*, p. 114)

Reference is given here to Gen. 5:1-3, the opening verses of the "Book of Generations".

195. The specific reference to GS,50 and the word "afterwards". Cf. *supra*, pp. 279-280.

temporary "social and cultural context". But it then goes on to explain that the reason this is true is not because there might be anything wrong with the teaching or its expression, but because society and culture are so evil and incapable of understanding it. Three reasons are given for this state of affairs: the growth of technology which leads not only to anxiety about the future but also to manipulation through imposed programs of family planning, the consumer mentality which is only concerned about material things, and a loss of the presence of God in our hearts. Although one could say these ideas are worthy of thought[196], they are stereotypes that lead us away from the point. Non-acceptance of HV is not always attributable to these "evil forces". The Synod had not said that was the case. But here their ideas are taken over as a general indictment of society. The text goes on, following Prop. 22, to set up a dichotomy: there is the prevailing "anti-life mentality" against which the Church gives its "yes", its "amen" to life. Therefore, finishing out a restatement of Prop. 22, the Pope leads quite naturally into the condemnation of contraception or, "still worse"[197] sterilization or procured abortion. In following the Proposition, FC, 30 is really only speaking about government intervention in these matters. But in the same way that the amended version of Prop. 22 ended up sounding like an unequivocal condemnation of contraception, sterilization, etc., in themselves, John-Paul continues the impression.

Following the same interpretive genre, FC, 31 is more or less a rewording of Prop. 23, with some interesting changes. First, the Proposition had quoted Paul VI on the need for further study on the many complex problems facing family life and for a "fuller, more organic and synthetic explanation" of the Church's teaching. FC left this out. Secondly, not only does John-Paul repeat the amended version's call upon theologians (rather than the Magisterium) to do the work of explanation, but he expands this even further to express his notion of the task of theologians. In a word. the theologian is a spokesperson for the Magisterium

The following two sections depart from following the Propositions and attempt to give John-Paul's own explanation of why he believes the

---

196. P. HEBBLETHWAITE, *The Pope on the Family*, in *The Tablet* 236 (1982) 29-30, recognized a very small influence of the Synod in these thoughts, but in general believed that "these pen-portraits are Pope John Paul's own work". In fact, the first (compound) and the last ideas are taken directly from Prop. 22. The second idea, that of the consumer mentality, had been elaborated in IL,54. Like a great deal of FC, there really is not much new here. The only thing original about the text is its "interpretation" of previously existing ideas.

197. FC,30 ends with a reference to number 5 of the bishops' closing "Message". The words used for moving from contraception to "still worse" sterilization, etc., appear to be the only specific reflection of that text. In reality, the text itself is much closer to Prop. 22 and we wonder why this alternative reference is given.

teaching of HV is correct. Most of the thought here, especially in the first section, can be found in the Pope's book of 1962[198]. It is based upon his notion of an "integral vision of the human person", a development that begins with a quote from GS, 51 but immediately moves to the two aspect theory of HV, 12 and the "exclusions" of HV, 14. Perhaps, like so many others before him, without realizing it, he has let the argument become trapped in the theory of the illusory "meanings" (*significationes*) of sexual intercourse, any "manipulation" of which "falsifies" personal communication. This is a philosophical argument, neither substantiated by experience nor convincing in its conclusions. We will only comment that the argument has been tried before. It becomes no more convincing because of papal endorsement, and it does not avoid the greatest objection against it: ultimately it divides the human person and dehumanizes sexuality[199]. The second interpretive section attempts to demonstrate that the Church has always shown compassion but is morally bound to stand fast for "the truth".

FC, 34 returns to the Pope's commentary on the Propositions. It should be recalled that Prop. 24 was originally addressed to the pastoral ministry to married couples and concentrated upon an "educational approach" that should follow the "law of gradualism". Reading the papal commentary, we find that every idea that was the result of an amendment in Prop. 24 is included in FC, 34, but some of the "original" ideas are left out. For instance, although pedagogy is seen as progressive, there is no repetition of this approach "mixing constancy with patience, courage, humility and complete confidence in God's mercy". Then, there is an allusion to the fact that "conjugal intimacy involves the wills of two persons" etc. (an amendment) which is followed by a call for all priests to demonstrate unity (also an amendment) but which leaves out the (original) intervening comment on the "law of gradualism". Of course, this topic had already been covered (FC, 9), but its introduction in the

198. Cf. *supra*, note 35.

199. The philosophical speculation on the "falsification" of sexual communication because of the use of contraception is not only weak but it also represents a misunderstanding of the conciliar insights. As we have already developed, according to GS, human sexuality is (should be) totally integrated in the person, not something "added on", the biological facticity of which functions as a moral norm. Talk of "respecting the cycle of the person, that is, the woman" (FC, 32) not only presumes the normative value of biology, it is also sexist and impersonal. It is sexist because it is a simplistic view of female sexuality as well as a throwback to placing all responsibility upon the woman. It is impersonal in a minor way because it allows the biological aspects of human sexuality to take on a (normative) life of their own; impersonal in a major way because it fails to integrate the aspects of love, care, tenderness, joy, responsibility, etc., *into* human sexuality. Ultimately, making biology the primary norm leads to a new form of manicheaism and completely avoids the more pressing responsibility of rebuilding a coherent teaching based upon human sexual integration. In short, it divides the human person and treats sexuality as a "thing".

synodal text at this point had some significance with respect to developing educational and pastoral programs. In the exhortation, only the moral law which reflects God's plan is important.

Finally, FC, 35 is an expansion of Prop. 25 which originally called for more study and the spread of information about scientific methods of regulating fertility. The fact that the synodal text was amended to specify this to the "natural methods" is not wasted in FC which gives its wholehearted endorsement to that movement. Then, in one more linguistic precision we find the core of papal thinking in this area. Whereas Prop. 25 had called upon developing methods that are "in conformity with human dignity and the Church's teaching", FC, 35 substitutes the norm of "respect for the structure and finalities of the conjugal act" (*observantes structuram ac fines actus coniugalis*, AAS, p. 125). Perhaps this was a slip of the pen. We tend to think that it is the logical conclusion of papal thinking. With all of FC's speculation on "an integral vision of the human person", it is clear that sexuality is something that remains apart from that integration. Human sexuality is equated with human genitality, something having its own (normative) "structure and finalities". This was not the perspective found in GS, nor was this form of biologism reflected in the episcopal contribution in the Synod. The ideas present in FC, 35 are much closer to pre-conciliar thought.

The second, classical, aspect of serving life follows procreation with education. The Synod had followed the same scheme (section 12) and so once again this division (FC, 36-41) is a sort of commentary on the Propositions (26-29), along with long quotations from *Gravissimum educationis*, the Vatican II "Declaration on Christian Education". However, it does not follow the same order as the Synod. The texts of the Propositions are dealt with piecemeal and sometimes sections are discussed elsewhere or simply left out[200]. This is not very significant Most of the basic ideas are represented and there really is nothing new in most of the text. The style is sometimes verbose and even mythical. When writing on the education for chastity, John-Paul uses the phrase "respecting and fostering the 'nuptial meaning' of the body", which is poetic but very unclear. The images of religious celibates being wedded either to the Church or to Christ are not far in the background, reminiscent of a traditional and very private spirituality. Nevertheless, the section ends with a somewhat original contribution on the "manifold service to life". This is an expansion of the idea expressed in the beginning of Prop. 20 and in Prop. 30, g: the mission of married couples involves much more than physical fruitfulness. A genuine community spirit is necessary for

---

200. Section 12 of the Propositions (26-29) is represented here with the rephrasing of 26, a-b, 28, a-c, 27, a-c, 29, a-b in that order. 26, c & d are not commented upon here.

families to share their resources and overcome social and cultural barriers.

The next two divisions (3 & 4) of Part III are broader in character, directed to social (FC, 42-48) and ecclesial (49-64) life. Section 3 is basically an expansion of the Synod's work; first in terms of the social role of the family (FC, 42 — Prop. 30, a; 43 — 30, d, c, b; 44 — 30, h, j; 45 — 30, k) and then in declaring a charter of family rights (46 = Prop. 42). This ends with the special mission the christian family has to those with special needs (FC, 47 — Prop. 30, h) and a call for a new international order in which the family as "domestic Church" mirrors the role of the universal Church in acting as a sign of peace, justice and reconciliation.

The fourth division, "sharing in the life and mission of the Church" is a long meditation which, after an introduction (49-50)[201], discusses three topics: the family as believing and evangelizing (51-54), in dialogue with God (52-62), and in service to man (63-64). The first is replete with quotations and repetition of the ideas put forth in Prop. 34 (and some parts of Prop. 12 on marital preparation being a journey of faith). The second represents a complete rethinking of Section 17 of the Propositions (36-38) on "Family Spirituality". Whereas the latter, in a relatively brief text, situated spirituality in the theology of marriage, the exhortation exhibits a kind of spirituality that is rare in the contemporary world, probably only found in what might be called a Catholic culture. Whereas the Synod was very social minded, FC is very private. Whereas the Synod did not neglect family prayer and liturgy (Prop. 37), FC concentrates on it[202]. Perhaps most significant of all is that the Synod saw one aspect of spirituality being the formation of conscience. That valuable text (Prop. 38) plays no part in FC.

The third sub-division on the relationship between the family and the community of man does in fact return to the development in Prop. 36 on the basis of this theology being the commandment to love. However, the

201. It might be noted that even in describing marriage and the family as the locus for religions mission, an opportunity is not missed for describing "the values of conjugal love" again as "totality, oneness, fidelity and fruitfulness" (FC,50) with appropriate reference to HV,9.

202. Concentrating upon the sacramental character of marriage, FC draws out its relation with the other sacraments, especially eucharist (FC,57) and penance (FC,58). The second of these raises a very good point about the practice of reconciliation beginning within the family itself. However, it also contains a curious reference to an ambiguous text of HV,25: "And if sin should still keep its hold over them, let them not be discouraged, but rather have recourse with humble perseverence to the mercy of God, which is abundantly poured forth in the sacrament of penance". This text is ambiguous because it constitutes the only mention of sin in that encyclical and implies a great deal of tolerance for recidivism if one wishes to classify the use of "artificial contraception" as sinful. Exactly what this quotation is doing in FC,58 remains a question. In any case, it testifies to the fact that FC was prepared with the encyclical HV in the other hand, so to speak.

two sections here appear to be more of an afterthought and the
fundamental insight of the Synod has been sacrificed to a basically
inward oriented spirituality. The theme of Part III on "The Role of the
Christian Family" is thus brought to a close. Looking back upon this
long text there is the feeling that very little was accomplished. With
endless quotations and paraphrases, we find a repetition of ideas that
remains very general and vague. We also find a somewhat selective use of
the wide variety of sources, all of which are utilized to build a picture of
the christian family that is perhaps too coherent, too neat and certainly
ideal. The sociological presumptions do not seem to fit the "modern
world" which was the point of inquiry of the Synod itself. That "world"
was characterized as problematic and pluralistic, but the "world" being
addressed by FC appears to be stable and basically homogeneous.
Without necessarily tracing it to specific words or expressions, one more
aspect of the Synod's perspective also appears to be missing, namely a
sense of urgency.

D. Part Four: Pastoral Care

Having put forth the scheme, "the plan of God", and drawn out its
conclusions, it now remains to deal with the "Pastoral Care of the
Family". Rather than turning immediately to specific issues, this Part is
an end in itself that attempts to construct a whole theory of pastoral care.
It has four sections:

1. Stages of Pastoral Care of the Family   (65-69)
2. Structures of Family Pastoral Care   (70-72)
3. Agents of the Pastoral Care of the Family   (73-76)
4. Pastoral Care of the Family in Difficult Cases   (77-85)

The first section, the idea for which is laid out in FC, 65[203] "The Church
accompanies the christian family on its journey through life", parallels
the stages of care with the stages in the growth of the conjugal union:
preparation (66), celebration (67), evangelization (68), and married life
(69). The third of these addresses the delicate issue of the need for faith
and the validity of the sacrament. First, however, is the question of
preparation for marriage.

203. In what appears to be a contrast with the closing words of our commentary on Part
III, FC,65 notes that "pastoral intervention of the Church in support of the family is a
matter of urgency". These words are a precis of John-Paul's own previous address (Puebla,
28 Jan. 1979) and do not address the urgency of problems rooted in conjugal and familial
experience. What is urgent in the mind of the Pope is really "pastoral intervention", as he
calls it, and not necessarily the problems themselves. That intervention is presumed to have
all the answers (drawn from God's plan) and creates no room for what might have to be
"urgent solutions" to pressing difficulties which refuse to fit into a predictable pattern.

FC, 66 parallels Prop. 35 but it does not begin with that text. Instead, the first two (in Latin, one) English paragraphs are a rewording of IL, 86 in its entirety. This is followed by a restatement of the first paragraph of Prop. 35, then returns to IL, 87 on general preparation through growth (here called remote preparation), and to IL, 88 on remote preparation for marriage in particular (here called proximate)[204]. The final stage of "immediate preparation" appears to be the Pope's own work and deals with the months and weeks preceding the ceremony. However, by developing his own contribution he is also omitting some good thoughts present in the Proposition. Namely, there is no repetition of the idea that the meaning of marriage as a sacrament is the experience of the presence of Christ in the lives of the couple; nor is there any reflection of the bishops' observation that the partners' sexual relationship "is an important part of their sacramental union". Instead, there is merely an emphasis upon the "meaning, content and form" of the premarital inquiry and a suggestion that this may reveal shortcomings and difficulties. Finally, there is the issue of setting up guidelines for preparation programs. This returns to a commentary on Prop. 35 that rewords mostly everything which was said there. But there is one curious twist. FC, 66 states that "it is to be hoped that the episcopal conferences... will take steps to see that there is issued a directory for the pastoral care of the family". When we examine Prop. 35 we find the statement that "bishops' conferences and dioceses should establish the minimal content, duration and methods for these programs". FC had included the same idea. But the bishops were speaking only about immediate marriage preparation. Elsewhere (Prop. 43) the Synod had called for each episcopal conference to draw up its own "pastoral directory" which "should explain Church teaching and discipline in a manner suitable for varying circumstances". The suggestion made by the Synod is here (FC, 66) given only veiled reference by use of the term "directory for pastoral care", and is contextually highly restricted to marriage preparation programs. Nowhere does FC credit the notion of independent "directories" dealing with all of "Church teaching and discipline". Legally speaking, FC recognizes the bishops' call for instituting "pastoral directories", but the spirit of that request has been mitigated by placing it in this very specific context.

The following number deals with the actual celebration of marriage in itself. There is little said here that is not already obvious. However, it can

204. Prop. 35 simply states that "remote preparation begins in the family. The Church should give attention to the pastoral role of christian initiation". It then goes on to proximate preparation for the sacrament itself. IL and FC divide these stages into three but use their own terminology. IL,86 is taken over completely by FC,66, though vocabulary and style are different. IL,87 & 88 are represented selectively, leaving out some ideas such as the endorsement of teaching the methods for a "natural regulation of conception" (IL,88).

be noted that FC, 67 takes care to remind everyone that any "cultural adaptation" must always be judged by "norms issued by the Apostolic See", and that the employment of cultural elements "contain nothing that is not in harmony with christian faith and morality". Again, the attitude toward inculturation is rather hesitent and very cautious (cf. FC, 10).

FC, 68 now addresses the problem of faith and the sacrament and must be read in direct comparison with Prop. 12. The latter text had signaled what apparently a large number of bishops had thought of or experienced as a problem. They even went so far as to suggest that the revision of canon law needs to take this problem into account. In response, John-Paul virtually dismisses the issue. In his mind, the only difficulty is when the pastor encounters an engaged couple who "reject explicitly and formally what the Church intends to do when the marriage of baptized persons is celebrated". Unlike the bishops, who were apparently struggling with the problem of exactly what it is that "the Church intends to do" in this instance, the papal document offers no further reflection on that issue nor attempts to link it with "the minimal intention of believing with the Church" (Prop. 12).

What we find in place of this question of faith is a naturalistic idea of marital sacramentality based, of course, on the "plan of God". Since God intended marriage to take place, anyone approaching marriage has "an attitude of profound obedience to the will of God". The only specific requirement is "the decision to commit by their irrevocable conjugal consent their whole lives in indissoluble love and unconditional fidelity". Therefore, any couple who commit themselves to marriage in a lasting way have a valid union because it is *de facto* in conformity with the will of God. If these persons are baptized, there is also a valid sacrament. Everything is automatic. There is no question of faith. The theological question raised by the bishops — how can we meaningfully speak of sacrament without at least a minimal understanding of faith — is completely ignored.

In one sense, the papal "solution" is pastoral. Indeed, the fact that he goes on to specifically reject any notion of drawing up guidelines for determining the faith of the engaged couple (a specific suggestion of the Synod, cf. Prop. 12, d) is explained on the grounds of the difficulties this might create not only for the engaged but also for those already married, both in the Roman Church and among the separated brethren[205]. One

205. While one has a tendency to read and classify the Pope's remarks here as "pastoral", we cannot forget what was signified by the bishops' own words, "This statement (with respect to faith and validity) has pastoral and juridical consequences". It is no secret that, at the time of the Synod, some officials were upset about the growing number of annulments which were being granted. (cf. *The Increased Number of Annulments*, a summary of the synodal intervention by Card. P. Felici on 6 Oct., in *Origins* 10 (1980) 314-315). If something more specific were said about the faith requirements to establish

can understand the solicitude, but the theological point appears too important to be dismissed so easily. According to the reasoning of FC, 68, any couple approaching marriage with a minimal intention to make this a lasting union, enters into a valid, although possibly not fruitful (cf. IL, 34), sacrament. Presumably, the title "sacrament" would only be applied to baptized christians. But would it also apply to non-baptized persons or non-christians? In terms of "jurisdiction" this is admittedly an irrelevant question. But the crux of the matter, as the bishops recognized, is not really baptism at all, but faith. The situation of the baptized but non-believing person(s) is the pastoral problem the bishops were addressing. Their concerns were not so much juridical (is this a valid sacrament) as ecclesial (what is the Church doing in such a situation: a variation on the problem of scandal).

In short, the crucial issue raised at the Synod was not faced in FC. It was not even admitted that the issue should be looked into or studied. In its place, John-Paul substituted the idea that approaching the Church for the solemnization of marriage vows was itself an indication of some form of recognition that the Church is "doing something" and thus an opportunity for further catechization. The idea is a worthy one, but it fails to address the issue. The pastoral implications of discussing that issue would obviously have been tremendous. What the Pope failed to acknowledge was that the pastoral implications of not addressing it may be even greater.

The final part of this section (FC, 69) provides words of encouragement for all families to work together and help in pastoral care throughout married life. This applies especially to young, i.e. newly married, couples who still have a great deal to learn about the experience of living the entire project which is married life. Older married couples can have a large role in this pastoral care and the entire community should help new families to acceppt new life (children) as a gift from the Lord.

The second section of Part IV attempts to outline "Structures of Family Pastoral Care". There is nothing new or striking in this text since it simply recounts what is an already existing situation. A couple small details may deserve mention insofar as they demonstrate the Pope's attitude present in the rest of the document. The first is in FC, 70 on "The ecclesial community and in particular the parish". This simply takes note of various organizations within the Church which are dedicated to studying and helping the family. A comment made in passing, however, is indicative of an idea we have already seen. "Communion with the universal Church does not hinder, but rather

marital validity, the result would inevitably lead to a broadening of the grounds for annulment. In the juridical approach to marriage, such an idea would probably not be acceptable.

guarantees and promotes the substance and originality of the various particular churches". The criterion here seems to speak of more than unity and imply the notion of conformity.

After a brief recognition of "The family" (FC, 71) as a source of pastoral care and concern, the final section turns to "Associations of families for families" (FC, 72). This incorporates most of the substance of Prop. 39, on the same topic, but it also goes further in giving some suggestions on what these associations can accomplish. One idea is that they can develop "knowledge of the problems connected with the responsible regulation of fertility in accordance with natural methods that are in conformity with human dignity and the teaching of the Church". Not only has John-Paul made one more plea for his moral position in this matter, he has also endorsed the whole Natural Family Planning movement. Considering the points made earlier and the development of events we have noted, this was no surprise.

The following section then moves to "Agents of the Pastoral Care of the Family". These are basically: bishops and priests (FC, 73), religious (74), lay specialists (75) and the entire media structure (76). The first discussion contains more than one might expect, as words of encouragement appear to be transformed into words of warning. After a fleeting mention of the role of bishops as principally responsible for pastoral care in the diocese and a remark about the new "Pontifical Council for the Family"[206], John-Paul turns his attention to priests and deacons and then to theologians. All of these persons are reminded to "be in full harmony with the authentic magisterium of the Church", and theologians in particular are given the specific advice "to recall that the proximate and obligatory norm in teaching the faith — also concerning family matters — belongs to the hierarchical magisterium". All this is necessary, it is said, to promote "legitimate pluralism".

These final words of FC, 73 remind us about the warning against "religious pluralism" present in IL, 21 that was said to constitute a threat to the Catholic family: "the plurality arises as much as anything from rejection of or dissension from the teaching of the magisterium, especially in the domain of sexual morality". However, it was not from this place but rather from IL, 48 that the expressions are taken. The last paragraph (in Latin, the last 3 in English) of FC, 73 is identical to the last paragraph of IL, 48. Again, it is not verbatim (e.g. IL: *genuinum pluralismum* becomes FC: *legitimum pluralismum*), but it may just as well have been.

The point here is not the employment of a previously existing text. If we could not refer to, summarize, borrow from or quote historical sources, our theology would hardly be able to progress. Rather, it is what

---

206. As we have already noted, this was not really a "new" idea or organisation. Cf. *supra*, note 166.

source and how it is used that is significant. The mentality of the IL has already been exposed, and it is evident that John-Paul agrees with it entirely[207]. The Magisterium is the only agency in the Church that has access to truth and creative thought. Priests are spokesmen for the Magisterium and theologians are its appointed defenders. Criticism and questioning have no place in this structure, even if it is a critique of the Magisterium being consistent with itself.

An example of that call for consistency can be given in reaction to the following number. FC, 74 is addressed to "Men and women religious" and their part in the care of the family. In what is an otherwise predictable text, we come accross a small point that was perhaps an accident but more likely a sign of the non-integration of conciliar theology. It is observed that men and women religious, by their consecration to God "are witnesses to that universal charity which, through chastity (*castitatem*, AAS, p. 172) embraced for the kingdom of heaven makes them even more available..." The term chastity is used here, in parallel with the traditional names for religious vows, as equivalent to celibacy. It is the state of celibacy, not being married, that provides the religious with the time "to be available". However, designating this with the traditional term can undermine the broader meaning of chastity as a dynamic virtue oriented to the integration of human sexuality in the whole life project, specifically in GS, 49 the marital project. It is not reducible to the "rational control of" or abstention from sexual-genital relations. Married persons practice chastity; and because virtue is oriented to the whole of christian life, they practice "chastity for the kingdom". The distinction between virtue and vow might be better respected by a different vocabulary.

FC, 75, on "Lay specialists" is a terse paragraph, half of which is a quote from one of John-Paul's previous addresses. It serves little more purpose than assigning a place for non-clerics to exercise their competence — and keeping them in that place. Similarly composed primarily of quotations (from Paul VI as well as John-Paul II) is FC, 76 on the "Recipients and agents of social communications". This is a section worth reading if one has never been exposed to problems concerning the media. However, its brevity is misleading and one should not look upon these throughts as the complete word on what in reality is an extremely complex issue. The message of FC itself is a rather paternalistic one: parents should control the use of the media and safeguard their children.

207. The fact that John-Paul II agrees with the ideas found in the IL does not imply that this is his only source. It has been evident from the beginning of his pontificate that the Pope sees theologians as the servants of the Magisterium. Here it is a simple matter of the thought of John-Paul and that of the IL coinciding perfectly. Any contribution which the bishops may have attempted to make in between the two (and we saw that the change in Prop. 23, placing all responsibility upon the theologians to conform, mitigated that contribution in any case) was a mere intervention.

Even though their own comment was brief in the Propositions (26, c), the bishops limited themselves to the parents' role in the use of the elements of communication with an aim to their children's socialization[208]. The solution to media problems will not be found in controlling the media itself. Such a task is not only impossible, it would be repressive and counterproductive. Rather, there is a desperate need for educational programs to teach a critical use of the media for adults as well as children. This is just one more project which deserves full time commitment and not simply an easy statement of words.

The final section of Part IV now comes to the "difficult cases". Structurally speaking it is significant that this has been left to the end of FC and not incorporated into the body of its — sometimes doctrinal — development The Propositions had attempted to combine theory and practice, even and especially in the difficult cases. But FC resembles the traditional approach in first laying out pure doctrine and then dealing with exceptions, all of which might be classified as deviant.

There are four sub-divisions here: particular circumstances (FC, 77), mixed marriages (78), irregular situations (FC, 79 introduces a five part treatment in numbers 80-84), and those without a family (85). The first is basically a rewording of Section 14 of the Propositions (31-33) along with an extended reflection on old age. At the end of a long list of the trials and tribulations of the elderly, it is written, "these are the circumstances in which, as the Synod fathers suggested, it is easier to help people understand and live the lofty aspects of the spirituality of marriage and the family". A search through the Propositions does not reveal what might be the source for this reflection, particularly not in Section 17 on "Family Spirituality" (Props. 36-38). One has the impression from FC of a spirituality of detachment which becomes "easier" in old age. This contrasts with the bishops' notion of a spirituality of engagement based on the commandment to love.

"Mixed marriages" (FC, 78) is the second topic considered to be a "difficult case" and can be compared with Prop. 19. In general, there is a positive evaluation of the thoughts which the bishops brought to the Synod: a recognition of and non-condemnatory attitude toward what is becoming a more common practice, an appreciation for the ecumenical aspects of mixed marriages, and an awareness of some of the potential difficulties. The last are mainly three in number. First, there is the question of freedom to practice one's religion. Prop. 19, c had urged that neither partner use undue force against the religious pursuasion of the

---

208. Prop. 33, on "the politically divided family", also observes that "since spokespersons for various beliefs often enter the home through the media, *the family* right from the beginning should be choosy about these 'guests' and *in common discussion* separate the good from the bad" (emphasis added). While the topic of Prop. 33 is not specifically about the media, it does relate to its importance. Note the ethic which the bishops are using. It is more educative and based upon dialogue than the paternalistic idea of FC, 76.

other either to covert them or impede their practice. FC, 78 is somewhat vague on specifying that the respect for religious freedom is reciprocal. Secondly, there is the issue of the baptism and religious upbringing of children by the Catholic partner. Both documents state that this should be pursued "as far as possible". This constitutes a realistic step forward from more traditional policy without giving up the idea that the Catholic partner has special responsibilities.

Thirdly, there is the issue of the celebration of the ceremony. John-Paul relies heavily on already existing documents and norms, especially with respect to the question of intercommunion. He also writes that, "with regard to the liturgical and canonical form of marriage, ordinaries can make wide use of their faculties to meet various necessities". This is all very well and good. But in Prop. 19, b it appears that the bishops had asked for more:

> Because conditions vary around the world, it seems useful to review the laws on mixed marriage with a view to granting bishops' conferences a greater power in setting norms for this type of marriage...

The statement made in FC, 78 is not a response to this request. It is a mere recognition of existing faculties governing liturgical celebration. Again, a specific request of the Synod had been passed over.

The third difficulty to be discussed for "pastoral action" is the problem of irregular situations". There are five in number. The introductory statement (FC, 79) gives the impression that the Synod had packaged all these together. We have seen that they did not do this, but handled each problem as it arose. Nevertheless, we must attend to John-Paul's "decisions" on these questions.

"Trial marriages" (FC, 80) and "De facto free unions" (FC, 81) were handled in Propositions 40 and 41 respectively. As for the first, John-Paul more or less takes over the Proposition — complete with a recognition of the need to study this phenomenon more deeply, which the bishops had suggested — but adds one argument against the practice, namely that, because it is a reflection of the Christ-Church relationship, marriage between two baptized persons can only be indissoluble. Although the Pope sided with the amended version of the Proposition in being cautious about actually calling this a marriage[209], he evidently believes that there really is a "marriage" present here. Because of his

---

209. Cf. *supra*, p. 291. The original expression was, "persons living in a marriage which is called experimental"; the amended version was, "persons living in a union which is called experimental marriage". We speculated that the change was due to a disagreement about what to call this phenomenon, whether or not to dignify it by calling it a marriage or simply to call it a union. In any case, taking Props. 40 & 41 together, the first appears to be speaking of what is really a trial marriage, i.e., one in which the promise of lastingness has not been made. The bishops obviously did not agree with this type of marriage, but called for more investigation before a solution could be found.

notion that any mutual commitment is a response to the will of God (FC, 68) and thus *de facto* a marriage which is also a sacrament for baptized persons, there is no way to "avoid" the character of indissolubility. One has the impression, by contrast, that the bishops believed in a certain role for human freedom in making the marital commitment. In that line of thought, indissolubility is something of a problematic. In FC, it is a foregone conclusion, simply in the nature of things, the plan of God (natural law).

The second irregular situation is the "de facto free union". The beginning of FC, 81 resembles the Proposition in noting that there can be various kinds of such unions and surrounding circumstances which are their cause. However, the rest of the papal text alternates between repeating what is in Prop. 41 and what is in IL, 93. The latter document places more emphasis upon the immaturity of these persons and the need for direct intervention. The Synod had brought out the need to search for the causes of these situations and deal with the more subtle problem of a loss of respect for marriage as an institution. FC combines the two but contributes nothing new. Prop. 41 is a better text.

"Catholics in civil marriages" is the next irregular situation to be dealt with (FC, 82), and it is something of a new aspect. The Synod had not given this any commentary in the Propositions, although one might justifiably raise the issue of betrothal ceremonies and the possibility of welcoming civil marriages into the Church as a first phase of catechesis. The latter was not specifically dealt with, nor does it seem to lie behind the Pope's thoughts here. Nevertheless, what he is writing about is perhaps becoming more widespread[210]. John-Paul apparently felt the need to express his disapproval. That was hardly a surprise, but the point seems to be even more explicit: pastors are reminded that they may not admit these people to the sacraments.

The next two situations concern separated or divorced persons, those who have not remarried (FC, 83) and those who have (FC, 84). The first begins by taking note of the reasons which might lead to the "breakdown of a valid marriage. These include mutual lack of understanding and the inability to enter into interpersonal relationships". There are numerous persons, clerics, theologians and canon lawyers included, who would question how one could speak of these factors and "valid marriage" in the same breath. The Pope presumes that a valid marriage can exist

---

210. The introduction of the issue of civilly married Catholics is somewhat superficial. Simply touching upon the question neither takes account of the really large numbers of people involved nor admits the delicate theological questions at stake. As for the first, there is the phenomenon of a drastically declining rate of church weddings in many African countries. See, A. HASTINGS, *Christian Marriage in Africa*, London, 1973. As for the second, there is the meaning of the phrase (pointed out by the bishops in the context of the need for faith in Prop. 12,d) "a valid marriage between baptized persons is always a sacrament". Does this apply to civil marriage?

without an interpersonal relationship. One wonders what happened to the "personalism" that is referred to every time there is talk about contraception. One may also wonder what happened to the analogies of the God-People, Christ-Church relationships. If marriage is a sacrament because it mirrors these love relationships, then it has to be a (love) relationship itself. If there is no ability to enter into a relationship (and some would say if there is no will to do so or if there is a total withdrawal from it) where is the sacrament? Where is the marriage? Where is the consistency in theological argumentation?

The inconsistency of this argumentation is frustrating and can perhaps explain the confusion and dissatisfaction that many have experienced with the thought of John-Paul II. When he has to establish sacramentality, he is a "personalist" and believes in marriage as relationship. When he has to prohibit divorce or remarriage, apparently *ratum et consumatum* (contract) is sufficient. The price of consistency would be heavy, for it would demand a fundamental rethinking of the basic concepts. The bishops saw the problem and called for more study and investigation. Whether or not John-Paul is sensitive to the problem, we may never know. We do know that he is not willing to discuss it in public.

The question of divorced-remarried persons was decided upon by the time of the Pope's "Closing Homily" — and obviously long before that. FC, 84 is therefore rather predictable in content. The text itself basically follows that of Prop. 14[211], with two exceptions. There is no mention of Prop. 14, f in which the bishops had called for a "new and extensive" study taking account of the practice of the Eastern Churches. Secondly, the repetition of the Proposition is broken at one point, between what would have been 14, d and 14, e.

In the English translation, the intervening text constitutes the seventh and eight paragraphs[212]. The new material has two parts. First, there is a quote from the Pope's own "Homily" (nr. 7), which we have already discussed, concerning the condition of total continence for readmission to the sacraments. Then, lest any doubt remain in one's mind about his opinion on these things, John-Paul becomes about as explicit as possible.

Similarly, the respect due to the sacrament of matrimony, to the couples themselves and their families, and also to the community of the faithful[213]

211. Again, to say that this text follows another is not to imply a verbatim quote. The occurrence of (multiple) translations has caused frequent differences in the Latin text. As we have studied these texts, we have become increasingly struck by a curious use of words. For instance, in the (questionable) remark that not admitting divorced-remarried persons to the eucharist is based upon Sacred Scripture, the Latin version of FC (*AAS*, p. 185) uses the term *Sacris Litteris*. Does this refer to the epistles in particular? Why does it depart from the simple mention of Scripture?

212. As usual, the Latin paragraph structure is different. There, the introduction of new material begins in the middle of the fourth paragraph and includes all of the fifth.

213. B. HÄRING, *The Synod of Bishops on the Family: Pastoral Reflections*, in *Studia*

forbids any pastor for whatever reason or pretext even of a pastoral nature to perform ceremonies of any kind for divorced people who remarry. Such ceremonies would give the impression of the celebration of a new, sacramentally valid marriage and would thus lead people into error concerning the indissolubility of a validly contracted marriage.

According to this, there appears to be absolutely no possibility for considering the issue any further. In the end, the reasoning is based upon impressions, scandal and the difficulty that would result in having to explain a change in practice.

Ultimately, this issue is going to have to be faced more directly. That will not simply be a form of accommodation to persons who do not believe in or do not respect marriage as an institution that is intended to be lasting. We are not speaking about persons who go from one relationship to another, changing partners like they might change a place of residence. Rather, we are speaking — and the Church must pastorally address the situation — of persons who sincerely entered and attempted to make a marital union work. While all the legal details had fit neatly into place, however, the relationship which was being called marriage either did not develop into the meaningful, interpersonal communion of love upon which its sacramentality is supposedly based, or for one reason or another the relationship came to an end or became humanly intolerable. Many such persons are victims, suffering from either abandonment or their own lack of moral strength. But, because of rigorist juridical practice and/or an unwillingness to instill into the community at large an attitude of reconciliation and understanding, those persons who are unable to "prove the grounds for annulment" become victims a second time as the ecclesial institution forces them to lead a celibate life. We cannot help but feel that the Church, as the People of God, is ready to accept a change in this practice. By taking the so-called hard line, the Church as institution is losing an opportunity to become a symbol for the compassion of Christ. Finally, we should not ignore the possibility that refusing to find some acceptable solution to this urgent pastoral problem will itself further undermine the credibility of the Church, especially in its pastoral activity as a means of reconciliation.

The last topic under the heading of "difficult cases" is a compassionate understanding of "those without a family" (FC, 85). This is a largely neglected group of persons to whom the Church should open itself as a family. But even more, christians should work socially and politically to alleviate the situation of those who are the victims of poverty, injustice

---

Moralia 19 (1981) 231-257, p. 237, points out that between the first and final version of Prop. 14, c a phrase was omitted which would have added to the reasons for not admitting divorced-remarried persons to the eucharist: that "good people" would be offended if they were. This, according to Häring, would have sounded very pharisaical and was therefore eliminated.

and oppression. This worthy theme should have come at the very beginning of the section on difficult cases and been extended to the so-called "irregularities".

The apostolic exhortation is concluded with a long paragraph (FC, 86) that gives encouragement, repeats the basic norm (God's plan) two more times, asks for cooperation between all concerned people of good will (as long as their pluralism is legitimate) and invokes the Holy Family whose "life was passed in anonymity and silence in a little town in Palestine". The text ends in a prayer and an apostolic blessing.

A. The Exhortation and the Propositions

As we have already explicitly stated, neither the Church nor the synodal process are democratic in the literal sense or in any way parliamentary. There is no imperative that the Pope must take the advice of the bishops in Synod or incorporate their findings and suggestions into (papal) magisterial teaching. These are the presumptions of the juridical view of the Church and its hierarchy. It is a traditional view, complete with its own reasoning, justification, and even to some extent we might add, necessity.

However, a strict interpretation of this view of the Church, in and of itself, would probably make the institution of the Synod of Bishops superfluous. That process, which grew out of the spirit of collegiality in Vatican II, has never really achieved definable status. Rather, it is always characterized as "advisory". The presumption has been that, although juridically totally independent and capable of acting alone, the papal magisterium needs the input of the experience of the universal Church in order to act and to speak in a way which would be relevant to the People of God. Since the Synod exists for the purpose of continuing the process of renewal set forth in Vatican II, drawing out the implications of conciliar theology and addressing pastoral issues and problems in light of that theology, its field of competence is directly related to magisterial teaching. If we were to apply the juridical view literally to the status of the Synod, it is hard to see how it could exercise its pastoral function. What would be the point of offering advice if the content of that advice is not taken seriously? However, if the Synod is to have any purpose or meaning, it should be possible to discern what impact it might have achieved. This is the question we must now examine.

The most explicit source for defining the accomplishment of the 1980 Synod is the text of the 43 Propositions. Although these statements did not achieve complete precision because of the rapid process in which they were drawn up and finalized, their content more or less represents the specifically synodal contribution. The preparatory documents were not synodal even in a loose sense, for they were almost purely the work of a few officials operating out of a very specific and "doctrinally oriented" perspective. We have already seen how the Propositions differed from those texts in both spirit and content. In the end, the bishops forged their own consensus and presented the result of their experience and pastoral practice to be considered for future development.

It has been demonstrated that FC exhibited a very close reliance upon the text of the Propositions. Many of the episcopal statements were substantially taken over and their insights incorporated into the papal teaching. However, the bishops had also made a number of very specific requests and suggested the initiation of certain studies before pastoral teaching or practice should further evolve. Some of these were taken into account. For instance, FC, 80 notes that it would be "useful to investigate the causes" of the phenomenon of trial marriage, including its psychological and sociological aspects, where Prop. 40 had also made that suggestion as preliminary to offering any concrete solutions. However, whereas Prop. 25 had originally called for more study, exchange of information and educational programs to promote scientifically established methods of regulating fertility, FC, 35 takes over the amended version of the Proposition that specifies only the "natural methods". John-Paul also expands this very explicitly, noting that these are based upon "the rhythms of woman's fertility", and gives the norm for respecting "the structure and finalities of the conjugal act". The bishops had not gone so far. In fact, the Propositions clearly recognized that this was to some extent a controverted issue. In the original version of Prop. 23, the bishops sided with Pope Paul VI in recognizing that the Magisterium should devote itself to providing "a fuller, more organic and more synthetic explanation" of the Church's teaching in this area. The amended version of that text limited this task to the work of theologians, and while FC, 31 expands upon this theme, FC, 73 is very explicit in warning priests and theologians to conform their thought to that of the Magisterium, as if no further study were needed. FC gave the impression that the Synod fully and absolutely endorsed the teaching of HV. The nuance and subtlety of the bishops' position in the question of regulating fertility had been lost and their predominant emphasis upon the social dimensions of this issue — especially the condemnation of government intervention in the family — was allowed to function as a judgment on the individual (private) moral issue itself.

Other issues raised by the Propositions were mentioned in FC but were then substantially changed. Prop. 43 had called for episcopal conferences to create pastoral directories to "explain Church teaching and discipline in a manner suitable for varying circumstances". In a separate place (Prop. 35), there was also a call for the conferences and dioceses to draw up guidelines for marriage preparation programs. FC, 66 recognizes these requests but contextually limits the scope of such "directories" to the preparation programs. It appears that the bishops had something else in mind. First, the directories to be drawn up by the episcopal conferences should encompass all Church teaching and discipline. FC presumes that the teaching in these areas should be determined by central authority. Secondly, the "suitability for varying circumstances" is clearly a reference for more inculturation. Teaching and discipline must be transmitted in ways that are appropriate for the local church situation. FC either does not recognize the distinction or has chosen not to deal with it.

The call for inculturation is not merely a singular interpretation of one small part of the Propositions. It is a recurrent theme throughout the text that parallels the episcopal call for more autonomy as well. Beginning with the recognition of the *sensus fidei* as a legitimate source for theological reflection and pastoral practice, the bishops take seriously the signs of the times which must be dealt with and an understanding of gradualism in order to construct educational and pastoral programs. This had influenced all of their thinking, including both global issues and their contextual expression. Thus, the need to understand the role of faith in the sacrament (Prop. 12) led to a call for local studies to investigate this phenomenon (Prop. 18, a) and the need for the local churches to have faculties which "would allow cultural adaptation and the creation of norms dealing with the celebration of marriage and its validity" (Prop. 18, b). In response, FC, 10 echoes the Pope's closing "Homily" in its concern for "the principle of communion with the universal Church" by stating that further study must pass the scrutiny of the "appropriate departments of the Roman curia". The papal reservations about inculturation are also evident in FC, 67 on the cultural adaptation for marital celebration following "norms issued by the Apostolic See" and FC, 70 on the local structures for pastoral care of the family being in "communion with the universal Church".

Similarly, Prop. 19, b called for a review of the laws on mixed marriages "with a view to granting bishops' conferences a greater power in setting norms for this type of marriage". While FC, 78 takes over a great deal of the substance of Prop. 19, it severely limits episcopal authority to determining "the liturgical and canonical form of marriage", faculties which the exhortation recognizes that local ordinaries already possess. Finally, at one point, in response to the pastoral problem of the growing number of broken marriages and the need to concretely instill an appreciation of the permanence of sacramental union, the Synod again made an appeal to local episcopal conferences suggesting that they might introduce some type of betrothal ceremony, presumably adapted to local customs. This suggestion received no response in FC.

Next, there are the synodal suggestions which have apparently had little or no influence upon the papal document. The first of these dealt with the relation between faith and the sacrament of marriage. Prop. 12, a had specifically called for an investigation to determine "to what extent the validity of this sacrament requires the faith of the contracting parties", and 12,d stated that,

We must investigate further if this statement applies to those who have lost the faith: a valid marriage between baptized persons is always a sacrament. The statement has pastoral and juridical consequences. Further we must investigate the pastoral criteria for discerning the couple's faith and the relationship between the intention of doing what the Church does and the minimal intention of believing with the Chruch.

We have seen that FC,68 almost completely refuses to pursue this issue. The bishops had been signaling an urgent pastoral problem which they felt needed further study and rethinking. In his exhortation, the Pope was willing to settle for the position that as long as there was no "explicit and formal rejection" of what the Church does in the sacrament of marriage, there was no problem.

Along the same lines, Prop. 14 exhibited a real willingness to make distinctions with respect to divorced and remarried persons and approached this issue with a great deal of pastoral solicitude. In his response (FC,84), the Pope agreed with the notion that these persons should still be treated as members of the Church. However, whereas the bishops appeared to be searching for a pastoral solution to this problem, the Pope was adamant and rigorous in defining what he felt to be acceptable pastoral practice. There was no possibility left open for such persons to be admitted to the sacraments while they maintained this second conjugal union, even if in good conscience there was some doubt about the validity of the first union. Furthermore, the bishops had taken an even more serious step in suggesting that a new study be launched in the pastoral care for this situation which "should take into account the practices of the Eastern Churches" (Prop. 14,f). This suggestion is not mentioned in FC, which probably signifies effectively closing off the issue for further investigation.

Two more concrete suggestions from the bishops also found no place in the papal response to the Synod. Prop. 12,e had proposed that the question of the relationship between faith and the sacrament not only needed further study but also that the observations of the bishops should be taken into account in the new code of canon law. Then, Prop. 16 had suggested that "while taking into account the differing vocations of men and women, the Church must promote as much as possible in her own life equal rights and dignity". Neither of these synodal conclusions are taken up in FC.

To read the Propositions is to encounter a spirit of inquiry and pastoral sensitivity to some of the more perplexing issues facing the Church with respect to marriage and family life. There are numerous calls for further study and investigations, and some concrete suggestions that would open the way to a fundamental reevaluation of Church teaching and practice: inculturation; faith and the sacrament; remarriage and the Eastern Churches; the rights and dignity of women in the

Church; and the autonomy of local episcopal conferences to draw up guidelines for determining the faith of the engaged couple, for sacramental celebration and validity of mixed marriages, and for "explaining Church teaching and discipline in a manner suitable for varying circumstances". One readily gets the impression that the bishops did not see their task to be one of providing solutions to problems but rather one of articulating what those problems were in the context of the pastoral experience of the Church. In studying and applying the theological insights of Vatican II, many areas of contemporary Church life, not the least of which is the experience of and ministry to marriage and family life, needed to be worked out and sometimes completely rethought.

Two particular contributions which the 1980 Synod, especially in the content of its 43 Propositions, made to contemporary theology in this area were in the form of clarifying issues and raising consciousness. The first had to do with the issue of marriage as a sacrament: how does the Church define this sacrament; what is its relation with faith, with law, with cultural values and customs; how can the Church, knowledgeable of the law of gradualism and the process of conversion, minister to the couple before, during and after the actual ceremonial event; what can be said about the special circumstances of mixed marriages, marital breakdown, and the cultural phenomena of trial marriage and unions which are not legally validated?

The second contribution dealt with the social dimensions of marriage and family life. Whereas most previous teaching on the matter had been rather privatized and concerned itself primarily with the inner workings of the family relationships, the Synod exhibited a much broader orientation. Not only is the good of society completely bound up with the well-being of marriage and the family, but the reciprocal relationships between society and the family are inextricably tied together. Positively, marriage and the family as institution are expressed in a cultural manner, conforming to as well as influencing the values, customs and norms of a given culture. It is also the transmittor of those values, etc., because it is a fundamental agent of socialization. Negatively, this relationship is the cause for limitation upon and threat to marriage and family life. Social, political and economic conditions have a tremendous impact upon family life which may make it impossible for persons to live the values which they hold from either social or religious conviction. It was almost exclusively within this social context that the Synod approached the question of the "transmission and safeguarding of life". Taking their cue from both GS and HV, the bishops presume the doctrine of responsible parenthood and go a step further in concentrating upon the social aspects of the question. While the final version of Props. 20-25 left much to be desired, situated in the context of the whole of their findings the Synod's position on the regulation of fertility is hardly absolutist. The single issue which received strong words was the threat of government intervention in the lives and decisions of the individual couple. Unfortunately, this single aspect became distorted because of the concern of some to repeat Paul VI's position on contraception.

Reading the apostolic exhortation which was supposedly a response to the Synod, the same impressions are not created. There is no spirit of inquiry, no initiation of further study or willingness to rethink fundamental presuppositions. The Propositions which represented the final conclusions of the Synod are represented selectively and interpretively. There is nothing taken positively from the Propositions which did not represent what was already established, official teaching and practice. The few controversial issues touched upon, such as the relation between faith and the sacrament of marriage, are answered with traditional solutions that hardly acknowledge the sense of urgency exhibited in the bishops' findings and suggestions. The need experienced by the bishops for greater inculturation in teaching and practicing the faith are given recognition but then placed under the conditions of conformity with the universal Church or the decisions of Roman authority. The calls for greater autonomy in legislation and forming guidelines are given no response except where there is an already existing recognition of episcopal faculties, such as the liturgical and canonical form of the marriage ceremony.

In short, one searches desperately for something in FC that emanated specifically from the Synod and was not already part of pre-synodal teaching or practice. The single "new idea" which appears to have been taken over from the Propositions is the attitude toward divorced and remarried persons, recognizing them as baptized Catholics who should participate in the life of the Church as fully as possible, albeit denying participation in the sacramental life of the community. Although this is a somewhat revolutionary idea, one can argue that it was an inevitable development in pastoral practice if the Church is to take seriously its role of reconciliation. Even so, while the bishops appeared to remain somewhat vague about the eventual outcome of such practice (Prop. 14,d: sacramental participation can be restored when divorced and remarried persons show themselves penitent and "sincerely pledge themselves to a way of life that does not contradict the indissolubility of the sacrament of marriage"), FC,84 removes any hint of vagueness and restores the traditional position that such persons are obliged to separate or, if that is not possible, to live in a state of absolute continence. It remains to be seen what the consequences of this "new" attitude will be. But as envisioned in FC, there is officially no room for evolution in pastoral practice.

The substance of these summary remarks leads to a rather clear and fundamental question: what was the purpose of the 1980 Synod? It appears to us that FC could have been written even if the Synod had not taken place. If one were to judge these events from a strictly "doctrinal" or juridical point of view, a case might be made that Church teaching is continuous and one should not expect "change" to occur in that teaching because of an episcopal Synod. But doctrine and teaching, the exercise of the Magisterium as Pope John XXIII saw it, is primarily pastoral. It must address real situations in a way that not only reflects the Gospel but also relates to and is understandable by the People of God.

The bishops, more or less representing the universal Church, had gathered in Synod to address a specifically pastoral issue: marriage and family life in the contemporary world. In doing so, they each contributed their pastoral experience on the state of the question. They articulated the problems which had to be faced and indicated some directions in which pastoral care should develop. Most significantly, the bishops called for further study and investigation on issues about which, in the present state of affairs, they at least implied that present teaching and practice were inadequate. The specific requests that they put forth in the Propositions were enunciated thoughtfully and calmly, yet not without a certain sense of urgency. In the last analysis, what the bishops had sought was an adequate response to genuine pastoral needs. In reading the apostolic exhortation, virtually none of these requests are fulfilled, nor are the suggestions for further study given credibility. In the end, while the event itself focused attention on the topic and provided a display of unity and collegiality among the hierarchy of the Church, the impact of the 1980 Synod on papal teaching was negligible.

B. The Theology of Marriage and the Family in Post-Conciliar Perspective

All this said about the substance of the 1980 Synod and its ultimate aftermath in the papal response, FC, we must not neglect the historical context in which these events took place. The Synod exists as an outgrowth of Vatican II, not simply as a forum for episcopal collegiality but more importantly as a vehicle for implementing the teachings of that Council. We have observed, at least in the content of the 43 Propositions, that the bishops of the 1980 Synod were inspired by conciliar theology and demonstrated a willingness to struggle with the problem of how to apply that theology to concrete pastoral needs. But we have also concluded that the results of the Synod itself have had little if any impact upon magisterial teaching as represented in the papal response. There remains the question of the present state of conciliar theology in the area of marriage and the family.

At the beginning of this study we listed twenty points which were believed to characterize the teaching of GS on marriage and family life. These included aspects of fundamental presuppositions such as the meaning of institutions, plurality in marriage and family life, the use of biblical terms and theology, etc., as well as more specific contributions on the relational meaning of marriage, the functional subordination of procreation to conjugal love, and the value oriented approach to the concept of responsible parenthood and the conflicts with which this project might be forced to contend in daily life. We also observed that there was a last minute attempt to change the direction of GS,47-52 by the introduction of four *modi* said to emanate from the papal office. The substance of these *modi* were characteristic of a certain school of thought, and, although their impact upon the conciliar teaching was highly mitigated, the ideas they represented were not laid to rest. Instead, this school, which might best be characterized as representing essentialist theology, maintained an idea of marriage and the family that could be said to have inspired the *modi* in the first place.

The main lines of this school of thought perpetuated the use of biological norms in sexual and conjugal morality, viewed the marital bond as an ontological reality containing its own intrinsic characteristics and conditions, implicitly reinstated the doctrine of the hierarchy of the ends of marriage, and dealt with the whole of human sexuality and the virtue of chastity that governs it as a mechanistic reflex which can and must be controlled simply by rational acts of the will. The foundation for this approach had traditionally been called "natural law". Since that terminology had become unacceptable, having been shunned by the Council itself, the ideas were eventually expressed in terms of the plan of God or God's will. This presupposed an absolute, essential pattern for human existence "intended" by God and imposed upon reality in the act of creation. The "plan" is thus taken as morally normative. This is not simply theoretical or ideal, but concrete and applicable in every instance. This rests upon the (classicist) view of a world that is basically stable and predictable. The arrival at moral and disciplinary norms then becomes a simple matter of deciphering the biblical account of creation and incorporating the data of experience which is compatible with the foregone conclusions. Ostensibly, the method is deductive. However, a very specific formulation of contemporary "experience" is allowed to play a submerged yet important role in elaborating the plan of God. The resulting picture is very much colored by Western ideals and rationalist philosophy. Elements of experience which deviate from the pattern are considered *ipso facto* evil and a threat to the existing situation.

Hence, marriage exists not primarily as a human relationship but as a functional, procreative unit. It is total, exclusive, lasting and procreative by design. The ontological status of the marital bond provides both a ground for elaborating the normative structure of conjugal behavior and a rationale for the normativeness itself. For instance, because the bond is an ontological reality it is unbreakable. Because it is part of the plan of creation, it pre-exists as a structured institution. The role of conjugal love is always subordinated to the institution. Therefore, when elaborating the "good points of christian marriage", one can speak of conjugal love or the institution of marriage interchangeably. Finally, the social dimensions of marriage and family life, whether actively described as their role in society or passively as the effect of existing conditions upon the unit, are incidental. Society, culture, history, politics and economics are appended considerations which never effectively alter the ontological scheme of things. They are even inconsequential on the level of moral decision making except when they create conditions "beyond one's control" which may affect human freedom or aggravate human weakness.

This view of marriage and the family is pre-conciliar. However, it did not pass away after the Council. It had a real but subtle influence in HV, where it has already been shown by others that the role of three of the four *modi* was significant in the formulation of the text of that encyclical. Whereas Paul VI utilized the concepts of that school of thought, he also had an appreciation for the teaching of the Council. We can speculate that it is for this reason that he never ventured to return to the topic of marriage and the family in a substantive way after the HV event. But he did call for a "fuller, more organic and synthetic explanation" of the Church's teaching to be elaborated by the Magisterium itself. The nature of the encyclical and the very specificity of its topic force us to classify this papal letter as a transitory teaching concerned more for the implications of a shift in the Church's position on the regulation of fertility than it is a definitive statement of that position itself. Pope Paul VI was not ready to change his thinking on the specific topic of contraception and probably accurately assessed the social dimensions of the question to the extent that he appreciated the complexity of the issue.

In contrast to what might here be called Paul VI's caution in at least implicitly respecting the contribution of the Second Vatican Council to the theology of marriage and the family, the essentialist view of some "interpreters" held firm to their perspective and resisted every attempt to read GS in non-traditionalist terms. Every statement and judgment from Rome on questions touching upon conjugal life and sexual morality exhibited the pre-conciliar mentality. Even where GS was quoted, its texts were used selectively and sometimes even inaccurately. This was not so much an effort to reinterpret the conciliar teaching as it was to substantiate the belief that the Council had not really said anything different from what had gone before. It was not so much a manipulation of texts as it was a basic misunderstanding of the teaching contained in those texts. It was a question of interpretation. The fact that a great number of people, including considerable episcopal opinion and a significant majority of theological analysis, did not agree with this interpretation begged for recognition and consideration from the Magisterium itself.

After the death of Paul VI, the opportunity to approach the questions concerning marriage and the family was at hand, and it is no surprise that this came to be the topic for the 1980 Synod, the first to be held after Paul's pontificate. The pastoral concerns were growing more and more urgent and the extent to which many episcopal conferences prepared for the Synod was indicative of a certain amount of enthusiasm and willingness to bring the issues out into the open. However, the preparatory work for the Synod was completely handled by a small group whose influence on the preparatory documents is unmistakable. The changes which took place between the *Lin* and IL clearly show the influence of episcopal reaction, but the main lines of theological interpretation remained the same. If the documents provided for the bishops had been followed literally, the outcome of the Synod would have been very different.

The content of the preparatory documents must be judged in light of the theology of Vatican II. It has been shown that there was a discrepancy between the conciliar perspective and that found in both the *Lin* and IL. The teaching of GS on marriage and the family had been reinterpreted in essentialist terms. Whereas conciliar theology itself had been put forth as a starting point, a fundamental restatement of teaching that was intended to be studied, worked out, applied and adapted to pastoral practice, in short, to evolve, the fate of that theology was submitted to the power of a certain group of interpreters. The re-reading of GS,47-52 was carried out to fit a preordained scheme. The assumption was that nothing had changed at the Council, except perhaps new words for an old doctrine. The ideas were those of Popes Pius XI and XII. The interpretations were made to fit those patterns of thought. The outcome was a restatement of traditionalist thinking. The words, phrases, ideas and insights did not evolve. They were interpreted to fit a previously existing pattern. The process was one of devolution.

What happened in October 1980 was something of a surprise. Not only did many bishops reject the set pattern of the IL, which itself claimed to be merely suggestive and not a schema for conclusion, but they also rejected its presuppositions. The interpretation of conciliar theology which guided the "official" teaching of the Magisterium between 1968 and 1980 and orchestrated its devolution into pre-conciliar thinking was recognized to be not merely inadequate for addressing contemporary problems, but we might even speculate that it was seen to be a cause of some of those problems themselves. The bishops knew that they were facing more than a set of complex issues in marriage and family life. They were also facing a problem of credibility. The language in which the Church was officially speaking was not being understood or accepted by large portions of the faithful. In response, it appears that the bishops themselves, consciously or unconsciously, attempted to resolve this problem by a return to the theological insights of Vatican II. Reading the 43 Propositions, it appears fair to say that in most all but one issue, the question of regulating fertility and the status of previous papal teaching in that area, they were successful.

In one sense, the momentum of devolution had been stopped. Against what might be called overwhelming odds, the bishops went their own way. They articulated the problems in their complexity, they suggested solutions inspired by conciliar theology, and they even singled out areas where they felt more study and possibly even concrete changes were necessary. This was not evident in their closing "Message", a document written before the final version of the Propositions and more closely reflecting the IL. It is clearly evident in the text of the Propositions themselves. When we read that text we can gain a whole new insight into the meaning of John-Paul II's closing "Homily" to the Synod. The bishops had come to Rome to discuss and investigate the pastoral needs of the Church. The Pope had rendered judgments before the episcopal contributions were even considered.

The "Homily" foreshadowed the ultimate papal response to the Synod, FC. That document did not reflect what the bishops had put forth. Rather, it simply restated what was already presumed teaching and Church policy. In some senses it was closer to IL than to the Propositions. If we compare FC and IL we find a number of concrete similarities.

FC,13 - IL,16: on the good points of christian marriage (unity, fidelity, permanence, procreation; cf. IL,29 & 63 on "the logical normal evolution of conjugal love")
FC,19 - IL,32: the marital bond (ontological reality) is a new communion resembling the mystical body of Christ
FC,28 - IL,35: fecundity is the "fruit and sign of conjugal love"
FC,30 - IL,54: the consumer mentality is one reason why persons do not accept the papal teaching on contraception
FC,66 - IL,86-88: on marriage preparation programs
FC,73 - IL,48(21): on legitimate pluralism in the Church
FC,81 - IL,93; on the immaturity of persons in free unions

These similarities are merely specific examples of a much deeper point of comparison. Namely, the theological perspective on marriage and the family which had been operative in Roman circles since the Council and which had attempted to interpret the contribution of Vatican II in pre-conciliar terms was chosen as normative.

It is not our intention here to challenge the prerogatives of the Pope in the fulfillment of his apostolic office. If John-Paul II, or any other Pope, decides to choose one theological perspective over another, this is simply a matter with which the Church and the bishops will have to contend. Papal authority is not at issue here. What is our concern, however, is the meaning or purpose of the synodal process. The Synod appears to have two principal tasks. One is to advise the Pope on practical and pastoral matters so that he can teach effectively for the universal Church. Another is to carry on the work of renewal set forth in Vatican II. Examining the events surrounding the 1980 Synod we have observed that the documents drawn up in preparation for that meeting, though they contained a number of references and quotations from conciliar texts, could have been written had Vatican II never taken place. Similarly, the apostolic exhortation, FC, could have been written had the 1980 Synod not taken place. In response to the first observation, we have seen that the bishops rejected the theology of the *Lin* and IL. In doing so, they reacted to the devolution of the conciliar teaching on marriage and the family and attempted to restate and apply what had been accomplished in GS, 47-52. Unfortunately, this achievement did not significantly effect official teaching. While FC is a response to the Synod, there simply is no forum for response to FC itself.

The advisory status of the Synod is a foregone juridical conclusion. The findings and suggestions of the bishops have no binding force. However, the Synod is a recognized forum for discussion and a structure for the exercise of collegiality. Fulfilling its role not only to advise the Pope but also to continue the work of Vatican II, it is within the context of these episcopal meetings that the evolution and unfolding of conciliar theology is expected to take place. It is incumbent upon the Church, therefore, and especially upon the bishops, to evaluate the work of the various Synods not simply with respect to the papal document given in response to the episcopal event. The meaning and purpose of the Synod, as well as its efficacy or ultimate impact, is to be judged according to how the entire process relates to the achievement of Vatican II and to the daily life of the Chruch. It remains for the People of God, and the bishops in particular, to reflect upon the state of the theology of marriage and the family in the contemporary Church.

APPENDIX

SENSUS GENERALIS CIRCA PROPOSITIONES

Propositio 1

Post disceptationem sive in Aula sive in Circulis Minoribus, Patribus Synodalibus placet ut Summo Pontifici praesententur — praeter documenta «De munere familiae christianae in mundo hodierno», quae in hoc labore synodali adhibita sunt, scilicet Lineamenta, Instrumentum laboris, Relationem introductoriam, Relationem syntheticam post disceptationem in Aula, Relationes Circulorum Minorum earumque discussionem — propositiones quaedam peculiares, quae Patribus maioris momenti visae sunt.

Rogant ergo Patres Synodales Beatissimum Patrem ut, tempore opportuno, Ecclesiae Universae documentum velit offerre de muneribus familiae christianae sicut per Adhortationem Apostolicam *Catechesi tradendae* fecit post Synodum anni 1977.

Hoc sensu votum humiliter proferunt.

Pars I

DE VOLUNTATE DEI
IN PEREGRINATIONE POPULI DEI COGNOSCENDA

1. DE SENSU FIDEI

Propositio 2

Christus Dominus munus suum propheticum usque ad consummationem saeculorum adimplet, *non solum per Pastores sed* «etiam per laicos, quos ideo et testes constituit et sensu fidei et gratia verbi instruit, ut virtus Evangelii in vita quotidiana, familiari et sociali eluceat» (*Lumen Gentium, 35*). Hic «supernaturalis sensus fidei» (*Lumen Gentium, 12*) non in solo consensu christianorum constat. Ecclesia sese dominio magni numeri non subiicit. Christum Dominum sequens veritatem quaerit, non numerum. Conscientiam audit, non potentiam et sic etiam infirmos et deiectos defendit. Qua de causa ex opinionum *tantum* inquisitione et ex statistica sensus fidei erui non potest, quamvis tales cognitiones *ad veritatem melius investigandam*, ad actionem pastoralem recte instituendam et ad signa temporum exploranda pro Ecclesia suum momentum habeant.

Propositio 3

Sensus fidei multum ad profectum fidei confert, i.e. ad illud itinerarium fidei in historia salutis, quo verbum Dei in dies profundius intellegitur et Ecclesia paulatim Spiritus Sancti virtute in omnem veritatem inducitur (cf. *Io.* 16, 13; 14, 26). Ille sensus ergo ibi maxime se manifestat, ubi «recta proficiendi regula» observatur (cf. Vincentius Lir., *Comm.*, cap. 23), i.e. ubi structura sua organica, proportio et relatio veritatum in nexu mysteriorum manet et clarescit (cf. Newman, *Development*). Qua de causa ad eius criteria pertinet cohaerentia profunda cum fide omnium saeculorum (i.e. catholicitas diachronica seu temporalis) et cum universitate fidelium (i.e. catholicitas synchronica seu spatialis): Fides non claudit hominem in aliquod tempus vel spatium, sed eum aperit. Quia catholicus, i.e. universalis, hic sensus semper docilis est erga Ecclesiam universalem eiusque magisterium. Quia autem fides hominem ad «rationabile obsequium» (cf. *Rom* 12, 1) incitat, eius sensus irrationalis non est, sed rationi verae correspondet, illi nempe rationi, quae a Creatore creaturae indita est.

Propositio 4

Sensus fidei fructus est fidei vivae. Qui autem secundum fidem vivunt, non conformantur huic saeculo, sed probant «quid sit bonum et bene placens et perfectum» (*Rom* 12, 2). Fructus spiritus et vita secundum beatitudines eius praesentiam testificant. Qua de causa praesertim apud sanctos invenitur et apud illos pauperes et humiles, de quibus Dominus dixit: «Confiteor tibi, Pater, Domine caeli et terrae, quia abscondisti haec a sapientibus et prudentibus et revelasti parvulis» (*Mt* 11, 25). Exemplar horum pauperum Mater Domini est, cuius «humilitatem respexit» Deus (*Lc* 1, 48). Profectus fidei nonnisi per totam Ecclesiam fieri potest. Quoad res familiares e familiis christianis praesertim pendet, in quibus sacramentum matrimonii experientia fidei realisatur et exponitur. Magisterii hierarchici est hunc sensum fovere et authentice interpretari.

2. DE SIGNIS TEMPORUM

Propositio 5

Signa temporum sunt ipsa «realitas», in qua vivimus in determinatis circumstantiis loci et temporis. Ut eorum significatio dignoscatur et propositum Dei ex iis aliquatenus inveniatur, interpretanda sunt attendendo ad continuitatem historiae salutis prout *eminentiori modo* in Scripturis Veteris et Novi Testamenti manifestantur, ad analogiam fidei, ad Magisterium Ecclesiae et ad rectam humanae prudentiae rationem (*Gaudium et Spes*, 4, 11, 37).

Alia ex his signis quid positivum continent et diversis gradibus praesentiam Dei operantis et mundum per Christum a servitute peccati liberantis apparere faciunt, ut v.gr. maior attentio ad libertatem et personalitatem, ad relationum qualitatem in matrimonio, ad promotionem dignitatis mulieris, ad paternitatem *maternitatemque responsabilem*, ad uberiorem curam circa pueros educandos, *mutuum inter familias auxilium tum in spiritualibus quam in materialibus*, conscientia vividior vocationis ecclesialis familiae eiusque responsabilitatis pro promotione iustitiae, *quae ducit ad transformationem structurarum iniustarum in mundo vigentium.* Alia autem non ex praesentia Dei in historia profluunt, sed ex resistentia peccati contra eius victoriam et exinde non profectum historiae salutis testificant, sed defectum hominis a Deo, i.e. processum degradationis culturatum atque amissionis valorum, ut v.gr. *status paupertatis et miseriae multarum familiarum in mundo ex structuris iniustis proveniens,* divortiorum et abortuum numerus crescens, mentalitas contraceptiva, violentia et iniustitia. Interdum in concretis adiunctis per se contraria etiam permixta esse possunt.

Haec duplicitas et permixtio signorum ex eo provenit, quia secundum mentem Sacrae Scripturae sanctorumque Patrum historia non simpliciter — sicut in philosophia hegeliana — progressus spiritus mundi («Weltgeist») est, qui cum necessitate viam suam dialectice progreditur, sed historia libertatum sibi oppugnantium sive historia «duarum civitatum», i.e. duorum amorum, amoris Dei usque ad contemptum sui et amoris sui ipsius usque ad contemptum Dei (cf. Augustinus, *De civ. Dei).* Quare discretio signorum discretio amorum est. Discretio haec nullo alio modo disci potest nisi educatione ad verum amorem, qui inter duo genera signorum distinguit.

Propositio 6

In mutatione structurarum et mentis (*Gaudium et Spes,* 7), quae hoc saeculo gressu rapido progreditur, Ecclesia invitatur, ut veritatem dynamicam propositi Dei cum homine recogitet. Culturae hucusque ad invicem clausae in mutuam penetrationem intrant et qui sibi procul fuerunt, vicini facti sunt. Ex una parte civilisatio universalis et uniformis (technica-rationalis) exsurgit, ex altera parte pluralismus intra singularum culturarum spatia acrior fit. In hac evolutione sociologica et culturali vita coniugalis et familiaris multas ob causas *celeribus mutationibus obnoxia est ideoque non raro* patitur et *periclitatur.* Ecclesiae est in his rerum adiunctis *novam emergentem culturam a suo initio evangelizare,* praesertim in campo educationis et mediorum communicationis socialis, ut veri valores dignoscantur et «humanismus novus» (*Gaudium et Spes,* 7), hominem non modo a Deo non avertat, sed potius ad Deum convertat. Ecclesiae imprimis locales cooperentur ad novos typos communionis interpersonalis inveniendos tali modo, ut familia locum firmum in nova se evolvendi societate consequatur. Necessaria est educatio continua conscientiae, quae aures hominis interioris aperit et hominem capacem reddit recta sapere et regulas discretionis spirituum in aedificationem Ecclesiae et totius familiae humanae bene applicare, *ita ut familiae possint positivum influxum exercere in creandis structuris mundi iusti et fraterni.*

3. DE GRADUALITATE

Propositio 7

Iniustitiae *quae in personali simul et sociali peccato originem habent,* et quae structuram huius mundi late penetrant, obsistendum est per continuam conversionem mentium et cordium, *quae etiam ad transformationem structurarum ducit.* In hac vero conversione mundus paulatim plenitudinem aetatis Christi adipiscitur.

Huius conversionis dantur gradus.

Est enim processus dynamicus, qui ab amore Dei, qui per Spiritum in corda effunditur et qui optionem pro Christo in mysterio paschali Patrem revelante inducit, paulatim procedit versus integrationem donorum Dei et exigentiarum eius amoris absoluti et definitivi in tota vita personali et sociali hominum.

Sic in vita, in oratione et in passione Ecclesiae Verbum Dei unum idemque remanens tamen etiam profundius in novis rerum adiunctis intellegitur (cf. *Dei Verbum*, 8).

Ductu paedagogio-*pastorali* opus est, ut fideles singuli et etiam populi atque civilisationes ab iis, quae de mysterio Christi iam receperunt, patienter adducantur ad uberiorem mysterii intellegentiam et ad pleniorem in eorum vita et moribus integrationem.

Ita fiat ut in spiritu amoris et timoris Dei, *cruce et sacrificio non exclusis*, sed non cum perturbatione, per progressivam mentis et cordis liberationem Christo corda et vita hominum plene aperiantur.

Pars II

DE PROPOSITIO DEI CIRCA FAMILIAS

4. DE FUNDAMENTO ANTHROPOLOGICO ET THEOLOGICO SACRAMENTI MATRIMONII

Propositio 8

Deus ipse amor exsistens hominem ad imaginem et similitudinem suam creavit (cf. *Gen* 1, 26 s.). Quia amor, ipse in tribus personis vivit, i.e. in relationibus sese dandi, sese accipiendi et reddendi, sese invicem donandi et amandi. Homo ad hanc imaginem creatus non ad solitudinem, sed ad relationem amoris destinatus est. Quia autem homo spiritus incarnatus est, i.e. anima sese in corpore exprimens et corpus anima immortali formatum, in hac sua totalitate ad amorem vocatur. Amor corpus hominis etiam penetrat et corpus amoris spiritualis particeps est.

Hac de causa sexualitas, qua homines ut vir et femina ad se referuntur nil mere biologicum est, sed ipsum nucleum destinationis humanae tangit. Sexualitas tunc modo vere humano realizatur, si pars integralis amoris fit, quo vir et mulier sese invicem usque ad mortem donant. Donatio totalis in corpore mendacium fit, nisi ei donatio personalis tota correspondet, in qua vere totus homo etiam cum dimensione temporis suae vitae adest; si sibi reservat in futuro aliter decidere, etiam nunc non totus se dat. Spatium hoc fidelitatis in amore creatum etiam fecunditati responsabili consonat, quae amori viri et mulieris intrinseca est.

Quia sexualitas ad nucleum existentiae hominis a Deo ad suam imaginem creati pertinet, matrimonium ut unicus locus eius realisationis vere humanae in omnibus culturis, *uti plurimum* inter res sacras numeratur. Matrimonium etenim forma concreta et publica illius fidelitatis est, quam sexualitas humana amorem fecundum exprimens per se postulat.

Quapropter in omnibus culturis semper celebratur magnitudo matrimonii necnon familiae et prolis. Societas quae arrham suae propriae perennitatis agnoscit in matrimonio et familia, formam institutionis eis confert et eo ipso focus (foyer) invitatur ut se transcendat et ut se ad ampliorem communitatem aperiat. Ita eo ipso quod familia et matrimonium institutiones deveniunt, novis valoribus et dimensionibus locupletantur.

5. DE THEOLOGIA SACRAMENTI MATRIMONII

Propositio 9

1. Quae in Veteri Testamento de homine ad imaginem Dei creato dicuntur, nos adiuvant in significatione mutuae donationis viri et mulieris profundius investiganda.

Etenim ad rationem imaginis pertinet:

1) diversitas profunda physica et psychologica coniugum qua eorum unio possibilis fit (*Gen* 2, 18-25);

2) dialogus et indispensabile commercium (échange, scambio) quae instauranda sunt inter personas differentes et tamen plene aequales;

3) *communio necnon eorum fecunditas* (*Gen* 1, 26-28).

2. Talis est amoris coniugalis excellentia, ut Deus per ipsum suum foedus amoris traducere et in ipso velut in speculo reflecti vellet. Per prophetas Deus continuo deordinationes et miserias populi electi in re amoris et sexualitatis denuntiavit. Per ipsos prophetas etiam revelavit *in connubii figura* quam profundus et sanctificans sit amor sponsalis quo ipse populum suum diligebat (*Os* 2, 18-21; *Ez* 16, 8; *Is* 54, 5).

3. Modus quo Deus se ipsum committit in foedus, tam profundus est, ut Christus — qui est definitivum Amen Dei hominibus datum (cf. 2 *Cor* 1, 20) — condicionem humanam in sua incarnatione totaliter assumat *absque peccato*.

4. Per donationem, qua ipse totus Ecclesiac sese dat, per mortem crucis et resurrectionem destruit «duritiam cordis» (*Mt* 19, 8) in amore (cf. *Eph* 5, 5) et ita fit pro viro et muliere exemplar et Salvator amoris coniugalis necnon cuiuslibet amoris humani, quia, ut dicit Scriptura, «maiorem caritatem nemo habet, ut animam suam ponat quis pro amicis suis» (*Io* 15, 13).

Propositio 10

In amore suo crucifixo Christus Ecclesiam *uti sponsam* Sibi ita coniunxit, ut in eius fidelitate permaneat usque ad consummationem saeculorum (cf. *Eph* 5, 26-33). Foedus novum aeternum est, et numquam dissolvitur (*Mt* 16, 18). Matrimonium iam in Veteri Testamento ut signum foederis Dei cum populo electo exsistens in Novum Foedus translatum eius sacrum signum, i.e. verum sacramentum Ecclesiae Christi fit.

Sane matrimonium non exhaurit divitias Christi mysterii; attamen a mysterio Christi totam suam veritatem primigeniam et plenam significationem recipit.

Amor coniugalis inter baptizatos est forma vivendi fecunditatem inter personas ex mysterio mortis et resurrectionis. Christi quod est fundamentum et exemplar cuiuslibet amoris et donationis (cf. *Eph* 5, 5). Haec est gratia sacramenti matrimonii *qua coniuges mutuo suo amore et relatione interpersonali sibi invicem tota vita instrumenta sanctificationis efficiuntur*.

Per revelationem Christi et vitae Dei Trini realitas iam excellens et perpulchra matrimonii humani novas divitias et inexspectatas dimensiones definitivas acquirit. In hoc etiam invenitur — modo speciali — illa solida fundamenta, quae ad veram promotionem mulieris quaeruntur.

Propositio 11

Virginitas *et coelibatus causa regni Dei* huic theologiae matrimonii non solum non contradicit sed eam praesupponit et confirmat. *Matrimonium et virginitas sunt duo modi exprimendi eamdem mysticam realitatem foederis Dei cum suo populo*. Ubi fides matrimonialis non aestimatur, ibi neque virginitas exsistere potest. Ubi sexualitas non ut magnum bonum homini a Creatore datum consideratur, ibi sensu caret hominem propter regnum caelorum eius usui renuntiare. In virginitate homo etiam corporaliter matrimonium Christi cum Ecclesia exspectat, sese totaliter donando Ecclesiae, ut Christus ei sese donat, i.e. secundum mensuram crucis *et anticipando iam in carne vitam futuri saeculi resurrectionis*. Veritatem huius spei cum tota sua existentia testificans amorem nuptialem Christi confitetur, et exinde matrimonii sacrum mysterium annuntiat et defendit. In sua *infecunditate physica spiritualiter fecundus fit* (cf. *Is* 54, 1; *Gal* 4, 27), pater sive mater multorum (cf *Mc* 10, 29s.), et ad vitam familiarem bene instaurandam multum confert. *Similia dici possunt de virginitate non consecrata sed in spiritu servitii electa vel circumstantiis vitae primum imposita et dein assumpta*.

6. DE FIDE ET SACRAMENTO

Propositio 12

1. Matrimonii sacramentum sicut et cetera sacramenta non solum fidem praesupponit, sed eam alit, roborat et exprimit (cf. *Sacrosanctum Concilium*, 59). Quamobrem *investigandum est, quonam modo* contrahentium fides ut Foederis expressio et ut conscia et personalis vocationis baptismalis actuatio ad huius sacramenti validitatem requiratur.

2. Intellegitur fidem non adesse si formaliter reiicitur.

Ipsa vero petitio matrimonii sufficiens est signum huius fidei, si motivis vere religiosis innititur. Attamen, quia celebratio sacramenti alicubi ut conventio socialis habetur potius quam ut eventus religiosus, necessaria videntur ex parte nupturientium, signa potiora fidei personalis.

3. Gradus maturitatis fidei et conscientia nupturientium faciendi, quod facit

Ecclesia, ponderentur. Haec intentio, quae ad sacramenti validitatem requiritur, adesse posse non videtur, nisi minima saltem intentio habetur credendi etiam cum Ecclesia, cum eius fide baptismali. Rigorismus simul et laxismus vitentur, fides infirma pro posse roboretur. Dynamica catechesis et adaequata ad matrimonium praeparatio tradantur *concurrente communitate* ad progressivam fidei maturitatem nupturientium et ad fructuosam receptionem sacramenti.

4. Profundius examenetur *an* affirmatio secundum quam *inter baptizatos matrimonium validum semper esse sacramentum applicetur etiam illis* qui fidem amiserunt. Indicentur postea consequentiae iuridicae et pastorales. *Insuper investigandum est quaenam sint criteria pastoralia discernendi fidem apud nupturientes et quomodo in intentione faciendi quod facit Ecclesia plusminusve haberi debeat minima intentio credendi etiam cum Ecclesia.*

5. Iterum affirmentur consequentiae unitatis et indissolubilitatis peculiares *matrimonii* naturalis. *Nova legislatio canonica rationem habeat de iis quae in hac propositione (12ª) continentur circa necessitatem fidei.*

7. DE INDISSOLUBILITATE MATRIMONII ET DE PROBLEMATE DIVORTIATORUM

Propositio 13

1. Synodus denuo affirmat doctrinam de indissolubilitate matrimonii rati et consummati inter christifideles. Iis quibus hodiernis temporibus difficile apparet definitiva assumere vincula, in mentem revocare vult bonum illud nuntium de fidelitate illius amoris, qui in Christo Iesu habet et virtutem et fundamentum (cf. *Phil* 1, 6; *2 Cor* 1, 8).

2. Indissolubilitas matrimonii in personali totali coniugum donatione radicatur et sustentatur, inquantum est fructus, signum et exigentia illius irreversibilis amoris Dei erga suum populum et Christi erga Ecclesiam donationis ac fidelitatis. Sacramentale enim donum simul est vocatio et mandatum, quae ad responsabilem libertatem coniugum dirigitur, ut inter se fideles pro semper maneant, secundum verba «Quod Deus coniunxit, homo non separet» (*Mt* 19, 6).

3. Christus, qui primordialem Dei Creatoris consilium in corde viri ac mulieris inscriptum renovavit, debilitatem humanam coniugum gratia sacramentali adiuvat, ut duritiam cordis vincant ac indissolubilis amoris testimonium hominibus praebeant.

4. Laudandi sunt complures illi coniuges, qui, licet gravibus afficiantur difficultatibus, in propria vita indissolubilitatem matrimonii testantur. Agnoscendus est etiam valor testimonii illorum, qui in christiana fide et spe fundati, quamvis a proprio coniuge derelicti sint, nullas nuptias denuo *attentaverunt. Isti et illi authentici sunt testes fidelitatis quibus hodie mundus indiget et ab Ecclesiae pastoribus et fidelibus adiuvandi sunt.*

5. *Propter intrinsecam dignitatem matrimonii et* cum in dies augeatur numerus

matrimoniorum, quae destructa sunt, ac declarationes nullitatis accrescant, urget insistere in apta instructione ac efformatione nupturientium, ita ut permanentiam unionis sacramentalis agnoscere valeant ac debita maturitate matrimonium inire possint. *Conferentiae episcopales urgentur ut quaetam forma sponsalium introduceretur qua tutius futuri coniuges conscii evadant de gravitate suae decisionis et pastores certi reddantur de adaequata dispositione nupturientium.*

Propositio 14

1. Ecclesia cum instituta sit, ut omnes *homines et praecipue* baptizatos in viam salutis ducat, illos qui *vinculo matrimonii sacramentalis coniuncti* ad secundas nuptias *transire attentaverunt (divortiati)*, in tali situatione derelinquere non potest et continuo conabitur ea salutis media procurare, quae eis praesto sint. *Sciant vero pastores sese ex veritatis amore obligatos esse ut bene discernant situationes. Differentia enim exsistit inter illos qui revera conati sunt ut salvent primum matrimonium et omnino iniuste derelicti sunt et illos qui ex gravi culpa matrimonium canonice validum destruxerunt. Sunt tandem illi qui secundum matrimonium attentaverunt propter educationem filiorum et quandoque in conscientia subiective certi primum matrimonium irreparabiliter destructum nunquam fuisse validum.*

2. Synodus pastores *et quidem totam communitatem fidelium* hortatur, ut divortiatos illos adiuvent, caritatis sollicitudine curando, ne ab Ecclesia separatos se considerent, sed cum sint baptizati de vita Ecclesiae participare *possunt et* debent. Audiant verbum Dei, *Missae sacrificium frequentent*, orationi instent, operam dent caritatis ac iustitiae promotionibus in communitate, filios in christiana fide instituant, poenitentiae mentem et opera alant, ita ut gratiam Dei in dies mereantur. Ecclesia pro illis oret ac eorum animos alat, matrem misericordem sese praebeat et sic eos in spe et fide sustentet.

3. Attamen Synodus praxim Ecclesiae Sacrae Scripturae innitentem de non admittendis divortiatis, irregulariter denuo coniugatis, ad Eucharisticam communionem confirmat. Etenim ad communionem eucharisticam admitti nequeunt cum eorum vitae status ac conditio obiective contradicant indissolubilitati illius foederis amoris inter Christum et Ecclesiam quae ab Eucharistia significatur et actuatur. Insuper adest specialis ratio pastoralis, quia in errorem et confusionem christifideles inducerentur circa Ecclesiae doctrinam de indissolubilitate matrimonii.

4. Reconciliatio sacramentalis in sacramento poenitentiae, quae viam ad eucharistici sacramenti participationem aperiret, eis solummodo praeberi potest, si poenitentes de violato signo foederis et fidelitatis Christi sese vivendi formae sincero corde aperiunt, quae indissolubilitati sacramenti matrimonii non contradicit.

5. Ita se gerens Ecclesia conatur fidelitatem erga Christum profiteri et materno animo erga filios se habere, *praesertim eos qui innocenter a legitimo coniuge derelicti fuerunt*, simul ac firma spe credit filios, qui a praecepto Domini digressi sunt, si in oratione, poenitentia et caritate perseveraverint, conversionis et salutis gratiam Dei obtinere posse.

6. Synodus cura pastorali de his fidelibus impulsa exoptat, ut nova et profundior investigatio, ratione habita etiam praxeos Ecclesiarum Orientalium, instituatur ad hoc, ut misericordia pastoralis plenior evadat.

8. DE MULIERE ET FAMILIA

Propositio 15

Dignitatem humanam in viro et in muliere aequo modo datam esse in Sacra Scriptura indicatur, ubi dicitur Deum hominem secundum suam imaginem creasse, «masculum et feminam creavit eos» (*Gen* 1, 27). Ambo a Deo possident iura inalienabilia et responsabilitates personae humanae.

In matrimonio modo particulari eorum relatio plene personalis exsistit, fundata in amore mutuo et mutua donatione sui ipsius. Tamquam aequales virtutem creatricem Dei participant in vita nova initianda et nutrienda. Dignitatem mulieris Deus in historia salutis mirabiliter expressit carnem assumendo ex Maria Virgine, quam Ecclesia ut Matrem Dei honorat *quamque novam Evam vocat atque exemplar mulieris redemptae proponit*. Dominus noster Iesus Christus, dignitatem aequalem viri et mulieris confirmavit reverentia sua erga mulieres, quas in sui sequelam et amicitiam vocavit (cf. e.gr. *Lc* 8, 1-3). Mulieri etiam ante discipulos post resurrectionem primum apparuit (cf. *Io* 20, 11-18) et mulieres vocavit, ut bonum nuntium resurrectionis apostolis ferrent (cf. *Mt* 28, 10). *Apostolus Paulus claris verbis asseritur: «Quicumque in Christo baptizati estis Christum induistis... non est masculus neque femina: omnes enim vos unus estis in Christo Iesu»* (*Gal* 3, 27 et 28).

Nostris temporibus haec omnia confirmata et amplius exposita sunt declarationibus Concilii Vaticani II et documentis subsequentibus magisterii (cf. etiam documentum praeparatum a Concilio pro Laicis ad Copenhagen-Conference 1980).

Propositio 16

Criterium morale authenticitatis relationum coniugalium et familiarium in promotione dignitatis et vocationis singularum personarum consistit, quae se dando seipsas plenius inveniunt. In traditione hucusque late vigente munus mulieris praesertim in ipso ambitu familiari, munus autem viri in rebus publicis situm suum habuit. In promotione iurium mulierum imprimis aequalitas muneris materni et familiaris cum muneribus publicis et aliis professionibus determinatis agnoscenda est. De cetero haec munera in evolutione culturali et sociali, sese compenetrare debent. Desideranda est quoad hanc rem theologia nova laboris, quae significationem laboris in vita christiana explanet eiusque relationem ad familiam determinet. Ecclesia societatem hodiernam iuvare possit recognoscendo valorem laboris domi peragendi et educationis prolis, sive de viro agatur sive de muliere. Haec omnia ad educationem liberorum magni momenti sunt, nam radix illa discriminis inter diversos labores et professiones evellitur, si clarum fit omnes in omnibus eodem adlaborare iure eademque responsabilitate. Ex his quoque imago Dei clarius apparebit.

De cetero ex dictis sequitur mulieribus aditum ad munera publica cuiusvis generis aequo modo sicut viris apertum esse debere. Ex altera parte societas ita instituenda est, ut mulieres non cogantur ad laborem externum professionalem, sed familia recte vivere possit etiamsi mater plene familiae sese vovet. Insuper impressio superanda est *honorem* mulieris magis ex labore externo quam ex amore familiari prodire. Hoc vero postulat, ut viri vere uxores suas in omni reverentia dignitatis earum aestiment et diligant.

Ecclesia debito cum respectu quoad vocationem differentem viri et mulieris aequalitatem iurium et dignitatis eorum *pro posse* in sua ipsius vita promovere debet, in bonum omnium: familiae, Ecclesiae et societatis.

Patet omnia haec non significare amissionem femineitatis et imitationem characteris viri, sed plenitudinem verae femineitatis et humanitatis in agendo tam in familia quam extra familiam, *ratione habita varietatum morum et culturarum.*

Propositio 17

Inter gravissima detrimenta societatis modernae adnumeranda est mentalitas illa, in cuius ambitu homo non ut persona, sed ut res *et quidem venalis* apparet, qua quis uti potest ad solam suam voluntatem adimplendam. Ex hac mentalitate in historia prodiit contemptus hominis, immoralitas, *servitus*, oppressio *debilium*. In societate moderna eadem mentalitas continuat hominem exinanire, imprimis in accrescente semper pornographia, *et prostitutione*, quae praesertim mulieris dignitatem gravissime laedunt; in *drogadictione*, in diversis discriminationis generibus quoad educationem, professionem, laboris pretium. *Multi etiam abusus connexi hodie inveniuntur cum praxi «tourismi» qui dicitur, quo saepe mulieres praesertim in nationibus sese evolventibus ad maximam degradationem ducuntur eo quod et organizationes touristicae et non raro gubernia ipsa prostitutionem organizatam, itinerantibus offerunt.*

Notanda est etiam *alia* discriminatio *valde* deploranda, quae haud raro *certis mulierum categoriis infertur: sponsis sine prole*, viduis, divortiatis, innuptis *puellis sic dictis matribus.* Tales mulieres, speciatim si familias *suo labore alere* debent, saepe iniuste tractantur a *cognatis, a* superioribus, a collaboratoribus, a diversis institutionibus nostrae societatis; etiam a christianis multoties haud bene aestimantur.

Synodus offensiones cuiusvis contra dignitatem humanae personae directas *condemnat* et ad aestimationem plenam imaginis Dei in omnibus hominibus vocat.

9. DE MATRIMONIO
SECUNDUM CONSUETUDINES CULTURARUM ANTIQUARUM ET DE MATRIMONIO CHRISTIANO

Propositio 18

Ratione habita ex una parte constantis Traditionis Ecclesiae Catholicae, quae semper a culturis populorum ea hausit, quae apta erant ad melius exprimendum ininvestigabile mysterium Christi, quaeque traditio nuper a Concilio Vaticano II confirmata fuit (*Gaudium et Spes,* 44; *Ad Gentes,* 15 et 22).

Ex alia parte characteris eschatologici Divinae Revelationis, qui indiget omnium culturarum concursu ad ipsius pleniorem comprehensionem tempore et spatio.

Firmo tamen manente principio de compatibilitate et conformitate valorum istarum culturarum cum Evangelio Christi necnon principio de communione cum Ecclesia universali, Synodus rogat,

a) ut Conferentiae Episcoporum studiis incumbant de elementis ex culturis haustis et ad matrimonium et familiam pertinentibus, eo fine ut vera fiat inculturatio fidei christianae in re theologica, pastorali, liturgica et disciplinari;

b) ut attenta diversitate culturarum et traditionum hac in materia facultates Ecclesiis particularibus necnon conferentiis Episcoporum concedantur, praesertim in iis quae ad concretam aestimationem illorum valorum spectant adque elaborationem normarum, quae ad celebrationem et validitatem matrimonii referuntur, ut statutum est in «Praenotandis» quae apud «Ordinem Celebrandi Matrimonium» inveniuntur (nn. 12, 16, 17, 18).

10. DE MATRIMONIIS MIXTIS

Propositio 19

1. Situatio

Propter indolem sacramentalem matrimonii et ad unitatem coniugalem fovendam Ecclesia semper cordi fuit, ut ambae partes in matrimonio catholicae sint. Attamen cum catholici cum aliis christianis et cum non-christianis in pluribus fere ubique communiter vivant, mirum non est matrimonia mixta non solum ubique oriri, sed immo multis in locis numero multo maiores esse.

Matrimonium mixtum duplicis est generis, nempe matrimonium partis catholicae sive cum parte acatholica christiana, sive cum parte non baptizata.

Difficultates speciales oriri possunt circa ipsam matrimonii celebrationem, circa futurae prolis religionem immo et circa fidem partis catholicae.

2. Legislatio recognoscenda

Cum condiciones diversae sint in diversis mundi regionibus, utile esse videtur, legislationem de matrimoniis mixtis recognosci ad hoc ut conferentiis episcopalibus maior tribuatur potestas normas statuendi circa huiusmodi matrimonia, in tuto autem posita obligatione partis catholicae *pro viribus* providendi de baptismo et educatione catholica prolis. Speciales normae requiri possunt e parte conferentiae episcopalis quando certis in adiunctis fides partis catholicae generatim in periculo constituitur. *Conferentiae episcopales autem curam exhibere debent et ad fidem partis catholicae tuendam et ad baptismum et educationem catholicam prolis fovendam.*

3. Libertas religiosa tuenda

Pastores qui nupturientes praeparant ad matrimonium mixtum omnem rationabilem conatum facere tenentur ne in futuro una vel alia pars vim indebitam exercat relate ad persuasionem religiosam coniugis, sive indebite quaerens conversionem sive impedimenta ponens contra liberam praxim religionis.

4. *Testimonium vitae*

Maximi momenti est ut pars catholica sit religione matura, ita ut fiet testis credibilis fidei. Imprimis huiusmodi testimonium dare debet intra ambitum familiae nempe per qualitatem amoris erga coniugem et prolem. Hac in re pars catholica auxilio communitatis indigebit (cf. *Evangelii Nuntiandi*, 71).

5. *Aspectus oecumenicus*

Matrimonium mixtum in quo ambo coniuges *christiani* propriam persuasionem religiosam plene vivunt qualitatem oecumenicam exhibere potest. Bona collaboratio inter ministrum catholicum et non-catholicum quaerenda est, quae iam a praeparatione et celebratione matrimonii initium sumere potuerit (cf. *Matrimonia mixta*, 14).

Pars III

DE MUNERIBUS FAMILIAE

II. DE VITA HUMANA TRANSMITTENDA *AC TUENDA*

Propositio 20

Creatio viri et mulieris coronavit opus Dei Creatoris et ipsam creationem ad suam perfectionem adduxit. In ipso actu creationis Deus constituit matrimonium et vocavit virum et mulierem ad unionem amoris in *servitium* vitae. Sic igitur sponsus et sponsa a Deo vocati sunt, ut participes fiant ipsius potestatis creatoris transmittendo donum vitae. Fructuositas amoris coniugalis autem minime restringitur ad *solam physicam* procreationem filiorum *sed etiam ad fructus supernaturales, morales et spirituales*. Nam sponsus et sponsa *quoque vocantur ad sua bona filiis simul et Ecclesiae et mundo communicanda*.

Propositio 21

Quia amor coniugalis est participatio in ipso mysterio vitae et amoris Dei, Ecclesia munus speciale habet protegendi dignitatem matrimonii et transmissionem vitae humanae quae creata est in imaginem et similitudinem Dei. Et sic tum Concilium Vaticanum II tum Encyclica Humanae Vitae nuntium profeticum nostris temporibus tradiderunt clare affirmantes Ecclesiae doctrinam semper antiquam *et* semper novam de matrimonio et de vitae humanae transmissione. Haec Sacra Synodus in unitate fidei cum Successore Petri congregata firmiter tenet quae in Concilio Vaticano II (cf. *Gaudium et Spes*, 50) *et postea* in Encyclica Humanae Vitae proponuntur et in specie quod amor coniugalis debet esse plene humanus, exclusivus et apertus ad novam vitam (*Humanae Vitae*, n. 11, et cf. 9 et 12).

Propositio 22

Dominium hominis super naturam arte technica semper crescens non solum spem creandi novam et meliorem humanitatem propulit, sed angorem etiam semper profundiorem futuri creat. Multi dubitant, num bonum sit vivere an melius forsan esset, natum non esse; dubitant hac de causa, num liceat alios in vitam vocare, qui forsan vitam suam condemnabunt in mundo crudeli, cuius terrores praevideri nequeunt. Alii cogitant se esse destinatarios quasi exclusivos beneficiorum technicorum cum exclusione aliorum, ad quos media contraceptiva fusius exportant. Ultima causa istius modi cogitandi absentia Dei in hominibus est, cuius amor solus fortior est quam omnes possibiles terrores saeculi. Sic mentalitas contra vitam directa (anti-life-mentality) orta est, quae multis quaestionibus hodiernis subest. *Etiam ut terrorismus ex studiis demograficis oecologorum et futurologorum exaggeratione insignitis periculum aggravando pro qualitate vitae ob incrementum populationis.* Ecclesia autem (   ) credit vitam etiam debilem et patientem donum Dei boni esse. Contra pessimismum et egoismum, qui mundum obscurat, pro vita stat; in unaquaque vita humana splendorem illius «Est» et «Amen» videt, quod Christus est. Illi «Non» quod late mundum pervadit, hoc «Est» opponit (cf. 2 *Cor* 1, 19) et sic hominem et mundum defendit contra *insidiatores* vitae.

Hanc voluntatem suam Ecclesia clara ac firma ratione rursus manifestet vitam humanam omni ope promovendi et eam defendendi contra insidias — cuiusmodi sunt contraceptio, sterilizatio, abortus, euthanasia, etc. — quae vitam ipsam attentant in quolibet eius stadio vel condicione.

Quare ut grave offensum contra dignitatem humanam et contra iustitiam *reprehendendae* sunt activitates qualescumque ex parte gubernii vel alius auctoritatis publicae, quae quaereret limitare quocumque modo libertatem Coniugatorum in determinatione liberorum. Et ideo quaecumque vis a talibus auctoritatibus exercita pro sterilisatione seu contraceptione *et procuratione abortus* omnino damnanda et reicienda est. Similiter in relationibus internationalibus prorsus exsecrandum et iniustum est, ut condicio auxilii *oeconomici ad promotionem* ligetur ad programma contraceptionis vel sterilisationis et *procurationis abortus.*

Propositio 23

Synodus quoque conscia est multiplicium et complexorum problematum quae coniugati experiri debent in multis locis hodie. Non nescia est etiam gravis problematis demografici nostrorum temporum. Conscientia omnium horum problematum quidem novam confirmationem praebet circa momentum doctrinae authenticae Ecclesiae *in Concilio Vaticano II* et in Encyclica *Humanae Vitae* prolatae. Praecise ut haec doctrina melius intellegatur, fiat magis effectiva et latius acceptetur, Synodus in memoriam revocat verba Pauli Papae VI dicentis Encyclicam *suam esse «clarificationem capituli cuiusdam fundamentalis vitae personalis, coniugalis, familiaris et socialis hominis, sed non esse* tractatum completum de homine et matrimonio, de familia et de probatione morali. Hic est enim campus immensus cui magisterium Ecclesiae posset et forsan debet regredi ad pleniorem, magis organicam et magis syntheticam expositionem proponendam» (*Allocutio*, die 31 Iulii 1968). *Synodus ergo theologos invitat, ut vires suas magisterio hierarquico coniungentes adlaborent, ut* fundamenta biblica et rationes personalisticae *huius doctrinae semper melius in lucem ponantur. Tali modo agentes eo intendant, ut in contextu «expositionis organicae et syntheticae» doctrina Ecclesiae de hoc capitulo fundamentali omnibus hominibus bonae volutatis vere accessibilis fiat, eius intellectus profundior in dies evadat et sic mandatum Dei semper plenius adimpleatur in salutem hominis et in laudem creatoris.*

Propositio 24

Synodus Episcoporum non ignorat situationem valde difficilem et vere tormentosam, tot christianorum coniugum qui, non obstante sincera voluntate, normas morales ab Ecclesia doctas adimplendo propter eorum infirmitatem et obiectivas difficultates ipsis oboediendo impares sentiunt.

In cura pastorali coniugatorum sacerdotes prae oculis teneant oportet legem gradualitatis. Paedagogia quaedam concreta doctrinae Ecclesiae cohaerere et numquam ab ea separari debet. Ad hanc paedagogiam *proinde pertinet ut coniuges imprimis clare doctrinam Humanae Vitae cognoscant utpote normativam propriae exercendae sexualitatis et sincere operam dent ad creandas condiciones necessarias pro hac norma adimplenda.* Pertinet *quoque* constantia non minus quam patientia, fortitudo non minus quam humilitas et plena confidentia in Dei misericordiam, quia «si reprehenderit nos cor, maior est Deus corde nostro et cognoscit omnia» (*1 Io* 3, 20). Quare timor in hoc itinere esse non debet nec angustiae, sed amor qui timorem foras pellit.

Haec paedagogia totam vitam coniugalem amplectitur. Transmittendae vitae officium integrari debet in visionem globalem vitae coniugalis, familiaris et socialis, immo in visionem globalem totius vitae christianae, quae sine cruce ad resurrectionem pervenire nequit. In hoc contextu intellegitur tolli non posse sacrificium e vita familiari, immo ex corde accipi debere et amorem coniugalem sic profundiorem fieri. Continentia, quae considerari debet ut habitudo positiva virtutis castitatis in ambitu sexualitatis convenit suo modo sive coniugibus sive personis, quae non sunt matrimonio coniunctae. Tali modo mutua donatio coniugum semper humanior et verior fit, vere «una caro» fiunt. Iter hoc commune postulat reflexionem, informationem et aptam educationem sacerdotum, religiosorum et laicorum, qui pastorali familiari favent, praesertim considerando necessitatem paedagogiae, quae manuducat coniuges in itinere humano et spirituali, quod involvit conscientiam peccati, desiderium *servandi legem non tanquam mere ideale in futurum* et ministerium reconciliationis.

Semper prae oculis habeatur necesse est voluntates duarum personarum in actu coniugali implicari alteramque alterius moribus ac sententiis se accommodare debere, quod ut eveniat haud raro patientia, sympathia ac tempore opus est.

Hanc legem gradualitatis sequens neque sacerdos neque coniuges dichotomiam quandam falsam inter doctrinam et praxim pastoralem erigunt, sed ea patientia viam in plenitudinem maturae fidei quaerunt, qua Dominus nos etiam quaerit.

Valde curanda est unitas in iudiciis sacerdotum ne fideles anxietates conscientiae patiantur.

Propositio 25

Oportet ut fiat profundior indagatio, communicatio informationis et conatus magis fortis ad educationem — *quae praesertim pauperibus accessibilis fiat* — latius *spargendam* de *naturalibus* methodis scientifice bene stabilitis regulationis natalium quae sunt conformes tum dignitati humanae *necnon* doctrinae Ecclesiae. *Agitur enim de vera educatione quae personam humanam cum omnibus suis exigentiis respexit.*

12. DE MUNERE EDUCATIONIS

Propositio 26

1. Munus educationis familiae radicatur in primordiali vocatione coniugum ad participandum opus creationis; ipsum, vi Sacramenti matrimonii, fit etiam participatio operis redemptionis Christi. Itaque baptizatorum familia, cum sit veluti ecclesia domestica a *Verbo Dei*, *fide et* Sacramento Baptismi convocata, simul invenitur quodammodo mater et magistra.

2. Munus educationis essentiale, nativum et primarium est et exinde venit quod terminus procreationis est persona, quae tum plene generatur cum rite educatur.

Responsabilitas educationis *imprimis* parentes afficit et constituit primum munus eorum ministerii coniugalis et quidem indeclinabile et *inalienabile*. Attamen omnia familiae membra pro cuiusque aetate et dono eiusdem muneris corresponsabilia sunt.

3. Quoniam schola, media socialis communicationis et ambitus vitae ad filiorum formationem cooperantur, parentes debent *in usu* horum elementorum, in quantum possunt, partes assumere, eorum influxum in filios discernere, eosque sollicite et cum amore in progressiva integratione in mundum comitari (cfr. *Instructio pastoralis «Communio et Progressio»*, 64-70).

4. Parentes filios educant:
1) Vitae testimonio,
2) ambitu austeritatis et responsabilitatis, iustitiae et amoris, pacis et orationis quem in domo familiari procurare possint;
3) doctrina *fidei christianae* simplici, apta, opportuna et progressiva inde a prima aetate;
4) intima cum filiis conversatione in atmosphaera respectus, fiduciae et amoris, ubi tum parentes *tum* filii et audiunt et discunt, *auctoritate parentum numquam neglecta*;
5) insertione et participatione *et fideli suorum munerum adimpletione* lente progressiva filiorum in communitatem ecclesialem et in communitatem civilem;
6) *colloquio fiduciali cum filiis de mysterio vitae (educatio conscientiae)*;
7) *adiutorium filiis prudenter praebendo in eorum vocatione seligenda* (cf. *Apostolicam Actuositatem*, 11).

Propositio 27

1. Missio educativa familiae per Matrimonii Sacramentum extollitur ad verum ministerium quo Evangelium transmittitur et irradiatur ita ut vita familiae fit itinerarium fidei et quodammodo initatio christiana; immo, familia fieri debet

schola dominicae sequelae. In familia quae sit huius doni conscia omnia membra evangelizant, sed et evangelizantur (*Evangelii Nuntiandi*, 71).

2. Parentes imprimis pro suo educationis ministerio, quod a generatione et a Sacramento oritur, per vitae testificationem inde ab infantia filiorum primi Evangelii praecones sunt. Immo cum eis orando necnon lectioni Verbi Dei incumbendo, per gressus Initiationis Christianae filios ducendo in interius corporis Christi — eucharistici nempe et ecclesialis — plene parentes fiunt, generatores non tantum vitae carnalis sed etiam eius, quae est per renovationem Spiritus Sancti, quae in cruce et resurrectione Christi fundatur.

3. Ad hos fines obtinendos utile est ut parentibus textus catechismi ad usum familiae praebeatur, qui clarus, brevis sit et facile memoriae tradatur.

Propositio 28

1. Educatio in fide educationem ad amorem verum comprehendit. Familia utpote communitas amoris et vitae locus praecipuus est educationis ad amorem, eiusque cursus cotidianus veluti paedagogia doni ipsius revera nuncupari potest (ad amorem scilicet qui vitam generat, sed etiam ad amicitiam necnon ad mutuam benevolentiam inter iuniores et seniores qua sibi animum pandant rationesque vitae conferant necnon ad servitium aliorum, etc.).

2. Ut haec educatio authentica et vere humana sit, compago unitatis animae et corporis videri debet, in qua sexualitas hominis sensum suum profundiorem monstrat: ordinationem ad donum sui ipsius secundum consilium Dei creatoris a Redemptore assumptum. Et sic in sexualitate et affectivitate educatio fiat; in statu tranquillitatis et pacis familiarum proprio. Qua de causa Ecclesia firmiter sese opponit educationi cuidam sexuali quae *frequentius* nil aliud est nisi introductio in methodos voluptatis acquirendae et sine periculo efficiendae. Inquantum schola in educatione sexuali cooperatur, legem subsidiaritatis strenuo observare et cum parentibus in eodem spiritu cooperari debet.

3. Quae omnia in familia ab infantia testimonio vitae potius quam verbis docentur, experientia cotidiana et conversatione gradatim apprehenduntur et ad maturationem perducuntur, illam capacitatem sese possidendi et donandi fovendo, quae in castitate semper vivitur, sive in donatione ad Regnum testificandum in virginitate, sive in matrimonio quod in Domino vivitur.

Propositio 29

1. In pastorali organica munus educationis locum pergrave obtinet. Hoc implicat novam indolem collaborationis inter *parentes* et *communitates christianas* diversos coetus educatorum et pastorum. In hoc sensu renovatio scholae catholicae specialiter attendere debet parentes *alumnorum et ad communitatem educativam plenam constituendam.* Ius parentum *eligendi educationem quae congruit fidei religiosae ipsorum parentum* omnino in tuto ponendum est. Status et Ecclesia tenentur ad omnia auxilia possibilia praebenda familiis in earum muneribus rite exercendis. Quapropter tam Ecclesia quam Status eas institutio-

nes et activitates creare et stabilire debent, quas familiae requirunt. Auxilium eo maius sit, quo minus sibi sufficiens est familia. Meminisse debent omnes qui in societate scholas regunt, Deum principaliter parentes educatores filiorum constituisse eorumque ius inalienabile esse.

2. Ubi in scholis ideologiae fidei christianae oppositae docentur, familia *una cum aliis familiis et, si fieri potest, cum associationibus familiarum*, omnibus viribus et sapienter contendere debet, ut iuvenibus succurrat, ne a fide discedant. In hoc casu specialibus subsidiis a pastoribus indiget, *memores quod parentes inviolabile ius habeant filios suos communitati ecclesiali committendi.*

13. DE MUNERE SOCIALI ET CULTURALI FAMILIAE

Propositio 30

1. Cum familia sit cellula primaria societatis, nexibus vitalibus et organicis cum ea connexa, aperta esse debet aliis familiis et communitatibus, ita ut non solum sibimetipsi provideat, sed et omnibus aliis, ut civilizatio amoris oriatur.

2. *Potissimum* munus solidae familiae est collaborare in mundi constructione ut vita proprie humana possibilis eveniat.

3. Familia potissimum humanizationis et personalizationis instrumentum est cuius ope culturae valores servantur et transmittuntur.

4. Experientia amoris et communionis in familia viget praesertim in efformatione personae humanae inde a primaeva aetate usque ad maturitatem.

Relationes interpersonales in familia maxime iuvant ut habitus veri dialogi et respectus erga alios oriatur et crescat.

5. Habitus et praxis communionis et participationis (bonorum spiritualium et materialium) et sensus intimus solidarietatis in familia discitur qui valores et fundamenta societatis constituunt.

6. *Ecclesia specialem curam habere debet de familiis incompletis, praesertim de viduis eorumque familiis, de matribus vel patribus derelictis, de orphanis.*

7. *Familiae vero, maxime si prole carent, ad prolem alienam auxiliandam provideant, inquantum possunt sive per adoptionem sive per affiliationem, iuxta leges proprii Status.*

8. Familia christiana in sequela Domini progrediens speciali dilectione erga omnes pauperes sensus habeat, praesertim erga famelicos, indigentes, senescentes, infirmos, drogadictos, familia carentes, *et id praesertim incipiendo a propriae familiae membris.*

9. Praeservatio bonorum naturalium (generis humani patrimonium) quae austeritatem et simplicitatem vitae exigit, in familia colenda est.

10. Peculiaritas familiae in munere socio-politico adimplendo in eo potius ponenda est ut convictiones et habitus ethicus qui decisiones politicas ad iustitiam et rectum ordinem obtinendum foveat, in quo homo, dignitate filii Dei praeditus, vivere possit.

11. Relationes Status ad familias regi debent principio subsidiarietatis, ita ut ne in interiora vitae familiae intromissio fiat (sterilizatio, abortus, contraceptio ...) sed potius iuvamen ad munera eorum adimplenda in procreatione atque educatione, etiam religiosa, filiorum praestet.

12. Familiae christianae etiam ad novum ordinem internationalem cooperari possunt, praesertim consociationibus peculiaribus unitae, ubi amor, veritas, iustitia et libertas in tuto ponantur.

14. DE FAMILIIS IN ADIUNCTIS SPECIALIBUS

Propositio 31

Supremum secuta Pastorem Ecclesia omnibus viribus unitis intendit succurrere familiis in specialibus adiunctis versantibus: uti sunt familiae migrantium, in specie operariorum migrantium, familiae militum, familiae profugae *ac exsules*; familiae emarginatae magnarum urbium, *familiae sine habitatione*, familiae incompletae; familiae quae habent filios handicapatos vel drogis assuefactos, familiae alcoholicorum, familiae quae perdunt radices culturales et sociales, familiae quae politice vel aliter discriminantur, familiae ideologice scissae, familiae quae haud faciliter contactum cum paroecia inveniunt; *familiae quae vim patiuntur propter fidem; familiae a coniugibus minoris aetatis compositae. Senes haud raro in solitudine et sine aptis subsidiis vivunt.*

Familiae in istis vel similibus difficultatibus versantes sint praesentes nostrae memoriae et respiciantur in omnibus dimensionibus curae pastoralis. Non possumus esse contenti cum cura symptomatica, sed omnes competentes in Ecclesia et societate cooperari debent, ut curentur ipsae causae. Necessaria est imprimis renovatio conscientiae publicae et exinde structurarum, culturalium, oeconomicarum, socialium et iuridicarum. Etiam omnes familiae inter se unitae sollicitae erunt his in rebus.

Propositio 32

Familiae migrantes, in specie operariorum migrantium, ubique in Ecclesia suam «patriam» invenire possint. Hoc est munus Ecclesiae connaturale, cum sit signum unitatis in diversitate. In quantum fieri potest assistantur a Sacerdotibus provenientibus ex earum *ritu*, cultura et lingua. Pars muneris Ecclesiae est appellare ad conscientiam publicam et auctoritates vitae socio-oeconomicae et politicae, ut operarii laborem invenire possint in propria regione et patria *et iusto salario gaudere valeant*; ut familiae quamprimum in eodem domicilio uniantur, in propria identitate culturali respiciantur ac tamquam aequales tractentur; ut filii aequas opportunitates in formatione professionali et in exercitio professionis habeant.

Propositio 33

Durum problema surgit, quando ipsa familia est ideologice scissa (cf. *Mt* 24, 10; *Mc* 13, 12-13; *Lc* 21, 16). His in circumstantiis peculiaris cura pastoralis requiritur, quaeque examen de nostra praxi pastorali postulat. Cum talibus familiis contactus personalis discrete servandus est. Credentes roborandi sunt in fide, ac in praxi vitae christianae adiuvandi. Etiamsi pars fidei catholicae fidelis minime cedere possit, dialogus cum parte dissidenti semper colendus.

Expressiones amoris et respectus augendae sunt, ut firma spes conservandae unitatis conservari possit. Multum dependet a relationibus, quae existunt inter parentes (patrem) et filios. Si filii ab ideologiis Ecclesiae inimicis attrahuntur, bonae relationes humanae inde ab initio exultae multum iuvare possunt, ut dialogus etiam de fide profundior iterum atque iterum instituatur. Ideologiae familiae extraneae urgent membra credentia, ut in fide et testimonio amoris crescant. Cum ideologiae disgregantes saepe intrent in domum per mass-media, inde ab initio tales «hospites» in familia magis discrete eligantur et communi consilio discernantur. Numquam autem oratio est omittenda, ex qua spes christiana alitur.

15. DE MUNERE APOSTOLICO FAMILIAE

Propositio 34

1. Futura evangelizatio magna ex parte ab ecclesia domestica pendet (Ioannes Paulus II, 28-2-79). Haec familiae apostolica missio in baptismo fundatur, gratia sacramentali matrimonii novam vim acquirit ad fidem transmittendam, ad sanctificandam et transformandam hodiernam societatem iuxta Dei propositum.

2. Familia filios ad vitam formare debet ut singuli suum opus plene adimpleant in statu vocationis a Deo acceptae. Familia ad transcendentes valores aperta, cum gaudio aliis serviens, fideliter munera adimplens et conscia suae participationis mysterii crucis Christi, primum et optimum est seminarium vocationis ad vitam consecratam.

3. Familia christiana, praesertim hodie, speciali vocatione testis esse debet paschalis foederis Iesu, laetitiam amoris et spei securitatem constanter irradiando, cuius rationem reddere debet. «Familia christiana vocationem etiam habet ut alta voce proclamet tum praesentes virtutes regni Dei, tum spem vitae aeternae» (*Lumen Gentium*, 11).

4. Obligatio evangelizandi familiae excellenti modo patefit praeferentiali erga pauperes amore.

5. Necessaria evangelizandi vocatio familiae etiam adimpleri potest, et quidem excellenti et efficaci modo, in motibus apostolicis. Hi motus constitui debent in relatione cum communitate ecclesiali *dioecesana et paroeciali*, ad Evangelii proclamationem et veritatis christianae transmissionem.

6. Familiaris pastoralis in pastoralem organicam inseritur et diversis eius partibus semper praesens esse debet.

7. *Familiae in territoriis missionum peculiare habent munus evangelizandi.*

8. *Munus presbyteri pars essentialis est ministerii Ecclesiae erga matrimonium et familiam. Responsabilitatem habet in rebus quam maxime personalibus necnon in rebus liturgicis, socialibus, moralibus. Familiam sustinere debet inter difficultates et angores et, intime coniunctus eius membris, eos adiuvare debet ad vitam suam in luce Evangelii considerandam. Hoc vinculum et familiae prodest et presbytero, cum familiae quibus servit eum confirmant et sustinent in eius vocatione sacerdotali.*

16. DE PRAEPARATIONE AD MATRIMONIUM

Propositio 35

Cum matrimonium christianum relationem humanam maxime profundam et complexam constituat, et bene esse et sanctitatem tam magnae partis hominum et mulierum afficiat, Ecclesia accuratiorem pastoralem praematrimonialem urgeat, ita ut in quantum possibile, situationes irregulares vitentur, in quibus tot matrimonia versantur. Hoc quidem implicat exigentiam fidei et humanam maturitatem ad responsabilitates familiares et sociales assumendas. Praeparatio haec tamquam processus continuus et progrediens concipienda est.

Praeparatio remota in sinu familiae incipit; ex parte Ecclesiae cura pastoralis de initiatione christiana detur.

Agnitio et interiorisatio mysterii Christi ac ipsius Ecclesiae, necnon cognitio realium exigentiarum ac responsabilitatum sacramenti in praeparatione proxima tradantur. Fines huius praeparationis considerari possunt: tum ut nupturientes amorem suum tamquam participationem amoris Dei, manifestati in amore Christi erga Ecclesiam, videant et vivant; tum ut profundiorem reddant eorum fidem utpote vocationem ad sactitatem et amorem oblativum sui ipsius; tum ut matrimonium intellegant tamquam sacramentum Christi praesentiae in vita eorum cotidiana; tum etiam ut relationes sexuales integrare valeant tamquam partem quandam magni momenti unionis eorum sacramentalis.

Praeparatio immediata magis magisque in usum venit et quidem fructuose; ut servitium pro nupturientibus omnibus, sed speciali ratione habita eorum qui sive doctrina, sive praxi fidei carere noscuntur. Bene perficitur auxilio laicorum, vitae et doctrinae ex corde deditorum atque melius in sinu *familiae et* propriae communitatis. *Haec praeparatio debet esse iter quoddam fidei ad instar catechumenatus.*

Episcoporum Conferentiae et Dioeceses in Directoriis pro pastorali familiari normas edant de minimo contentu, duratione et methodis adhibendis pro cursibus praeparationis. Ibi, aspectus doctrinales Sacramenti, paedagogici, iuridici, atque medicinales inveniantur. Praeparatio nupturientium non potest esse solummodo intellectualis, sed debet esse vitalis, ita ut ipsi nupturientes inserantur ad modum cuiusdam catechumenatus in communitate ecclesiali viva, v.gr. in paroeciis.

Ita tamen haec fiat praeparatio, ut ipsa novum pro nupturientibus non constituat impedimentum.

17. DE SPIRITUALITATE FAMILIAE

Propositio 36

Spiritualitas familiae ex theologia familiae derivatur. Uno verbo, fundatur in amore Dei pro nobis et in mandato evangelico amoris Dei et proximi. Vere est vocatio ad sanctitatem — invitatio divina exspectans responsum. Familia est «ecclesia domestica». Communitas amoris et fidei est. Familia responsabilitatem habet pro vita familiari et sua spiritualitate.

Familia est tamquam schola primaria doctrinae, spiritualitatis et apostolatus. Iste aspectus apostolatus laicorum clarissime enuntiatur in documentis *Lumen Gentium*, *Gaudium et Spes*, necnon in decreto de apostolatu laicorum, *Apostolicam Actuositatem*.

Imago amoris Christi erga Ecclesiam confortat et provocat familias quae conantur adimplere mandatum eius: «Ut diligatis invicem». Familia sic assumitur ad amorem et vocationem Dei. Recognita hac dignitate, circumstantiae vitae cotidianae determinant responsionem uniuscuiusque personae huic amori et vocationi. Haec responsio emphatice manifestat pro familia spiritualitatem creationis, foederis, crucis, resurrectionis et signi.

1) *Spiritualitas creationis*

Coniuges libere procreationi servientes, electionem fundamentalem et simplicem faciunt pro vita potius quam pro nihil. Sunt iidem coniuges qui etiam creant pro unaquaque vita novam initialem experientiam amoris. Ita aedificant communitatem. Vivunt spiritualitatem eorum qui historiam faciunt, eorum qui responsabilitatem suscipiunt, etiam responsabilitatem pro propria vita familiari.

2) *Spiritualitas foederis*

Coniuges fiunt una caro, et ita *secundum quandam analogiam* etiam parentes cum prole. Exemplar huius dedicationis mutuae est dedicatio Christi erga Ecclesiam.

3) *Spiritualitas crucis*

In imitatione Iesu, spiritualitas familiae consistit in donatione vitae ad invicem. In familia adimpletur passio liberatrix et sacrificium crucis. Attingit modo quidem speciali coniuges separatos, senes, infirmos, minoratos, et etiam ipsos qui amorem non rependunt.

4) *Spiritualitas resurrectionis*

Spiritualitas resurrectionis quae suum fundamentum habet in eventu Paschali, adimpletur per tribulationes uniuscuiusque diei, in conatu denuo incipiendi, veniam dandi, iniuriasque animo excidendi *necnon profundam excolendi laetitiam*.

5) *Spiritualitas signi*

Huiusmodi spiritualitas familiam provocat ut sit testis amoris, signum responsionis ad Dei vocationem. Sed amor protendit ad alios, et quidem ad indigentes. Responsabilitatem socialem pro iustitia et pace manifestat.

Adsunt elementa quaedam quae magnopere favere videntur hanc spiritualitatem familiae:

— Familiaris conversatio ex qua cognitio et affectus oriuntur ac nutriuntur.
— Mutuus respectus, dialogus et auctoritas participata *necnon spatia silentii*.
— Austeritas, sobrietas, simplicitas adversus hodiernum consumismum.
— Aura puritatis contra erotismum.

6) *Spiritualitas eschatologica.*

Vita aeterna terminus est omnium membrorum familiae.

Propositio 37

Atmosphaera, aptus locus, tempus genuinae spiritualitatis saepe deest familiis. Propitiandae sunt ergo novae condiciones quae a mutationibus mentalitatum et structurarum oriuntur; quaeque spiritualitatem et actionem pastoralem foveant.

In spiritualitae familiarum quae vocari possunt «incompletae» praevalet revera aspectus crucis, qui spem et certitudinem facit familias istas non esse alienas a vita Ecclesiae non obstante condicione sua, immo Ecclesiam illas accipere in caritate Christi.

Inter media proposita, quae ad spiritualitatem familiarum fovendam adiuvare possunt, notanda sunt quae sequuntur:

— in primis, adimpletio necessaria et fidelis munerum familiae propriorum;

— oratio quae in familia quatenus familia habetur, v.gr.: lectio et meditatio Verbi Dei, praeparatio in familia ad sacramenta recipienda, recitatio Rosarii *marialis*, etc.;

— *observatio pietatis popularis, quia valores emotionales et traditionis religiosae continet;*

— participatio familiae qua talis in celebrationibus communitariis, praesertim temporibus liturgicis praestantioribus sicut Adventus, Nativitas Domini, Quadragesima, Hebdomada Sancta, Festa Sanctorum Patronorum, diebus Dominicis, *itemque in eventibus praestantioribus familiae;*

— haec omnia maximi momenti sunt ut vocationes ad vitam religiosam et sacerdotalem in ambitu familiae christianae oriantur et multiplicentur *et ut laici zelo apostolico ferveant.*

Propositio 38

Familia tandem est locus praecipuus in qua personae humanae veniunt ad experientiam conscientiae. Unusquisque cognoscit semetipsum in relatione ad alios, quae cognitio conducit ex sese ad Alium, ad Deum. Talis conscientia, quae oritur ex amore et solidaritate et semper magis elucidatur intuitu amoris et omnium virtutum quibus se exprimit, est via salutis et eodem tempore via ad conscientiam vere maturam, si conscientiae formatio organice unitur educationi fidei, et quidem educationi reciprocae inter coniuges et filios. Fides aperiet horizontes ad iustitiam socialem et omnes virtutes sociales; quia conscientia in ipsa familia, quae est ecclesia domestica, facit omnes conscientes se non posse confiteri fidem in unum Deum, Patrem omnium, in Christum Redemptorem omnium, et in Spiritum Sanctum qui vocat omnes ad unitatem, nisi sese consociat cum omnibus hominibus quarendo veritatem et vias amoris et iustitiae. Talis educatio conducit ad sensum Ecclesiae et corresponsabilitatem in Ecclesia, quae nobis indicat maximum respectum personae eiusque intimi sanctuarii, id est conscientiae. Normae morales elucescunt e visione integrativa et profunda cognitione valorum moralium et spiritualium. Conscientia excolenda est in omnibus dimensionibus, ut sit et semper magis fiat matura, fide illuminata et capax discernendi.

18. DE ASSOCIATIONIBUS FAMILIARUM

Propositio 39

Communitates familiares hodie multis in locis fundantur. Fideles inveniunt consensum solidarietatis ad vitam suam ex inspiratione Evangelii et fide Ecclesiae ducendam; ad conscientiam a valoribus christianis et non ab opinione publica formandam; ad se invicem exercitae pietatis et erga homines ac societatem responsabilitatis causa corroborandos. Experientiae formatae ac consuetudines cotidianae cum religiosis connexae (i.e. «cultura familiaris») curae pastorali transmittendae sunt.

Propterea haec Synodus valorem egregium coetuum seu associationum spiritualium qui vitam christianam apud coniuges et familias fulcire volunt, confirmant, non autem ut membra semetipsos a ceteris fidelibus segregent, sed ut sint «lux» seu «fermentum» omnibus familiis.

19. DE CONIUNCTIONIBUS EXTRA MATRIMONIUM

Propositio 40

Phaenomenon se coniungendi in *unione* sic dicto «*matrimonium* ad experimentum» in dies magis magisque grassatur, immo non desunt qui huic *unioni* quemdam valorem tribuant.

Iam sub luce ipsius humanae rationis omnino reiciendum est experimentum circa personas immo nec dari potest. Nam res cadunt sub ratione experimenti, personae vero sunt termini amoris seu oblationis sine tempore suiipsius ad alterum.

Sub luce fidei donatio corporis symbolum reale est adeo profundum totius personae, ut nequeat effici sine auxilio caritatis Christi per sacramentum matrimonii receptum (cf. *Prop.* 8-11). Alioquin haec donatio continuo in periculo versatur praesumptionis et mendacii.

Synodus proinde in mentem vocat hanc tentationem superari *ordinarie* non posse, nisi ab infantia persona humana educetur, gratia Christi et sine formidine, ad nascentem concupiscentiam superandam et ad relationes veri amoris cum ceteris instituendas. Quae omnia fieri nequeunt absque vera educatione sexuali, ita ut persona humana, in sua totalitate et proinde etiam in suo corpore, in mysterium Christi plene introducatur.

Investigandae sunt causae huius phaenomeni etiam sub aspectu psychologico et sociologico, ut apta therapia inveniatur.

Propositio 41

Phaenomenon quod non potest non suscitare attentionem Pastorum est crescens in dies numerus unionum s.d. liberarum. Situationes vero sunt sat diverse: aliqui non obstante sensu maritali renuntiant matrimonium socialiter sancitum ad evitandum damnum quoddam; alii vero repudiant matrimonium, etiam civile, propter contemptum societatis vel protestando contra ordinem socio-politicum; alii autem intendunt nonnisi coniunctionem ad libidinem sexualem explendam vel consumismo utilem. Gravitas situationis magis adhuc apparet ex tendentiis aequiparandi tales uniones liberas ipsi matrimonio.

Consequentiae morales et sociales sunt funestae: irreparabile vulnus infligitur sensui fidelitatis etiam socialiter testificandae; ipsa cellula societatis destruitur. *Condicio liberorum saepe miseranda evadit, et traumatibus, ut aiunt psychologicis, afferuntur per totam vitam.* Cum familia sit domicilium humanitatis, tales uniones fiunt diversorium egoismi. Sensus religiosus in luce foederis Dei cum suo populo colendus amittitur; et qui sic agunt privant seipsos gratia sacramentali et insuper dant grave scandalum.

Cura pastoralis non solum magna cum sollicitudine quaerat homines viventes in tali situatione, sed maiore etiam cohaerentia colat sensum fidelitatis in tota educatione morali et religiosa, instruendo homines etiam de condicionibus et structuris faventibus spiritum fidelitatis, sine qua non potest existere vera libertas.

Auctoritates etiam politicae interpellantur, ut talibus tendentiis efficaci modo resistant non solum propter stabilitatem ipsius societatis, sed etiam propter dignitatem, securitatem et sanitatem civium. *Alia tamen est situatio illorum iuvenum et illarum puellarum qui hodie multis in regionibus ob summam paupertatem a praesentibus structuris socio-oeconomicis causatam, vix decenter nubere possunt. Qui coadiuvandi sunt ne ex hac paupertate obstaculum huiusmodi veniat.*

PARS IV

ANNEXA

20. CHARTA IURIUM FAMILIAE
(Elementa)

Propositio 42

Synodus exopat, ut Sancta Sedes edendam curet chartam iurium familiae illamque proponat etiam Nationibus Unitis (UNO).

Fundamentum:

1. Familia est cellula basica societatis, subiectum iurium et officiorum, prior quam Status et quaelibet alia communitas.

2. Status debet legibus et institutionibus familiam agnoscere et protegere respectu eius libertatis eique subsidium praebere eam non substituens.

Contentus

Ius:

1. Existendi et progrediendi ut familia, *i.e. ius omnis hominis, praesertim etiam pauperum ad familiam condendam et aptis susidiis sustentandam.*

2. Exercendi suum munus in vita transmittenda inde ab eius conceptione atque filios educandi.

3. Intimitatis vitae et coniugalis et familiaris.

4. Stabilitatis vinculi atque institutionis matrimonialis.

5. Credendi et profitendi propriam fidem, eamque propagandi.

6. Educandi filios iuxta proprias traditiones et valores religiosos, necnon culturales, instrumentis, mediis atque institutionibus necessariis.

7. Obtinendi securitatem physicam, socialem, politicam, oeconomicam, praesertim pauperum et infirmorum.

8. *Ius ad habitationem aptam vitae familiae rite ducendae.*

9. Expressionis et repraesentationis coram publicis auctoritatibus oeconomicis, socialibus et culturalibus eisque subiacentibus, sive per se, sive ope consociationum.

10. Consociationes creandi cum aliis familiis et institutionibus, ut apte et sollerter suum munus adimpleat.

11. Protegendi minorennes ope adaequatarum institutionum et legislationum, contra nociva pharmaca, pornographiam, alcoholismum, etc.

12. Honesti otii quod simul valores familiae foveat.

13. *Ius senum ad dignam vitam et dignam mortem.*

14. *Ius emigrandi tamquam familia ad meliorem vitam quaerendam.*

21. DIRECTORIUM PASTORALE

Propositio 43

Familia, in quantum sibiectum (agens) actionis pastoralis, assumere debet munus et responsabilitatem evangelizandi semetipsam ac ceteras familias necnon diversas areas apostolicas in societate. Expressio huiusmodi muneris et instrumentum ad hoc obtinendum sunt institutiones sive consociationes familiarum totalitati Ecclesiae locali apertae.

Cum multiplex sit in mundo situatio pastoralis, Synodus nonnisi principia maiora tradere potest, ex quibus unaquaeque Conferentia Episcoporum Directorium Pastorale de re familiari conficere possit, *in quo doctrina Ecclesiae eiusque disciplina apto modo pro circumstantiis diversis exponatur.*

Huiuscemodi Directorium comprehendere debet:

a) doctrinam de sacramento Matrimonii et de familia christiana necnon de illorum divitiis et exigentiis in vita cotidiana;

b) principia de praeparatione ad matrimonium;

c) instructiones de ipsa nuptiarum celebratione;

d) principia de cura et actione pastorali sic dicta «d'accompagnement»;

e) elementa de spiritualitate familiae;

f) principia de educatione liberorum in fide.

Quaeque omnia rationem habebunt de munere familiae in opere evangelisationis.

INDEX OF NAMES

BIBLIOTHECA EPHEMERIDUM THEOLOGICARUM LOVANIENSIUM

* Out of print

1. *Miscellanea dogmatica in honorem Eximii Domini J. Bittremieux*, 1947. 235 p. FB 220.
*2-3. *Miscellanea moralia in honorem Eximii Domini A. Janssen*, 1948.
 *4. G. PHILIPS, *La grâce des justes de l'Ancien Testament*, 1948.
 *5. G. PHILIPS, *De ratione instituendi tractatum de gratia nostrae sanctificationis*, 1953.
 6-7. *Recueil Lucien Cerfaux*, 1954. 504 et 577 p. FB 500 par tome. Cf. *infra*, n° 18.
 8. G. THILS, *Histoire doctrinale du mouvement œcuménique*. Nouvelle édition, 1963. 338 p. FB 135.
 *9. J. COPPENS et al. *Études sur l'Immaculée Conception. Sources et sens de la doctrine*, 1955. 110 p. FB 150.
*10. J.A. O'DONOHOE, *Tridentine Seminary Legislation. Its Sources and its Formation*, 1957.
*11. G. THILS, *Orientations de la théologie*, 1958.
*12-13. J. COPPENS, A. DESCAMPS, É. MASSAUX (éd), *Sacra Pagina, Miscellanea Biblica Congressus Internationalis Catholici de Re Biblica*, 1959.
*14. *Adrien VI, le premier Pape de la contre-réforme. Sa personnalité — sa carrière — son œuvre*, 1959.
*15. F. CLAEYS BOUUAERT, *Les déclarations et serments imposés par la loi civile aux membres du clergé belge sous le Directoire (1795-1801)*, 1960.
*16. G. THILS, *La «Théologie Œcuménique». Notion-Formes-Démarches*, 1960.
 17. G. THILS, *Primauté pontificale et prérogatives épiscopales. «Potestas ordinaria» au Concile du Vatican*, 1961. 104 p. FB 50.
*18. *Recueil Lucien Cerfaux*, t. III, 1961. Cf. *supra*, n°ˢ 6-7.
*19. *Foi et réflexion philosophique. Mélanges F. Grégoire*, 1961.
*20. *Mélanges G. Ryckmans*, 1963.
 21. G. THILS, *L'infaillibilité du peuple chrétien «in credendo»*, 1963. 66 p. FB 50.
*22. J. FÉRIN et L. JANSSENS, *Progestogènes et morale conjugale*, 1963.
*23. *Collectanea Moralia in honorem Eximii Domini A. Janssen*, 1964. FB 200.
 24. H. CAZELLES (éd.), *L'Ancien Testament et son milieu d'après les études récentes. De Mari à Qumrân* (Hommage J. Coppens, I), 1969. 158*-370 p. FB 800.
 25. I. DE LA POTTERIE (éd.). *De Jésus aux évangiles. Tradition et rédaction dans les évangiles synoptiques* (Hommage J. Coppens, II), 1967. 272 p. FB 500.

26. G. THILS et R.E. BROWN (éd.), *Exégèse et théologie* (Hommage J. Coppens, III), 1968. 328 p. FB 550.

27. J. COPPENS (éd.), *Ecclesia a Spiritu sancto edocta. Hommage à Mgr G. Philips*, 1970. 640 p. FB 580.

28. J. COPPENS (éd.), *Sacerdoce et Célibat. Études historiques et théologiques*, 1971. 740 p. FB 600.

29. M. DIDIER (éd.), *L'évangile selon Matthieu. Rédaction et théologie*, 1971. 432 p. FB 750.

*30. J. KEMPENEERS, *Le Cardinal van Roey en son temps*, 1971.

*31. F. NEIRYNCK, *Duality in Mark. Contributions to the Study of the Markan Redaction*, 1972.

*32. F. NEIRYNCK (éd.), *L'évangile de Luc. Problèmes littéraires et théologiques. Mémorial Lucien Cerfaux*, 1973.

*33. C. BREKELMANS (éd.), *Questions disputées d'Ancien Testament. Méthode et théologie*, 1974.

*34. M. SABBE (éd.), *L'évangile selon Marc. Tradition et rédaction*, 1974.

*35. *Miscellanea Albert Dondeyne. Godsdienstfilosofie. Philosophie de la religion*, 1974.

*36. G. PHILIPS, *L'union personnelle avec le Dieu vivant*, 1974.

37. F. NEIRYNCK, in collaboration with T. HANSEN and F. VAN SEGBROECK, *The Minor Agreements of Matthew and Luke against Mark with a Cumulative List*, 1974. 330 p. FB 800.

*38. J. COPPENS, *Le Messianisme et sa relève prophétique*, 1974.

39. D. SENIOR, *The Passion Narrative according to Matthew. A Redactional Study*, 1975; new impression, 1982. 440 p. FB 1000.

*40. J. DUPONT (éd.), *Jésus aux origines de la christologie*, 1975.

*41. J. COPPENS (éd.), *La notion biblique de Dieu*, 1976.

42. J. LINDEMANS – H. DEMEESTER (éd.), *Liber Amicorum Monseigneur W. Onclin*, 1976. 396 p. FB 900.

43. R.E. HOECKMAN (éd.), *Pluralisme et œcuménisme en recherches théologiques. Mélanges offerts au R.P. Dockx, O.P.*, 1976. 316 p. FB 900.

44. M. DE JONGE (éd.), *L'Évangile de Jean*, 1977. 416 p. FB 950.

45. E.J.M. VAN EIJL (éd.), *Facultas S. Theologiae Lovaniensis 1432-1797. Bijdragen tot haar geschiedenis. Contributions to its History. Contributions à son histoire*, 1977. 570 p. FB 1500.

46. M. DELCOR (éd.), *Qumrân. Sa piété, sa théologie et son milieu*, 1978. 432 p. FB 1550.

47. M. CAUDRON (éd.), *Faith and Society. Foi et Société. Geloof en maatschappij. Acta Congressus Internationalis Theologici Lovaniensis 1976*, 1978. 304 p. FB 1150.

48. J. KREMER (éd.), *Les Actes des Apôtres. Traditions, rédaction, théologie*, 1979. 590 p. FB 1600.

49. F. NEIRYNCK, avec la collaboration de J. DELOBEL, T. SNOY, G. VAN BELLE, F. VAN SEGBROECK, *Jean et les Synoptiques. Examen critique de l'exégèse de M.-É. Boismard*, 1979. XII-428 p. FB 950.

50. J. COPPENS, *La relève apocalyptique du messianisme royal. I. La royauté – Le règne – Le royaume de Dieu. Cadre de la relève apocalyptique*, 1979. 325 p. FB 848.

51. M. GILBERT (éd.), *La Sagesse de l'Ancien Testament*, 1979. 420 p. FB 1700.

52. B. DEHANDSCHUTTER, *Martyrium Polycarpi. Een literair-kritische studie*, 1979. 296 p. FB 950.

53. J. LAMBRECHT (éd.), *L'Apocalypse johannique et l'Apocalyptique dans le Nouveau Testament*, 1980. 458 p. FB 1400.

54. P.-M. BOGAERT (éd.), *Le Livre de Jérémie. Le prophète et son milieu. Les oracles et leur transmission*, 1981. 408 p. FB 1500.

55. J. COPPENS, *La relève apocalyptique du messianisme royal. III. Le Fils de l'homme néotestamentaire*, 1981. XIV-192 p. FB 800.

56. J. VAN BAVEL & M. SCHRAMA (éd.), *Jansénius et le Jansénisme dans les Pays-Bas. Mélanges Lucien Ceyssens*, 1982. 247 p. FB 1000.

57. J.H. WALGRAVE, *Selected Writings – Thematische geschriften. Thomas Aquinas, J.H. Newman, Theologia Fundamentalis*. Edited by G. DE SCHRIJVER & J.J. KELLY, 1982. XLIII-425 p. FB 1000.

58. F. NEIRYNCK & F. VAN SEGBROECK, avec la collaboration de E. MANNING, *Ephemerides Theologicae Lovanienses 1924-1981. Tables générales. Bibliotheca Ephemeridum Theologicarum Lovaniensium 1947-1981*, 1982. 400 p. FB 1600.

59. J. DELOBEL (éd.), *Logia. Les paroles de Jésus – The Sayings of Jesus. Mémorial Joseph Coppens*. 1982. 647 p. FB 2000.

60. F. NEIRYNCK, *Evangelica. Gospel Studies – Études d'évangile. Collected Essays*. Edited by F. VAN SEGBROECK, 1982. XIX-1036 p. FB 2000.

61. J. COPPENS, *La relève apocalyptique du messianisme royal. II. Le Fils d'homme vétéro- et intertestamentaire*. Édition posthume par J. LUST, 1982. XVII-272 p. FB 1000.

62. J.J. KELLY, *Baron Friedrich von Hügel's Philosophy of Religion*. 1983. 232 p. FB 1500.

63. G. DE SCHRIJVER, *Le merveilleux accord de l'homme et de Dieu. Étude de l'analogie de l'être chez Hans Urs von Balthasar*. 1983. 344 p. FB 1500.

64. J. GROOTAERS & J. SELLING, *The 1980 Synod of Bishops: «On the Role of the Family»*. Preface by Prof. emeritus L. JANSSENS. 372 p. FB 1500.

In preparation:

65. F. NEIRYNCK & F. VAN SEGBROECK, *New Testament Vocabulary. A Companion Volume to the Concordance.*